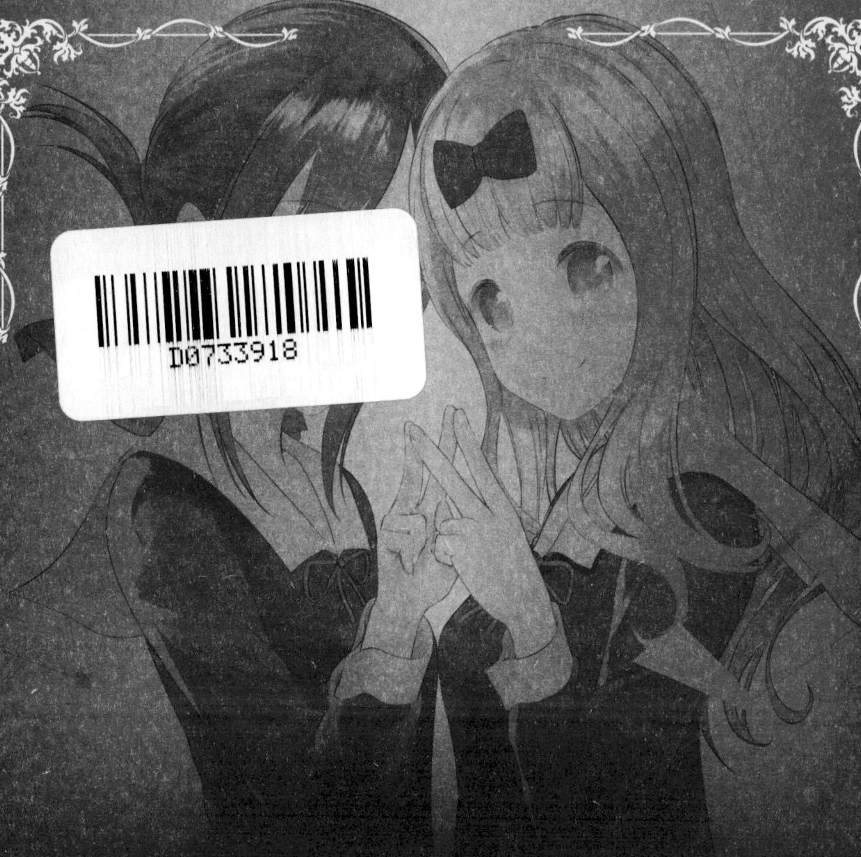

KAGUYA-SAMA
LOVE IS WAR

22

AKA AKASAKA

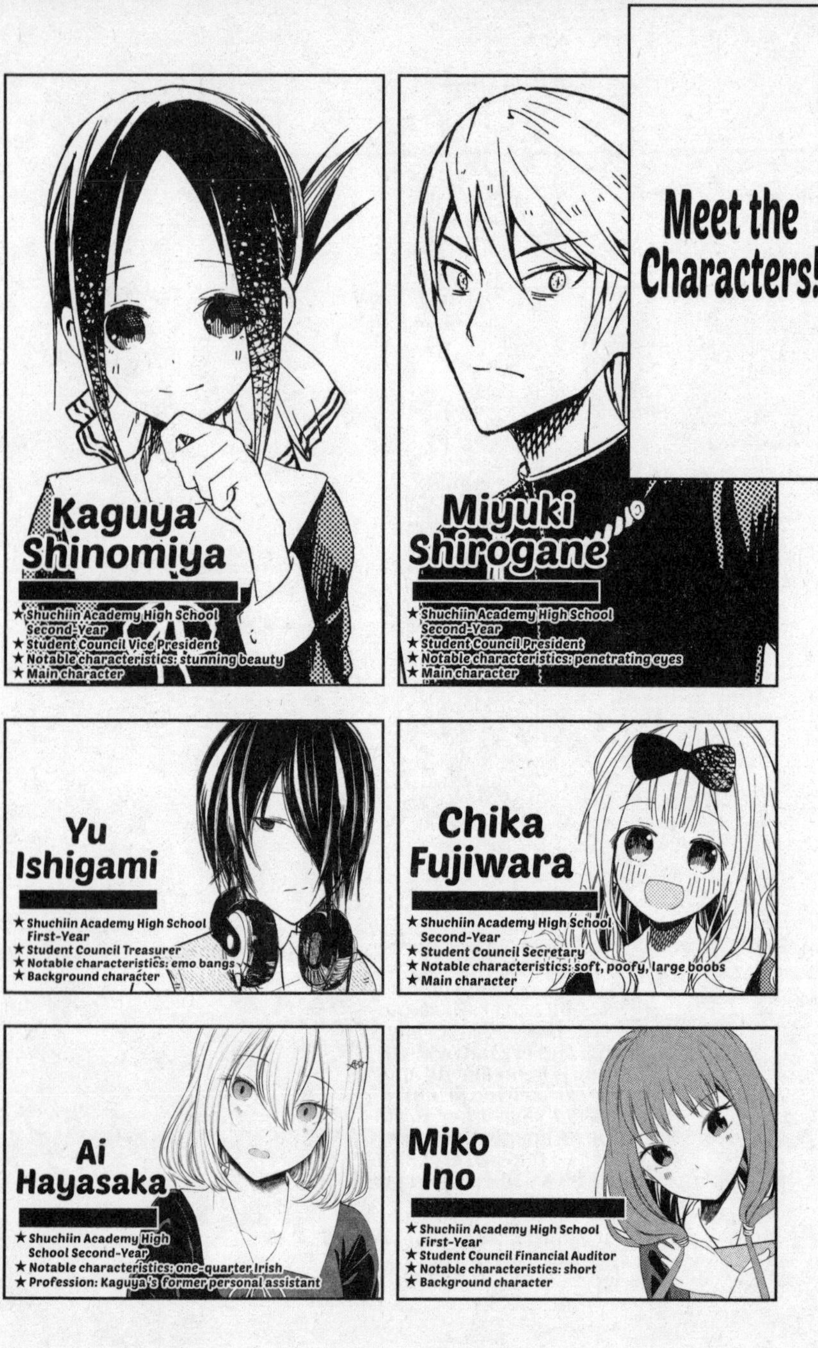
Meet the Characters!
Miyuki Shirogane
★ Shuchiin Academy High School Second-Year
★ Student Council President
★ Notable characteristics: penetrating eyes
★ Main character
Kaguya Shinomiya
★ Shuchiin Academy High School Second-Year
★ Student Council Vice President
★ Notable characteristics: stunning beauty
★ Main character
Chika Fujiwara
★ Shuchiin Academy High School Second-Year
★ Student Council Secretary
★ Notable characteristics: soft, poofy, large boobs
★ Main character
Yu Ishigami
★ Shuchiin Academy High School First-Year
★ Student Council Treasurer
★ Notable characteristics: emo bangs
★ Background character
Miko Ino
★ Shuchiin Academy High School First-Year
★ Student Council Financial Auditor
★ Notable characteristics: short
★ Background character
Ai Hayasaka
★ Shuchiin Academy High School Second-Year
★ Notable characteristics: one-quarter Irish
★ Profession: Kaguya's former personal assistant

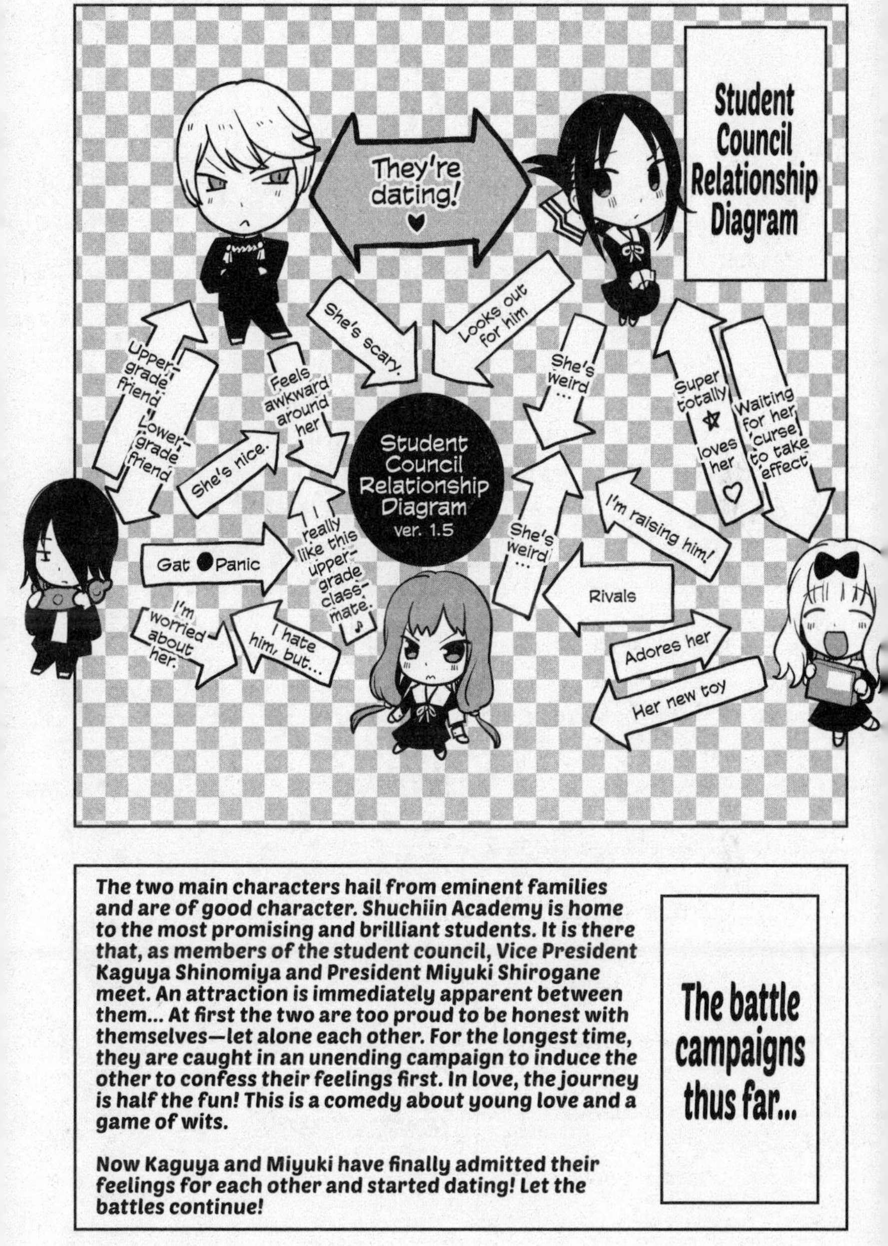
Student Council Relationship Diagram
They're dating! ♥
She's scary.
Looks out for him
Upper-grade friend
Lower-grade friend
Feels awkward around her
She's nice.
Student Council Relationship Diagram ver. 1.5
She's weird...
Super totally ✩ loves her ♡
Waiting for her "curse" to take effect
Gat ● Panic
I really like this upper-grade classmate. ♪
She's weird...
I'm raising him!
Rivals
I'm worried about her.
I hate him, but...
Adores her
Her new toy

The battle campaigns thus far...

The two main characters hail from eminent families and are of good character. Shuchiin Academy is home to the most promising and brilliant students. It is there that, as members of the student council, Vice President Kaguya Shinomiya and President Miyuki Shirogane meet. An attraction is immediately apparent between them... At first the two are too proud to be honest with themselves—let alone each other. For the longest time, they are caught in an unending campaign to induce the other to confess their feelings first. In love, the journey is half the fun! This is a comedy about young love and a game of wits.

Now Kaguya and Miyuki have finally admitted their feelings for each other and started dating! Let the battles continue!

KAGUYA-SAMA LOVE IS WAR

BATTLE CAMPAIGNS

22

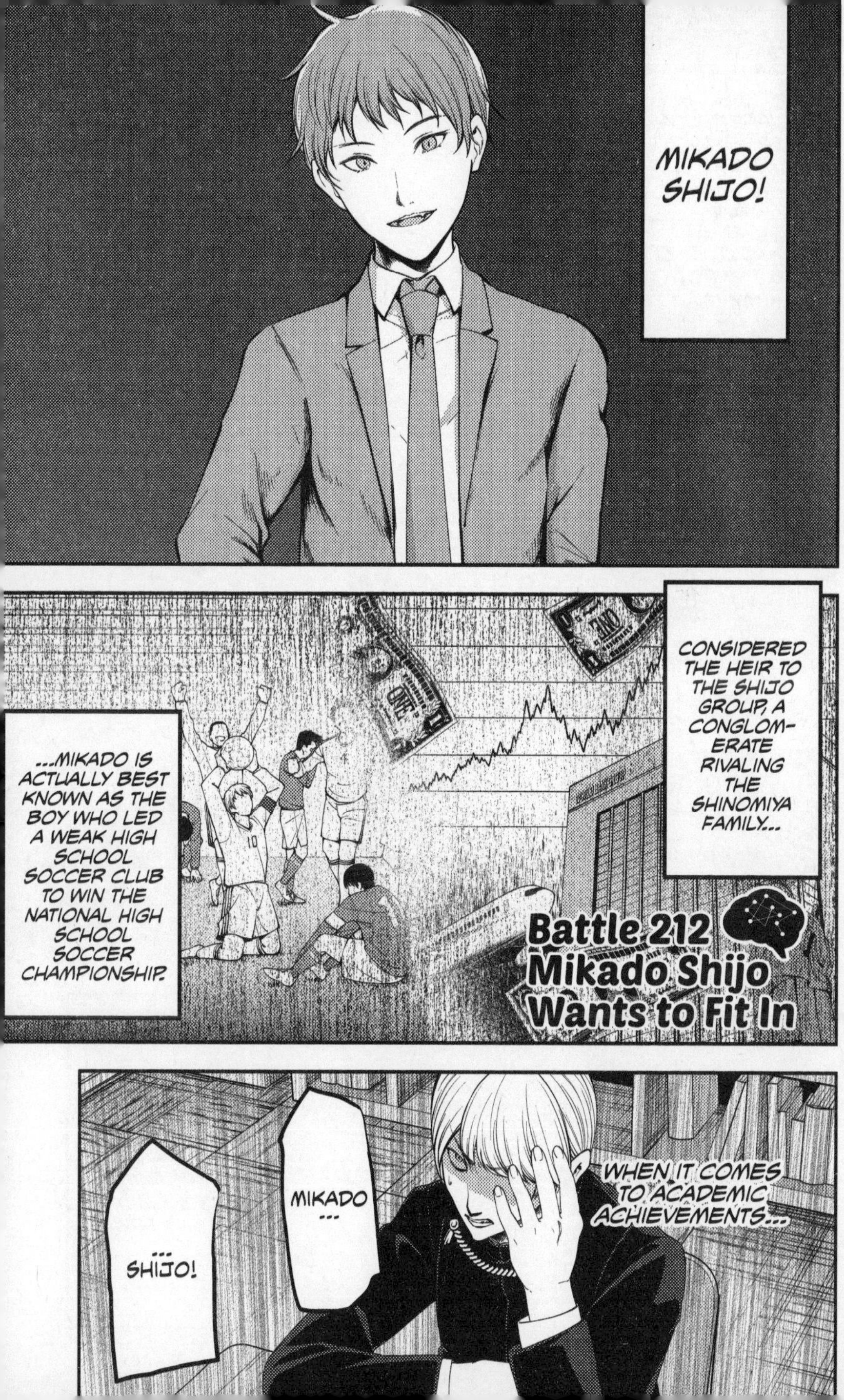
MIKADO SHIJO!
CONSIDERED THE HEIR TO THE SHIJO GROUP, A CONGLOM-ERATE RIVALING THE SHINOMIYA FAMILY...
...MIKADO IS ACTUALLY BEST KNOWN AS THE BOY WHO LED A WEAK HIGH SCHOOL SOCCER CLUB TO WIN THE NATIONAL HIGH SCHOOL SOCCER CHAMPIONSHIP.
Battle 212 Mikado Shijo Wants to Fit In
WHEN IT COMES TO ACADEMIC ACHIEVEMENTS...
MIKADO ...
... SHIJO!

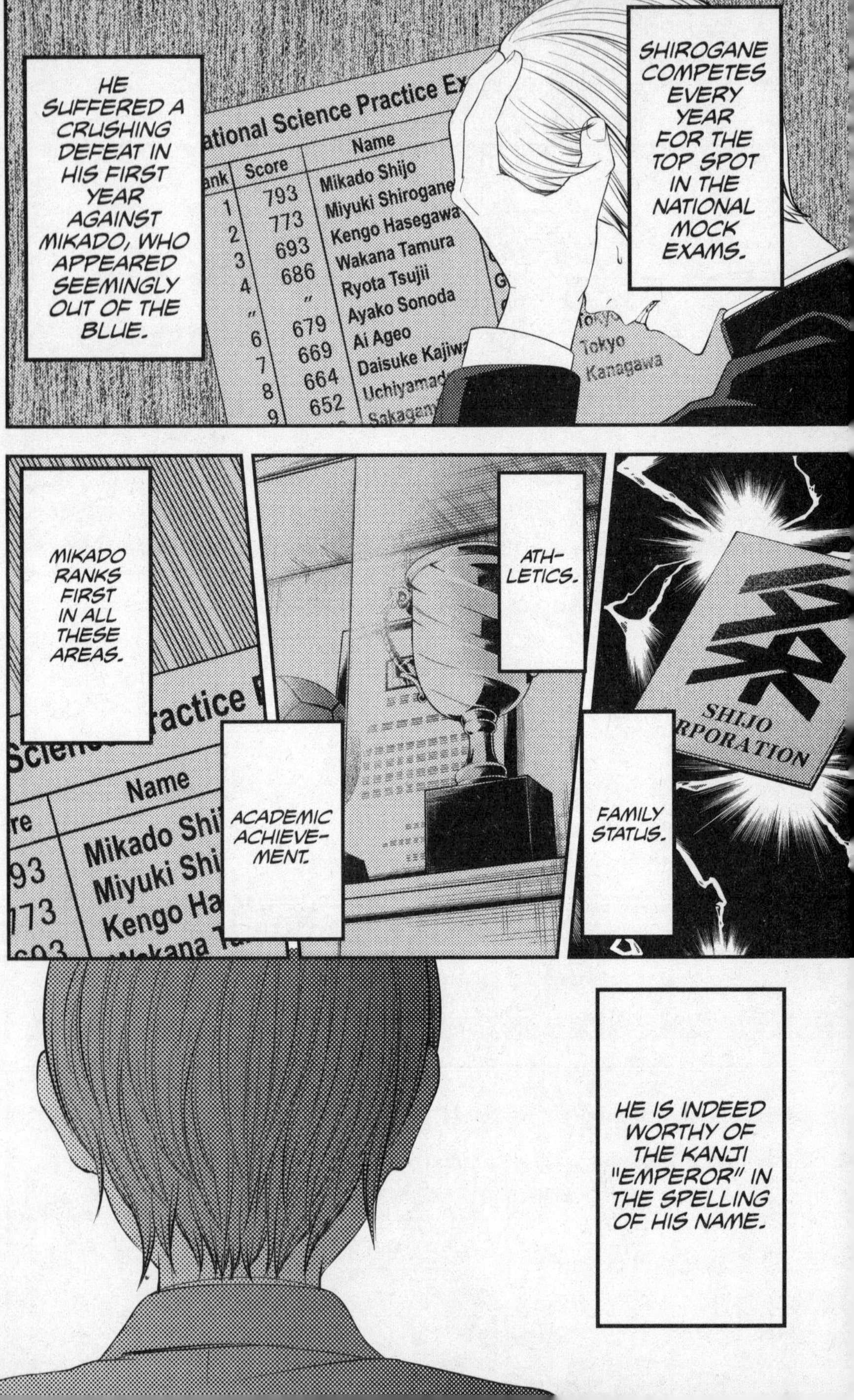

SHIROGANE COMPETES EVERY YEAR FOR THE TOP SPOT IN THE NATIONAL MOCK EXAMS.
HE SUFFERED A CRUSHING DEFEAT IN HIS FIRST YEAR AGAINST MIKADO, WHO APPEARED SEEMINGLY OUT OF THE BLUE.
ational Science Practice Ex
Score
Name
1 793 Mikado Shijo
2 773 Miyuki Shirogane
3 693 Kengo Hasegawa
4 686 Wakana Tamura
Ryota Tsujii
6 679 Ayako Sonoda
7 669 Ai Ageo
8 664 Daisuke Kajiw
9 652 Uchiyamad
Tokyo
Kanagawa
FAMILY STATUS.
SHIJO
ATH-LETICS.
ACADEMIC ACHIEVE-MENT.
MIKADO RANKS FIRST IN ALL THESE AREAS.
HE IS INDEED WORTHY OF THE KANJI "EMPEROR" IN THE SPELLING OF HIS NAME.

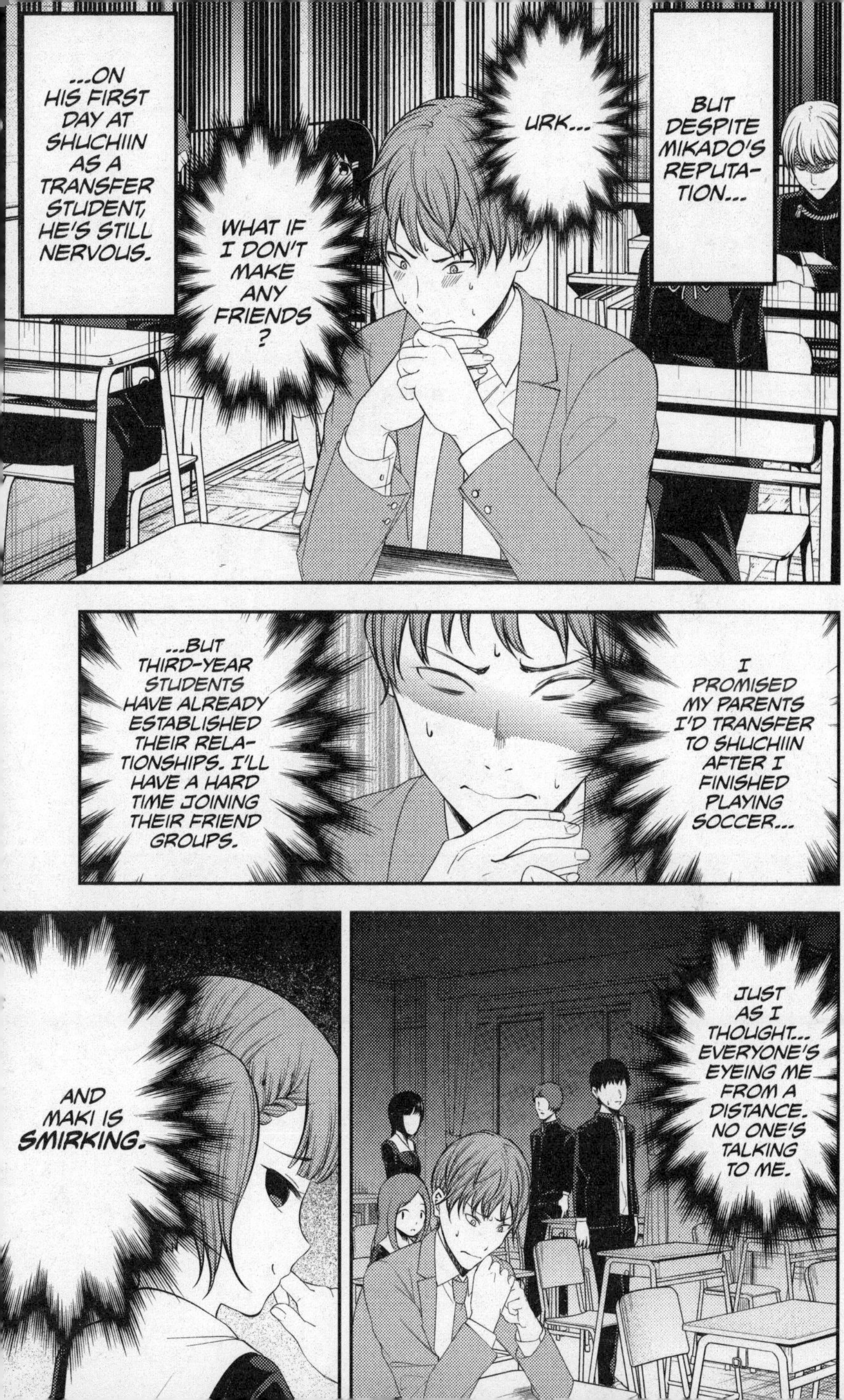
BUT DESPITE MIKADO'S REPUTATION...
URK...
WHAT IF I DON'T MAKE ANY FRIENDS?
...ON HIS FIRST DAY AT SHUCHIIN AS A TRANSFER STUDENT, HE'S STILL NERVOUS.
I PROMISED MY PARENTS I'D TRANSFER TO SHUCHIIN AFTER I FINISHED PLAYING SOCCER...
...BUT THIRD-YEAR STUDENTS HAVE ALREADY ESTABLISHED THEIR RELATIONSHIPS. I'LL HAVE A HARD TIME JOINING THEIR FRIEND GROUPS.
JUST AS I THOUGHT... EVERYONE'S EYEING ME FROM A DISTANCE. NO ONE'S TALKING TO ME.
AND MAKI IS SMIRKING.

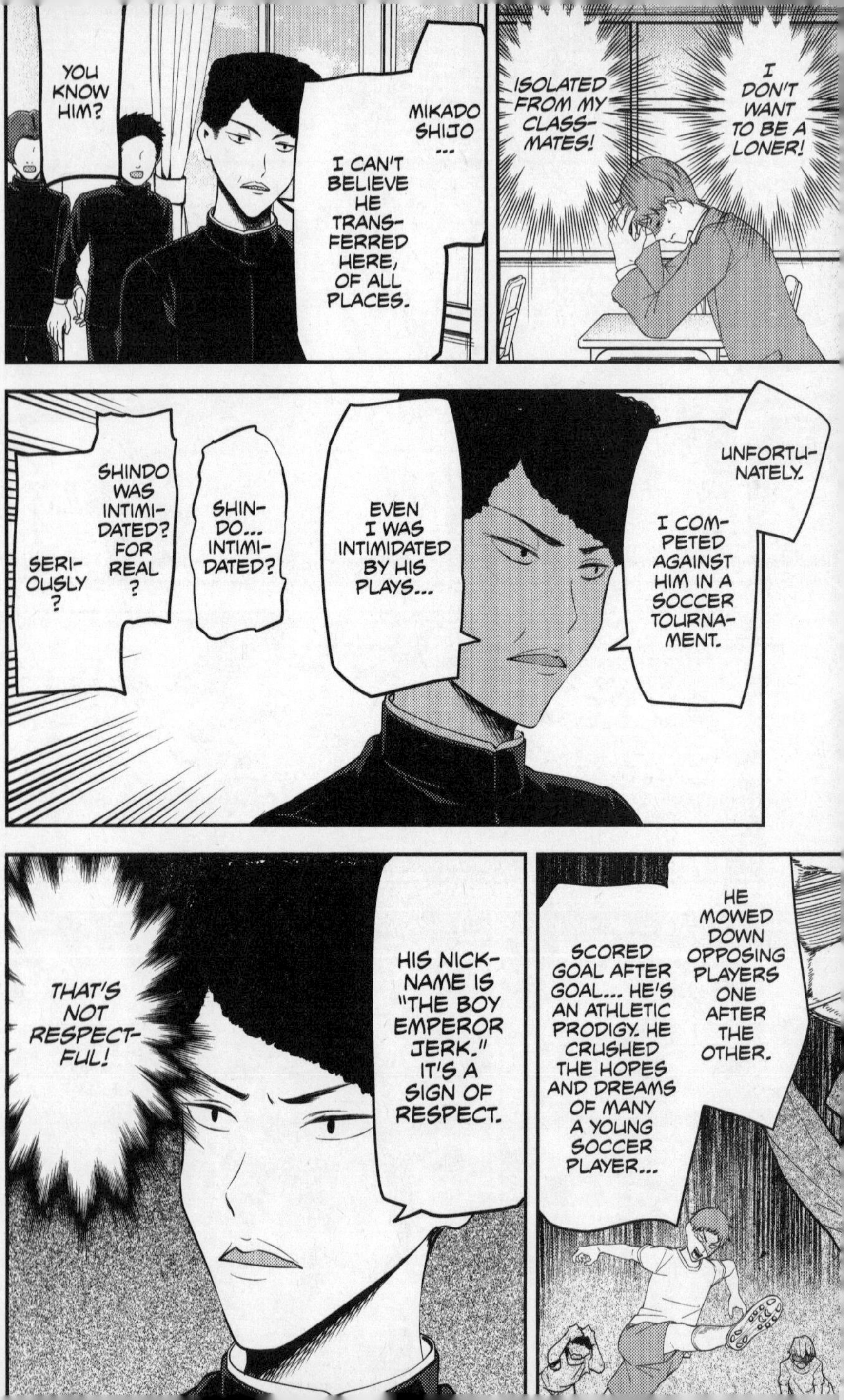
I DON'T WANT TO BE A LONER!
ISOLATED FROM MY CLASSMATES!
MIKADO SHIJO...
I CAN'T BELIEVE HE TRANSFERRED HERE, OF ALL PLACES.
YOU KNOW HIM?
UNFORTUNATELY.
I COMPETED AGAINST HIM IN A SOCCER TOURNAMENT.
EVEN I WAS INTIMIDATED BY HIS PLAYS...
SHINDO... INTIMIDATED?
SHINDO WAS INTIMIDATED? FOR REAL?
SERIOUSLY?
HE MOWED DOWN OPPOSING PLAYERS ONE AFTER THE OTHER.
SCORED GOAL AFTER GOAL... HE'S AN ATHLETIC PRODIGY. HE CRUSHED THE HOPES AND DREAMS OF MANY A YOUNG SOCCER PLAYER...
HIS NICKNAME IS "THE BOY EMPEROR JERK." IT'S A SIGN OF RESPECT.
THAT'S NOT RESPECTFUL!

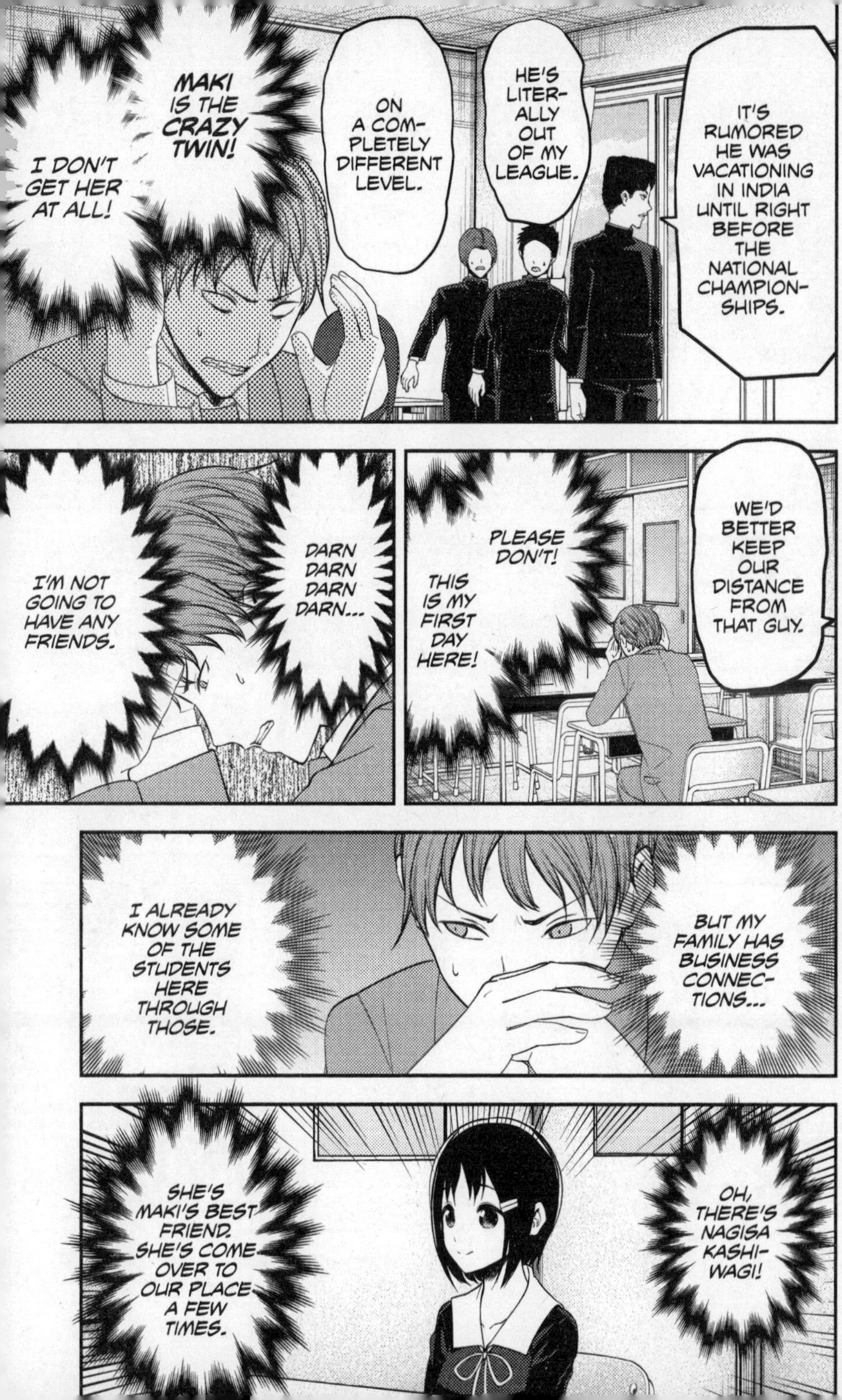
IT'S RUMORED HE WAS VACATIONING IN INDIA UNTIL RIGHT BEFORE THE NATIONAL CHAMPIONSHIPS.
HE'S LITERALLY OUT OF MY LEAGUE.
ON A COMPLETELY DIFFERENT LEVEL.
MAKI IS THE CRAZY TWIN!
I DON'T GET HER AT ALL!
WE'D BETTER KEEP OUR DISTANCE FROM THAT GUY.
PLEASE DON'T!
THIS IS MY FIRST DAY HERE!
DARN DARN DARN DARN...
I'M NOT GOING TO HAVE ANY FRIENDS.
BUT MY FAMILY HAS BUSINESS CONNECTIONS...
I ALREADY KNOW SOME OF THE STUDENTS HERE THROUGH THOSE.
OH, THERE'S NAGISA KASHIWAGI!
SHE'S MAKI'S BEST FRIEND. SHE'S COME OVER TO OUR PLACE A FEW TIMES.

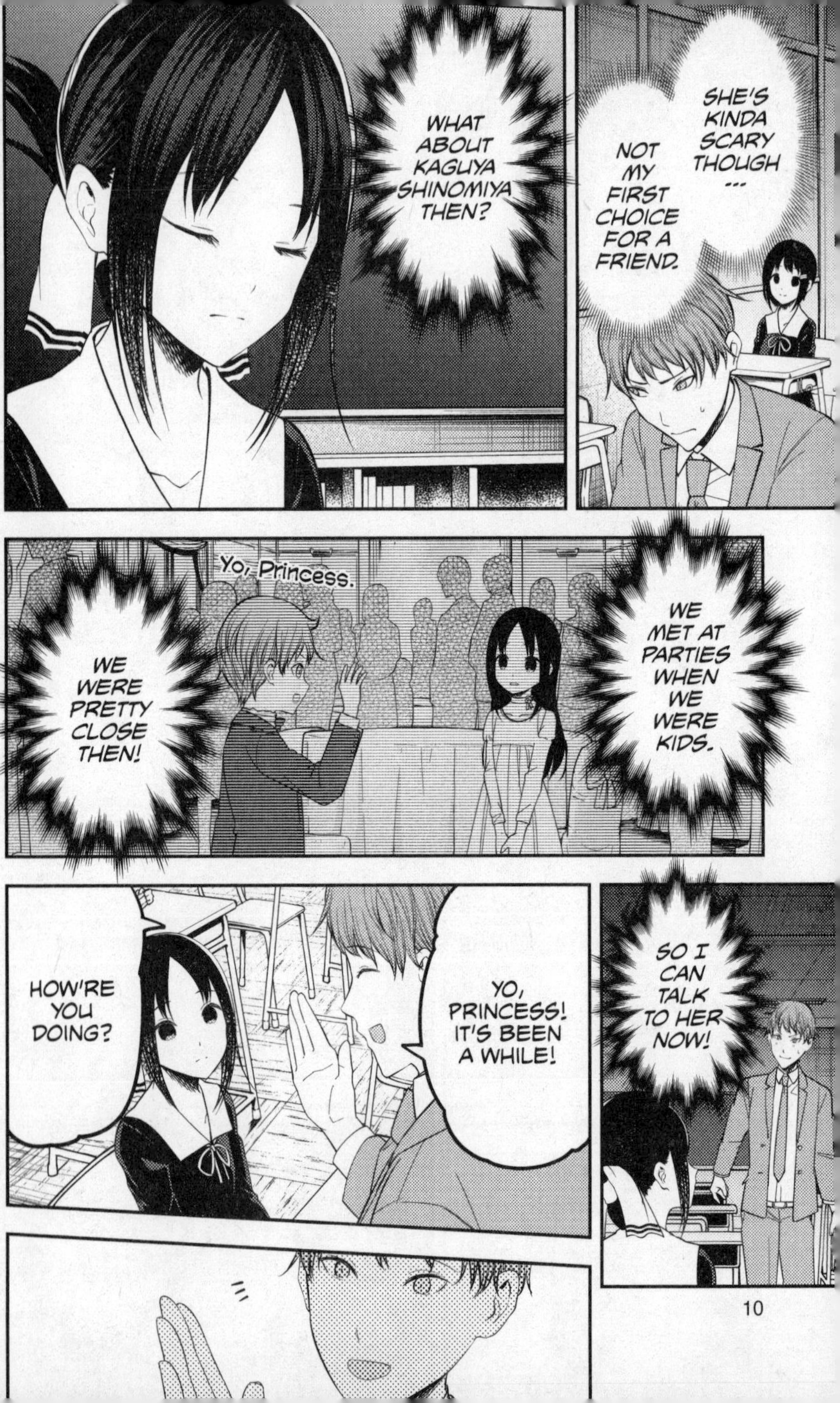
SHE'S KINDA SCARY THOUGH...
NOT MY FIRST CHOICE FOR A FRIEND.
WHAT ABOUT KAGUYA SHINOMIYA THEN?
WE MET AT PARTIES WHEN WE WERE KIDS.
Yo, Princess.
WE WERE PRETTY CLOSE THEN!
SO I CAN TALK TO HER NOW!
YO, PRINCESS! IT'S BEEN A WHILE!
HOW'RE YOU DOING?

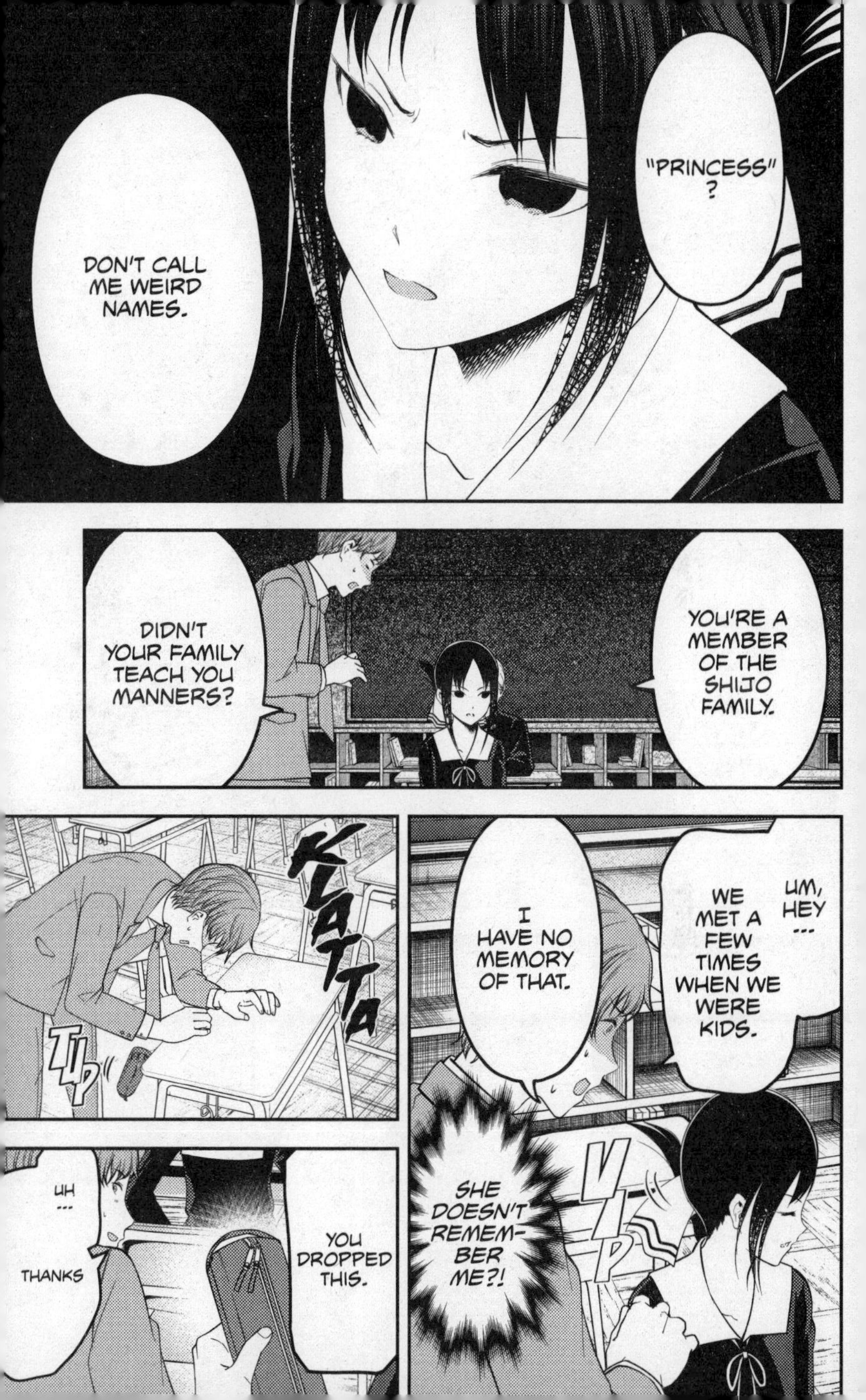
"PRINCESS"?
DON'T CALL ME WEIRD NAMES.
YOU'RE A MEMBER OF THE SHIJO FAMILY.
DIDN'T YOUR FAMILY TEACH YOU MANNERS?
UM, HEY ...
WE MET A FEW TIMES WHEN WE WERE KIDS.
I HAVE NO MEMORY OF THAT.
VIP
SHE DOESN'T REMEMBER ME?!
KLATTA
TUP
YOU DROPPED THIS.
UH ...
THANKS

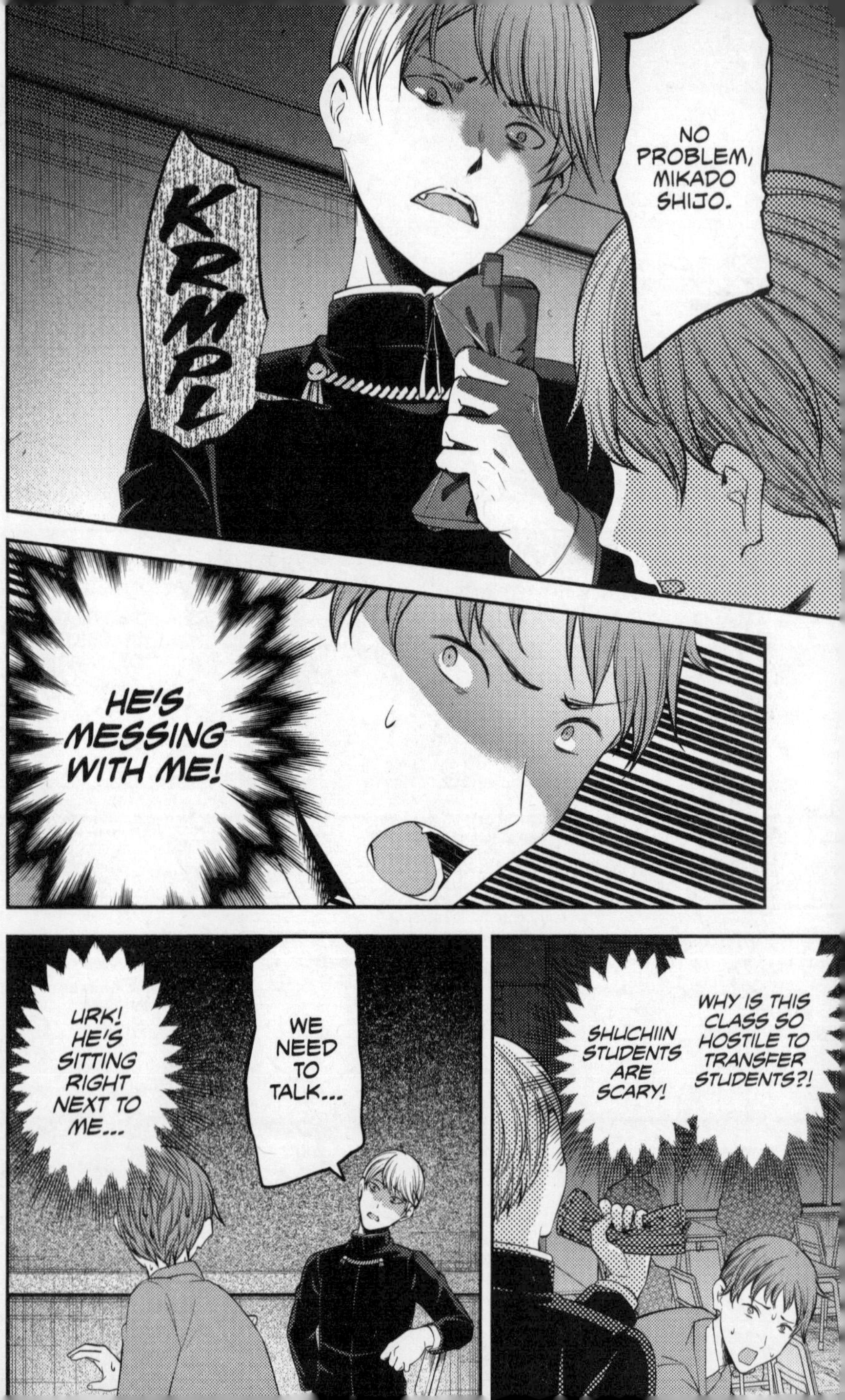
NO PROBLEM, MIKADO SHIJO.
KRMPL
HE'S MESSING WITH ME!
WHY IS THIS CLASS SO HOSTILE TO TRANSFER STUDENTS?!
SHUCHIIN STUDENTS ARE SCARY!
WE NEED TO TALK...
URK! HE'S SITTING RIGHT NEXT TO ME...

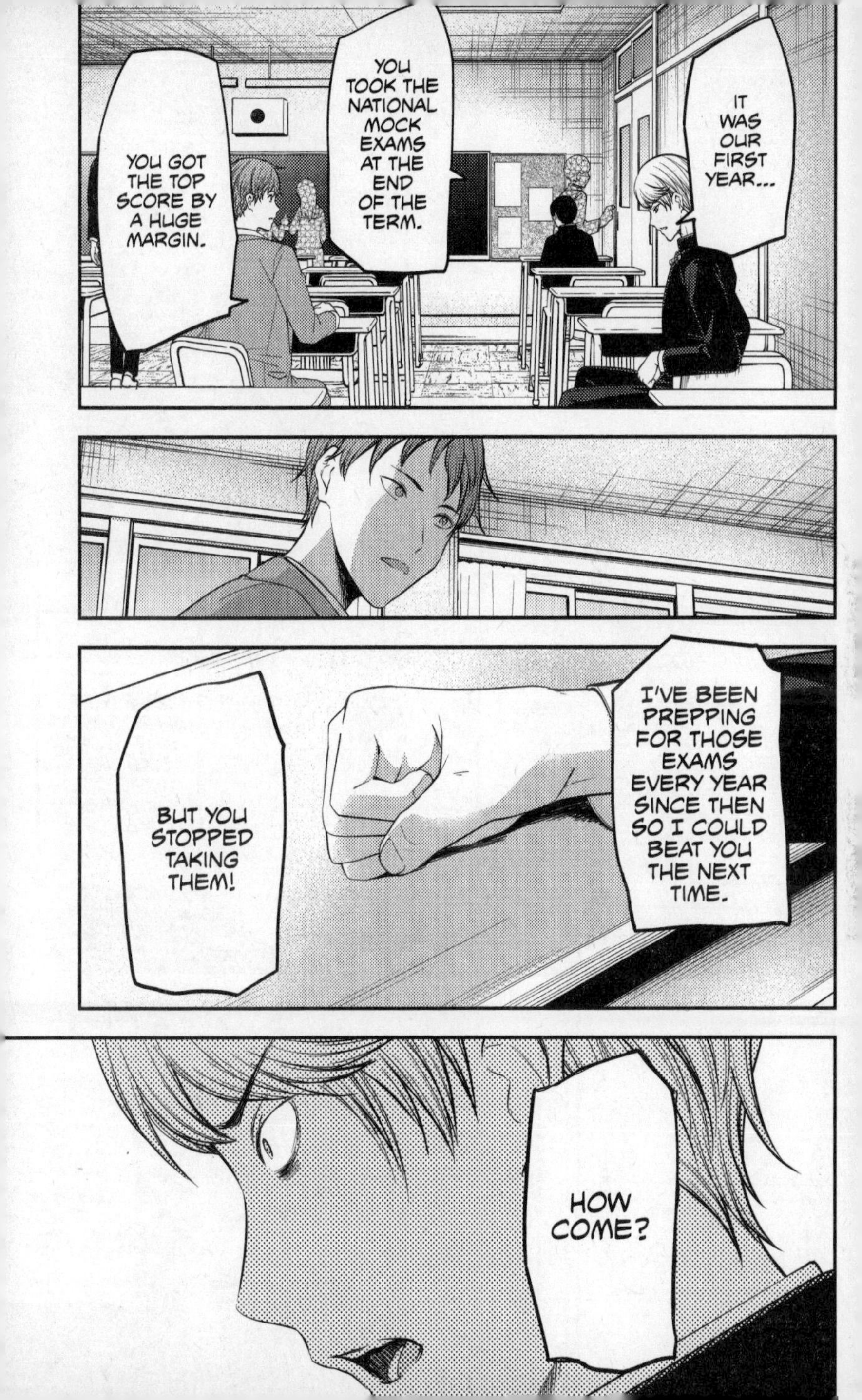
IT WAS OUR FIRST YEAR...
YOU TOOK THE NATIONAL MOCK EXAMS AT THE END OF THE TERM.
YOU GOT THE TOP SCORE BY A HUGE MARGIN.
I'VE BEEN PREPPING FOR THOSE EXAMS EVERY YEAR SINCE THEN SO I COULD BEAT YOU THE NEXT TIME.
BUT YOU STOPPED TAKING THEM!
HOW COME?

MIYUKI SHIROGANE IS USUALLY MILD MANNERED ...
...BUT HE DEFINITELY HAS IT IN FOR MIKADO SHIJO.
THE BASIS OF SHIROGANE'S SELF-WORTH IS HIS ACADEMIC ACHIEVEMENTS.
THE ONLY BOY WHO HAS MERCILESSLY CRUSHED HIM...
...IS SITTING BEFORE HIM NOW.
Defeat Mikado!
ONLY THOSE WHO KNOW SHIROGANE'S TRUE NATURE...
MRMR
...SENSE THE ELECTRICAL CHARGE IN THE ATMOSPHERE.
UM...

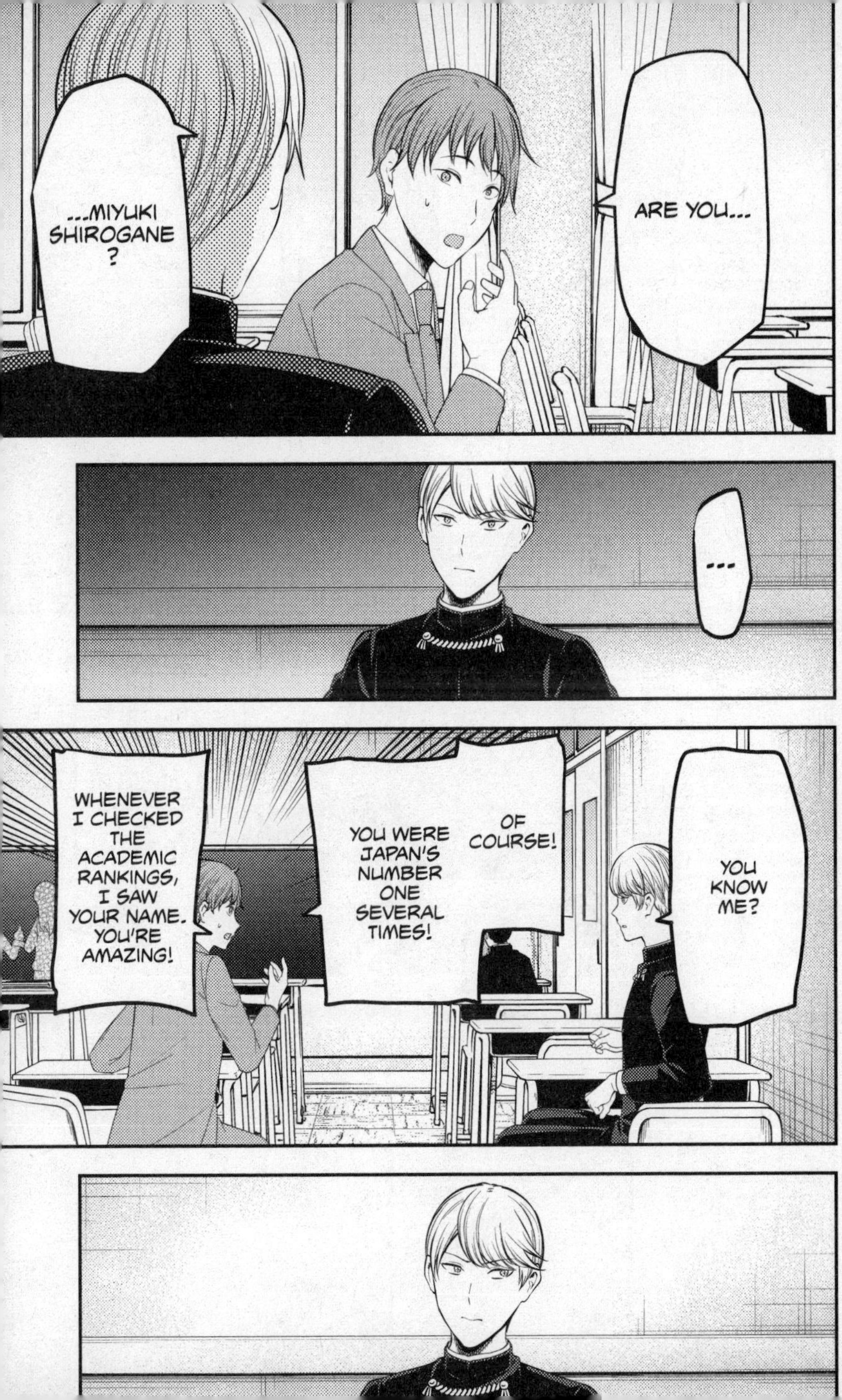
ARE YOU...
...MIYUKI SHIROGANE?
...
YOU KNOW ME?
OF COURSE!
YOU WERE JAPAN'S NUMBER ONE SEVERAL TIMES!
WHENEVER I CHECKED THE ACADEMIC RANKINGS, I SAW YOUR NAME. YOU'RE AMAZING!

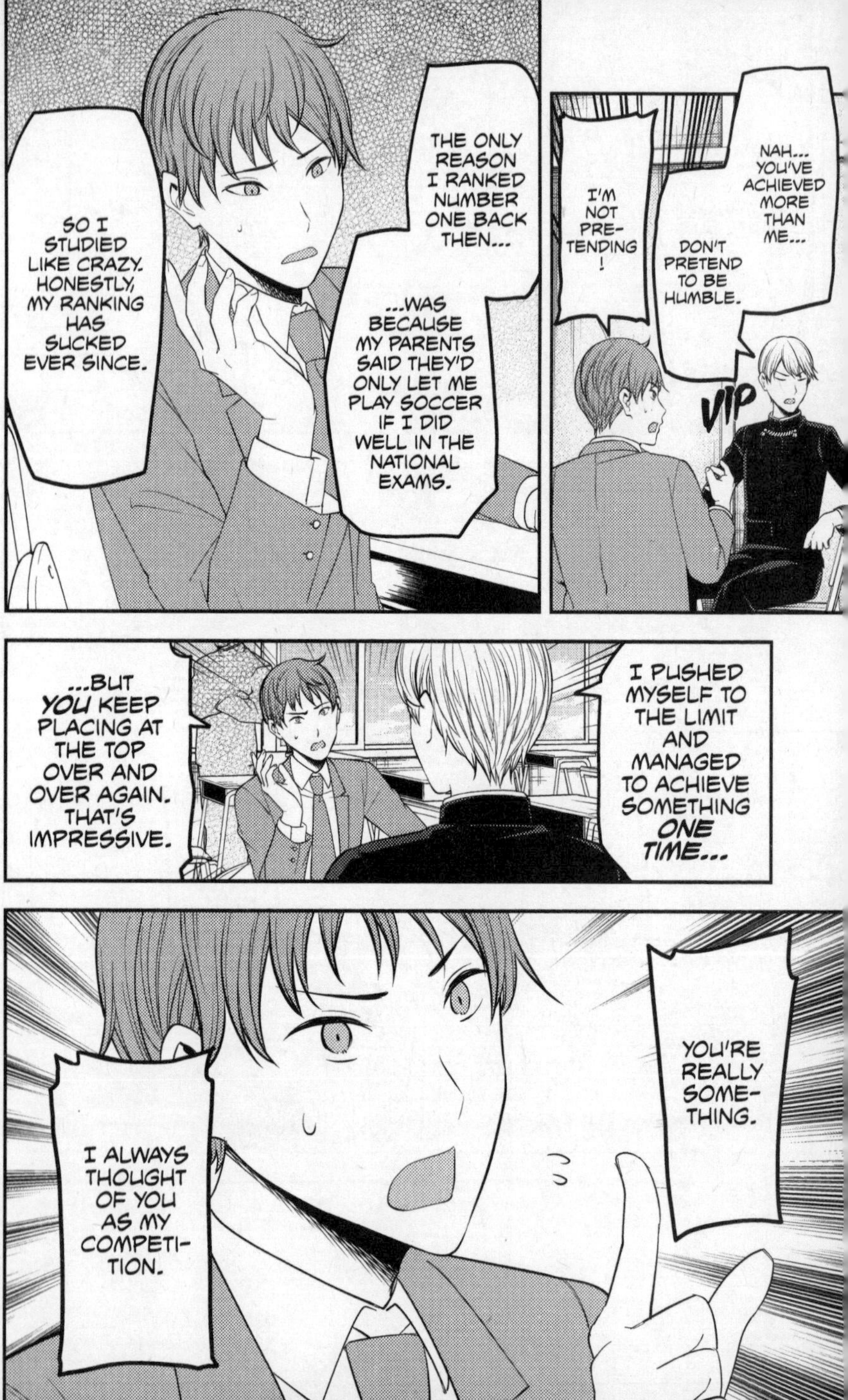
NAH... YOU'VE ACHIEVED MORE THAN ME...
DON'T PRETEND TO BE HUMBLE.
I'M NOT PRETENDING!
VIP
THE ONLY REASON I RANKED NUMBER ONE BACK THEN...
...WAS BECAUSE MY PARENTS SAID THEY'D ONLY LET ME PLAY SOCCER IF I DID WELL IN THE NATIONAL EXAMS.
SO I STUDIED LIKE CRAZY. HONESTLY, MY RANKING HAS SUCKED EVER SINCE.
I PUSHED MYSELF TO THE LIMIT AND MANAGED TO ACHIEVE SOMETHING *ONE TIME*...
...BUT *YOU* KEEP PLACING AT THE TOP OVER AND OVER AGAIN. THAT'S IMPRESSIVE.
YOU'RE REALLY SOMETHING.
I ALWAYS THOUGHT OF YOU AS MY COMPETITION.

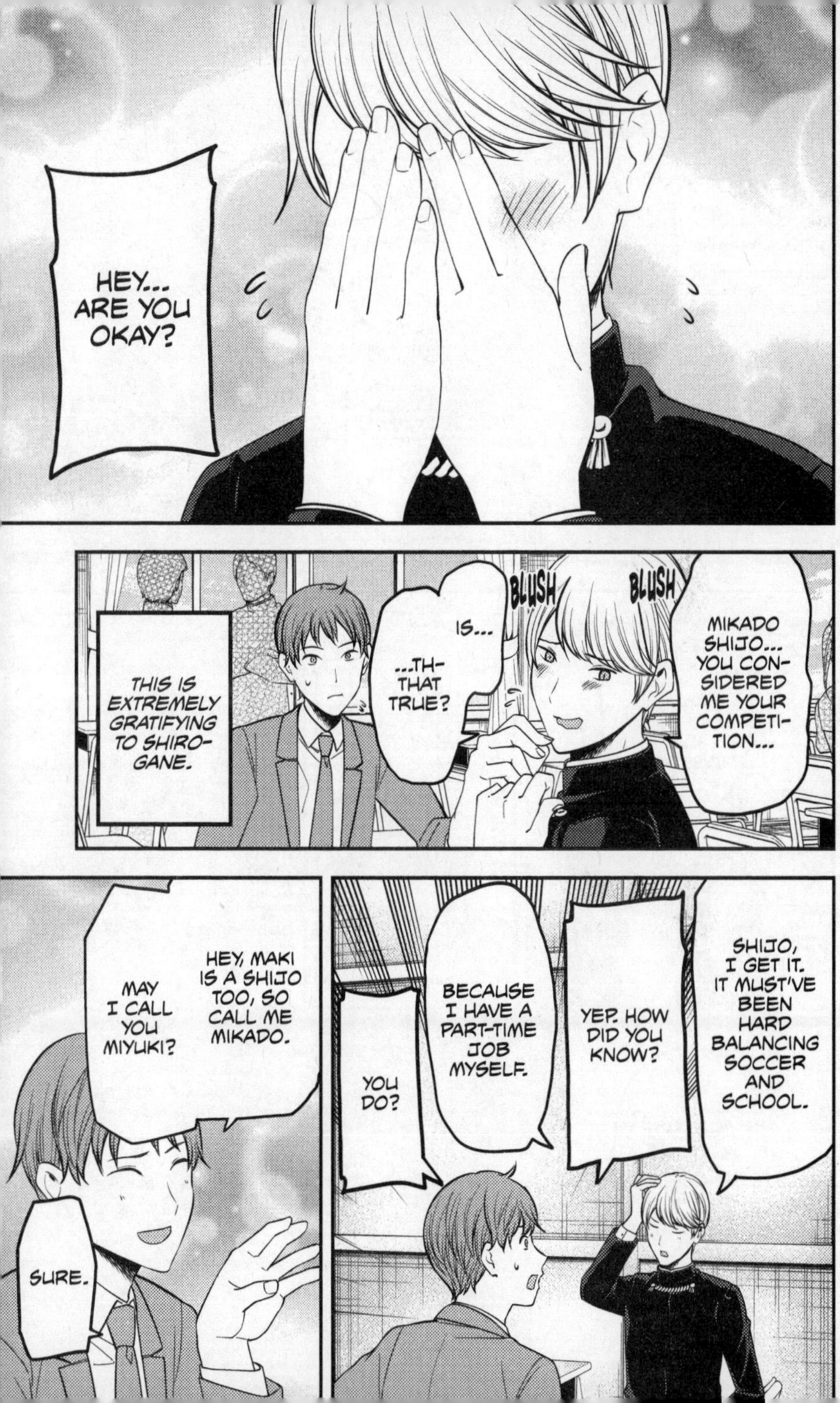
HEY... ARE YOU OKAY?
MIKADO SHIJO... YOU CONSIDERED ME YOUR COMPETITION...
BLUSH
BLUSH
IS...
...TH-THAT TRUE?
THIS IS EXTREMELY GRATIFYING TO SHIROGANE.
SHIJO, I GET IT. IT MUST'VE BEEN HARD BALANCING SOCCER AND SCHOOL.
YEP. HOW DID YOU KNOW?
BECAUSE I HAVE A PART-TIME JOB MYSELF.
YOU DO?
HEY, MAKI IS A SHIJO TOO, SO CALL ME MIKADO.
MAY I CALL YOU MIYUKI?
SURE.

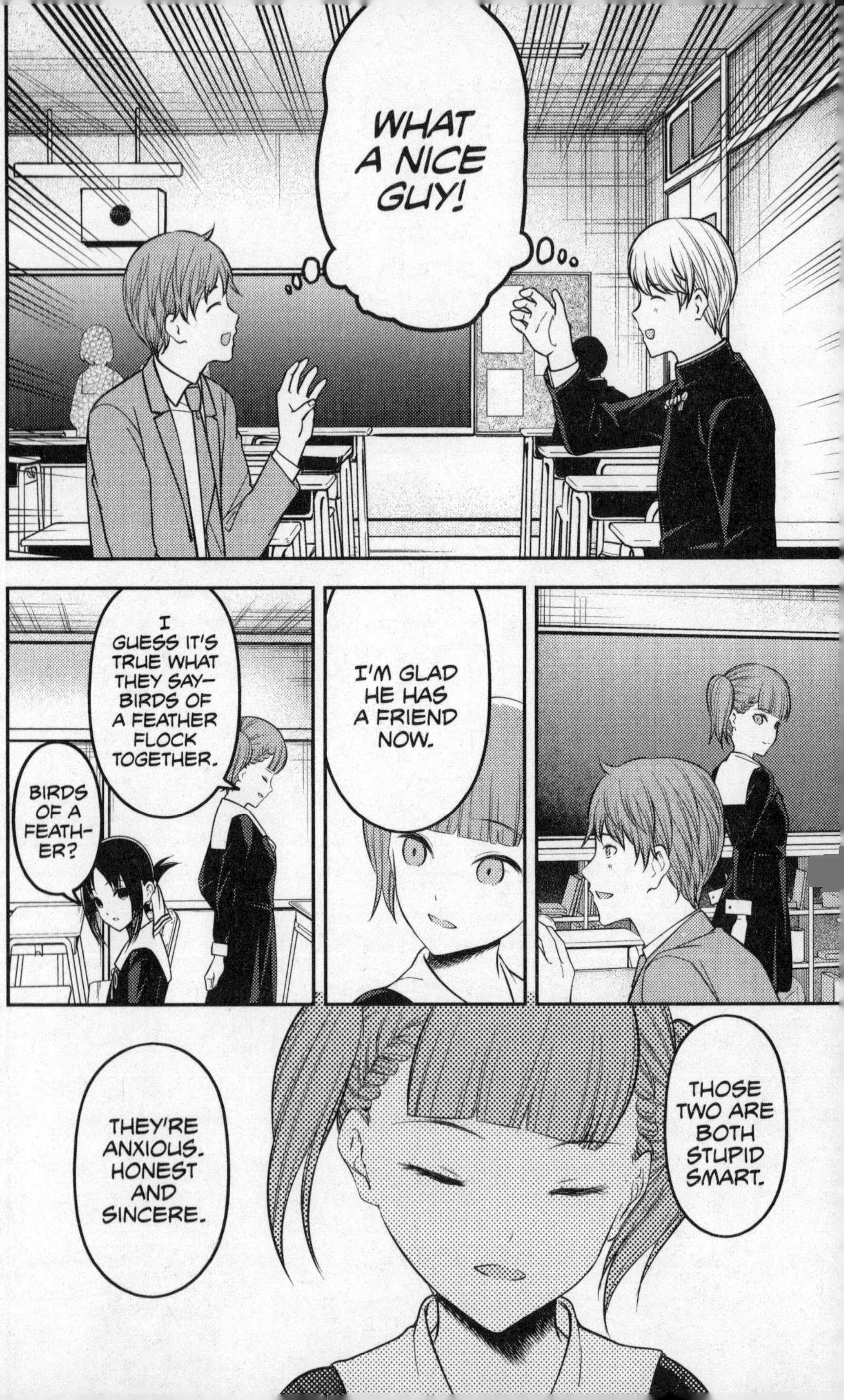
WHAT A NICE GUY!
I'M GLAD HE HAS A FRIEND NOW.
I GUESS IT'S TRUE WHAT THEY SAY—BIRDS OF A FEATHER FLOCK TOGETHER.
BIRDS OF A FEATH-ER?
THOSE TWO ARE BOTH STUPID SMART.
THEY'RE ANXIOUS. HONEST AND SINCERE.

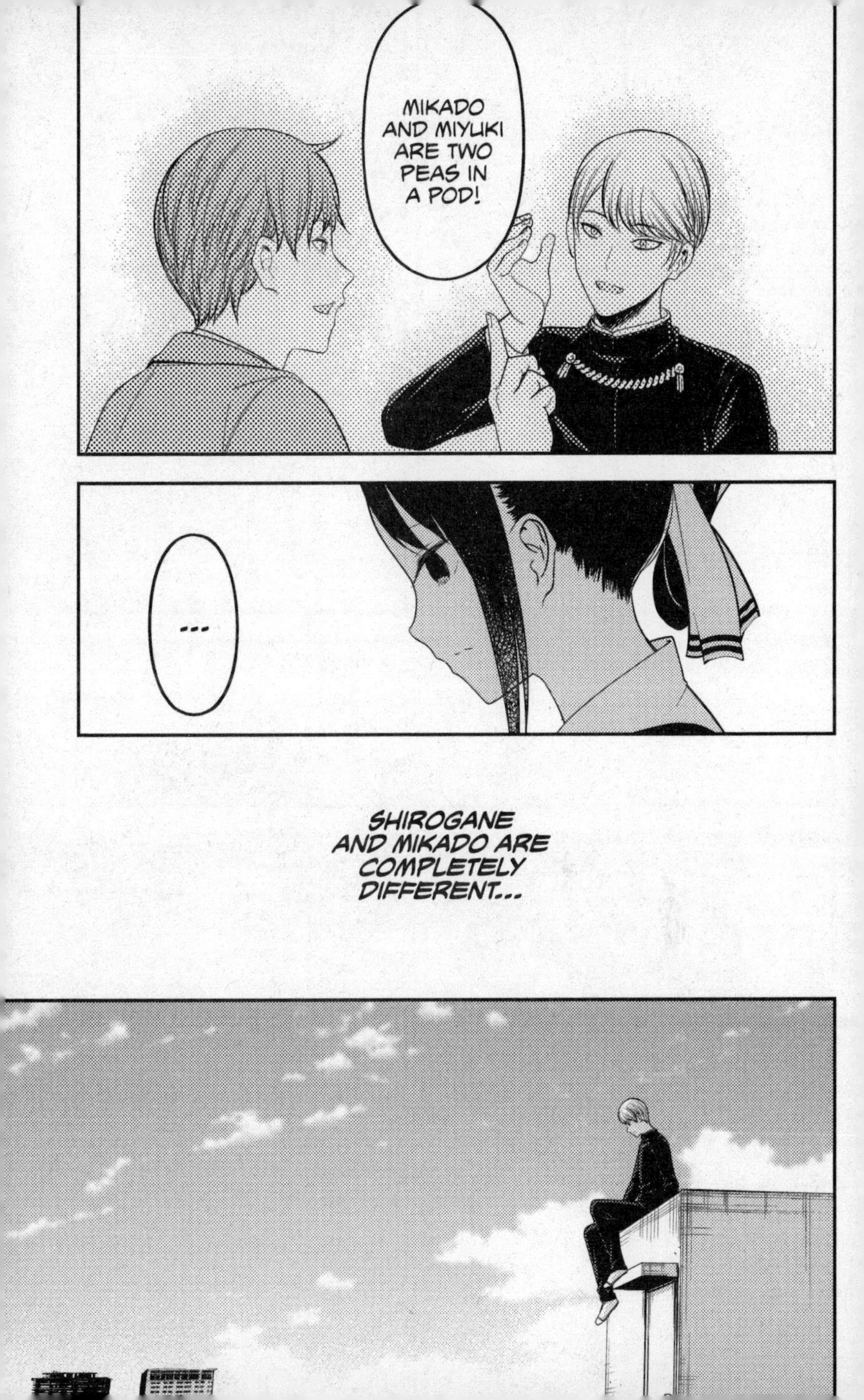
MIKADO AND MIYUKI ARE TWO PEAS IN A POD!
...
SHIROGANE AND MIKADO ARE COMPLETELY DIFFERENT...

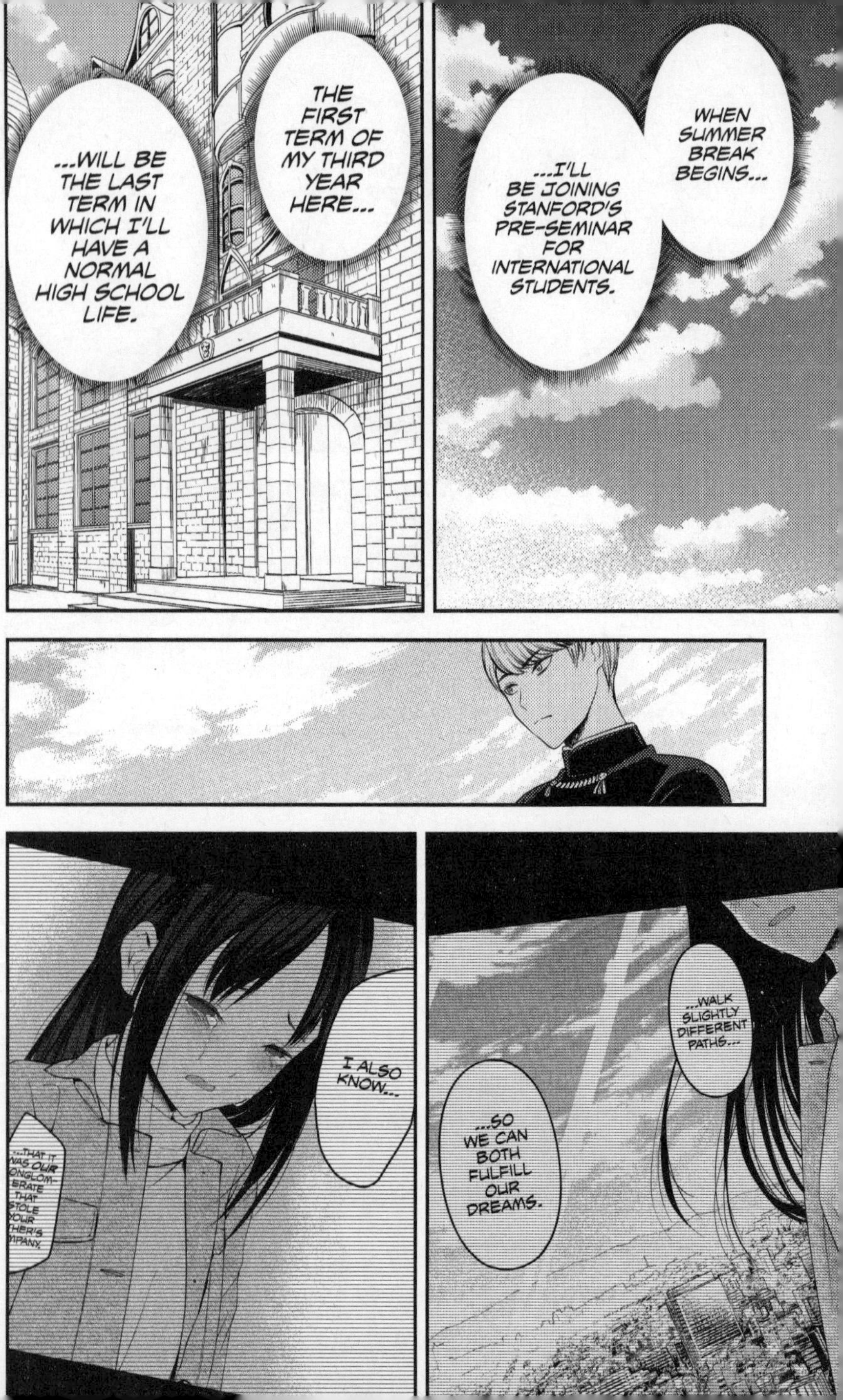
WHEN SUMMER BREAK BEGINS...
...I'LL BE JOINING STANFORD'S PRE-SEMINAR FOR INTERNATIONAL STUDENTS.
THE FIRST TERM OF MY THIRD YEAR HERE...
...WILL BE THE LAST TERM IN WHICH I'LL HAVE A NORMAL HIGH SCHOOL LIFE.
...WALK SLIGHTLY DIFFERENT PATHS...
...SO WE CAN BOTH FULFILL OUR DREAMS.
I ALSO KNOW...
...THAT IT WAS OUR ONGLOM-ERATE THAT STOLE OUR THER'S MPANY.

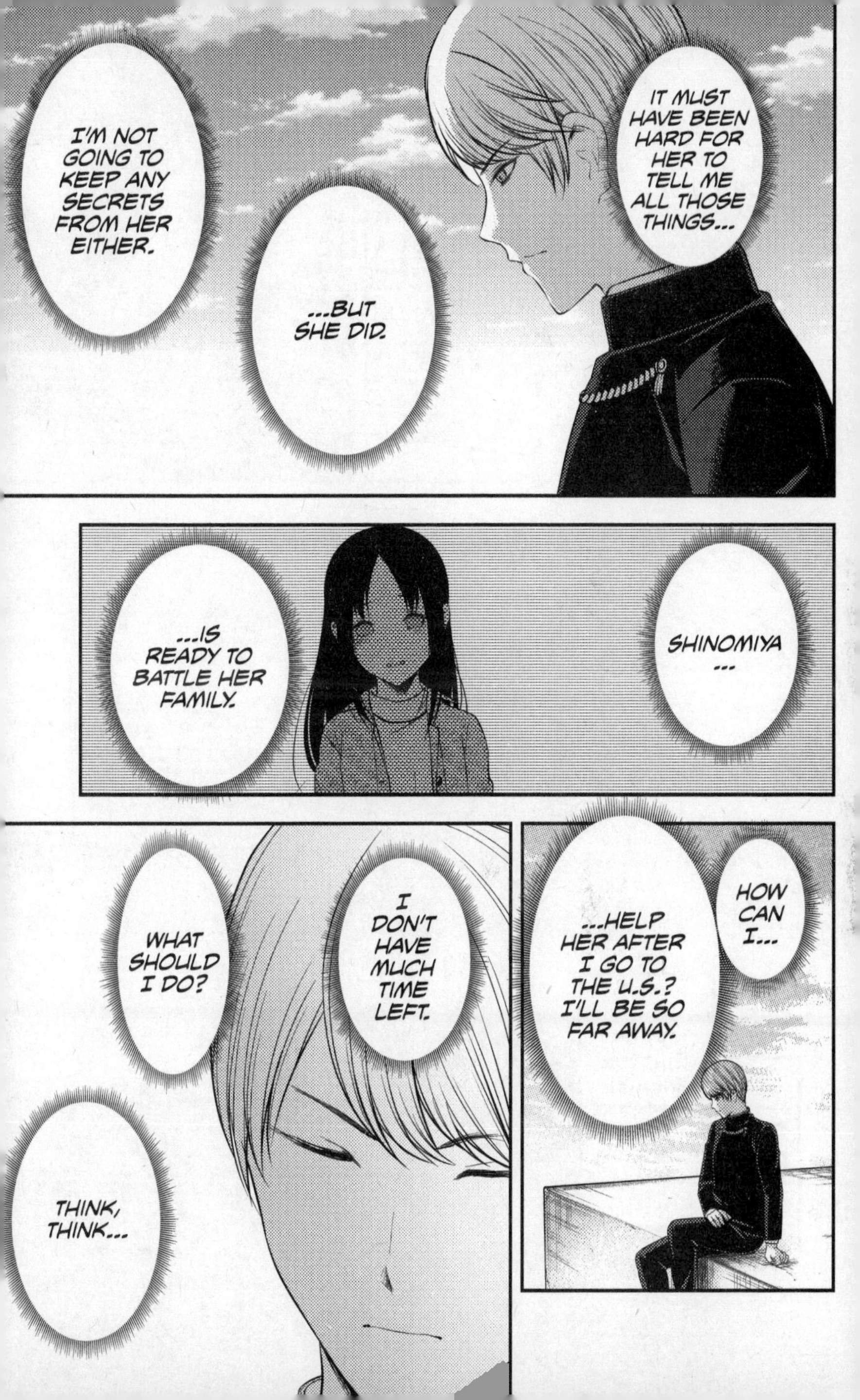
IT MUST HAVE BEEN HARD FOR HER TO TELL ME ALL THOSE THINGS...
...BUT SHE DID.
I'M NOT GOING TO KEEP ANY SECRETS FROM HER EITHER.
SHINOMIYA ...
...IS READY TO BATTLE HER FAMILY.
HOW CAN I...
...HELP HER AFTER I GO TO THE U.S.? I'LL BE SO FAR AWAY.
I DON'T HAVE MUCH TIME LEFT.
WHAT SHOULD I DO?
THINK, THINK...

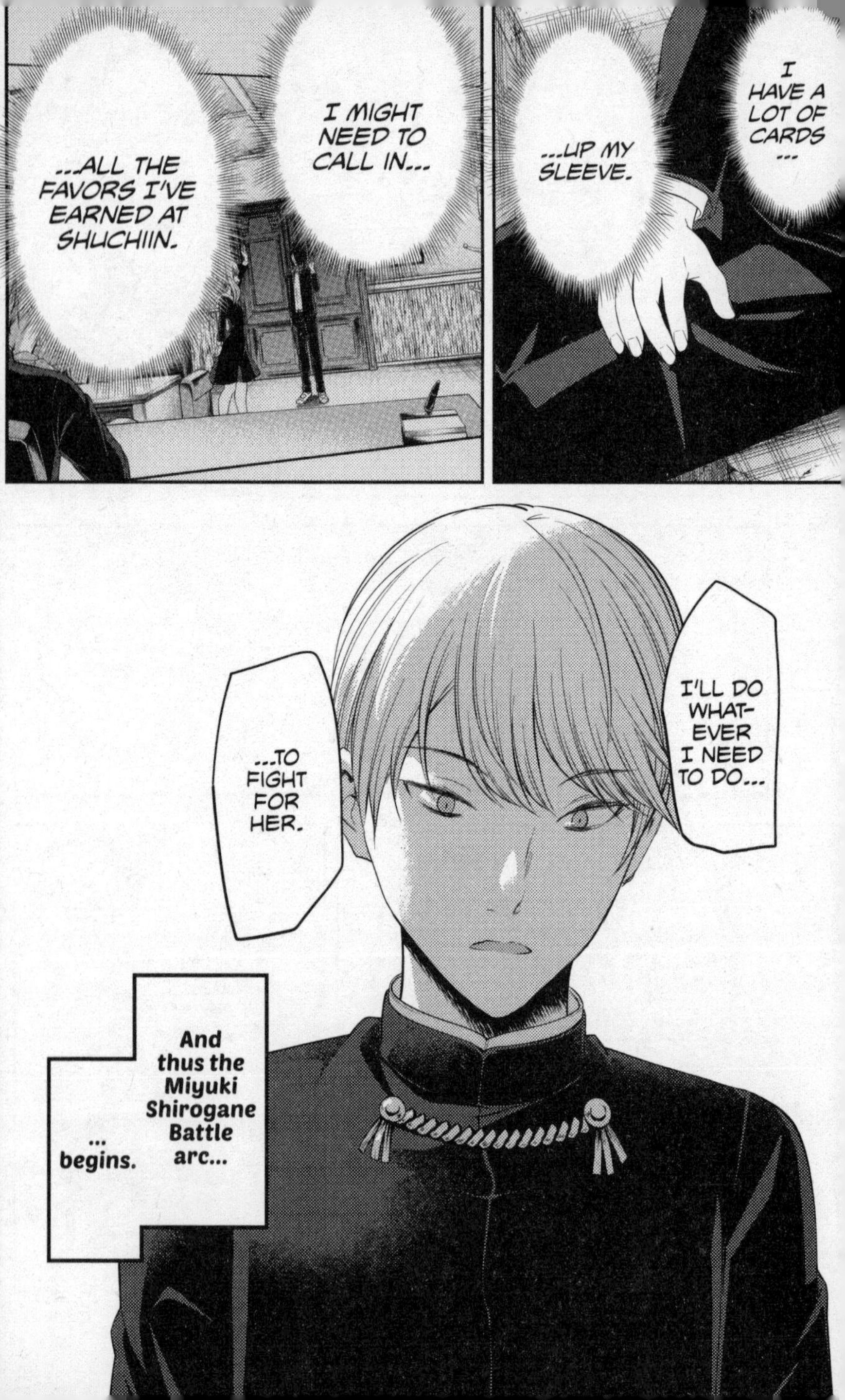
I HAVE A LOT OF CARDS...
...UP MY SLEEVE.
I MIGHT NEED TO CALL IN...
...ALL THE FAVORS I'VE EARNED AT SHUCHIIN.
I'LL DO WHATEVER I NEED TO DO...
...TO FIGHT FOR HER.
And thus the Miyuki Shirogane Battle arc...
...begins.

KAGUYA-SAMA
LOVE IS WAR

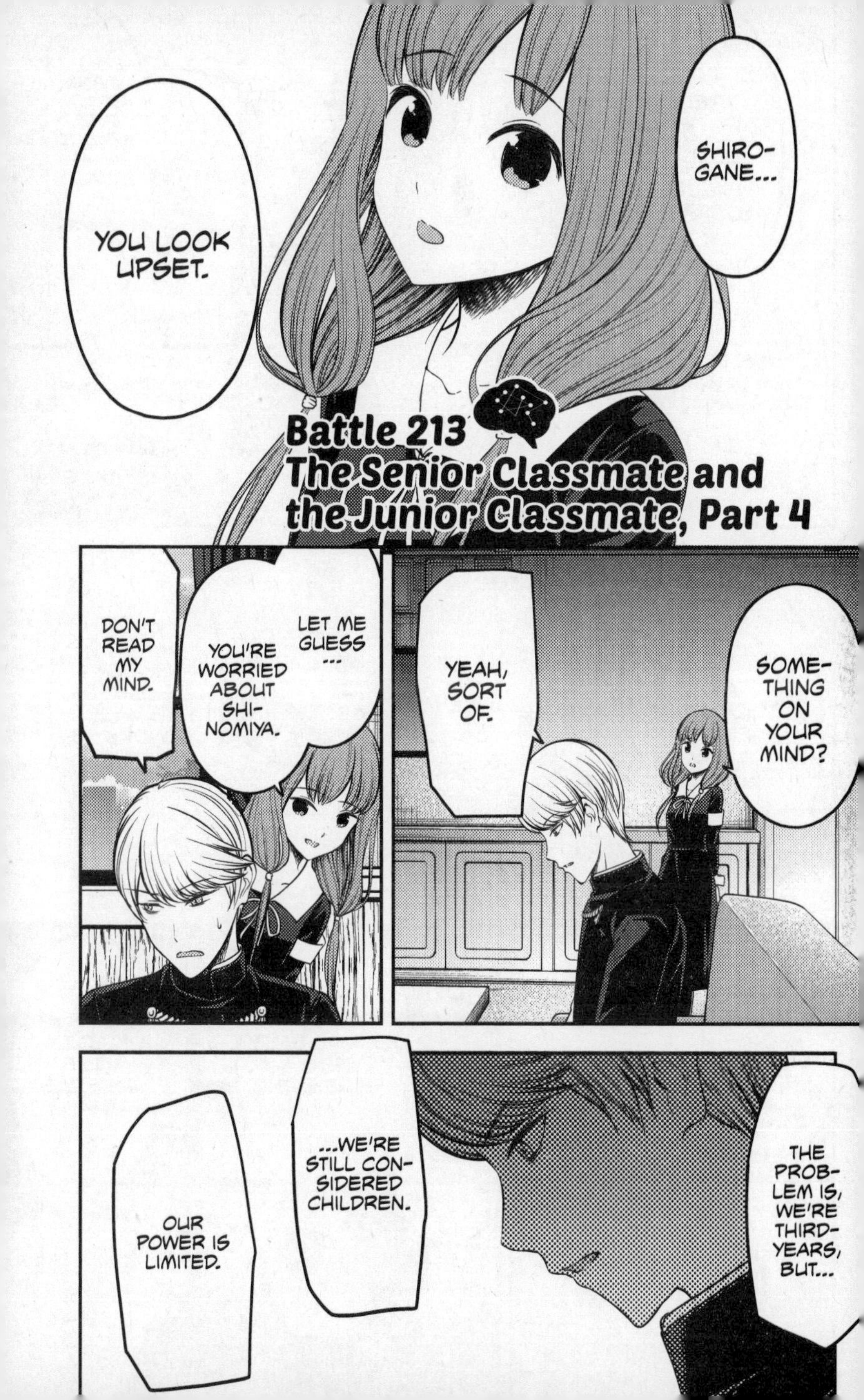
SHIROGANE...
YOU LOOK UPSET.
Battle 213 The Senior Classmate and the Junior Classmate, Part 4
SOMETHING ON YOUR MIND?
YEAH, SORT OF.
LET ME GUESS...
YOU'RE WORRIED ABOUT SHINOMIYA.
DON'T READ MY MIND.
THE PROBLEM IS, WE'RE THIRD-YEARS, BUT...
...WE'RE STILL CONSIDERED CHILDREN.
OUR POWER IS LIMITED.

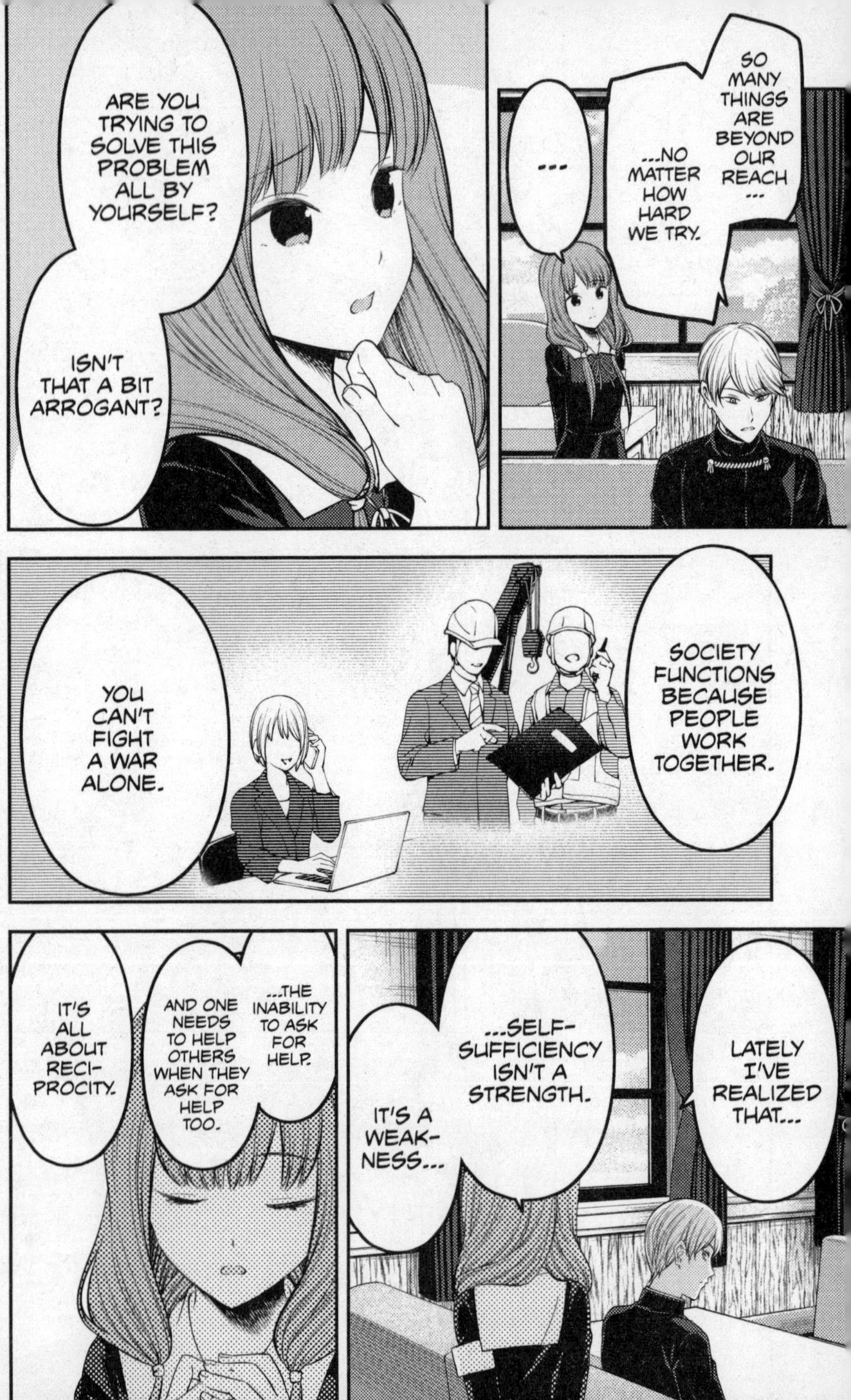
SO MANY THINGS ARE BEYOND OUR REACH...
...NO MATTER HOW HARD WE TRY.
...
ARE YOU TRYING TO SOLVE THIS PROBLEM ALL BY YOURSELF?
ISN'T THAT A BIT ARROGANT?
SOCIETY FUNCTIONS BECAUSE PEOPLE WORK TOGETHER.
YOU CAN'T FIGHT A WAR ALONE.
LATELY I'VE REALIZED THAT...
...SELF-SUFFICIENCY ISN'T A STRENGTH.
IT'S A WEAKNESS...
...THE INABILITY TO ASK FOR HELP.
AND ONE NEEDS TO HELP OTHERS WHEN THEY ASK FOR HELP TOO.
IT'S ALL ABOUT RECIPROCITY.

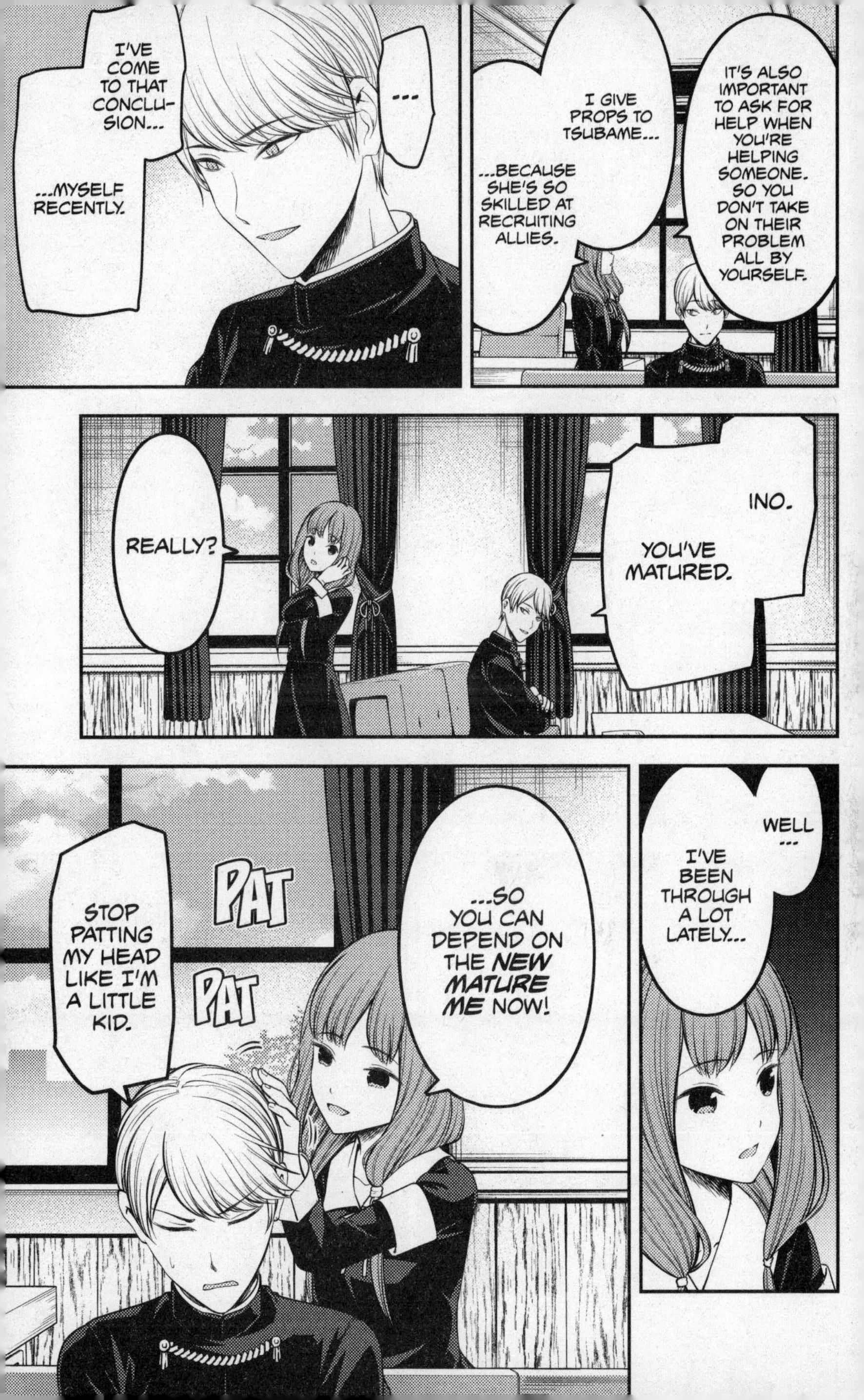
IT'S ALSO IMPORTANT TO ASK FOR HELP WHEN YOU'RE HELPING SOMEONE. SO YOU DON'T TAKE ON THEIR PROBLEM ALL BY YOURSELF.
I GIVE PROPS TO TSUBAME...
...BECAUSE SHE'S SO SKILLED AT RECRUITING ALLIES.
...
I'VE COME TO THAT CONCLUSION...
...MYSELF RECENTLY.
INO.
YOU'VE MATURED.
REALLY?
WELL...
I'VE BEEN THROUGH A LOT LATELY...
...SO YOU CAN DEPEND ON THE *NEW MATURE ME* NOW!
PAT
PAT
STOP PATTING MY HEAD LIKE I'M A LITTLE KID.

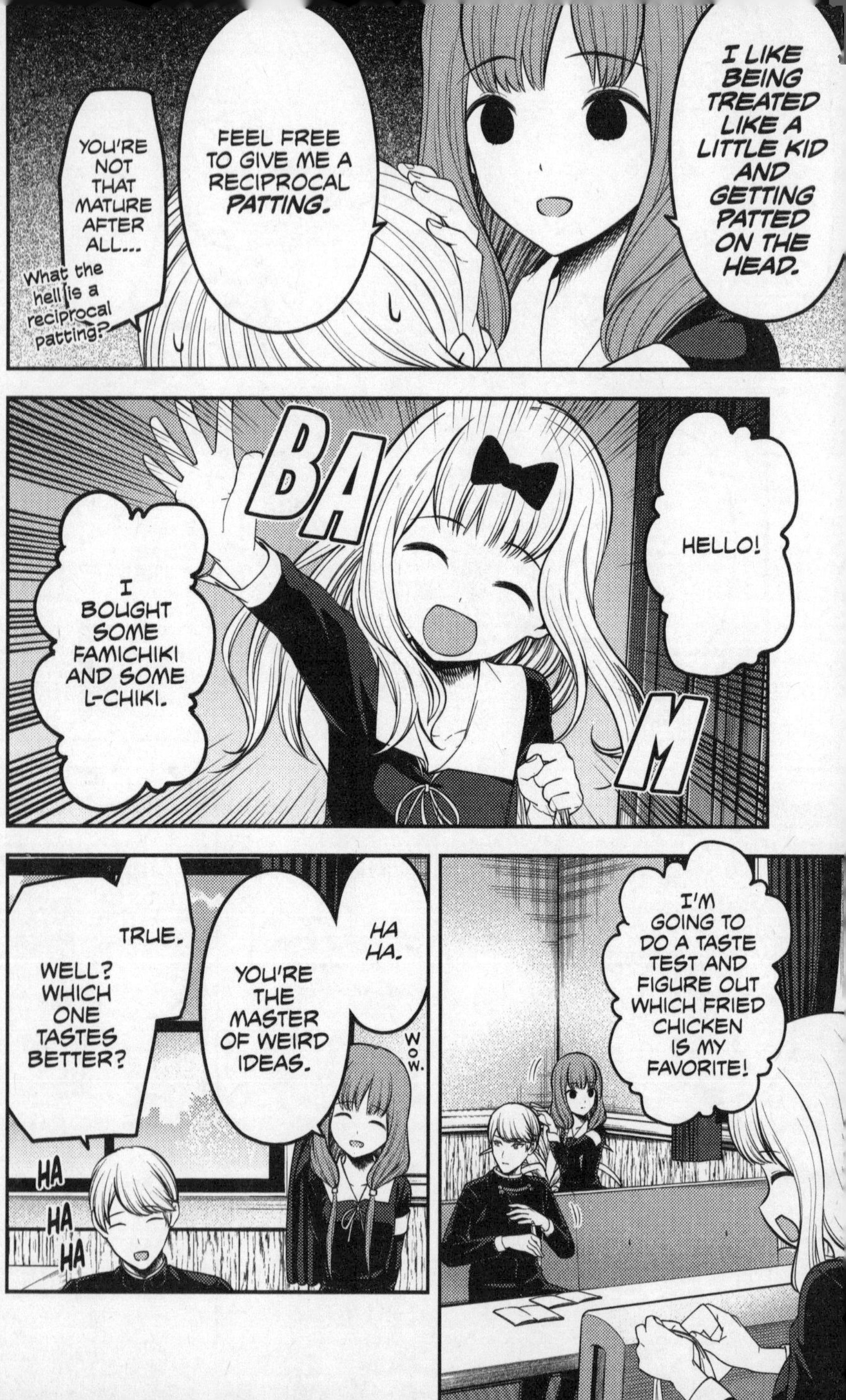
I LIKE BEING TREATED LIKE A LITTLE KID AND GETTING PATTED ON THE HEAD.
FEEL FREE TO GIVE ME A RECIPROCAL PATTING.
YOU'RE NOT THAT MATURE AFTER ALL...
What the hell is a reciprocal patting?
HELLO!
BAM
I BOUGHT SOME FAMICHIKI AND SOME L-CHIKI.
I'M GOING TO DO A TASTE TEST AND FIGURE OUT WHICH FRIED CHICKEN IS MY FAVORITE!
HA HA.
YOU'RE THE MASTER OF WEIRD IDEAS.
WOW.
TRUE.
WELL? WHICH ONE TASTES BETTER?
HA HA HA

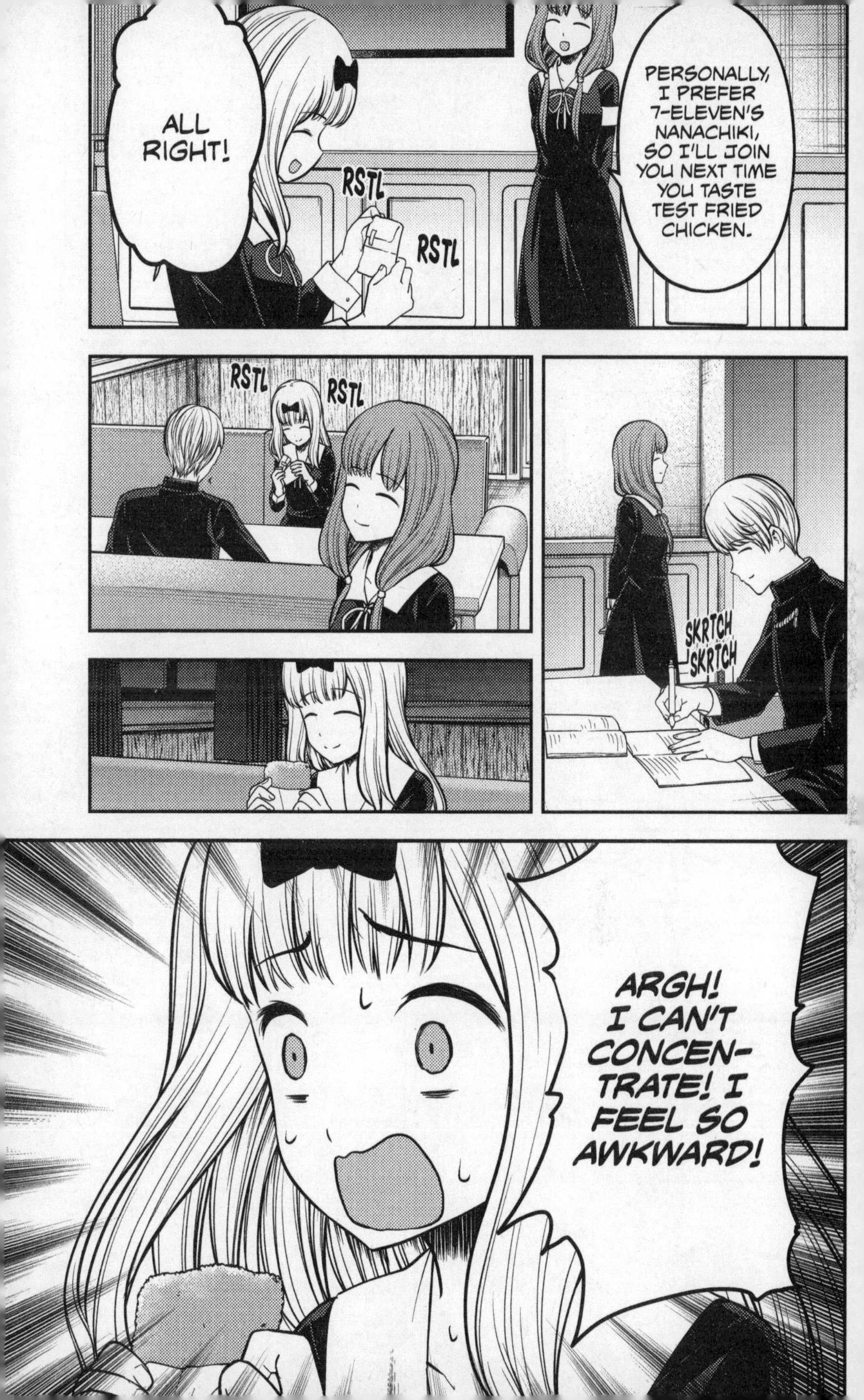
PERSONALLY, I PREFER 7-ELEVEN'S NANACHIKI, SO I'LL JOIN YOU NEXT TIME YOU TASTE TEST FRIED CHICKEN.
ALL RIGHT!
RSTL
RSTL
SKRTCH
SKRTCH
RSTL
RSTL
ARGH! I CAN'T CONCEN-TRATE! I FEEL SO AWKWARD!

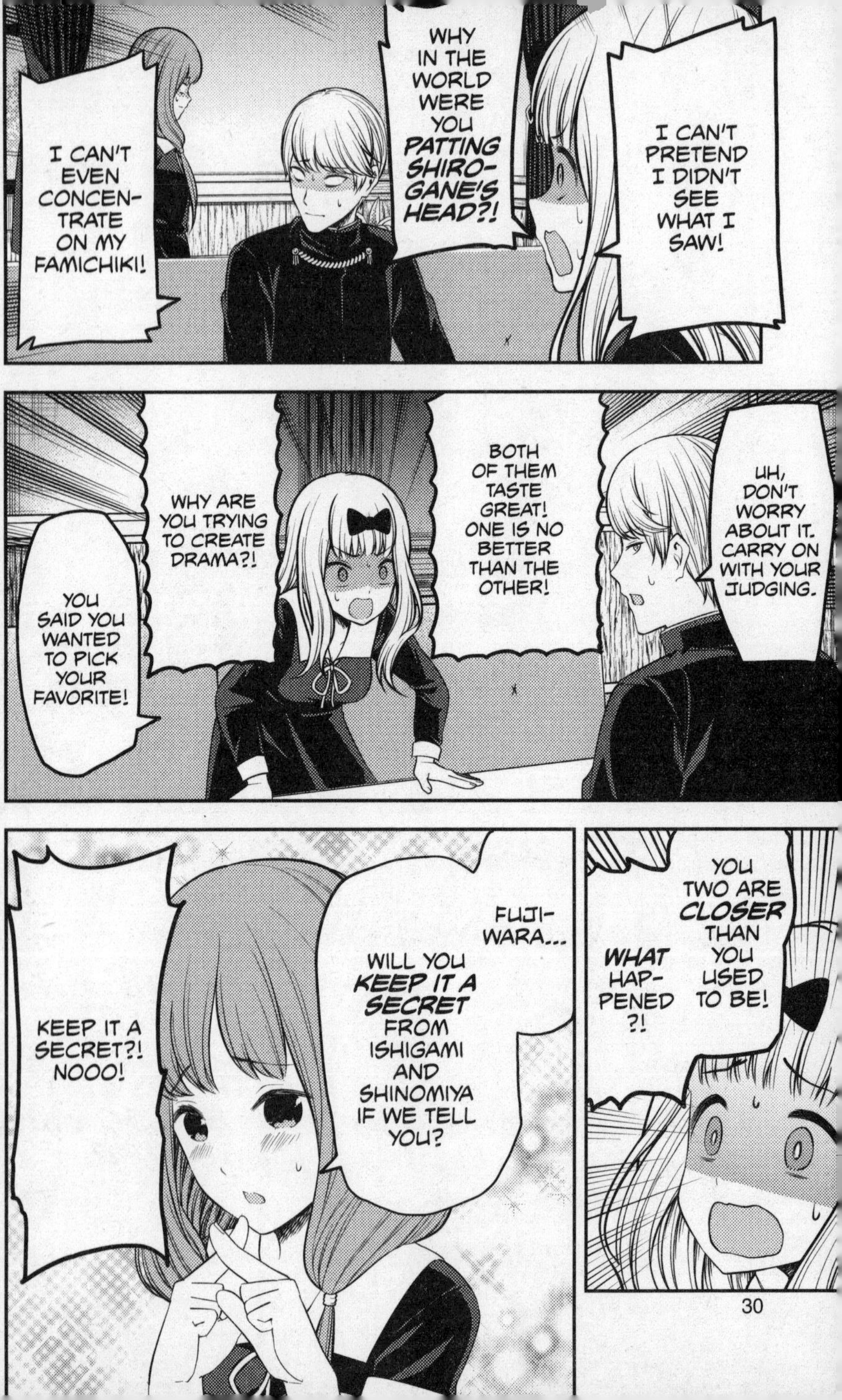

I CAN'T PRETEND I DIDN'T SEE WHAT I SAW!
WHY IN THE WORLD WERE YOU PATTING SHIROGANE'S HEAD?!
I CAN'T EVEN CONCENTRATE ON MY FAMICHIKI!
UH, DON'T WORRY ABOUT IT. CARRY ON WITH YOUR JUDGING.
BOTH OF THEM TASTE GREAT! ONE IS NO BETTER THAN THE OTHER!
WHY ARE YOU TRYING TO CREATE DRAMA?!
YOU SAID YOU WANTED TO PICK YOUR FAVORITE!
YOU TWO ARE CLOSER THAN YOU USED TO BE!
WHAT HAPPENED?!
FUJIWARA... WILL YOU KEEP IT A SECRET FROM ISHIGAMI AND SHINOMIYA IF WE TELL YOU?
KEEP IT A SECRET?! NOOO!

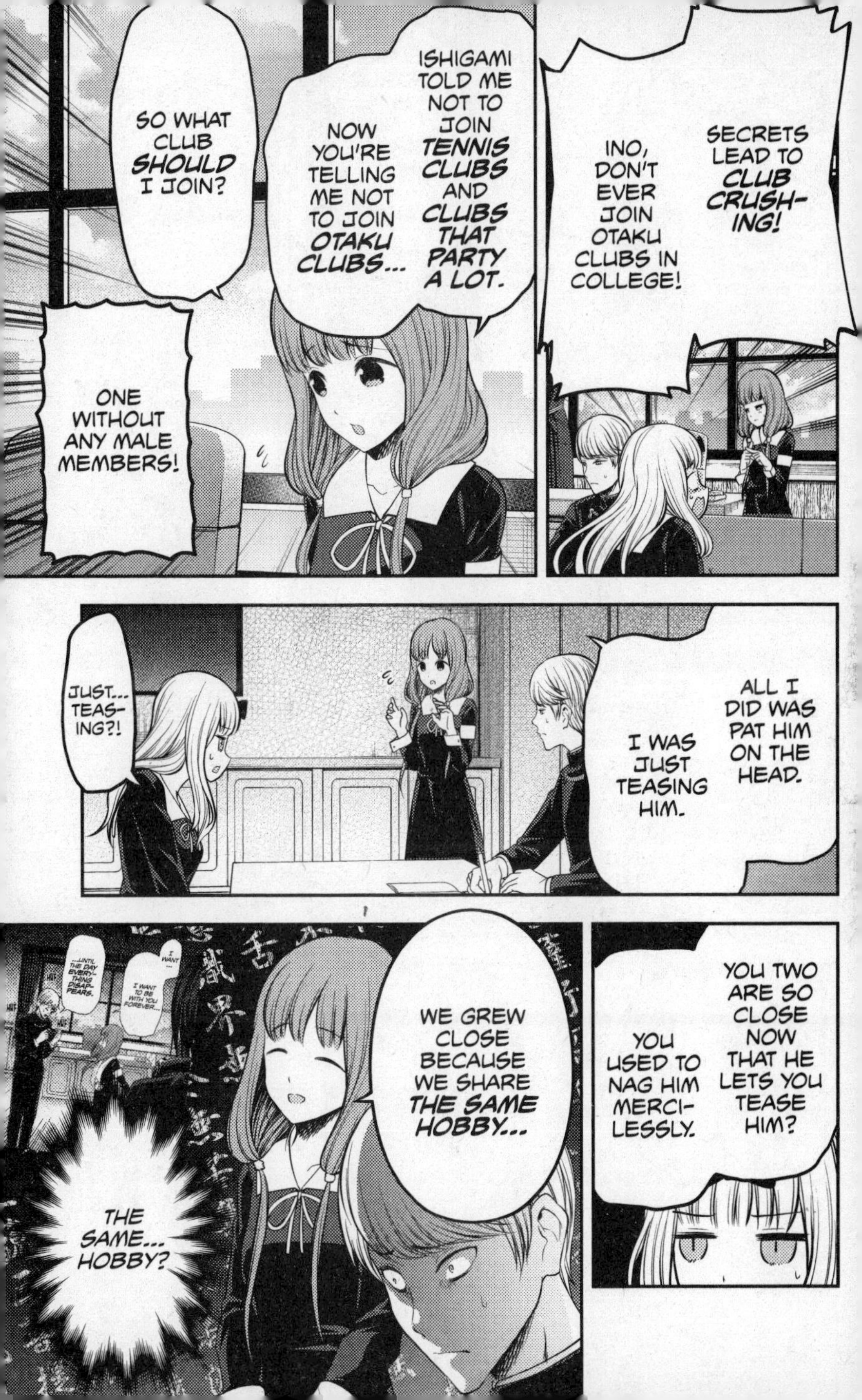
SECRETS LEAD TO CLUB CRUSHING!
NO, DON'T EVER JOIN OTAKU CLUBS IN COLLEGE!
ISHIGAMI TOLD ME NOT TO JOIN TENNIS CLUBS AND CLUBS THAT PARTY A LOT.
NOW YOU'RE TELLING ME NOT TO JOIN OTAKU CLUBS...
SO WHAT CLUB SHOULD I JOIN?
ONE WITHOUT ANY MALE MEMBERS!
ALL I DID WAS PAT HIM ON THE HEAD.
I WAS JUST TEASING HIM.
JUST... TEASING?!
YOU TWO ARE SO CLOSE NOW THAT HE LETS YOU TEASE HIM?
YOU USED TO NAG HIM MERCILESSLY.
WE GREW CLOSE BECAUSE WE SHARE THE SAME HOBBY...
I WANT...
I WANT TO BE WITH YOU FOREVER...
...UNTIL THE DAY EVERYTHING DISAPPEARS.
THE SAME... HOBBY?

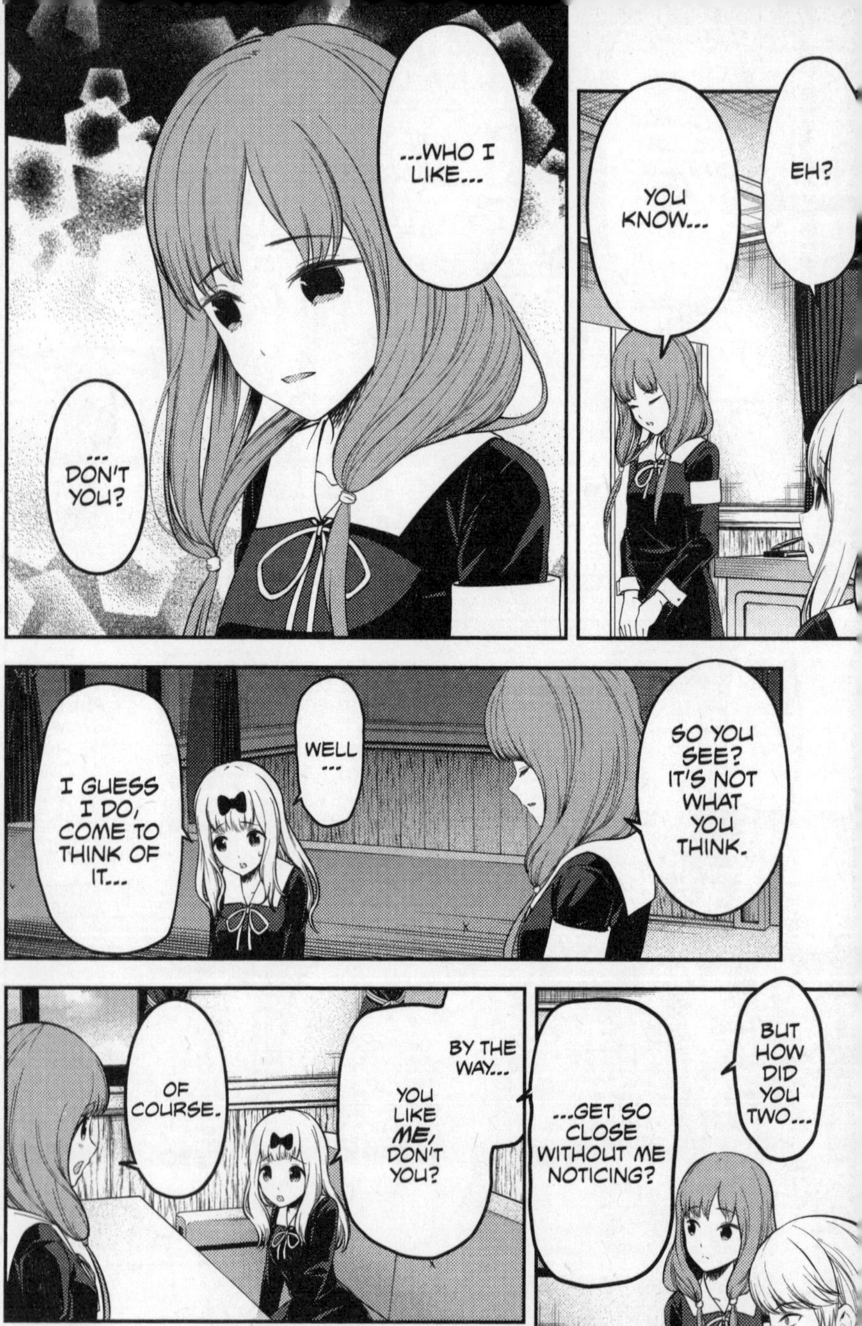
EH?
YOU KNOW...
...WHO I LIKE...
...DON'T YOU?
SO YOU SEE? IT'S NOT WHAT YOU THINK.
WELL...
I GUESS I DO, COME TO THINK OF IT...
BUT HOW DID YOU TWO...
...GET SO CLOSE WITHOUT ME NOTICING?
BY THE WAY...
YOU LIKE *ME*, DON'T YOU?
OF COURSE.

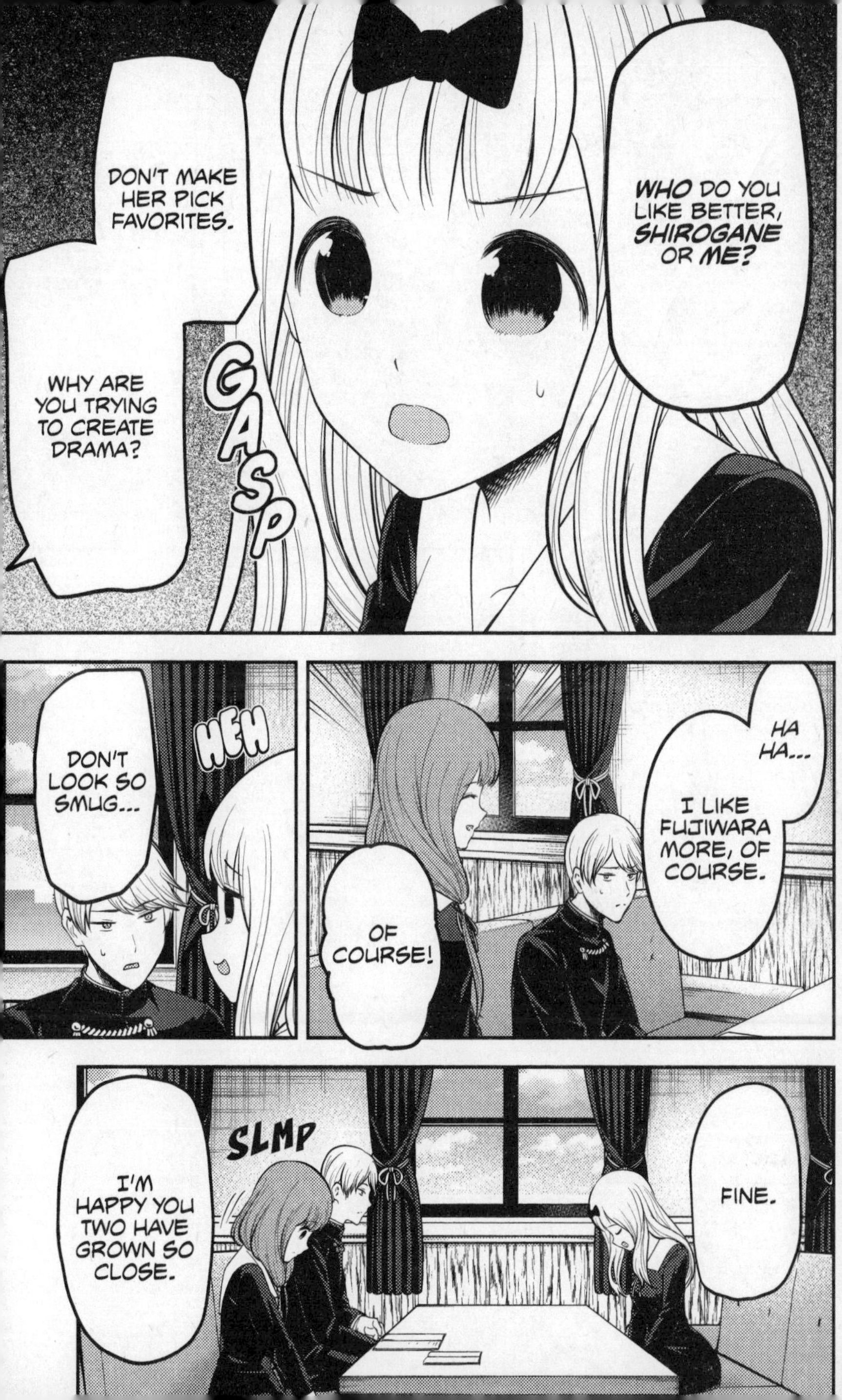
WHO DO YOU LIKE BETTER, SHIROGANE OR ME?
GASP
DON'T MAKE HER PICK FAVORITES.
WHY ARE YOU TRYING TO CREATE DRAMA?
HA HA...
I LIKE FUJIWARA MORE, OF COURSE.
OF COURSE!
HEH
DON'T LOOK SO SMUG...
FINE.
SLMP
I'M HAPPY YOU TWO HAVE GROWN SO CLOSE.

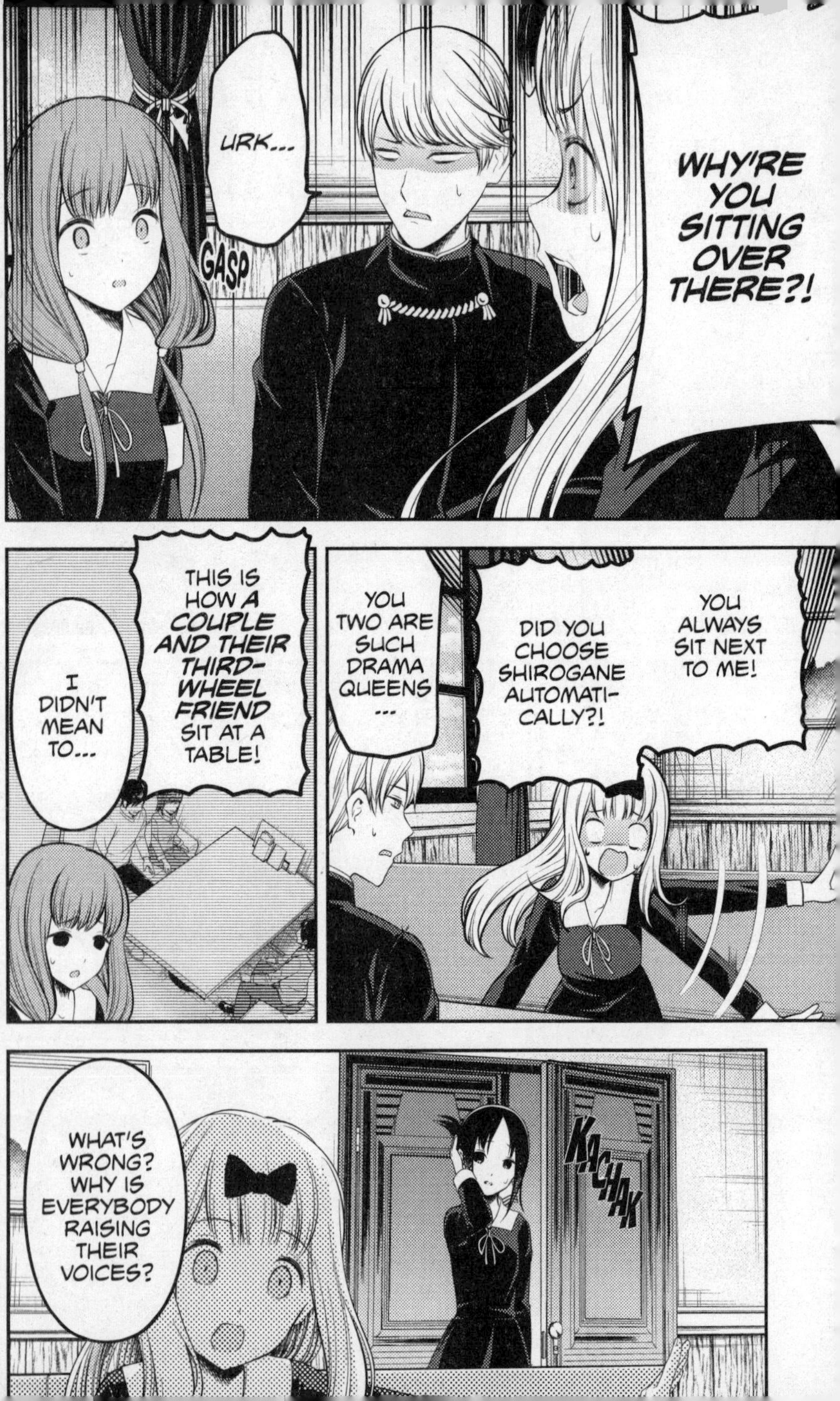
WHY'RE YOU SITTING OVER THERE?!
URK...
GASP
YOU ALWAYS SIT NEXT TO ME!
DID YOU CHOOSE SHIROGANE AUTOMATI-CALLY?!
YOU TWO ARE SUCH DRAMA QUEENS...
THIS IS HOW A COUPLE AND THEIR THIRD-WHEEL FRIEND SIT AT A TABLE!
I DIDN'T MEAN TO...
KACHAK
WHAT'S WRONG? WHY IS EVERYBODY RAISING THEIR VOICES?

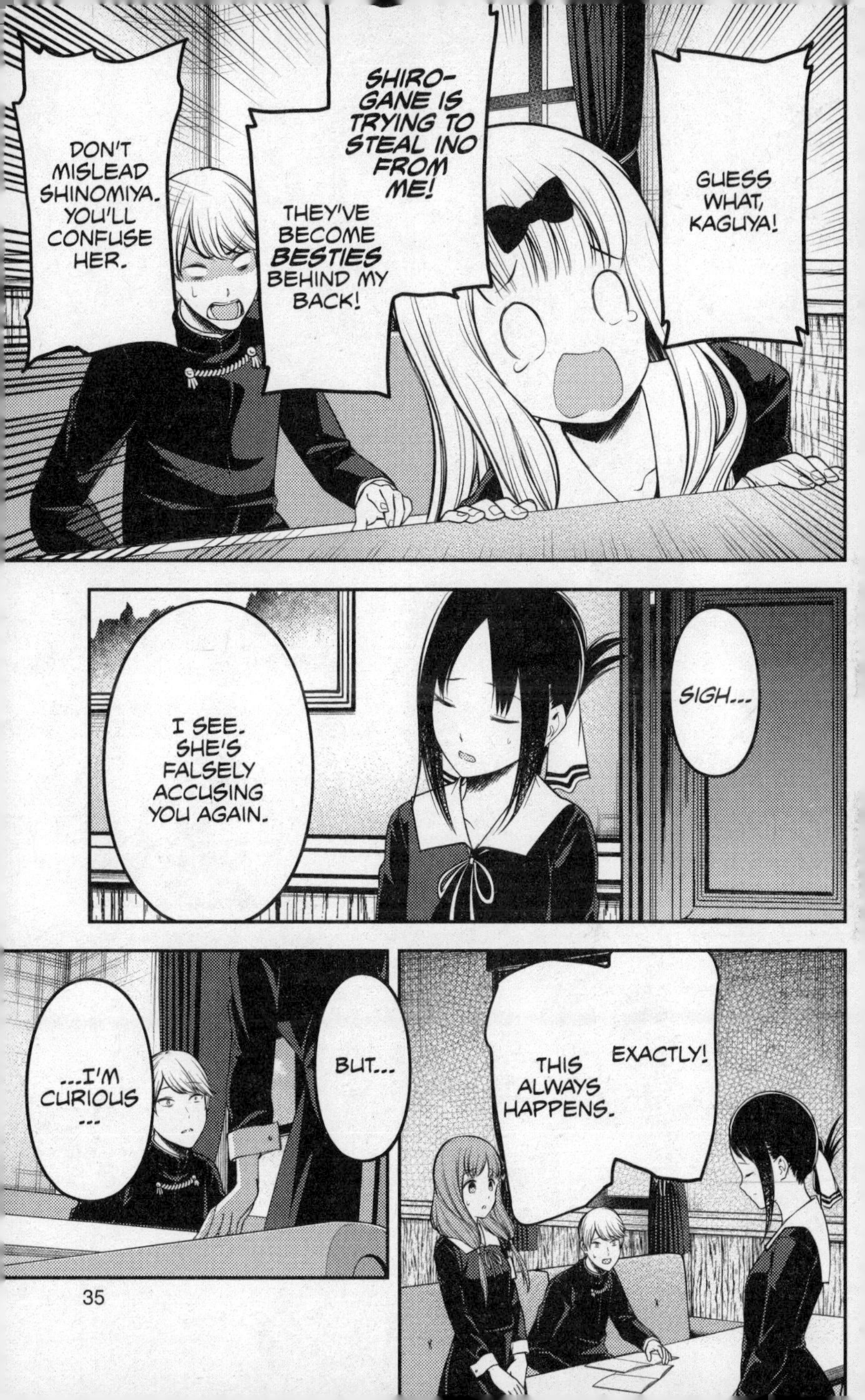
GUESS WHAT, KAGUYA!
SHIRO-GANE IS TRYING TO STEAL INO FROM ME!
THEY'VE BECOME **BESTIES** BEHIND MY BACK!
DON'T MISLEAD SHINOMIYA. YOU'LL CONFUSE HER.
SIGH...
I SEE. SHE'S FALSELY ACCUSING YOU AGAIN.
EXACTLY!
THIS ALWAYS HAPPENS.
BUT...
...I'M CURIOUS...

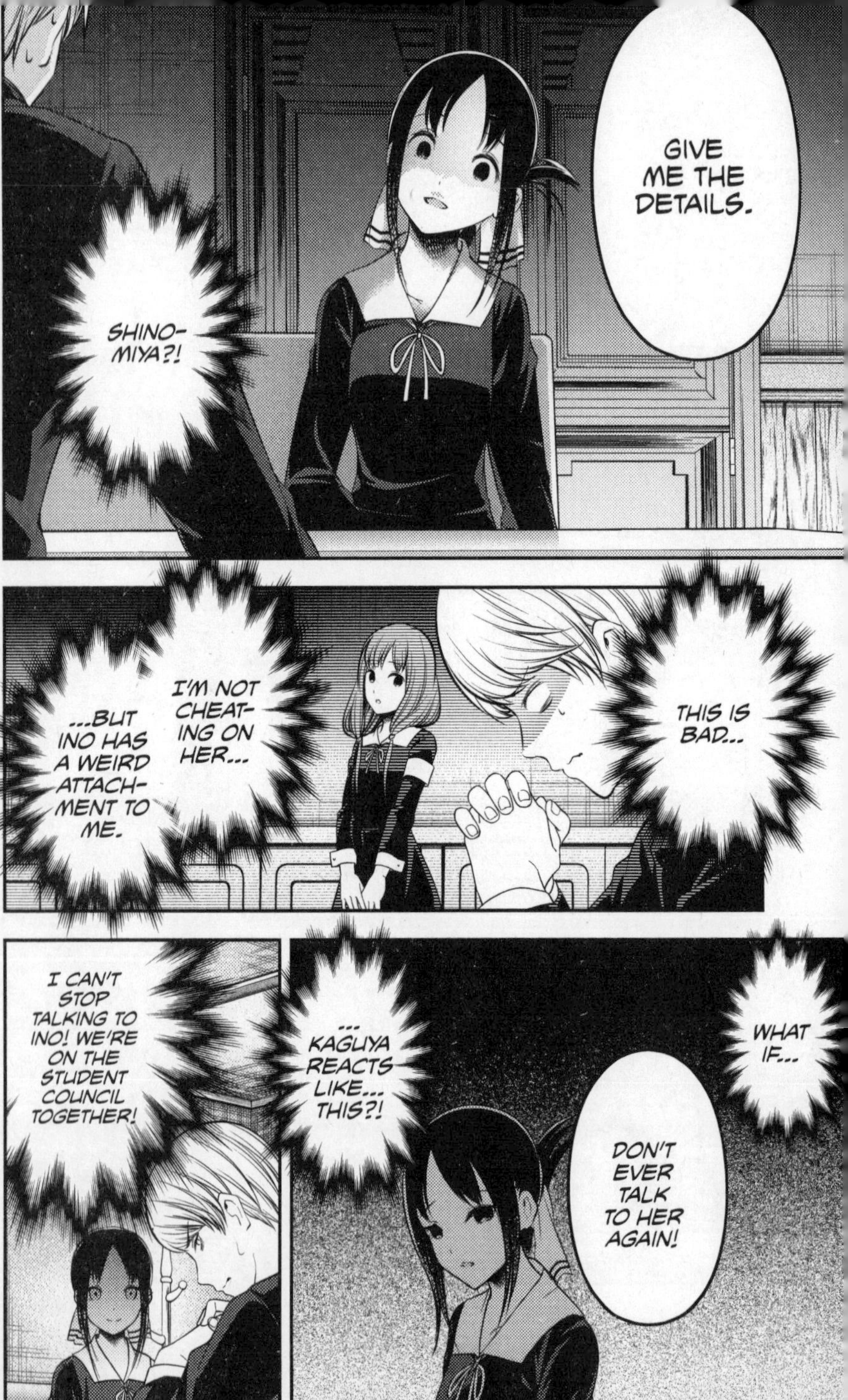
GIVE ME THE DETAILS.
SHINO-MIYA?!
THIS IS BAD...
I'M NOT CHEAT-ING ON HER...
...BUT INO HAS A WEIRD ATTACH-MENT TO ME.
WHAT IF...
...KAGUYA REACTS LIKE... THIS?!
DON'T EVER TALK TO HER AGAIN!
I CAN'T STOP TALKING TO INO! WE'RE ON THE STUDENT COUNCIL TOGETHER!

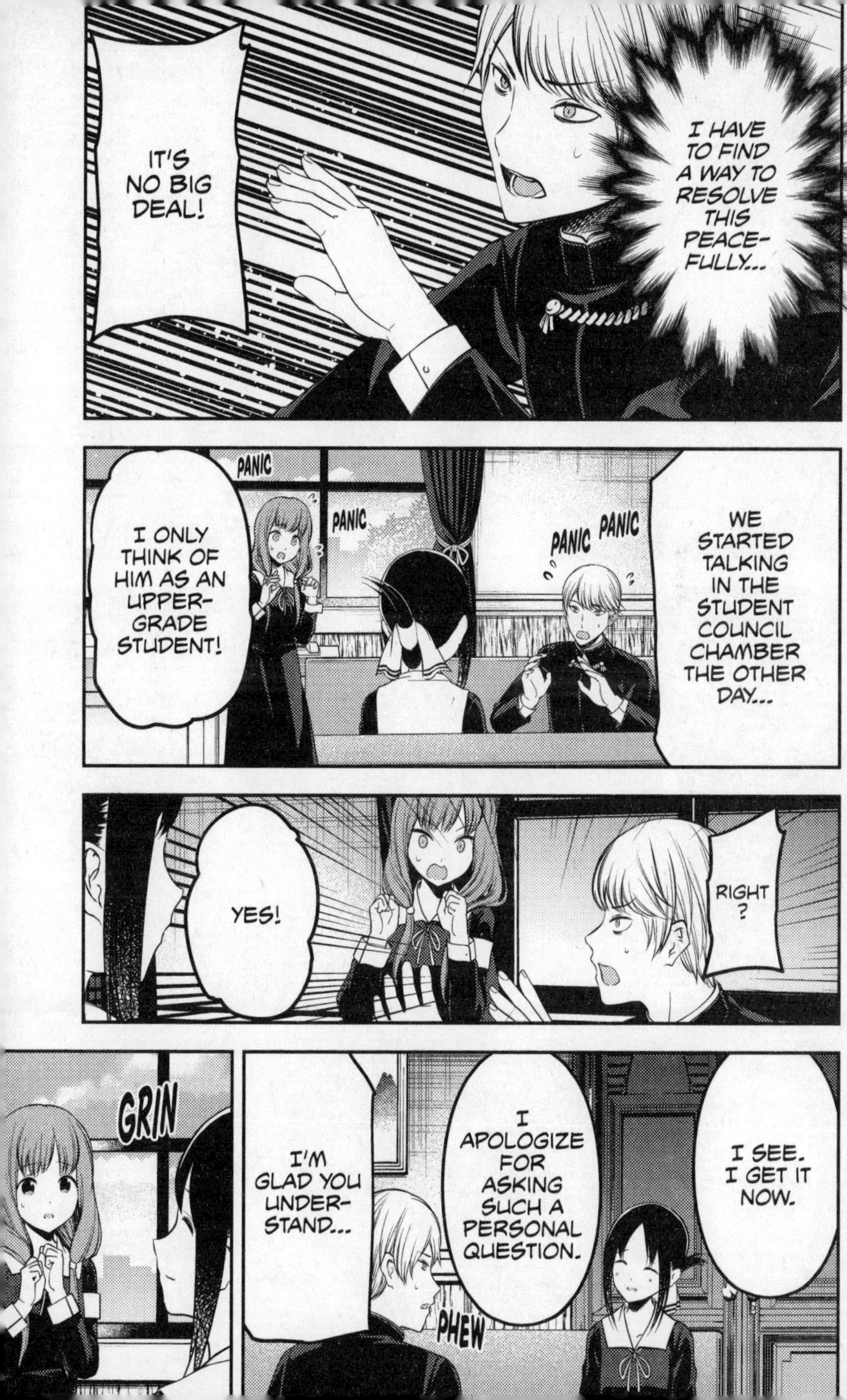
I HAVE TO FIND A WAY TO RESOLVE THIS PEACE-FULLY...
IT'S NO BIG DEAL!
WE STARTED TALKING IN THE STUDENT COUNCIL CHAMBER THE OTHER DAY...
PANIC PANIC
PANIC
PANIC
I ONLY THINK OF HIM AS AN UPPER-GRADE STUDENT!
RIGHT?
YES!
I SEE. I GET IT NOW.
I APOLOGIZE FOR ASKING SUCH A PERSONAL QUESTION.
I'M GLAD YOU UNDER-STAND...
PHEW
GRIN

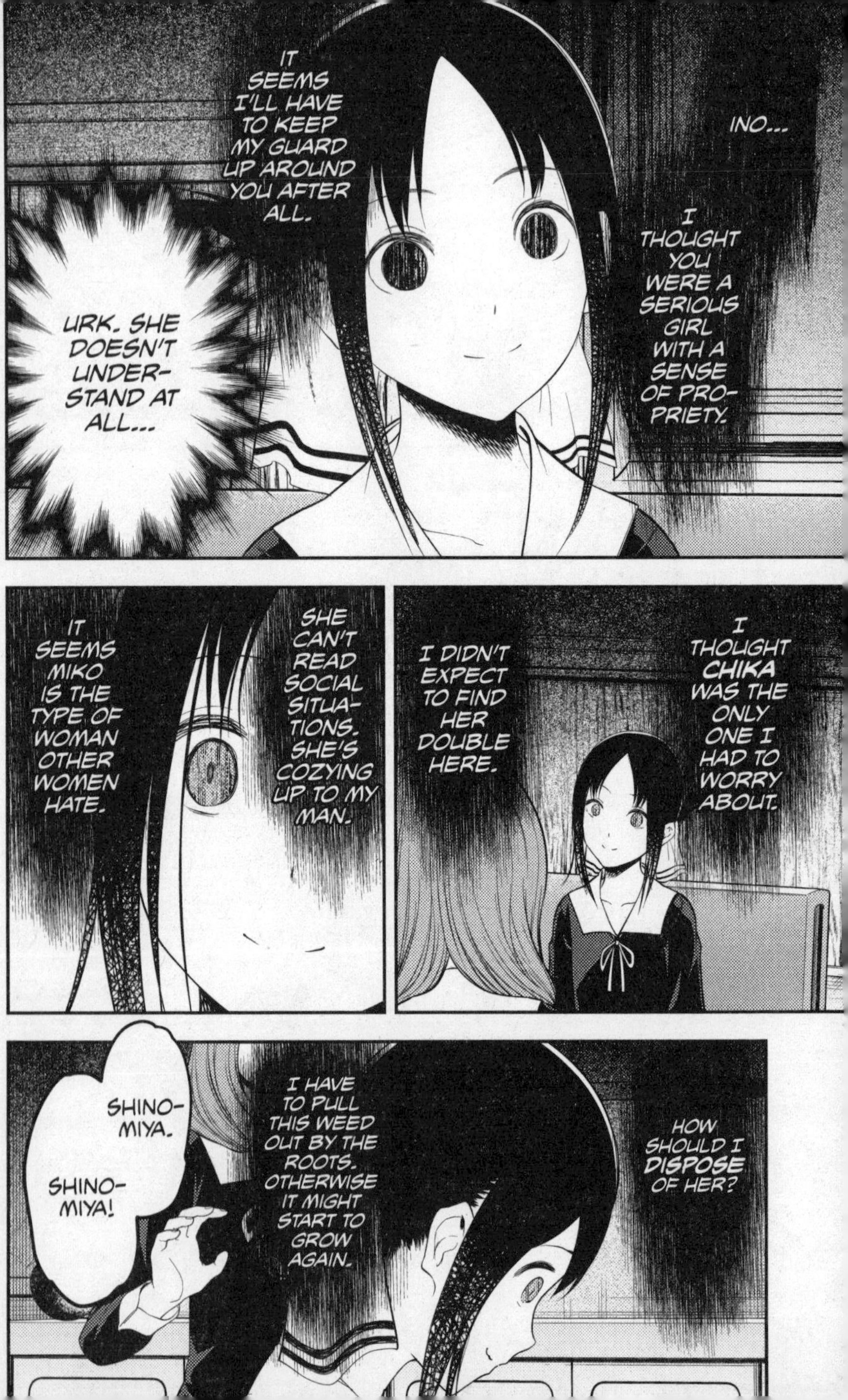
INO...
I THOUGHT YOU WERE A SERIOUS GIRL WITH A SENSE OF PROPRIETY.
IT SEEMS I'LL HAVE TO KEEP MY GUARD UP AROUND YOU AFTER ALL.
URK. SHE DOESN'T UNDERSTAND AT ALL...
I THOUGHT **CHIKA** WAS THE ONLY ONE I HAD TO WORRY ABOUT.
I DIDN'T EXPECT TO FIND HER DOUBLE HERE.
SHE CAN'T READ SOCIAL SITUATIONS. SHE'S COZYING UP TO MY MAN.
IT SEEMS MIKO IS THE TYPE OF WOMAN OTHER WOMEN HATE.
HOW SHOULD I **DISPOSE** OF HER?
I HAVE TO PULL THIS WEED OUT BY THE ROOTS. OTHERWISE IT MIGHT START TO GROW AGAIN.
SHINOMIYA.
SHINOMIYA!

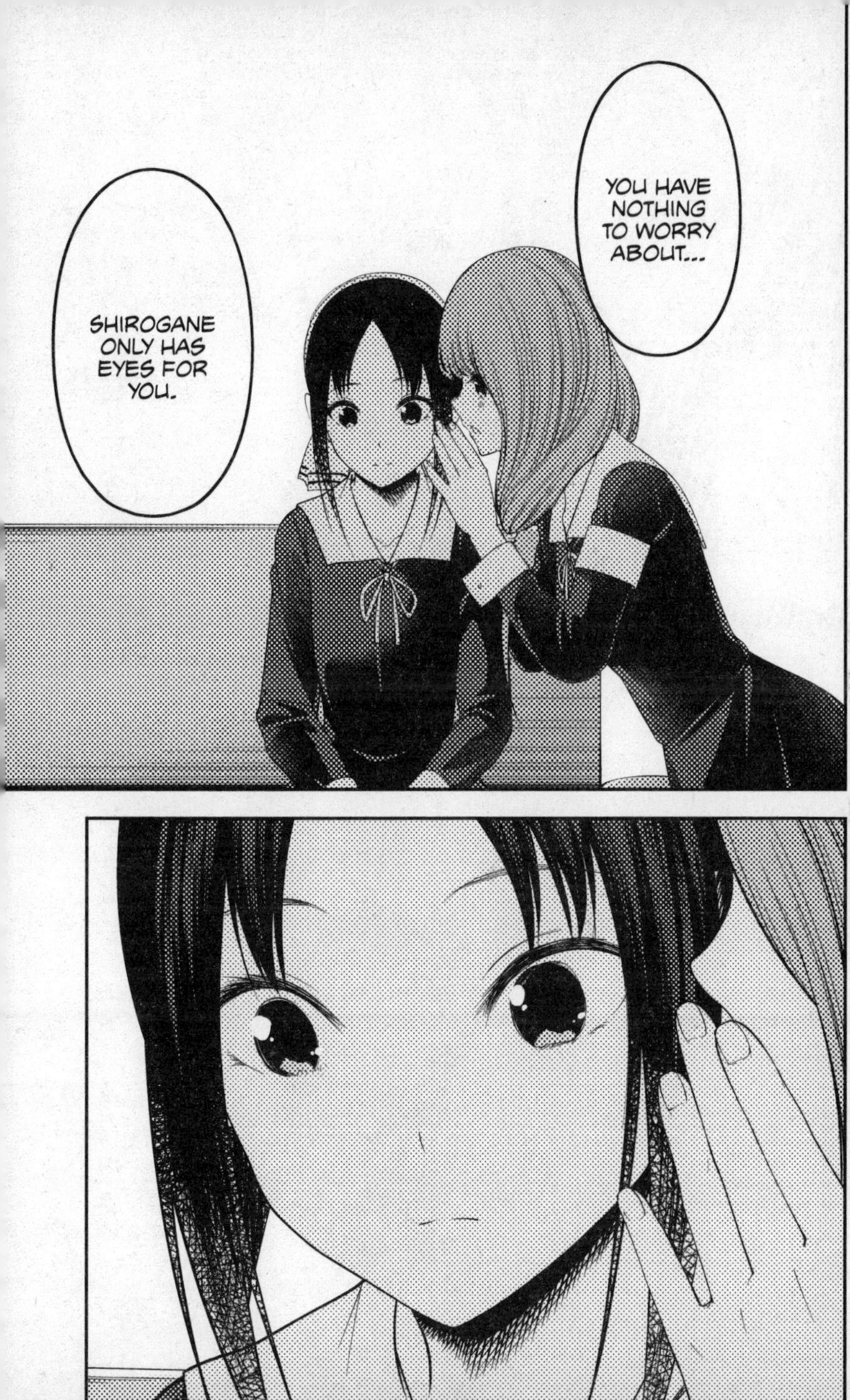
YOU HAVE NOTHING TO WORRY ABOUT...
SHIROGANE ONLY HAS EYES FOR YOU.

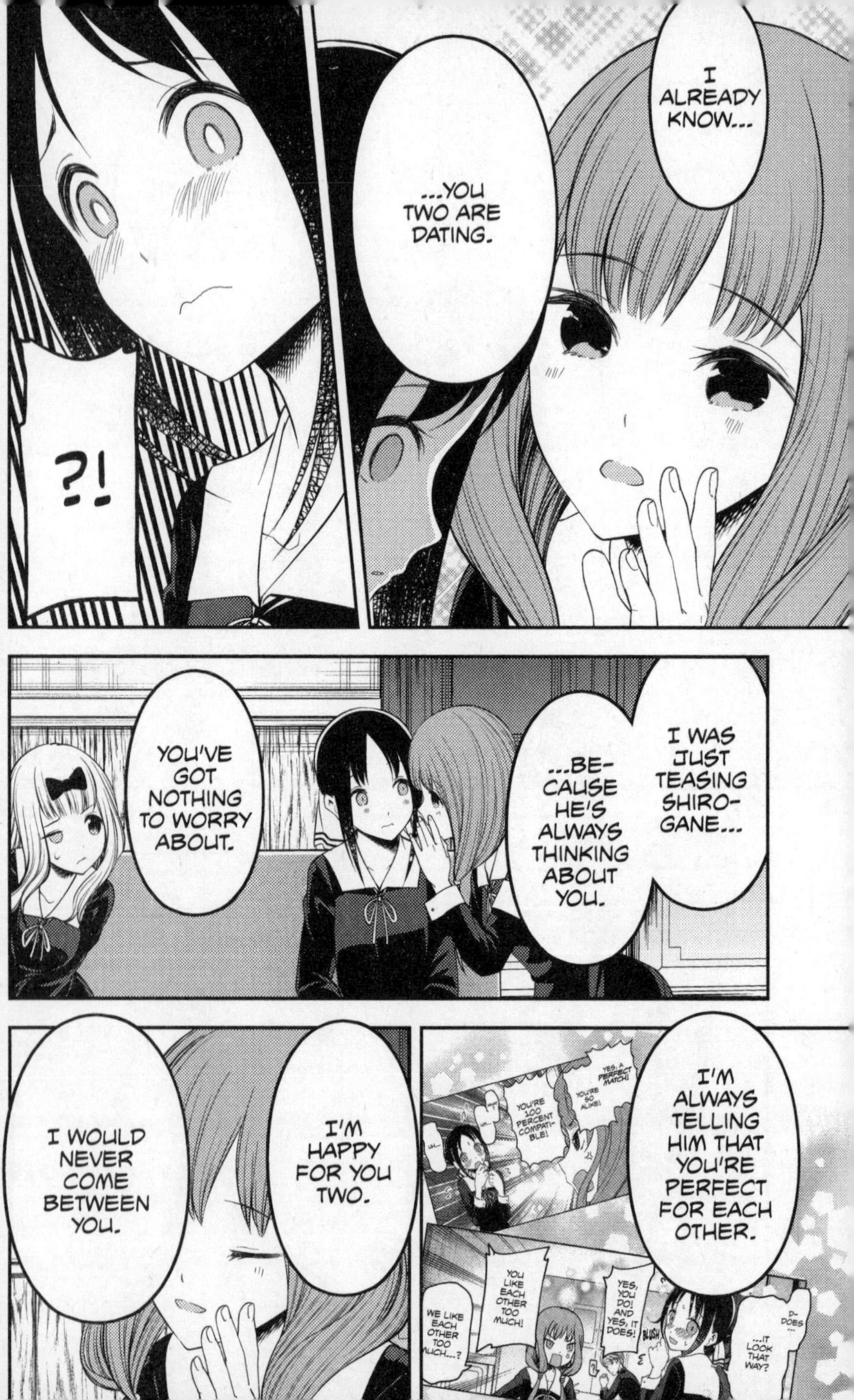
I ALREADY KNOW...
...YOU TWO ARE DATING.
?!
I WAS JUST TEASING SHIRO-GANE...
...BE-CAUSE HE'S ALWAYS THINKING ABOUT YOU.
YOU'VE GOT NOTHING TO WORRY ABOUT.
I'M ALWAYS TELLING HIM THAT YOU'RE PERFECT FOR EACH OTHER.
YES, A PERFECT MATCH!
YOU'RE SO ALIKE!
YOU'RE 100 PERCENT COMPATI-BLE!
UH...
D-DOES...
...IT LOOK THAT WAY?
YES, YOU DO! AND YES, IT DOES!
BLUSH
YOU LIKE EACH OTHER TOO MUCH!
WE LIKE EACH OTHER TOO MUCH...?
I'M HAPPY FOR YOU TWO.
I WOULD NEVER COME BETWEEN YOU.

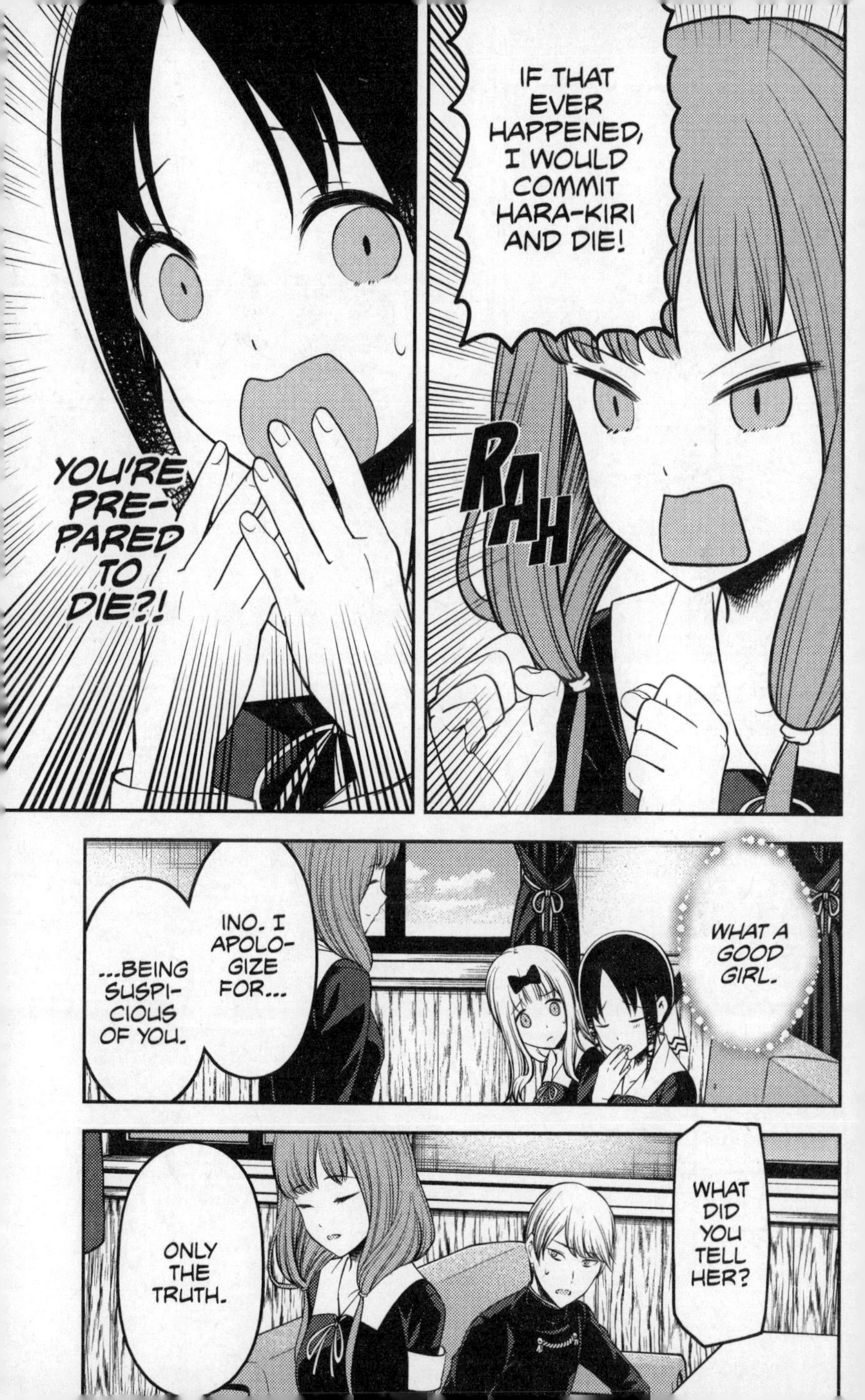
IF THAT EVER HAPPENED, I WOULD COMMIT HARA-KIRI AND DIE!
RAH
YOU'RE PRE-PARED TO DIE?!
WHAT A GOOD GIRL.
INO. I APOLO-GIZE FOR...
...BEING SUSPI-CIOUS OF YOU.
WHAT DID YOU TELL HER?
ONLY THE TRUTH.

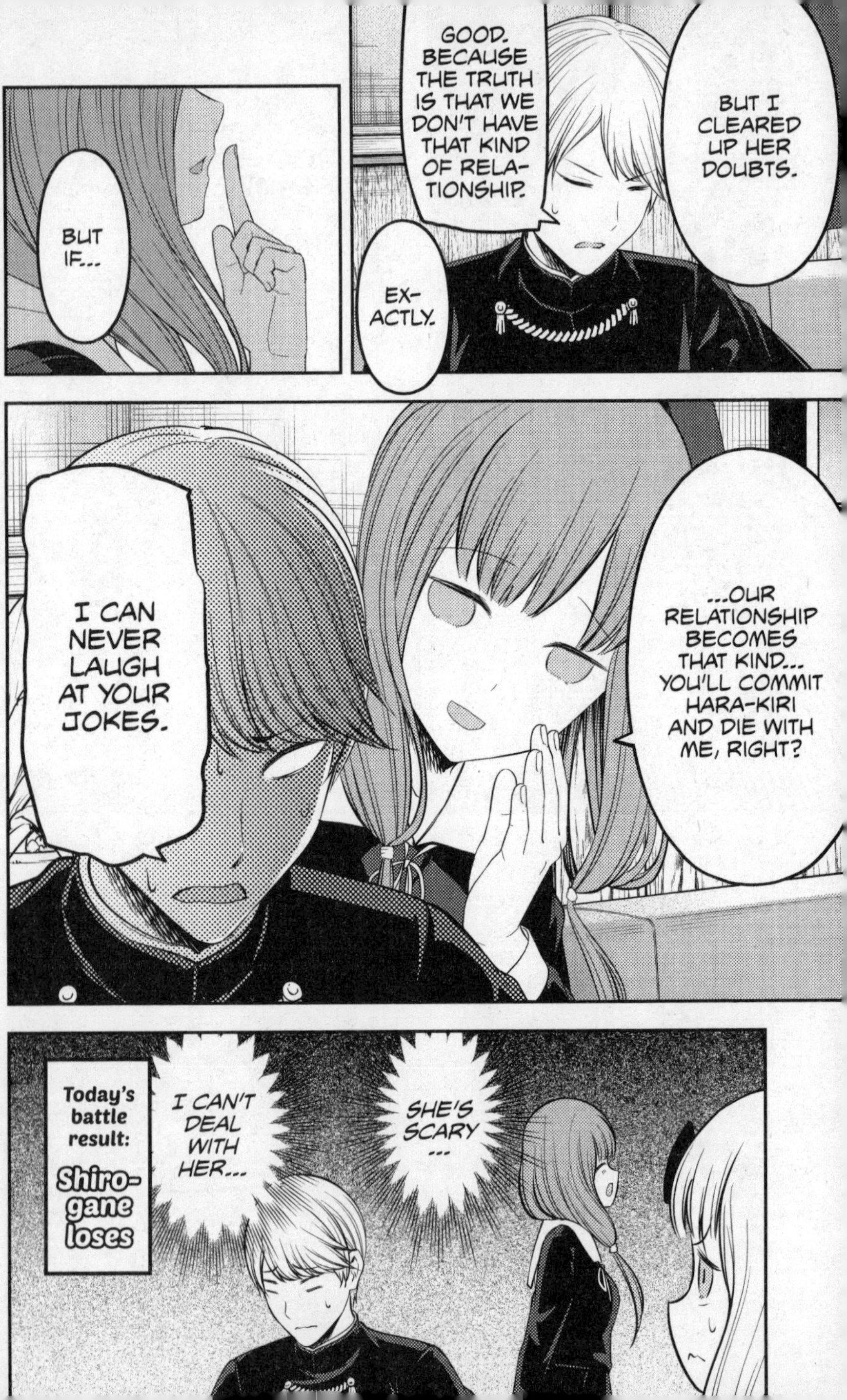
BUT I CLEARED UP HER DOUBTS.
GOOD. BECAUSE THE TRUTH IS THAT WE DON'T HAVE THAT KIND OF RELA-TIONSHIP.
EX-ACTLY.
BUT IF...
...OUR RELATIONSHIP BECOMES THAT KIND... YOU'LL COMMIT HARA-KIRI AND DIE WITH ME, RIGHT?
I CAN NEVER LAUGH AT YOUR JOKES.
SHE'S SCARY...
I CAN'T DEAL WITH HER...
Today's battle result:
Shiro-gane loses

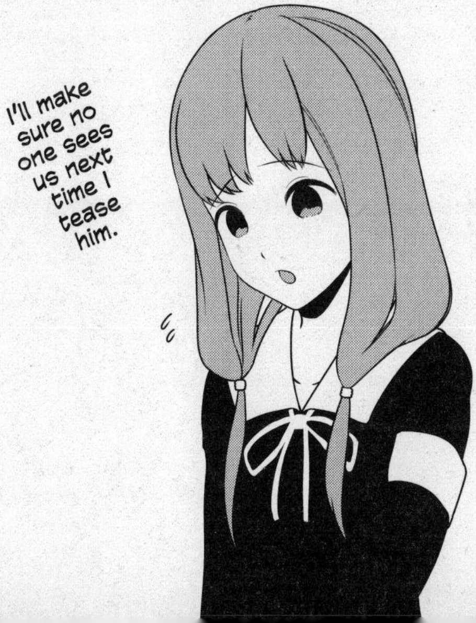
I'll make sure no one sees us next time I tease him.

KAGUYA-SAMA
LOVE IS WAR

Battle 214 Kaguya Hates Cats

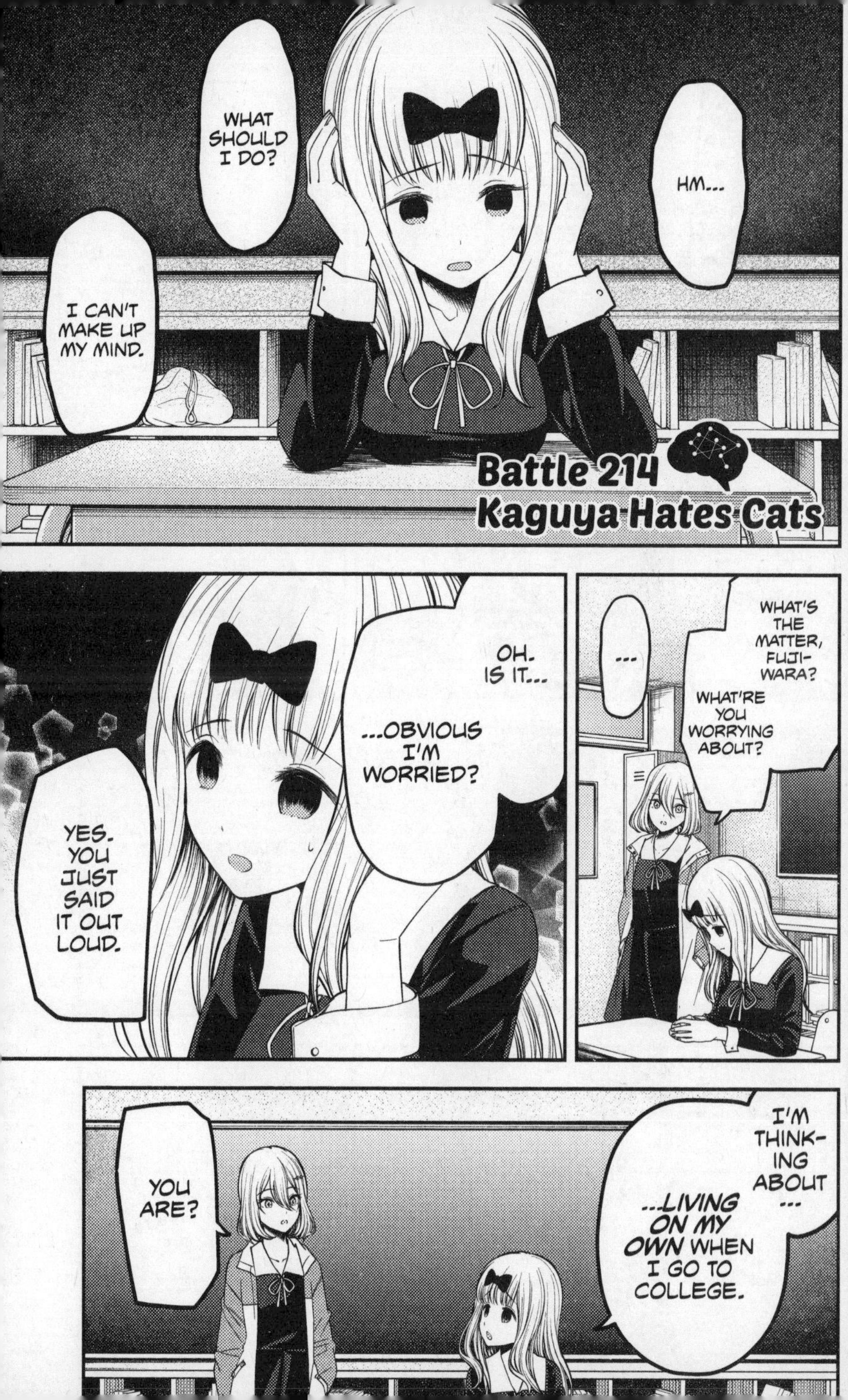
HM...
WHAT SHOULD I DO?
I CAN'T MAKE UP MY MIND.
WHAT'S THE MATTER, FUJIWARA? WHAT'RE YOU WORRYING ABOUT?
...
OH. IS IT... ...OBVIOUS I'M WORRIED?
YES. YOU JUST SAID IT OUT LOUD.
I'M THINKING ABOUT... ...*LIVING ON MY OWN* WHEN I GO TO COLLEGE.
YOU ARE?

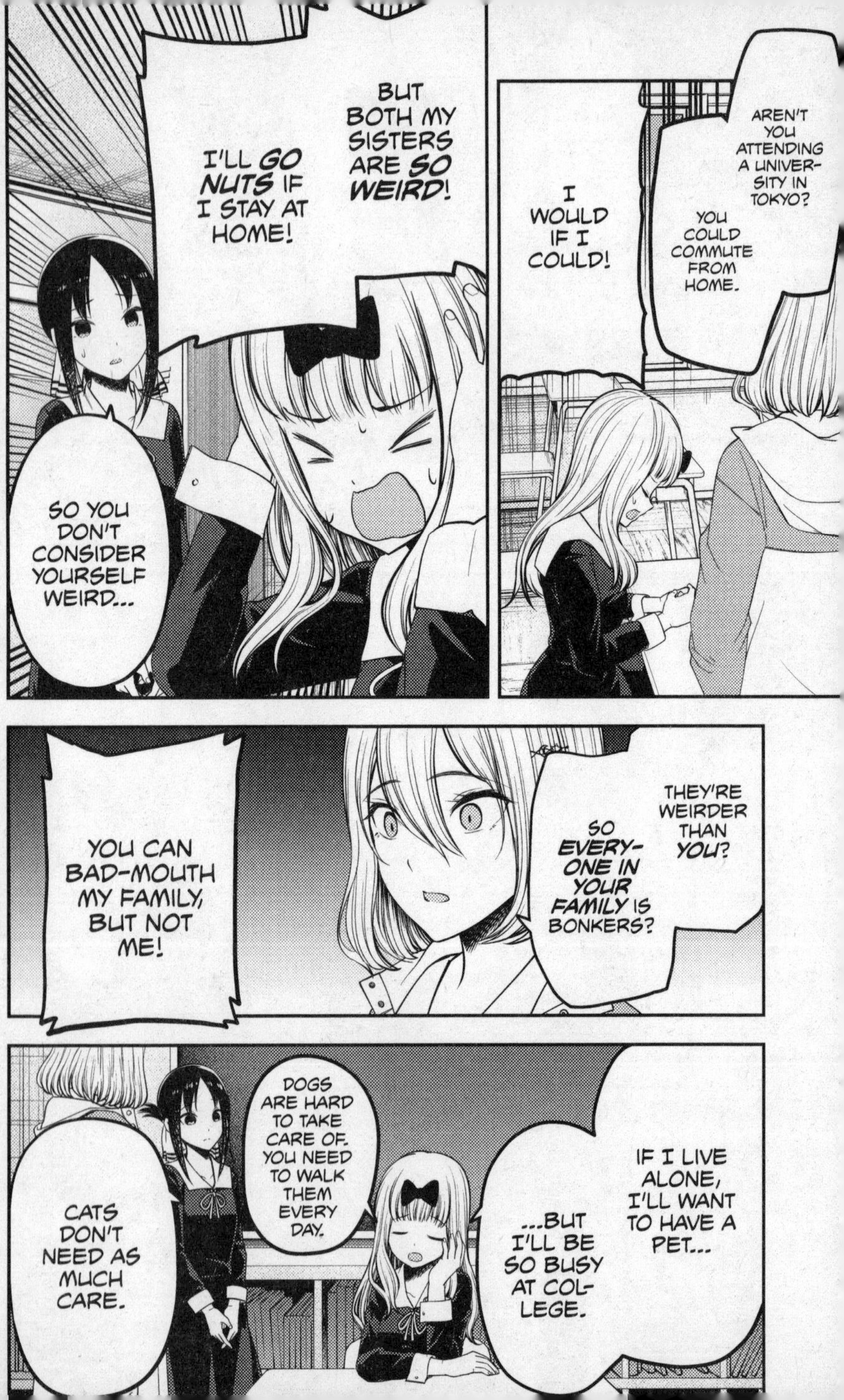
AREN'T YOU ATTENDING A UNIVERSITY IN TOKYO?
YOU COULD COMMUTE FROM HOME.
I WOULD IF I COULD!
BUT BOTH MY SISTERS ARE SO WEIRD!
I'LL GO NUTS IF I STAY AT HOME!
SO YOU DON'T CONSIDER YOURSELF WEIRD...
THEY'RE WEIRDER THAN YOU?
SO EVERYONE IN YOUR FAMILY IS BONKERS?
YOU CAN BAD-MOUTH MY FAMILY, BUT NOT ME!
IF I LIVE ALONE, I'LL WANT TO HAVE A PET...
...BUT I'LL BE SO BUSY AT COLLEGE.
DOGS ARE HARD TO TAKE CARE OF. YOU NEED TO WALK THEM EVERY DAY.
CATS DON'T NEED AS MUCH CARE.

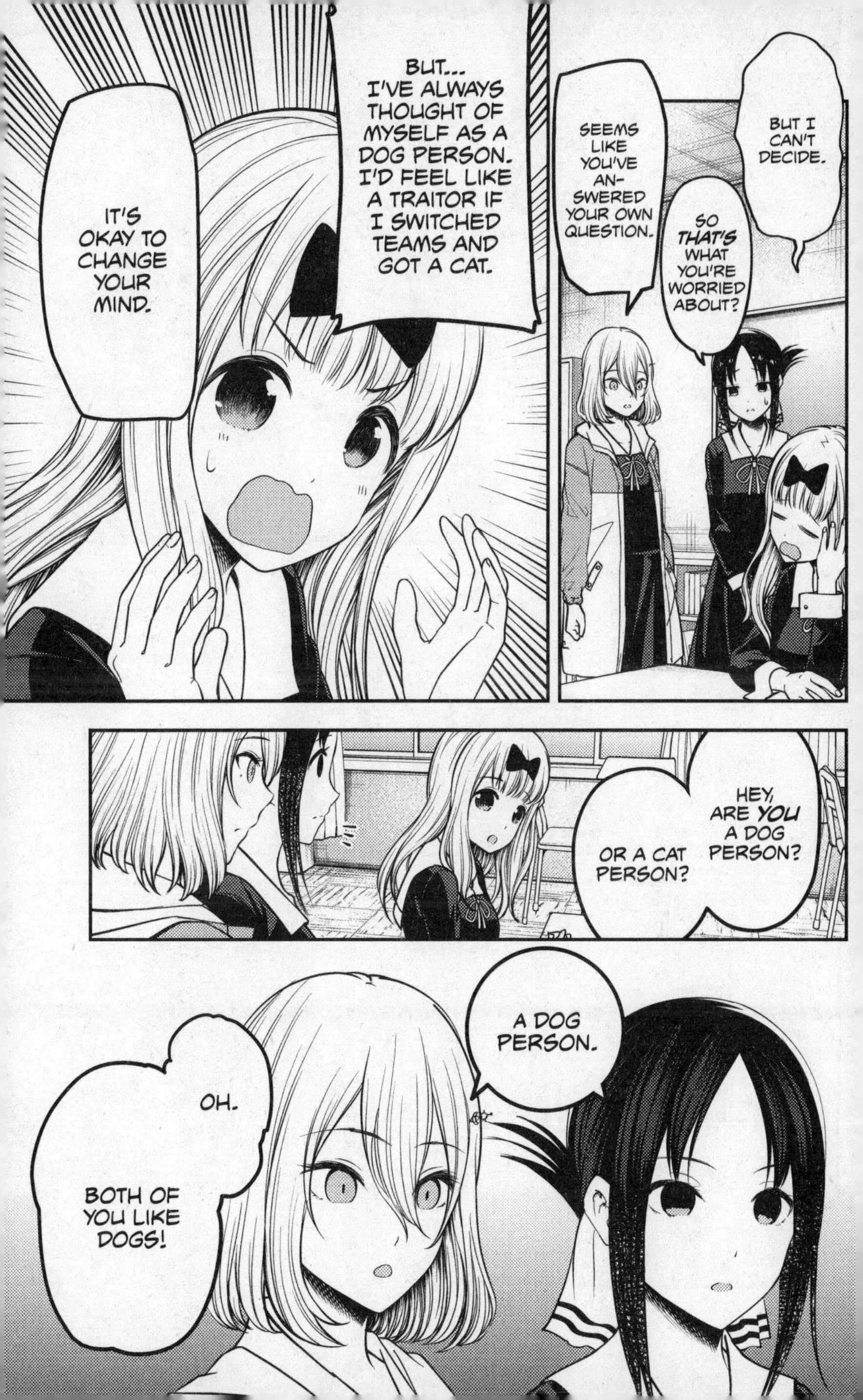
BUT I CAN'T DECIDE.
SO *THAT'S* WHAT YOU'RE WORRIED ABOUT?
SEEMS LIKE YOU'VE AN-SWERED YOUR OWN QUESTION.
BUT... I'VE ALWAYS THOUGHT OF MYSELF AS A DOG PERSON. I'D FEEL LIKE A TRAITOR IF I SWITCHED TEAMS AND GOT A CAT.
IT'S OKAY TO CHANGE YOUR MIND.
HEY, ARE *YOU* A DOG PERSON?
OR A CAT PERSON?
A DOG PERSON.
OH.
BOTH OF YOU LIKE DOGS!

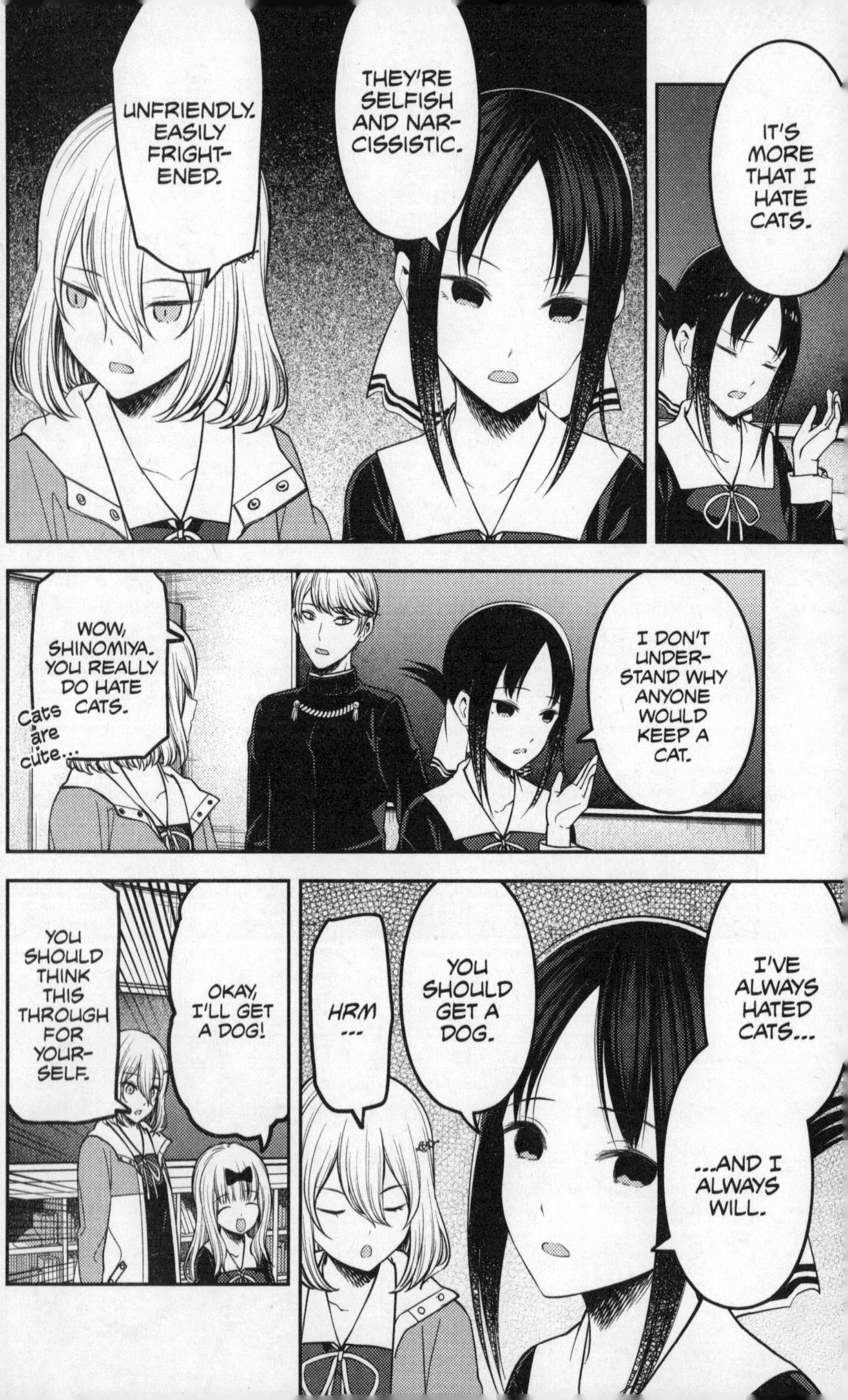
IT'S MORE THAT I HATE CATS.
THEY'RE SELFISH AND NARCISSISTIC.
UNFRIENDLY. EASILY FRIGHTENED.
I DON'T UNDERSTAND WHY ANYONE WOULD KEEP A CAT.
WOW, SHINOMIYA. YOU REALLY DO HATE CATS.
Cats are cute...
I'VE ALWAYS HATED CATS...
...AND I ALWAYS WILL.
YOU SHOULD GET A DOG.
HRM...
OKAY, I'LL GET A DOG!
YOU SHOULD THINK THIS THROUGH FOR YOURSELF.

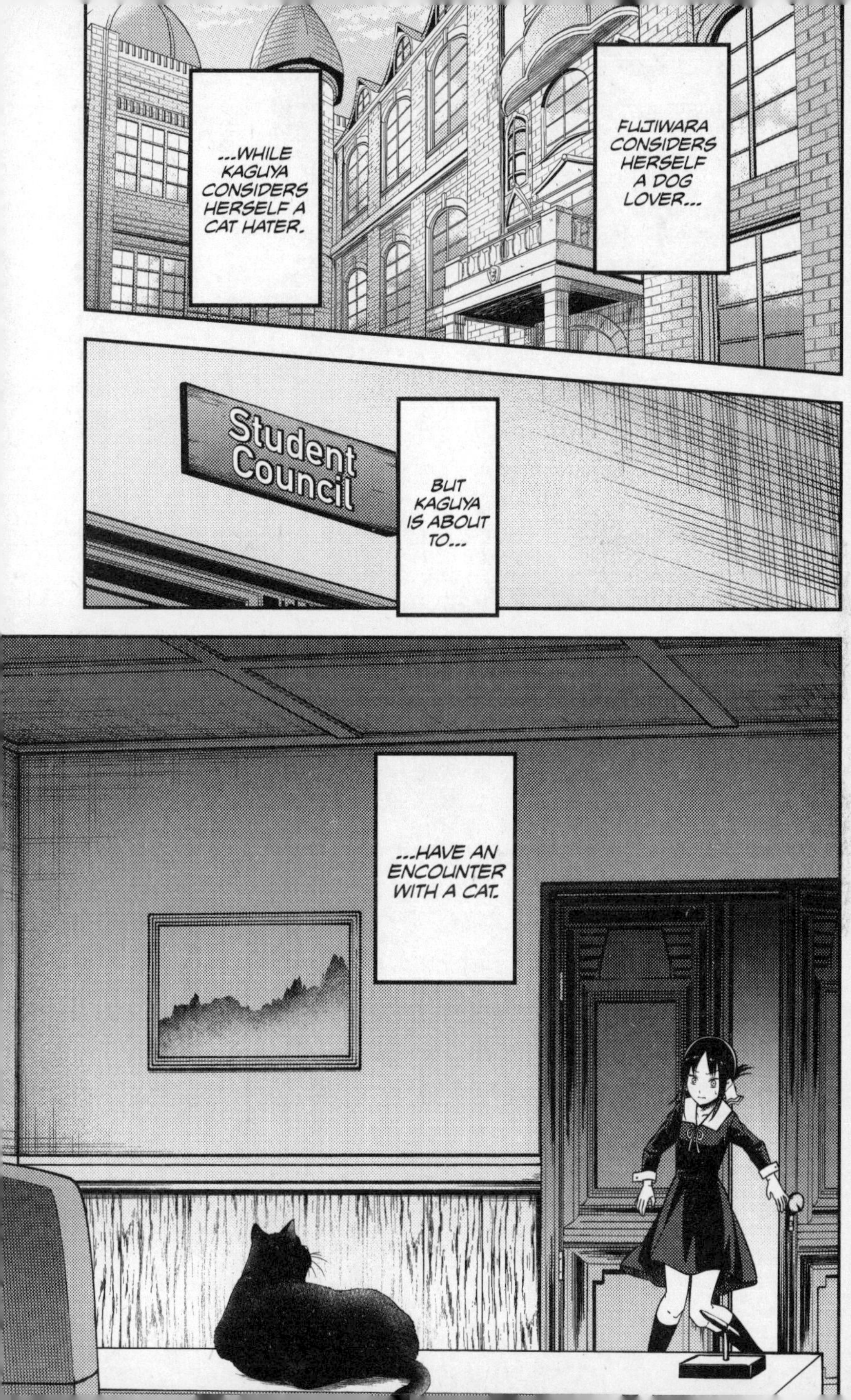
FUJIWARA CONSIDERS HERSELF A DOG LOVER...
...WHILE KAGUYA CONSIDERS HERSELF A CAT HATER.
BUT KAGUYA IS ABOUT TO...
Student Council
...HAVE AN ENCOUNTER WITH A CAT.

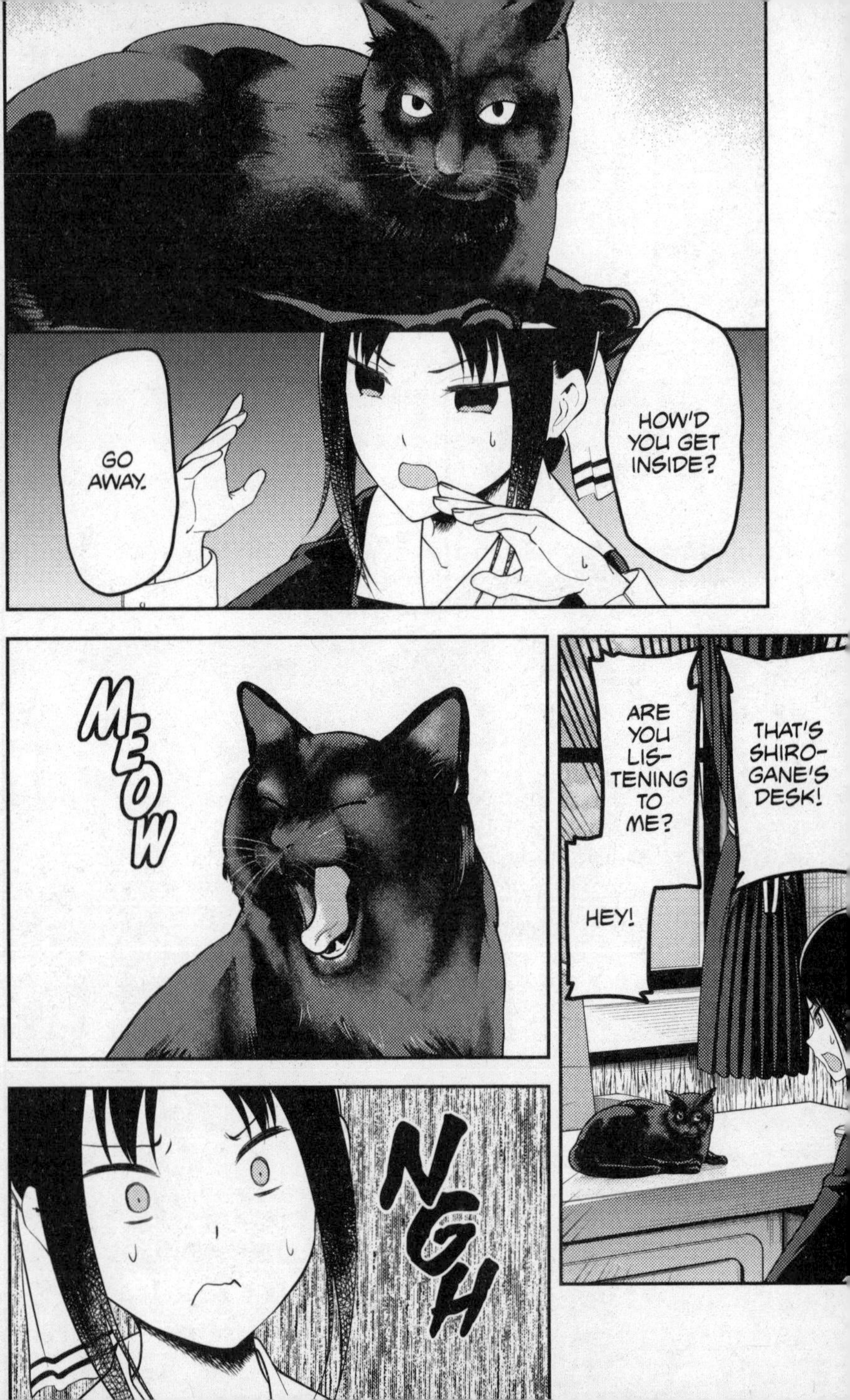
HOW'D YOU GET INSIDE?
GO AWAY.
THAT'S SHIRO-GANE'S DESK!
ARE YOU LIS-TENING TO ME?
HEY!
MEOW
NGH

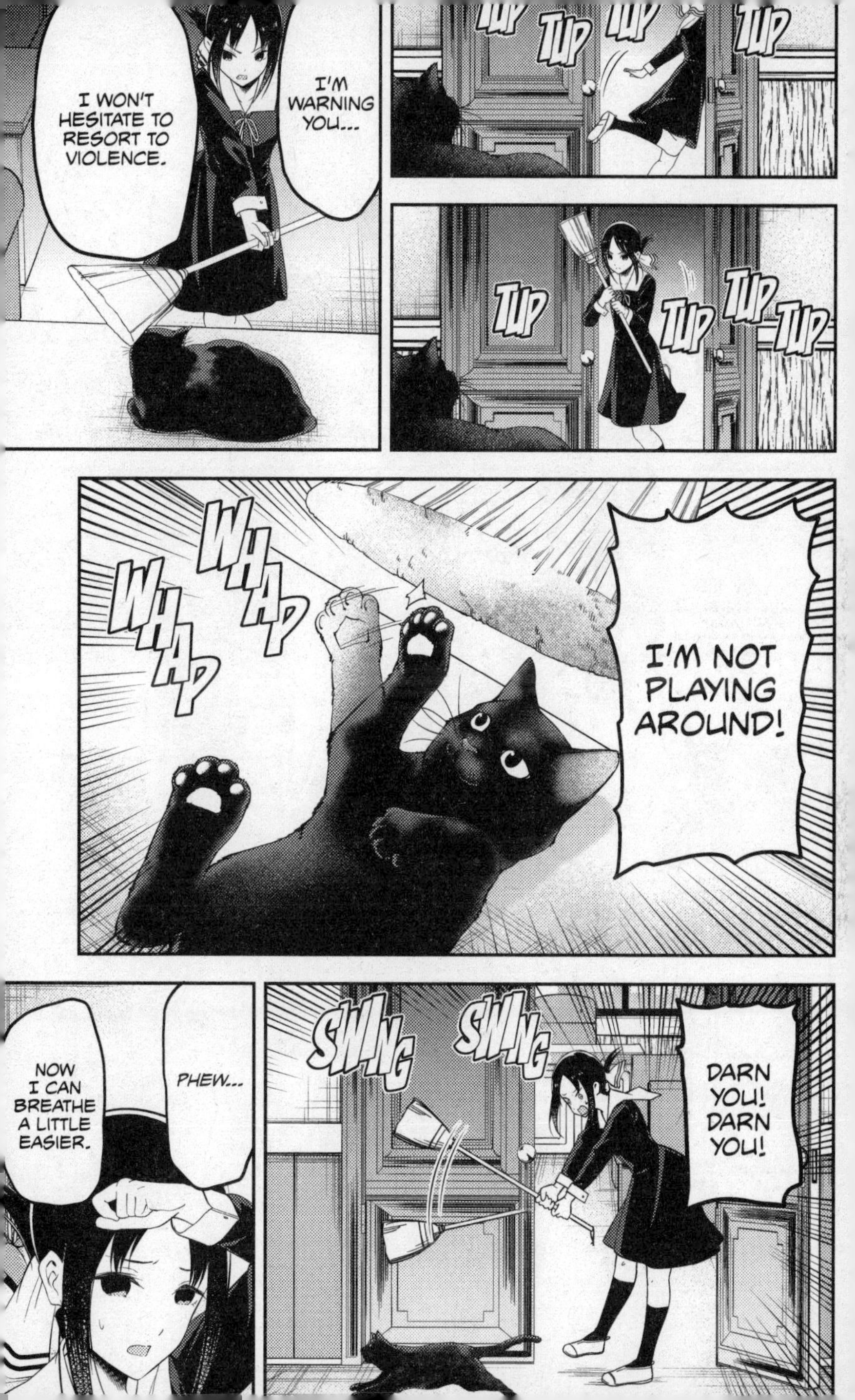
TUP TUP TUP TUP
TUP TUP TUP TUP
I'M WARNING YOU...
I WON'T HESITATE TO RESORT TO VIOLENCE.
I'M NOT PLAYING AROUND!
WHAP
WHAP
DARN YOU! DARN YOU!
SWING
SWING
PHEW...
NOW I CAN BREATHE A LITTLE EASIER.

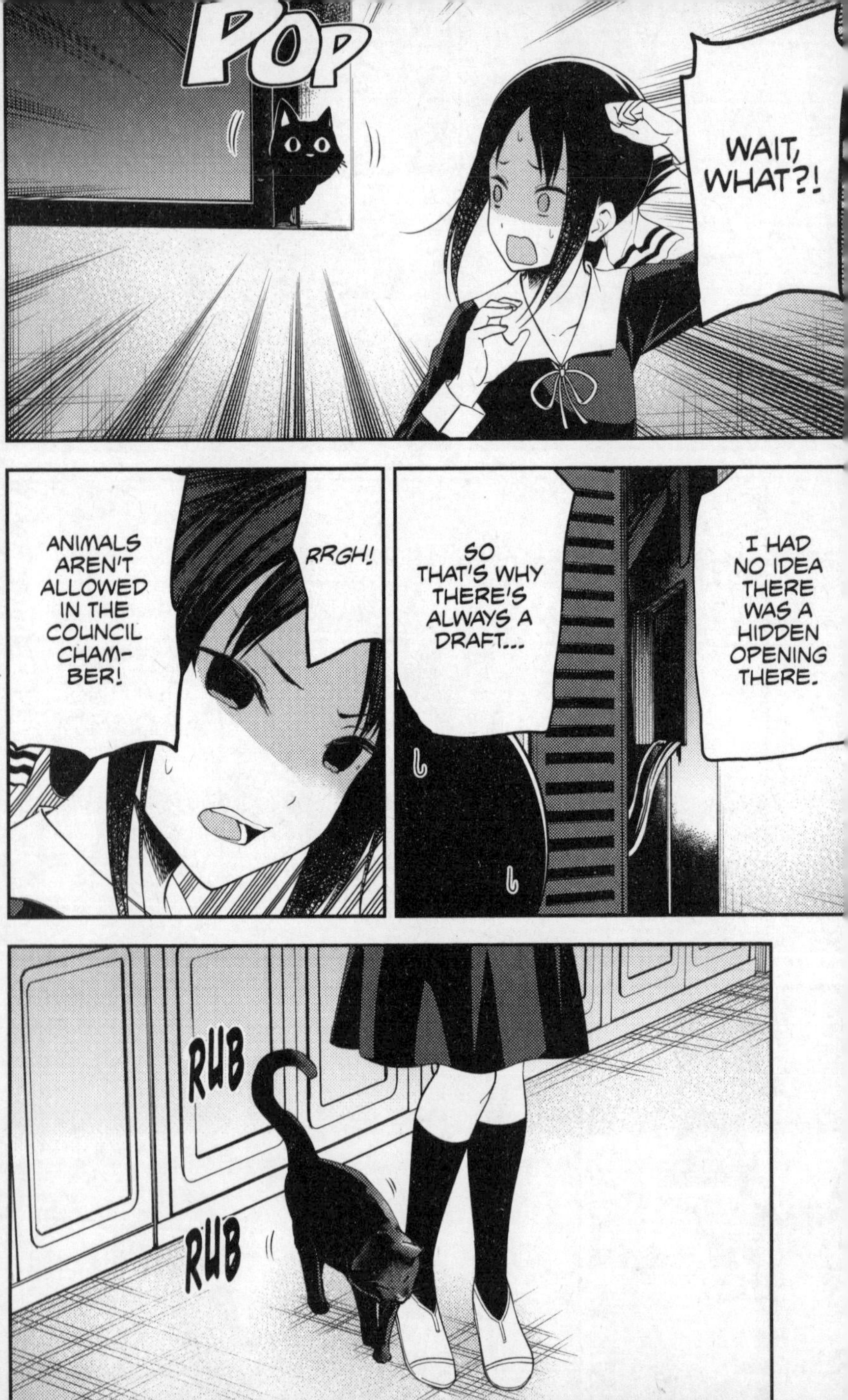
POP
WAIT, WHAT?!
I HAD NO IDEA THERE WAS A HIDDEN OPENING THERE.
SO THAT'S WHY THERE'S ALWAYS A DRAFT...
RRGH!
ANIMALS AREN'T ALLOWED IN THE COUNCIL CHAM-BER!
RUB
RUB

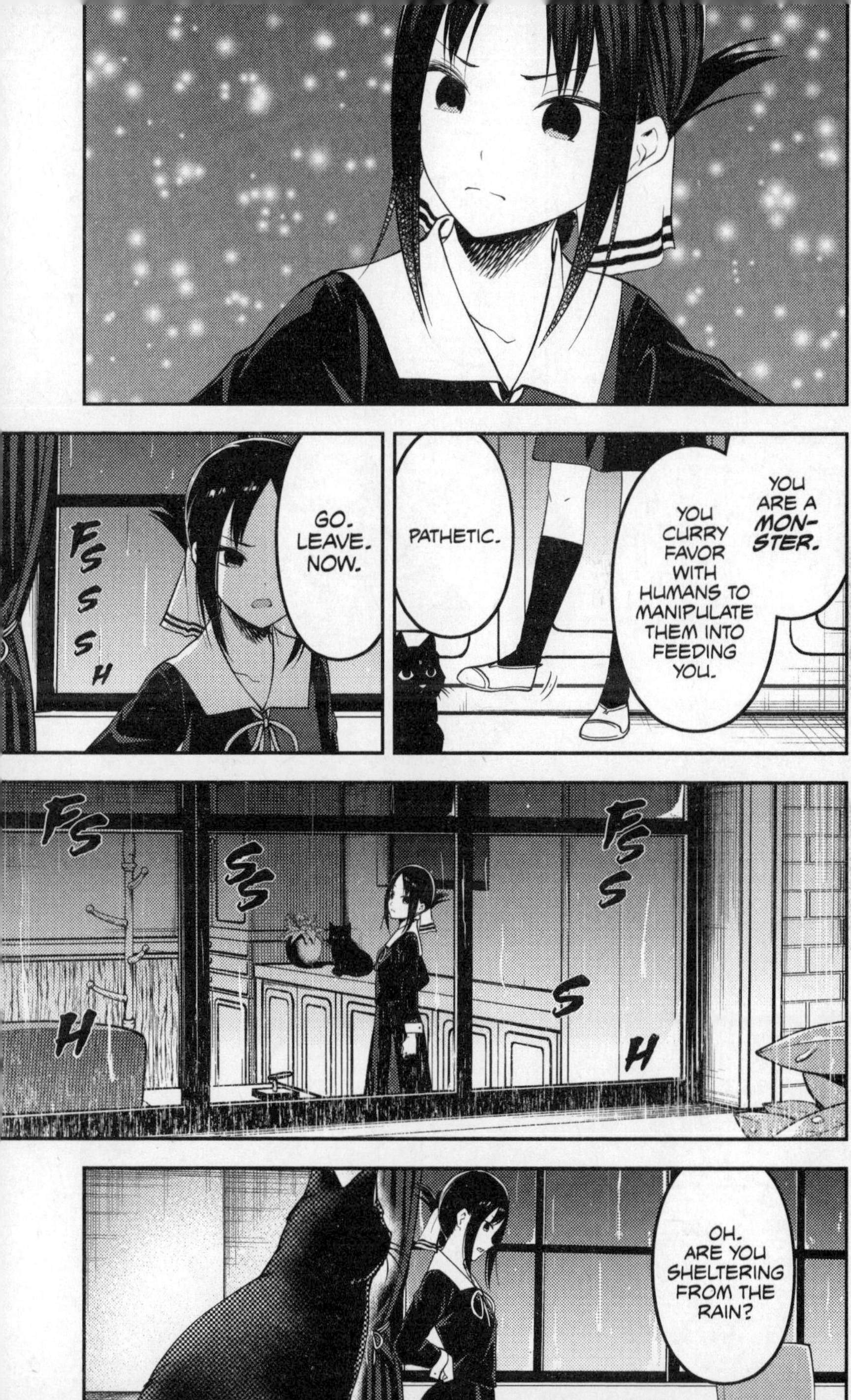

YOU ARE A MONSTER.
YOU CURRY FAVOR WITH HUMANS TO MANIPULATE THEM INTO FEEDING YOU.
PATHETIC.
GO. LEAVE. NOW.
FSSSH
FSSSH
FSSSH
OH. ARE YOU SHELTERING FROM THE RAIN?

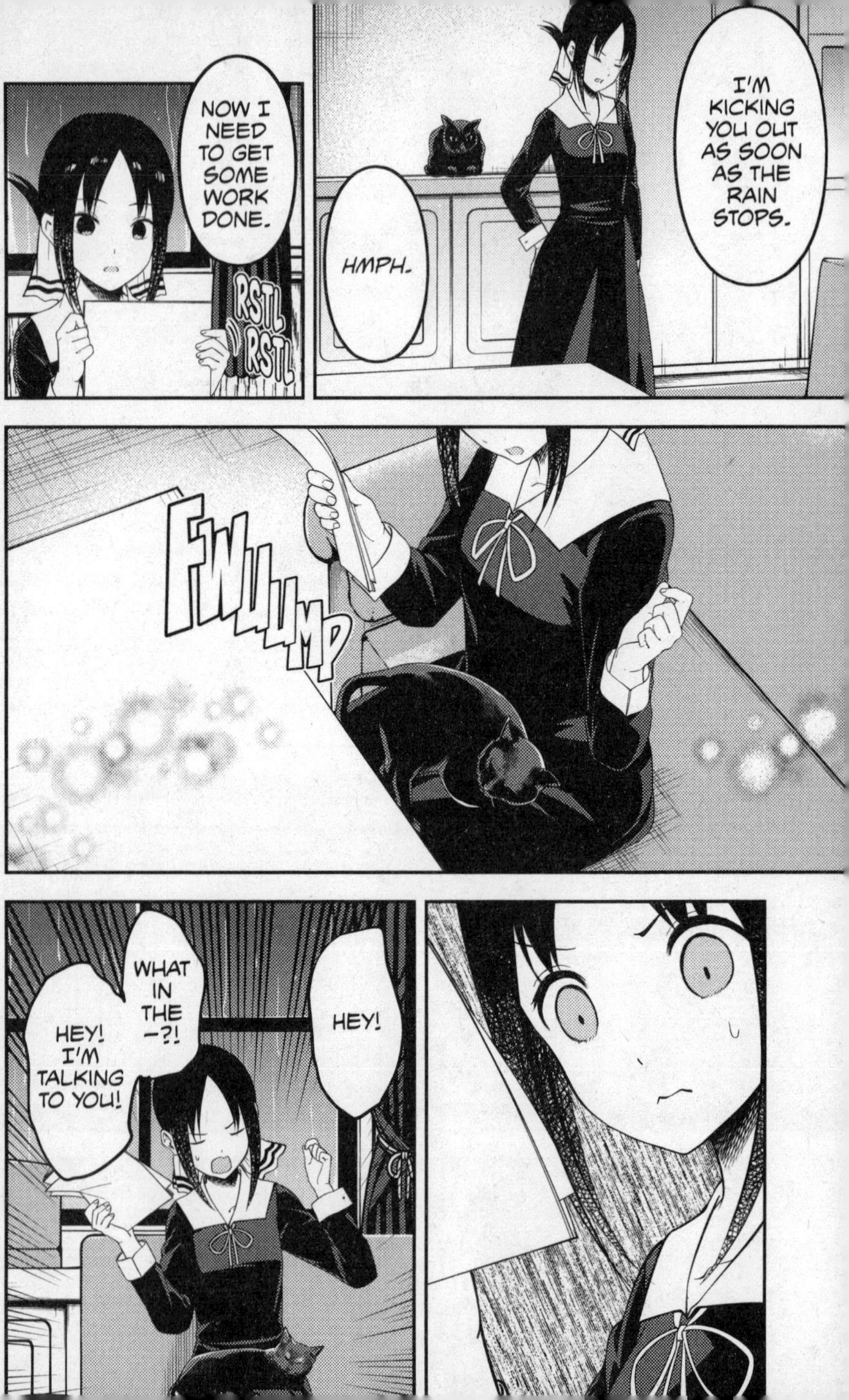
I'M KICKING YOU OUT AS SOON AS THE RAIN STOPS.
HMPH.
NOW I NEED TO GET SOME WORK DONE.
RSTL RSTL
FWUUMP
HEY!
WHAT IN THE—?!
HEY! I'M TALKING TO YOU!

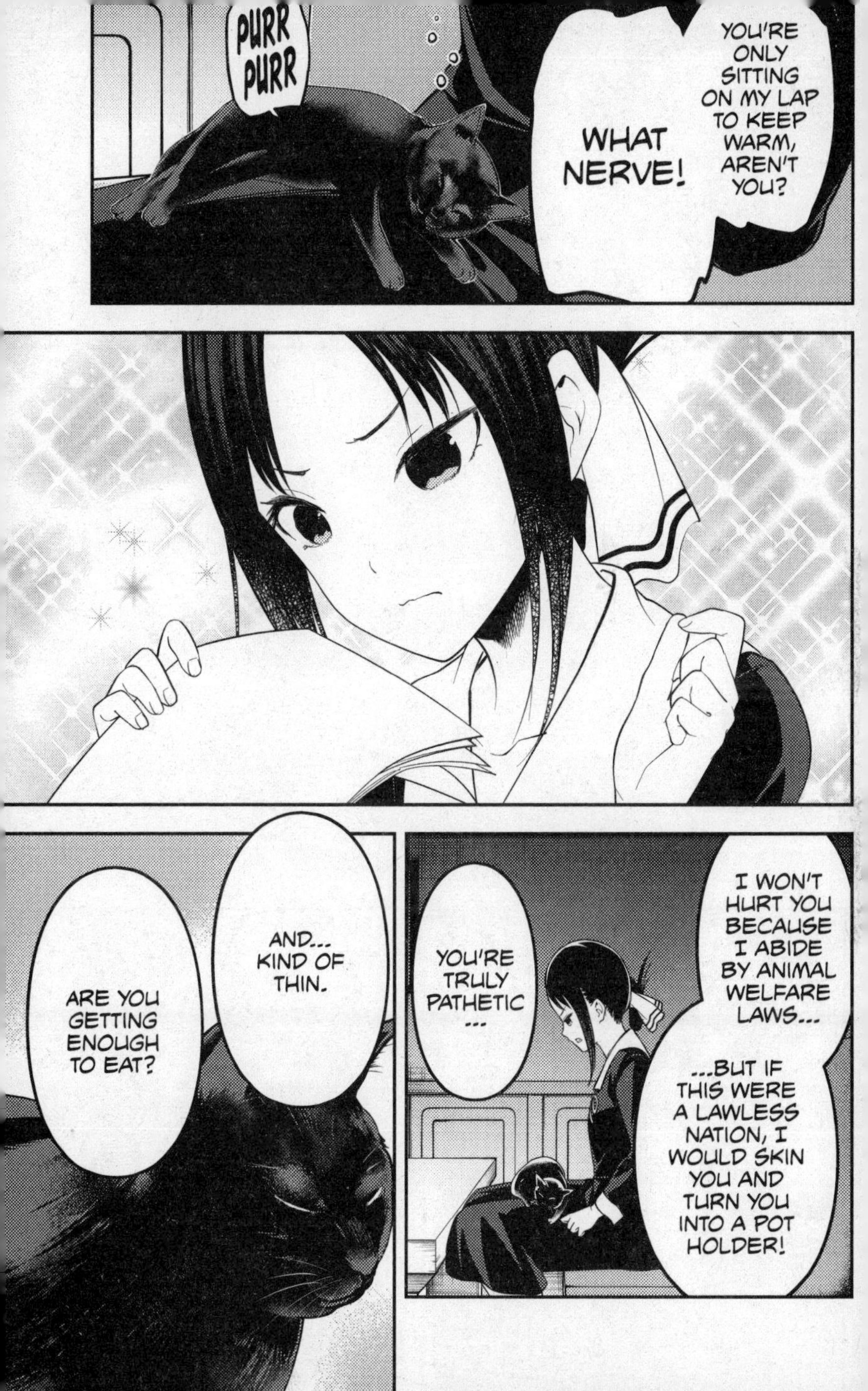
YOU'RE ONLY SITTING ON MY LAP TO KEEP WARM, AREN'T YOU?
WHAT NERVE!
PURR PURR
I WON'T HURT YOU BECAUSE I ABIDE BY ANIMAL WELFARE LAWS...
...BUT IF THIS WERE A LAWLESS NATION, I WOULD SKIN YOU AND TURN YOU INTO A POT HOLDER!
YOU'RE TRULY PATHETIC...
AND... KIND OF THIN.
ARE YOU GETTING ENOUGH TO EAT?

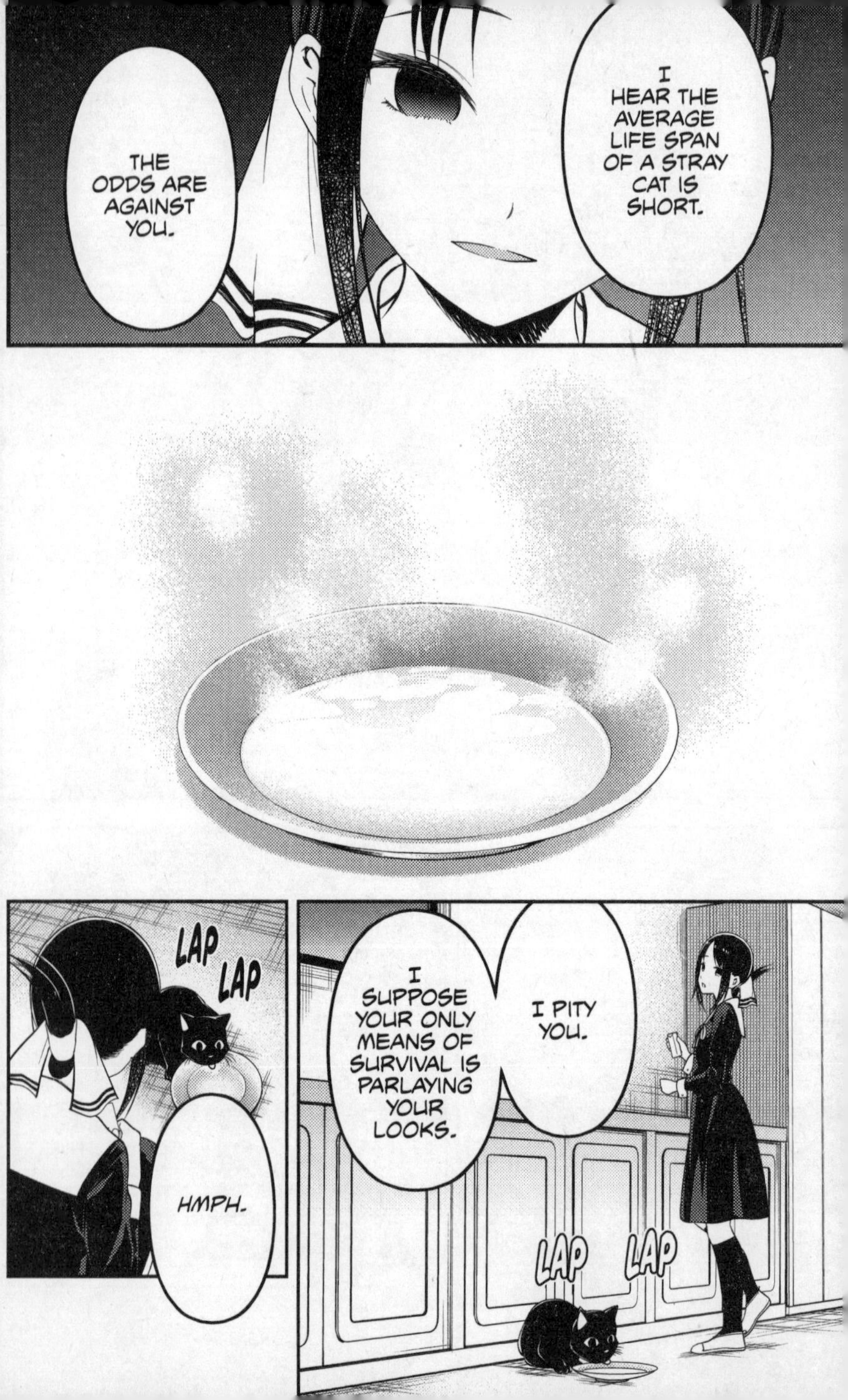
I HEAR THE AVERAGE LIFE SPAN OF A STRAY CAT IS SHORT.
THE ODDS ARE AGAINST YOU.
I PITY YOU.
I SUPPOSE YOUR ONLY MEANS OF SURVIVAL IS PARLAYING YOUR LOOKS.
LAP LAP
LAP LAP
HMPH.

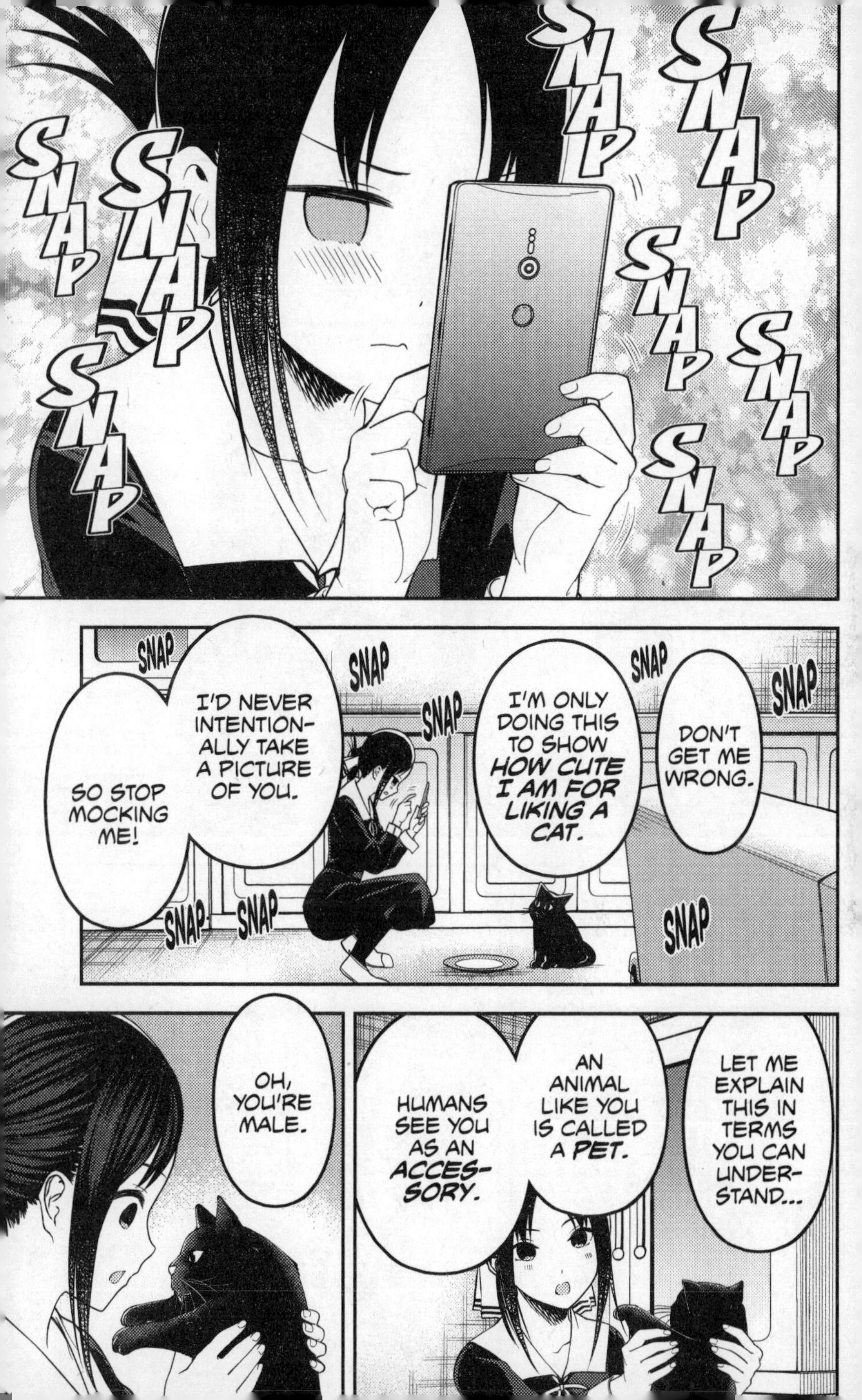
SNAP SNAP SNAP SNAP SNAP SNAP SNAP SNAP
SNAP SNAP SNAP SNAP SNAP SNAP SNAP
DON'T GET ME WRONG.
I'M ONLY DOING THIS TO SHOW *HOW CUTE I AM FOR LIKING A CAT.*
I'D NEVER INTENTIONALLY TAKE A PICTURE OF YOU.
SO STOP MOCKING ME!
LET ME EXPLAIN THIS IN TERMS YOU CAN UNDERSTAND...
AN ANIMAL LIKE YOU IS CALLED A *PET.*
HUMANS SEE YOU AS AN *ACCESSORY.*
OH, YOU'RE MALE.

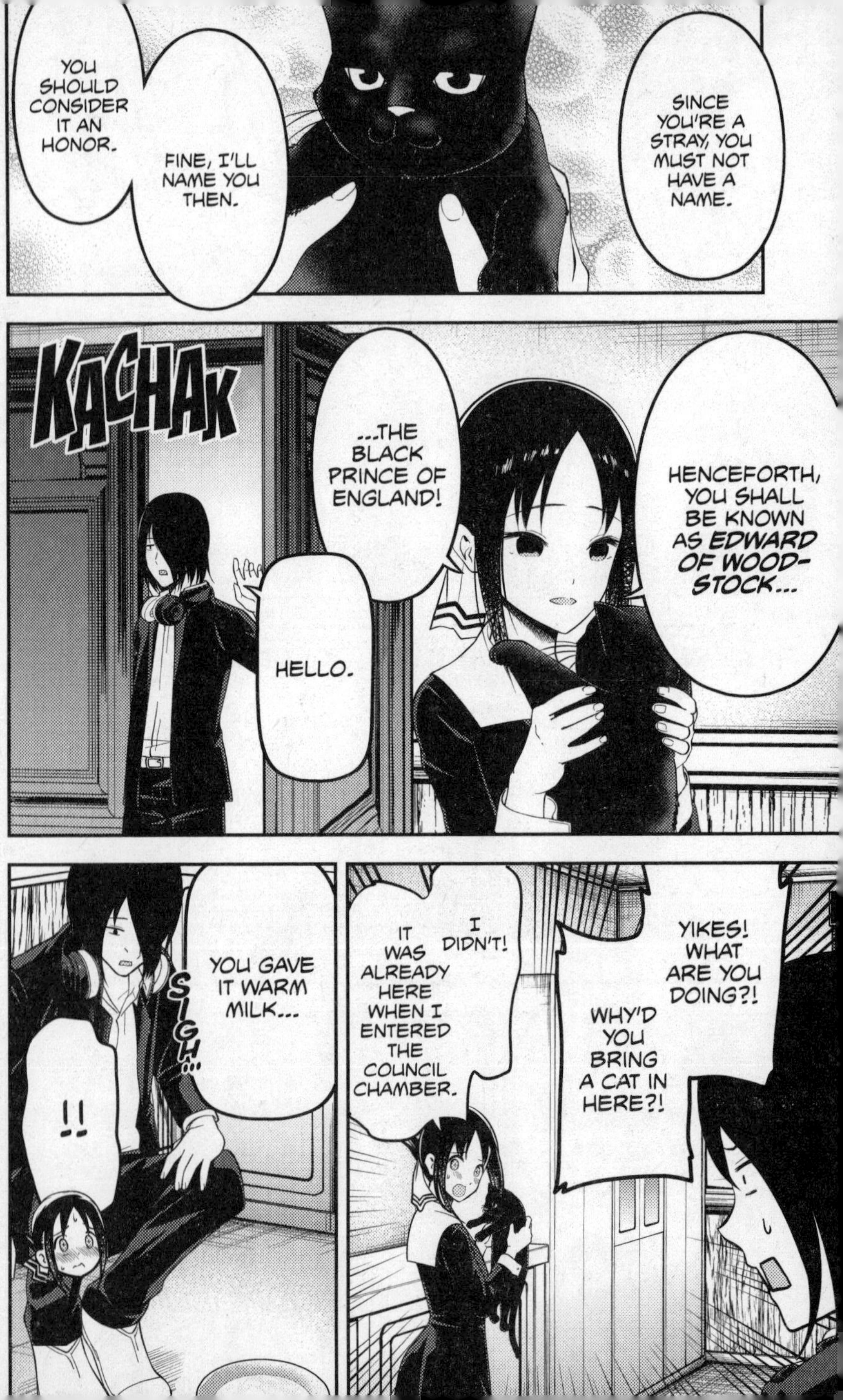
SINCE YOU'RE A STRAY, YOU MUST NOT HAVE A NAME.
FINE, I'LL NAME YOU THEN.
YOU SHOULD CONSIDER IT AN HONOR.
HENCEFORTH, YOU SHALL BE KNOWN AS EDWARD OF WOOD-STOCK...
...THE BLACK PRINCE OF ENGLAND!
KACHAK
HELLO.
YIKES! WHAT ARE YOU DOING?!
WHY'D YOU BRING A CAT IN HERE?!
I DIDN'T!
IT WAS ALREADY HERE WHEN I ENTERED THE COUNCIL CHAMBER.
YOU GAVE IT WARM MILK...
SIGH...
!!

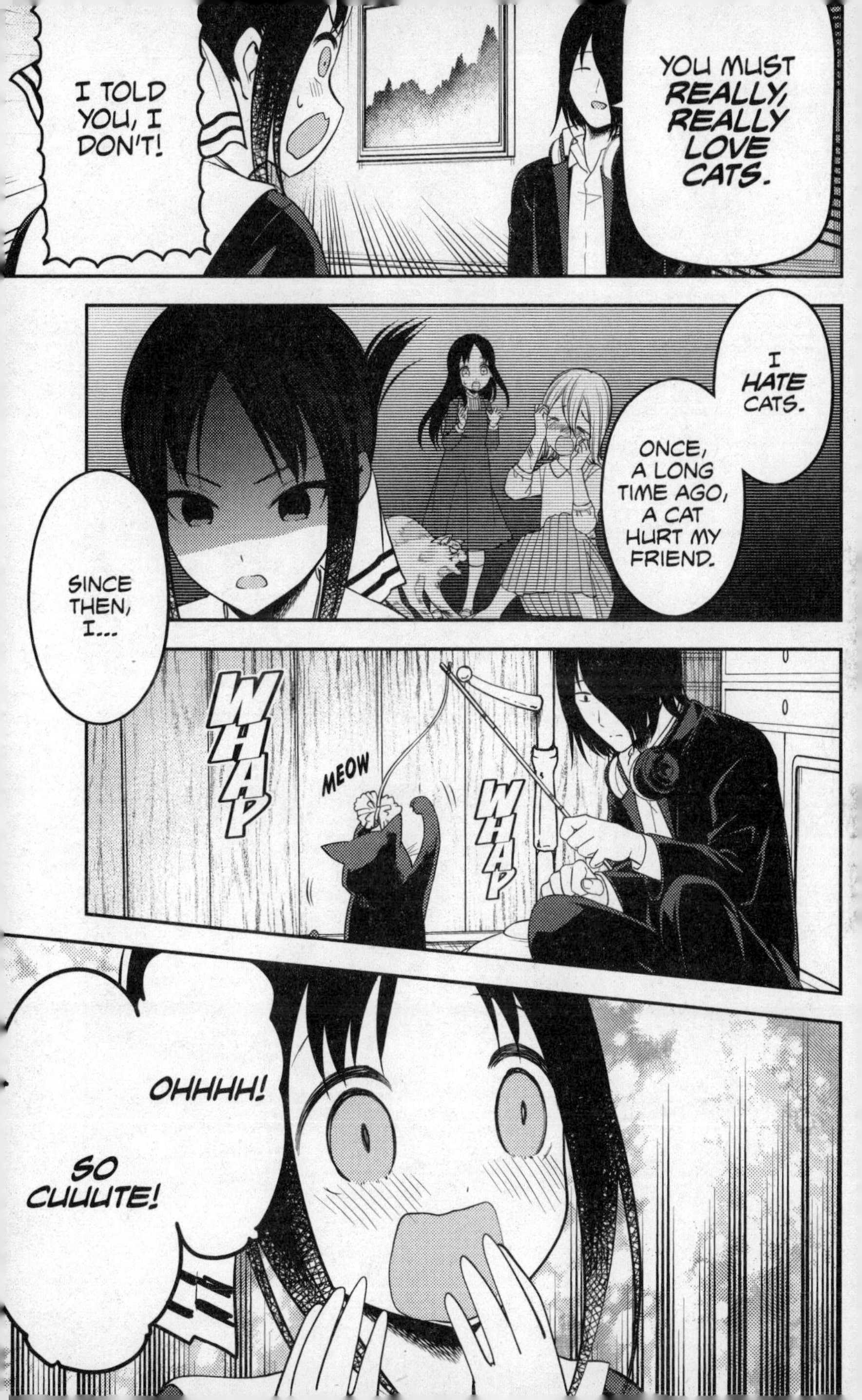
YOU MUST REALLY, REALLY LOVE CATS.
I TOLD YOU, I DON'T!
I HATE CATS.
ONCE, A LONG TIME AGO, A CAT HURT MY FRIEND.
SINCE THEN, I...
WHAP
MEOW
WHAP
OHHHH!
SO CUUUTE!

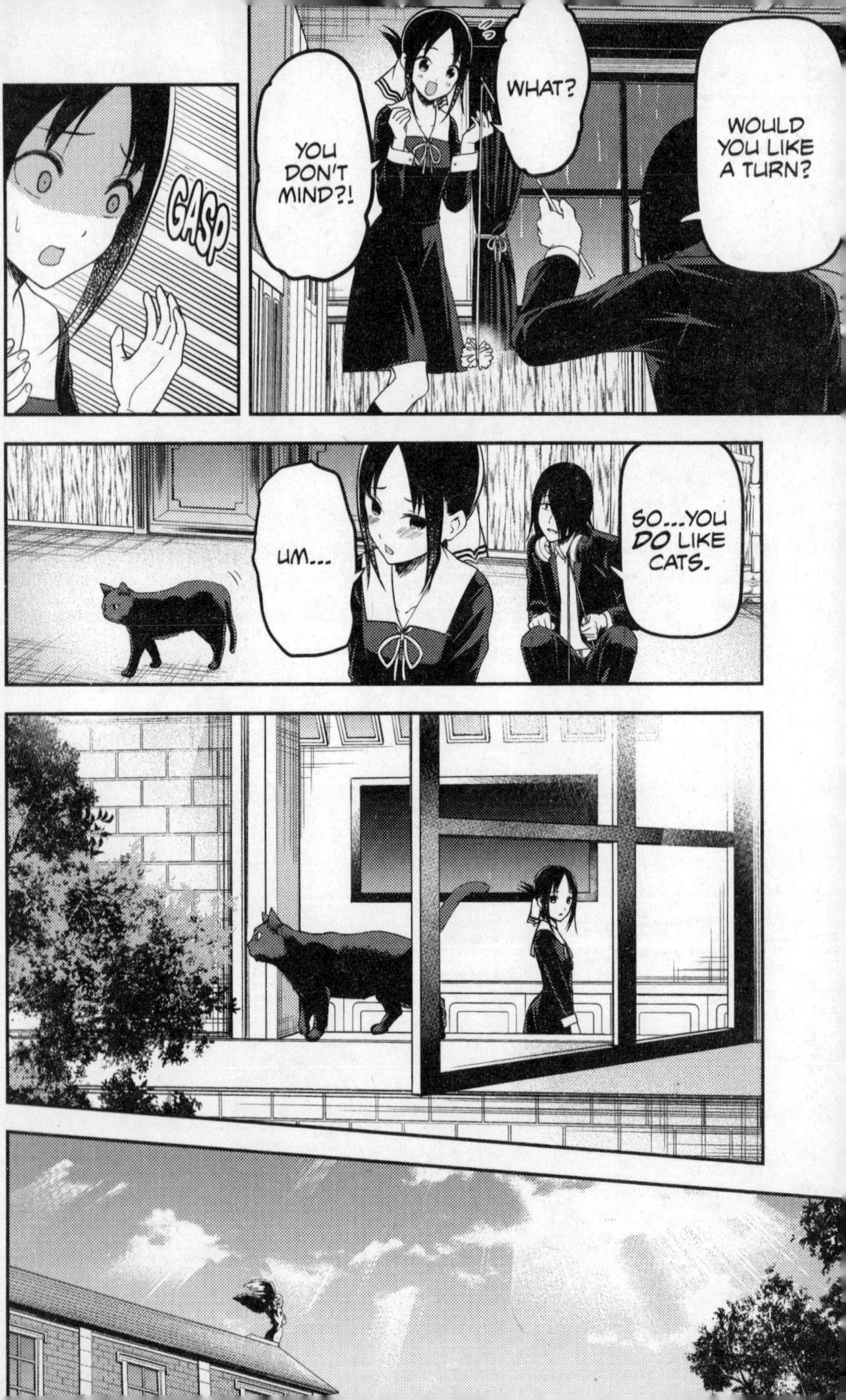
WOULD YOU LIKE A TURN?
WHAT?
YOU DON'T MIND?!
GASP
SO...YOU DO LIKE CATS.
UM...

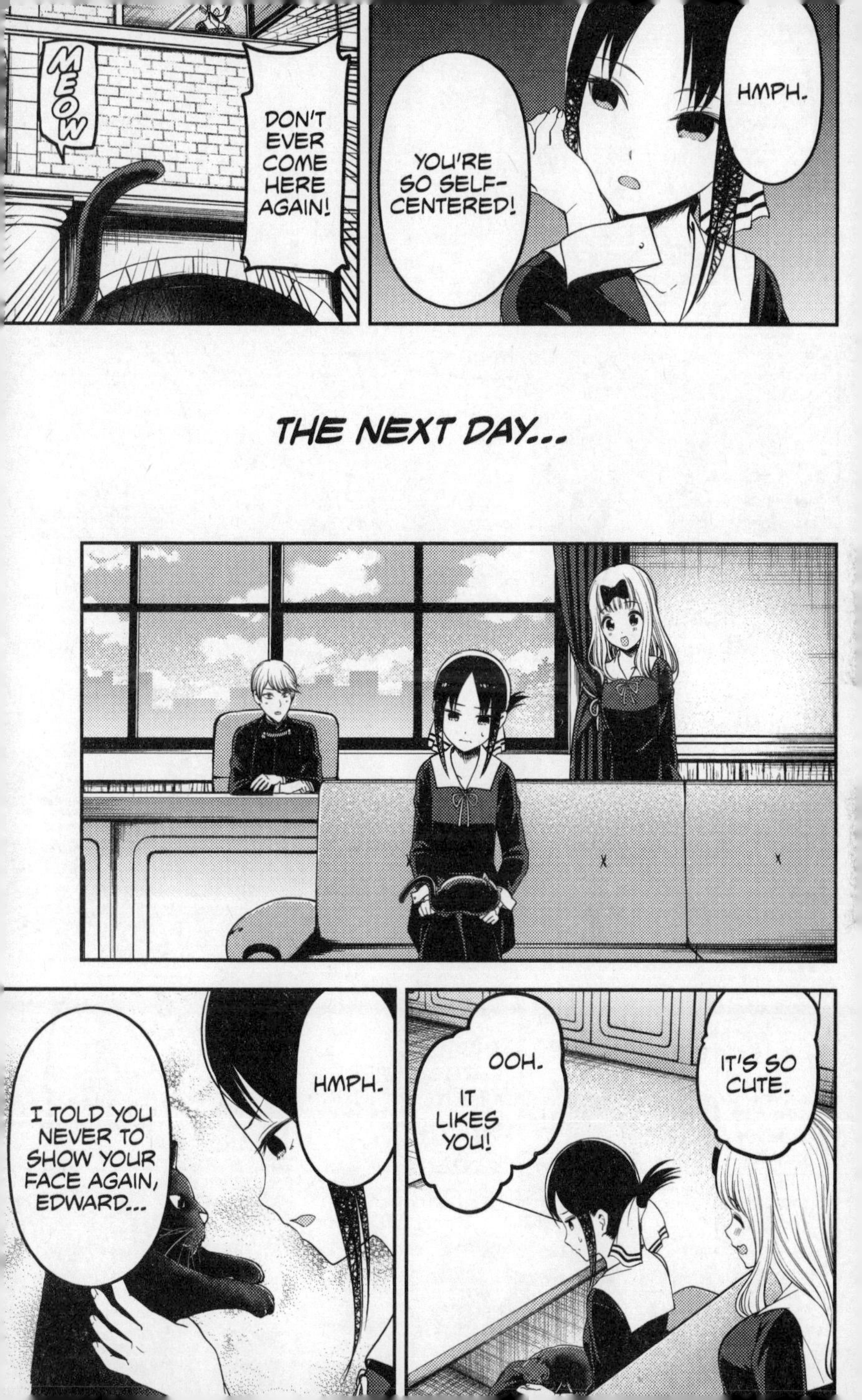
HMPH.
YOU'RE SO SELF-CENTERED!
DON'T EVER COME HERE AGAIN!
MEOW
THE NEXT DAY...
IT'S SO CUTE.
OOH.
IT LIKES YOU!
HMPH.
I TOLD YOU NEVER TO SHOW YOUR FACE AGAIN, EDWARD...

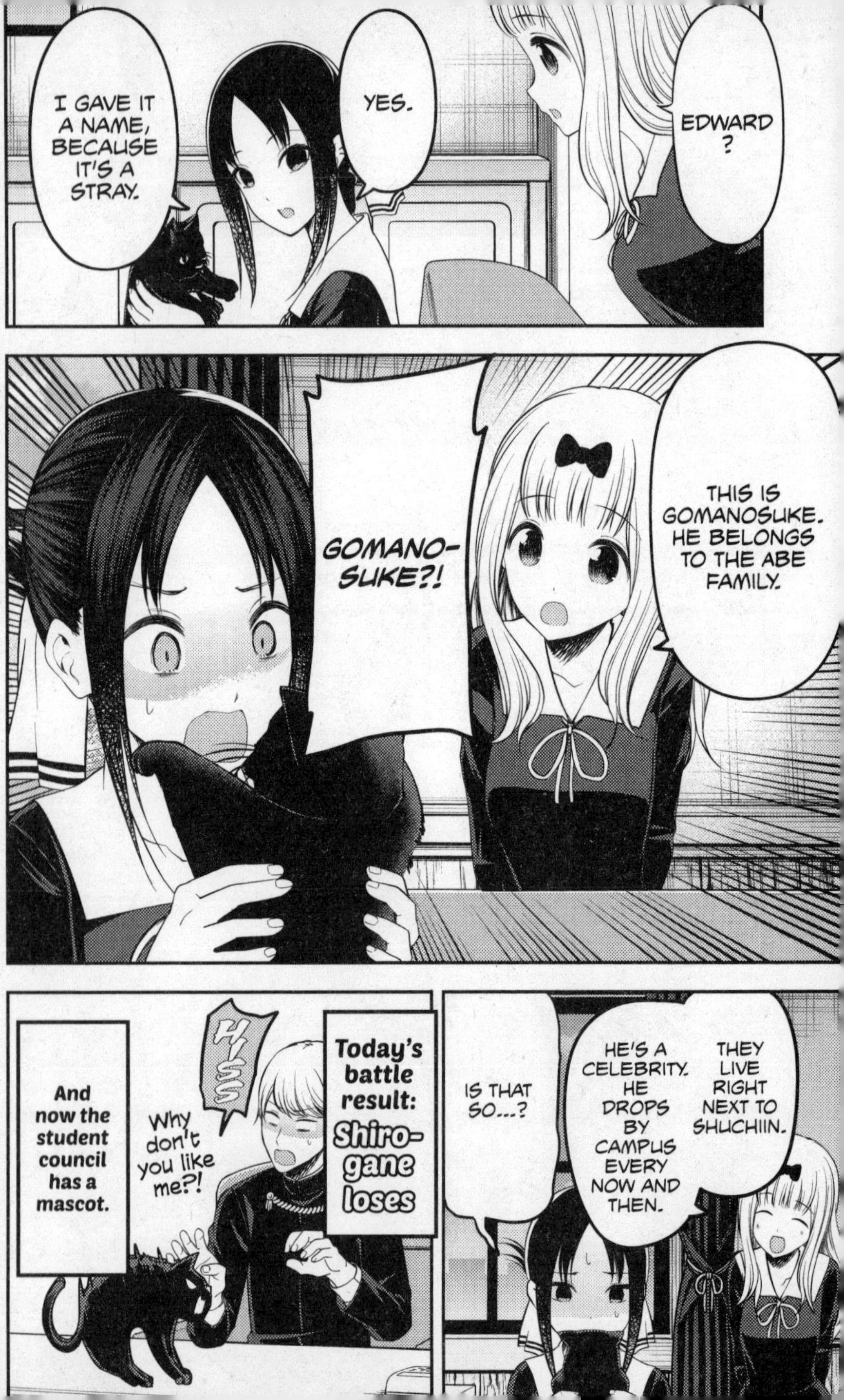
EDWARD?
YES.
I GAVE IT A NAME, BECAUSE IT'S A STRAY.
THIS IS GOMANOSUKE. HE BELONGS TO THE ABE FAMILY.
GOMANO-SUKE?!
THEY LIVE RIGHT NEXT TO SHUCHIIN.
HE'S A CELEBRITY. HE DROPS BY CAMPUS EVERY NOW AND THEN.
IS THAT SO...?
Today's battle result: Shiro-gane loses
HISS
Why don't you like me?!
And now the student council has a mascot.

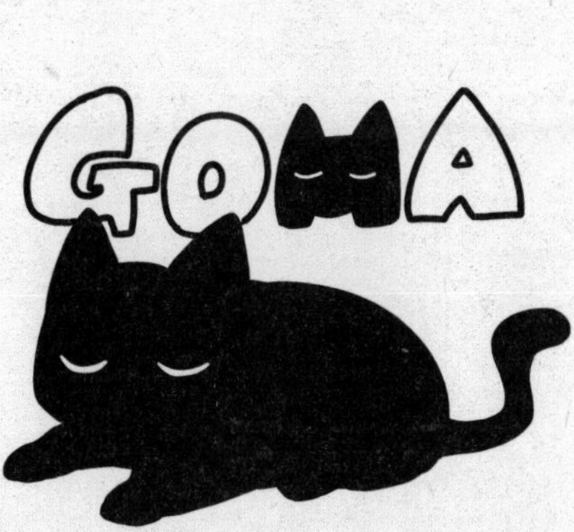
GOMA

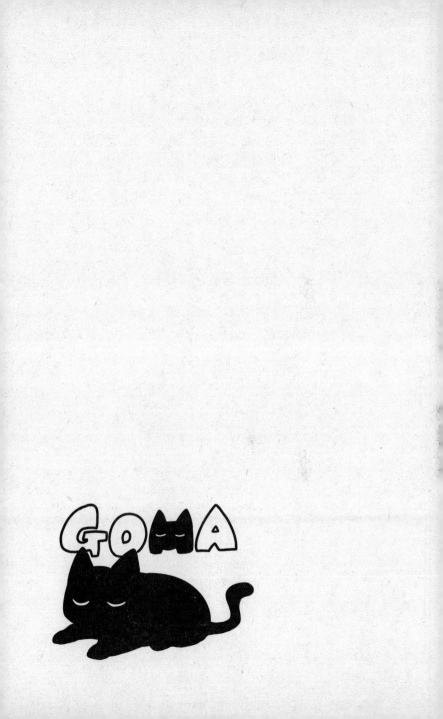

KAGUYA-SAMA
LOVE IS WAR

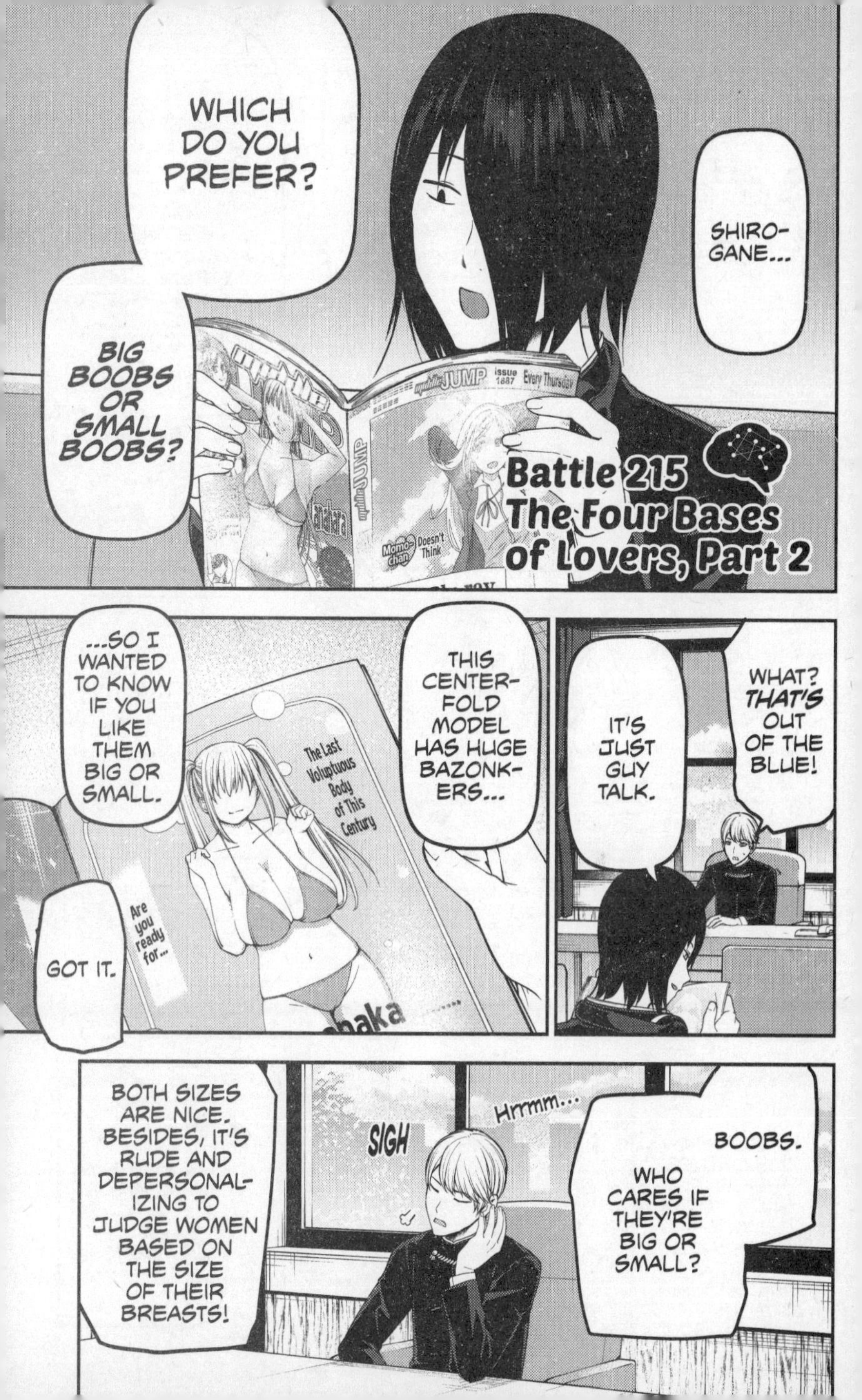
SHIRO-GANE...
WHICH DO YOU PREFER?
BIG BOOBS OR SMALL BOOBS?
JUMP issue 1887 Every Thursday
Momo-chan Doesn't Think
Battle 215 The Four Bases of Lovers, Part 2
WHAT? THAT'S OUT OF THE BLUE!
IT'S JUST GUY TALK.
THIS CENTER-FOLD MODEL HAS HUGE BAZONK-ERS...
The Last Voluptuous Body of This Century
...SO I WANTED TO KNOW IF YOU LIKE THEM BIG OR SMALL.
Are you ready for...
GOT IT.
BOOBS.
WHO CARES IF THEY'RE BIG OR SMALL?
Hrrmm...
SIGH
BOTH SIZES ARE NICE. BESIDES, IT'S RUDE AND DEPERSONAL-IZING TO JUDGE WOMEN BASED ON THE SIZE OF THEIR BREASTS!

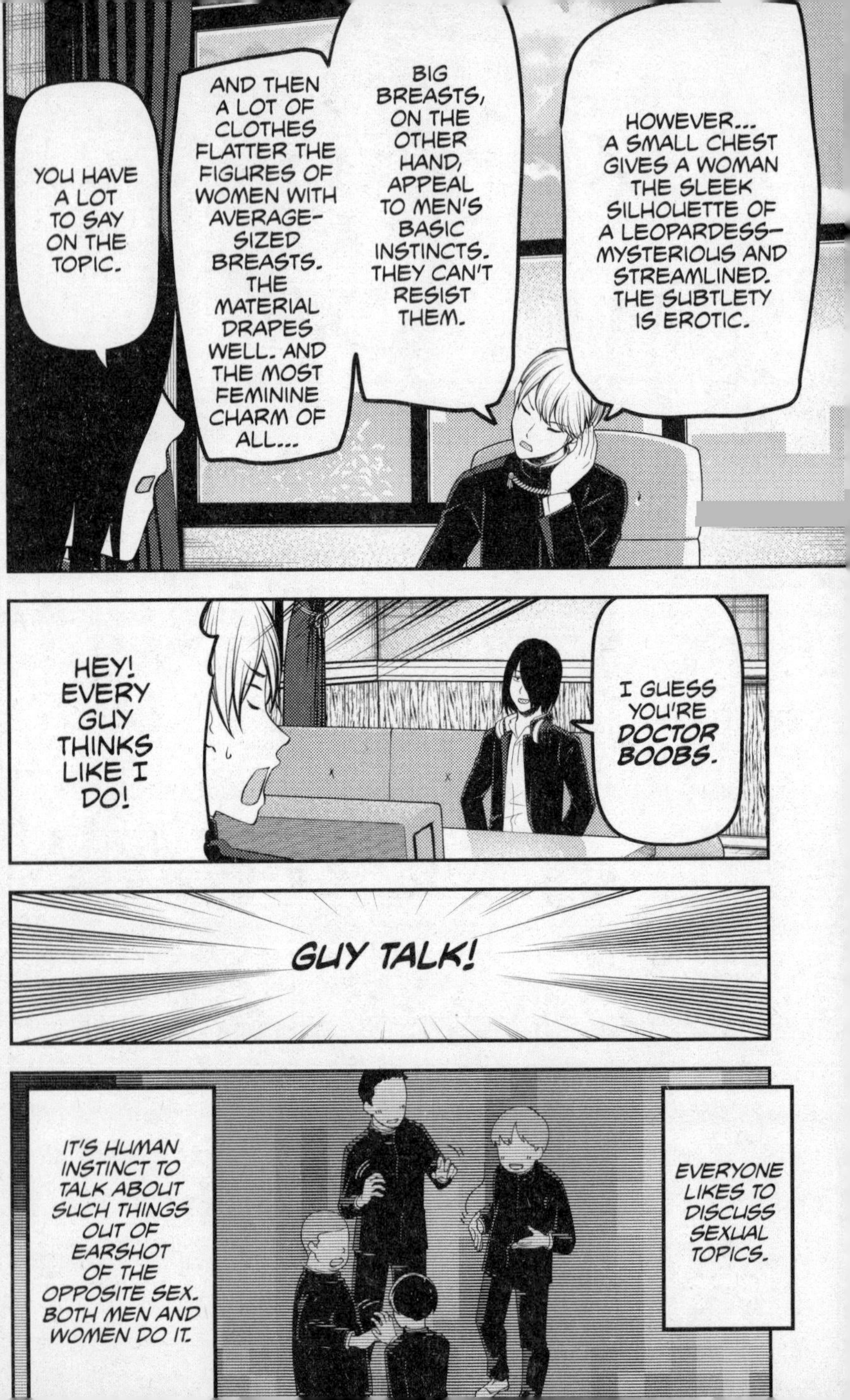
HOWEVER... A SMALL CHEST GIVES A WOMAN THE SLEEK SILHOUETTE OF A LEOPARDESS—MYSTERIOUS AND STREAMLINED. THE SUBTLETY IS EROTIC.
BIG BREASTS, ON THE OTHER HAND, APPEAL TO MEN'S BASIC INSTINCTS. THEY CAN'T RESIST THEM.
AND THEN A LOT OF CLOTHES FLATTER THE FIGURES OF WOMEN WITH AVERAGE-SIZED BREASTS. THE MATERIAL DRAPES WELL. AND THE MOST FEMININE CHARM OF ALL...
YOU HAVE A LOT TO SAY ON THE TOPIC.
I GUESS YOU'RE DOCTOR BOOBS.
HEY! EVERY GUY THINKS LIKE I DO!
GUY TALK!
EVERYONE LIKES TO DISCUSS SEXUAL TOPICS.
IT'S HUMAN INSTINCT TO TALK ABOUT SUCH THINGS OUT OF EARSHOT OF THE OPPOSITE SEX. BOTH MEN AND WOMEN DO IT.

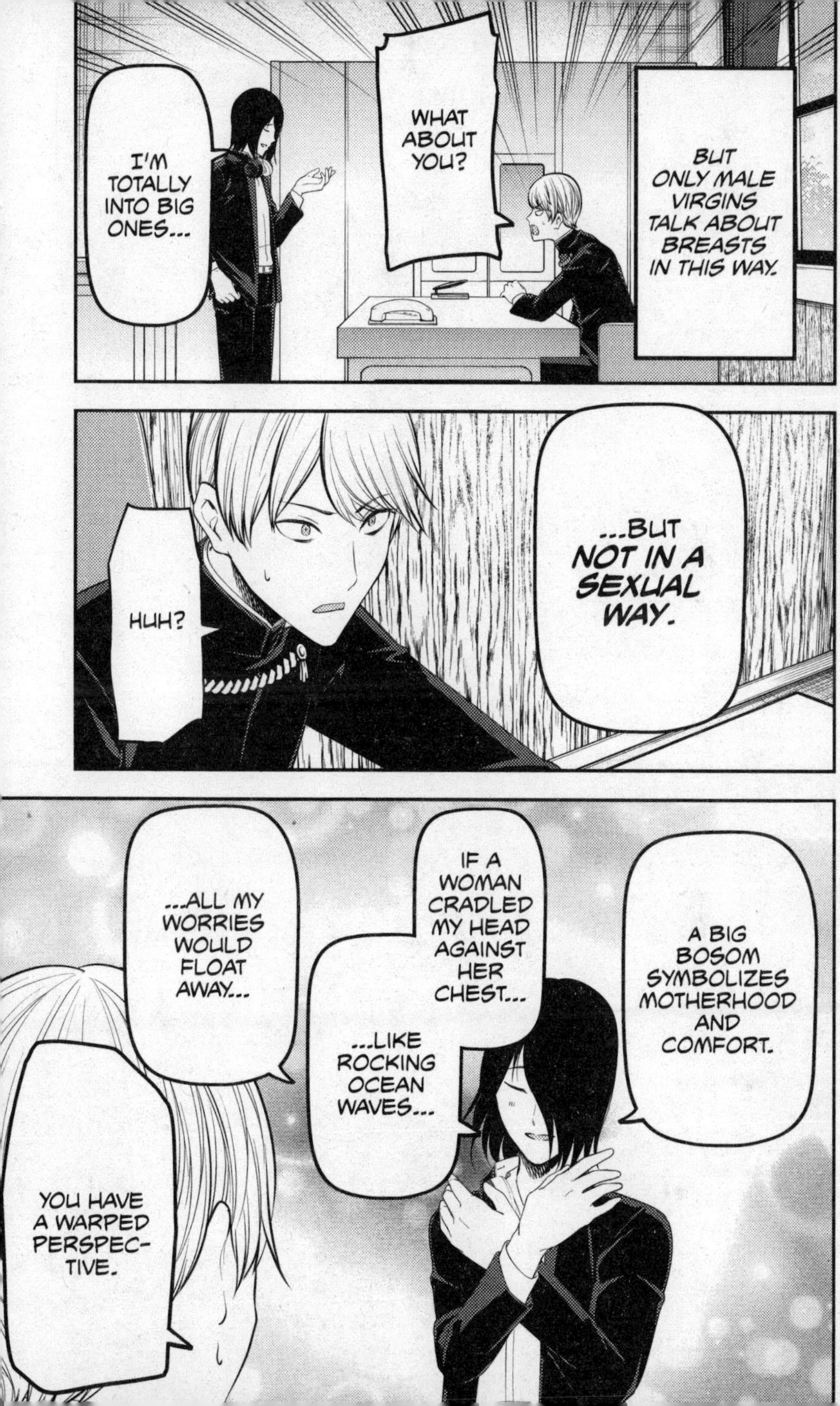
BUT ONLY MALE VIRGINS TALK ABOUT BREASTS IN THIS WAY.
WHAT ABOUT YOU?
I'M TOTALLY INTO BIG ONES...
...BUT NOT IN A SEXUAL WAY.
HUH?
A BIG BOSOM SYMBOLIZES MOTHERHOOD AND COMFORT.
IF A WOMAN CRADLED MY HEAD AGAINST HER CHEST...
...LIKE ROCKING OCEAN WAVES...
...ALL MY WORRIES WOULD FLOAT AWAY...
YOU HAVE A WARPED PERSPECTIVE.

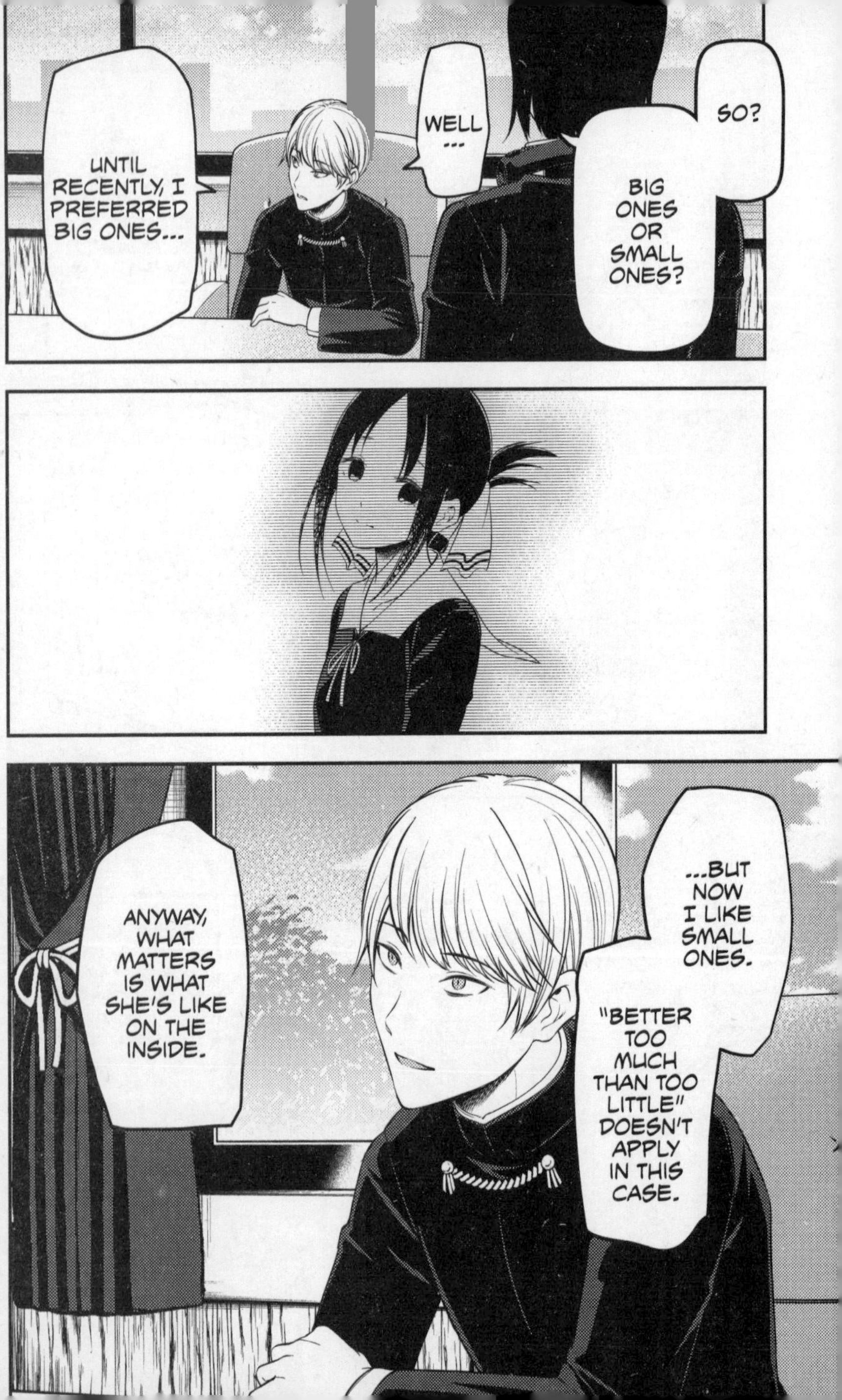
SO?
BIG ONES OR SMALL ONES?
WELL...
UNTIL RECENTLY, I PREFERRED BIG ONES...
...BUT NOW I LIKE SMALL ONES.
"BETTER TOO MUCH THAN TOO LITTLE" DOESN'T APPLY IN THIS CASE.
ANYWAY, WHAT MATTERS IS WHAT SHE'S LIKE ON THE INSIDE.

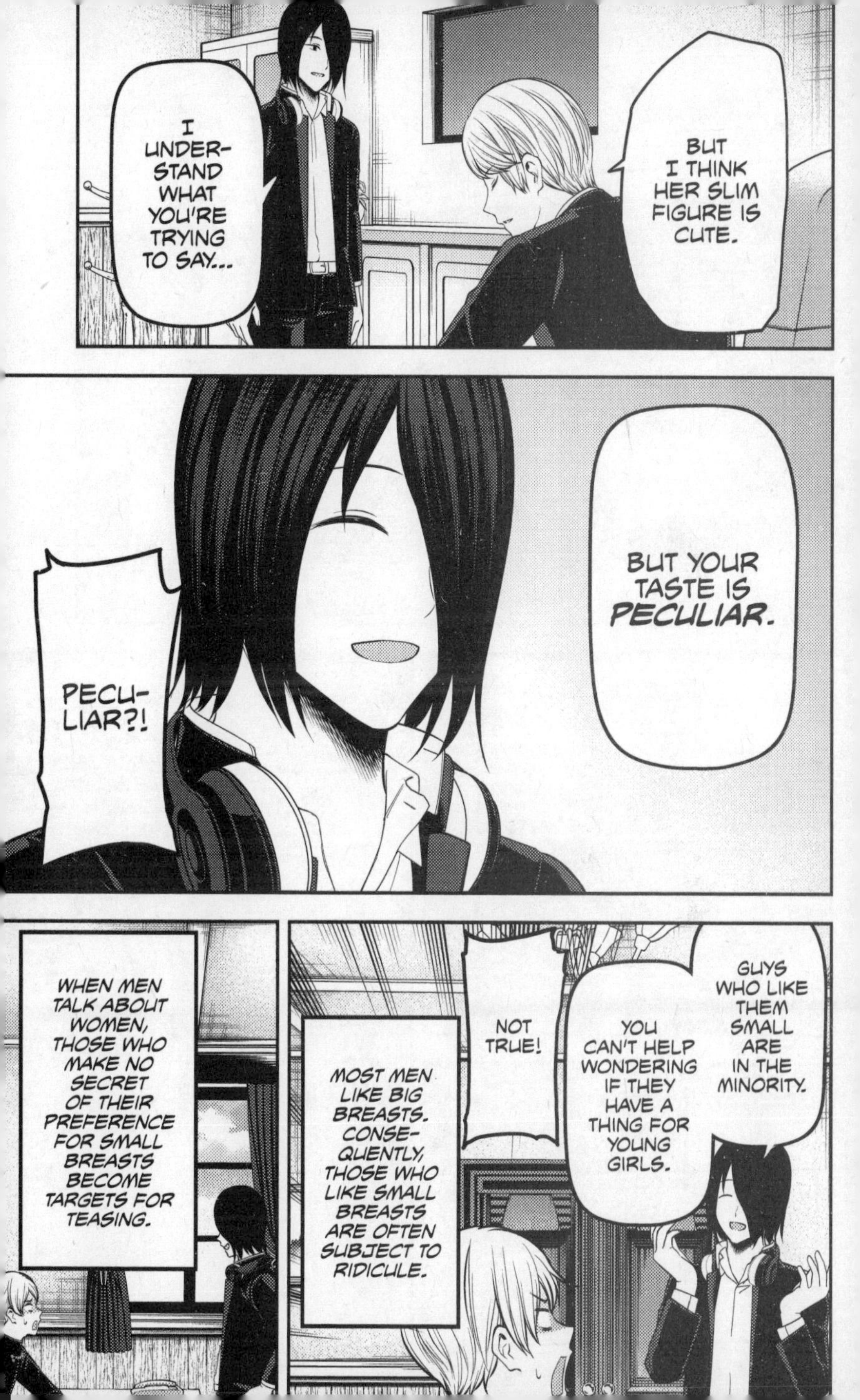
BUT I THINK HER SLIM FIGURE IS CUTE.
I UNDERSTAND WHAT YOU'RE TRYING TO SAY...
BUT YOUR TASTE IS PECULIAR.
PECULIAR?!
GUYS WHO LIKE THEM SMALL ARE IN THE MINORITY.
YOU CAN'T HELP WONDERING IF THEY HAVE A THING FOR YOUNG GIRLS.
NOT TRUE!
MOST MEN LIKE BIG BREASTS. CONSEQUENTLY, THOSE WHO LIKE SMALL BREASTS ARE OFTEN SUBJECT TO RIDICULE.
WHEN MEN TALK ABOUT WOMEN, THOSE WHO MAKE NO SECRET OF THEIR PREFERENCE FOR SMALL BREASTS BECOME TARGETS FOR TEASING.

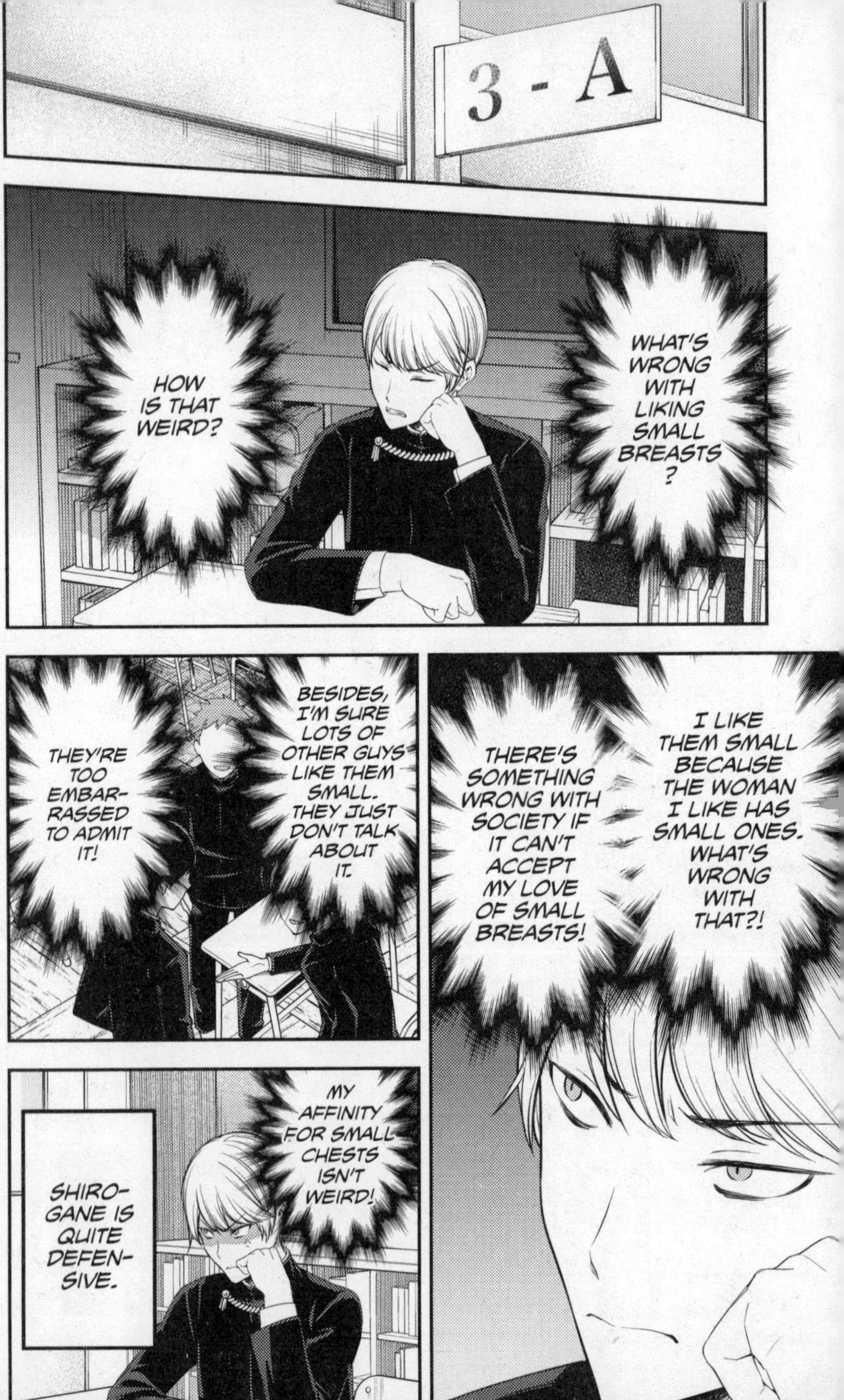
3 - A
WHAT'S WRONG WITH LIKING SMALL BREASTS?
HOW IS THAT WEIRD?
I LIKE THEM SMALL BECAUSE THE WOMAN I LIKE HAS SMALL ONES. WHAT'S WRONG WITH THAT?!
THERE'S SOMETHING WRONG WITH SOCIETY IF IT CAN'T ACCEPT MY LOVE OF SMALL BREASTS!
BESIDES, I'M SURE LOTS OF OTHER GUYS LIKE THEM SMALL. THEY JUST DON'T TALK ABOUT IT.
THEY'RE TOO EMBAR-RASSED TO ADMIT IT!
MY AFFINITY FOR SMALL CHESTS ISN'T WEIRD!
SHIRO-GANE IS QUITE DEFEN-SIVE.

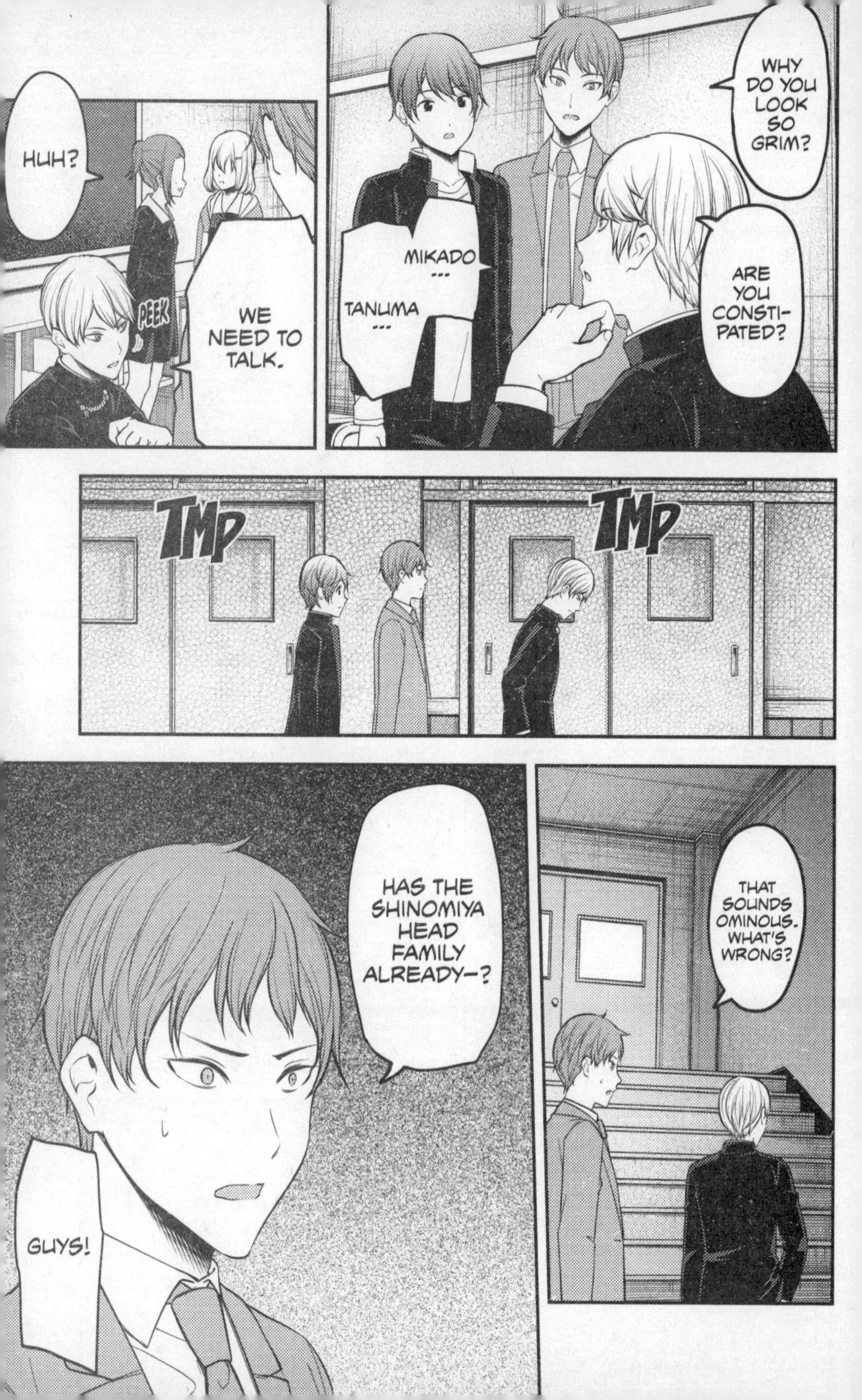
WHY DO YOU LOOK SO GRIM?
ARE YOU CONSTIPATED?
MIKADO...
TANUMA...
HUH?
PEEK
WE NEED TO TALK.
TMP
TMP
THAT SOUNDS OMINOUS. WHAT'S WRONG?
HAS THE SHINOMIYA HEAD FAMILY ALREADY—?
GUYS!

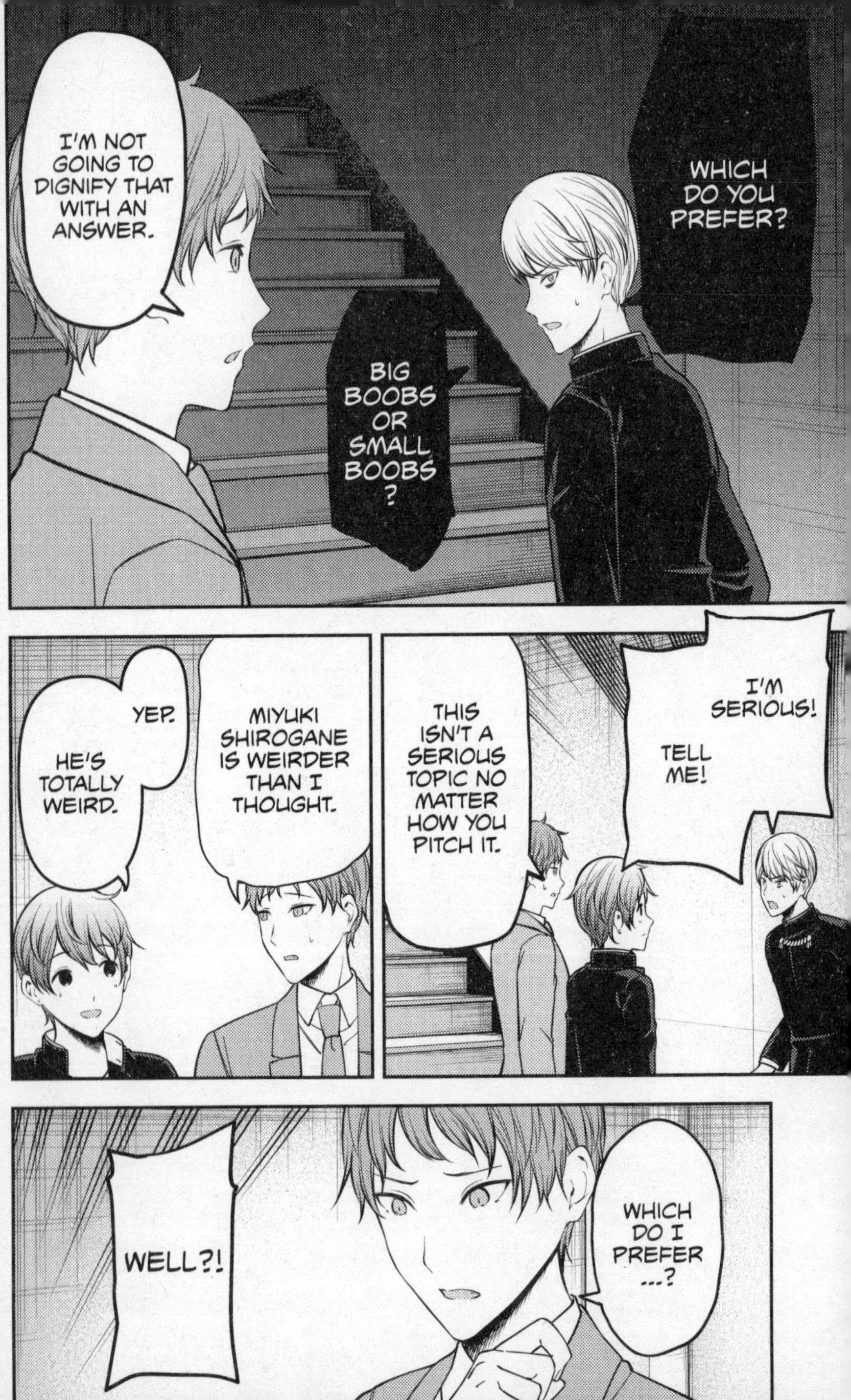
WHICH DO YOU PREFER?
BIG BOOBS OR SMALL BOOBS?
I'M NOT GOING TO DIGNIFY THAT WITH AN ANSWER.
I'M SERIOUS!
TELL ME!
THIS ISN'T A SERIOUS TOPIC NO MATTER HOW YOU PITCH IT.
MIYUKI SHIROGANE IS WEIRDER THAN I THOUGHT.
YEP.
HE'S TOTALLY WEIRD.
WHICH DO I PREFER ...?
WELL?!

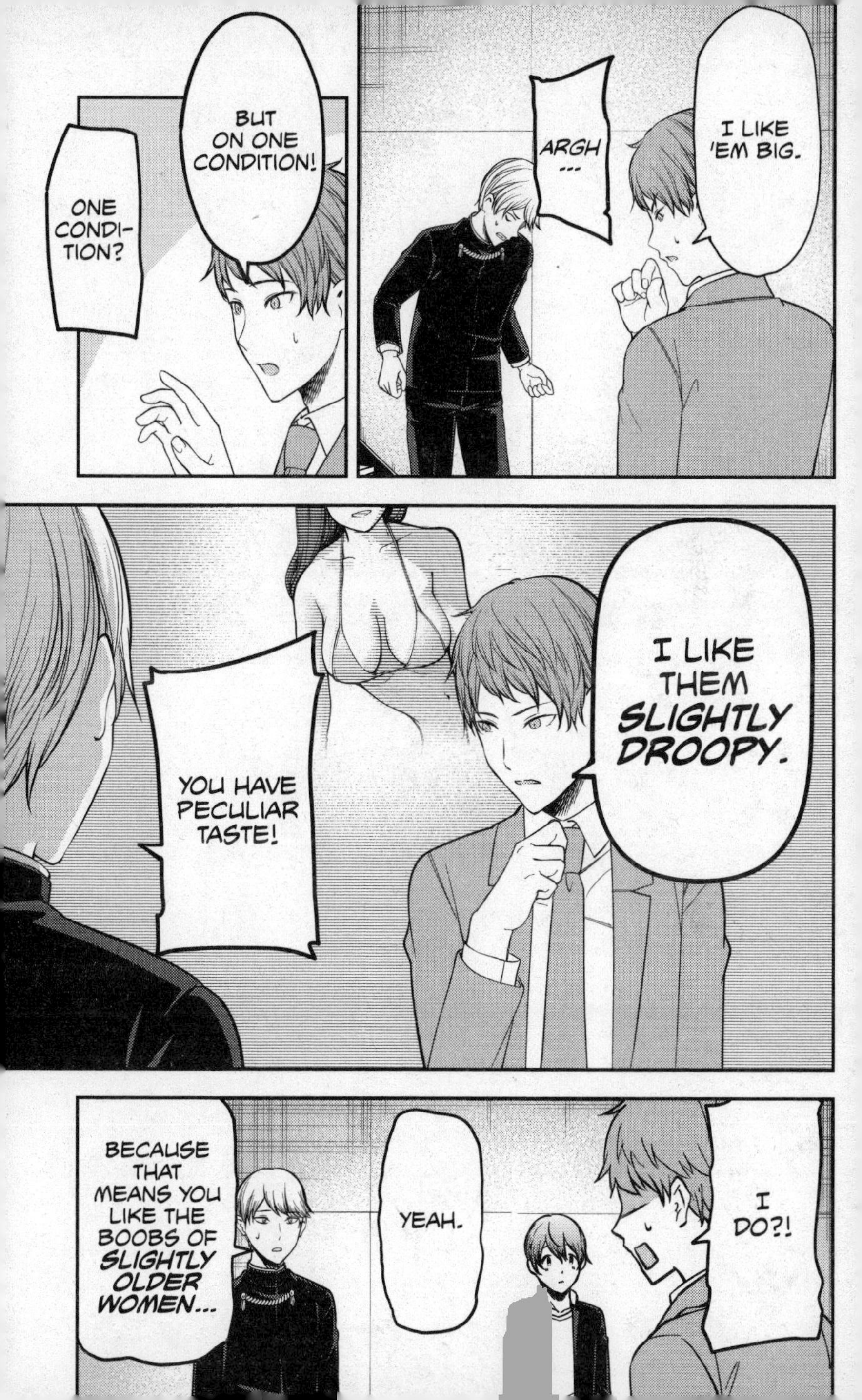

I LIKE 'EM BIG.
ARGH...
BUT ON ONE CONDITION!
ONE CONDITION?
I LIKE THEM SLIGHTLY DROOPY.
YOU HAVE PECULIAR TASTE!
I DO?!
YEAH.
BECAUSE THAT MEANS YOU LIKE THE BOOBS OF SLIGHTLY OLDER WOMEN...

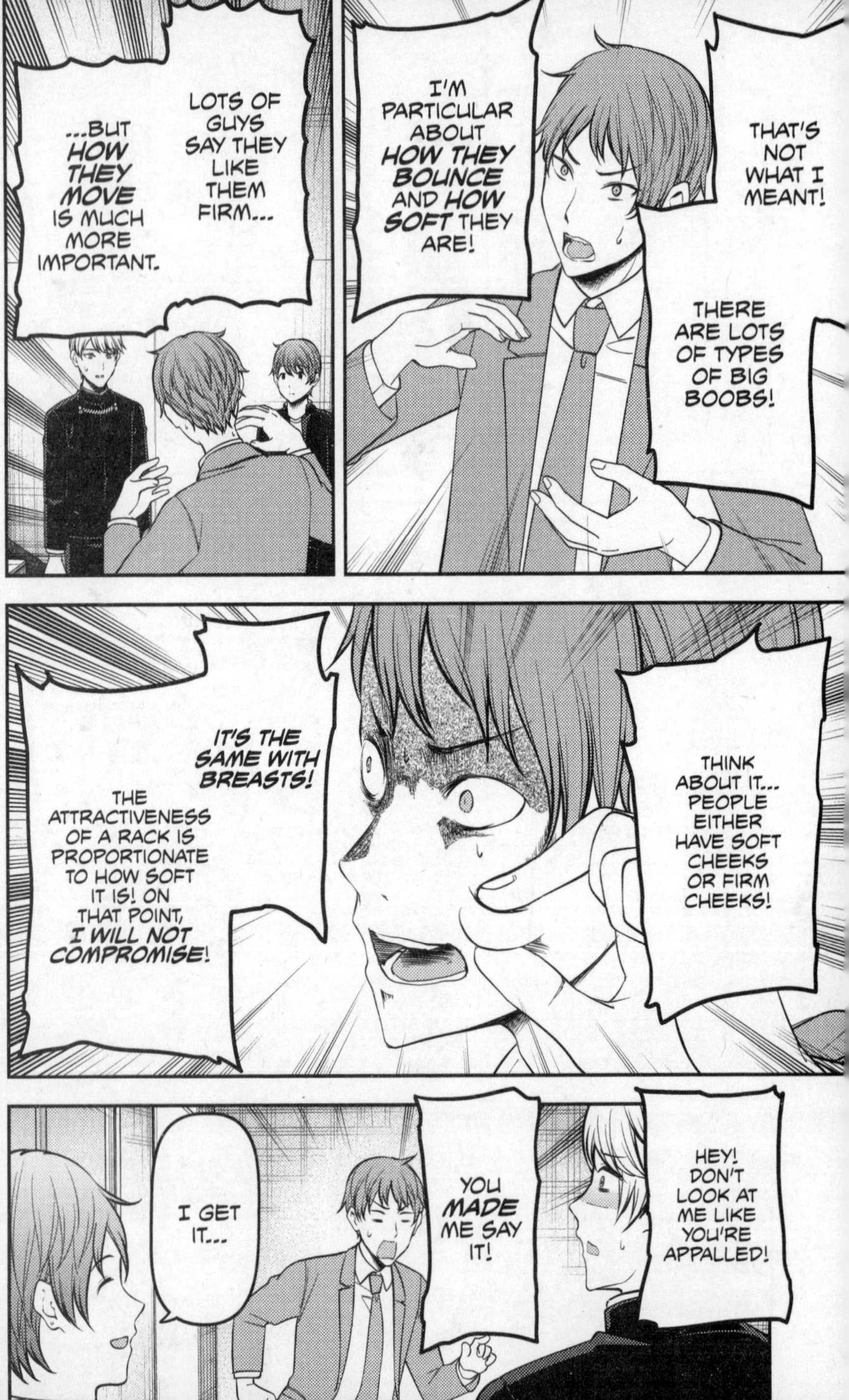
THAT'S NOT WHAT I MEANT!
THERE ARE LOTS OF TYPES OF BIG BOOBS!
I'M PARTICULAR ABOUT HOW THEY BOUNCE AND HOW SOFT THEY ARE!
LOTS OF GUYS SAY THEY LIKE THEM FIRM...
...BUT HOW THEY MOVE IS MUCH MORE IMPORTANT.
THINK ABOUT IT... PEOPLE EITHER HAVE SOFT CHEEKS OR FIRM CHEEKS!
IT'S THE SAME WITH BREASTS!
THE ATTRACTIVENESS OF A RACK IS PROPORTIONATE TO HOW SOFT IT IS! ON THAT POINT, I WILL NOT COMPROMISE!
HEY! DON'T LOOK AT ME LIKE YOU'RE APPALLED!
YOU MADE ME SAY IT!
I GET IT...

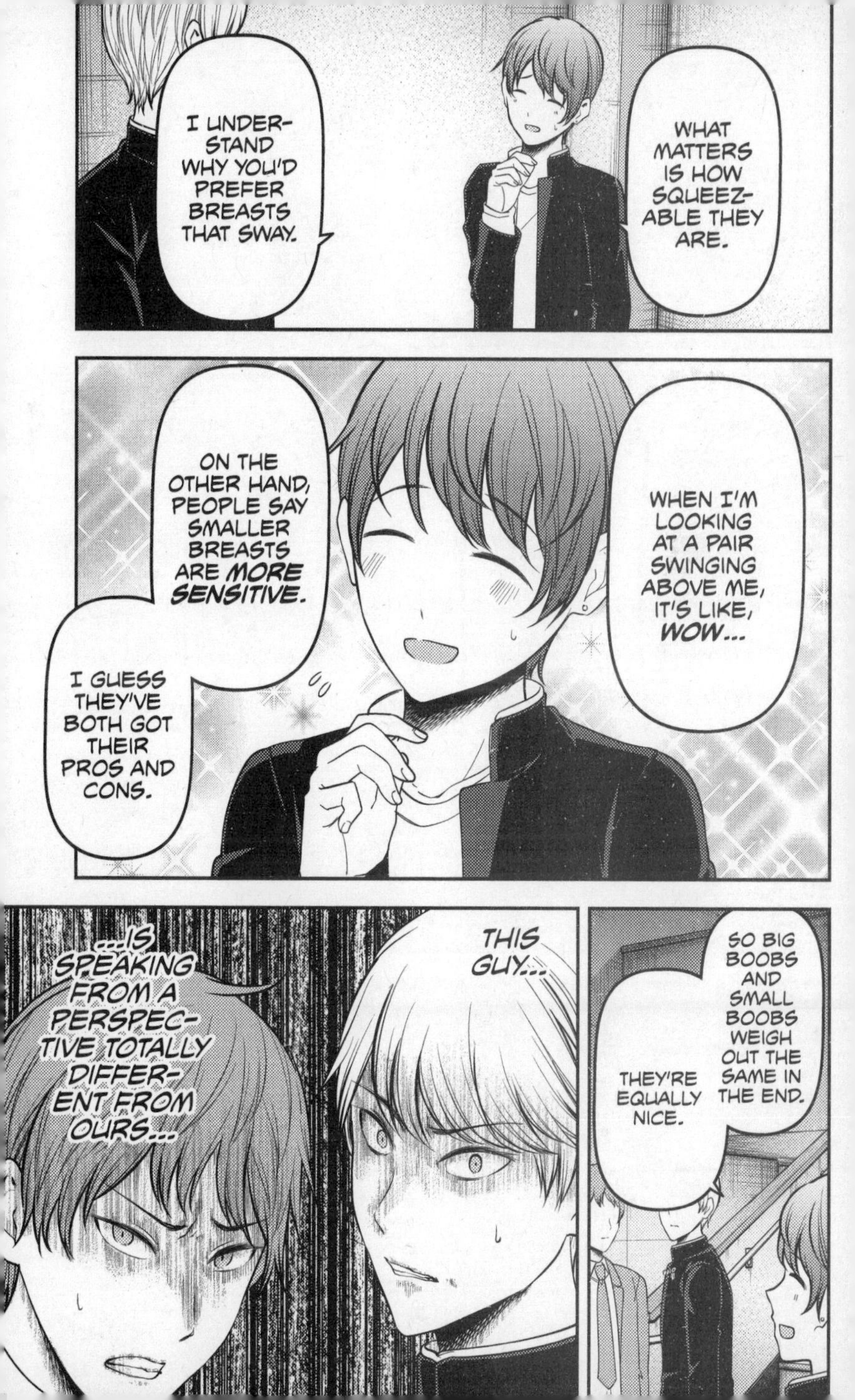
WHAT MATTERS IS HOW SQUEEZABLE THEY ARE.
I UNDERSTAND WHY YOU'D PREFER BREASTS THAT SWAY.
WHEN I'M LOOKING AT A PAIR SWINGING ABOVE ME, IT'S LIKE, *WOW*...
ON THE OTHER HAND, PEOPLE SAY SMALLER BREASTS ARE *MORE SENSITIVE*.
I GUESS THEY'VE BOTH GOT THEIR PROS AND CONS.
SO BIG BOOBS AND SMALL BOOBS WEIGH OUT THE SAME IN THE END.
THEY'RE EQUALLY NICE.
THIS GUY...
...IS SPEAKING FROM A PERSPECTIVE TOTALLY DIFFERENT FROM OURS...

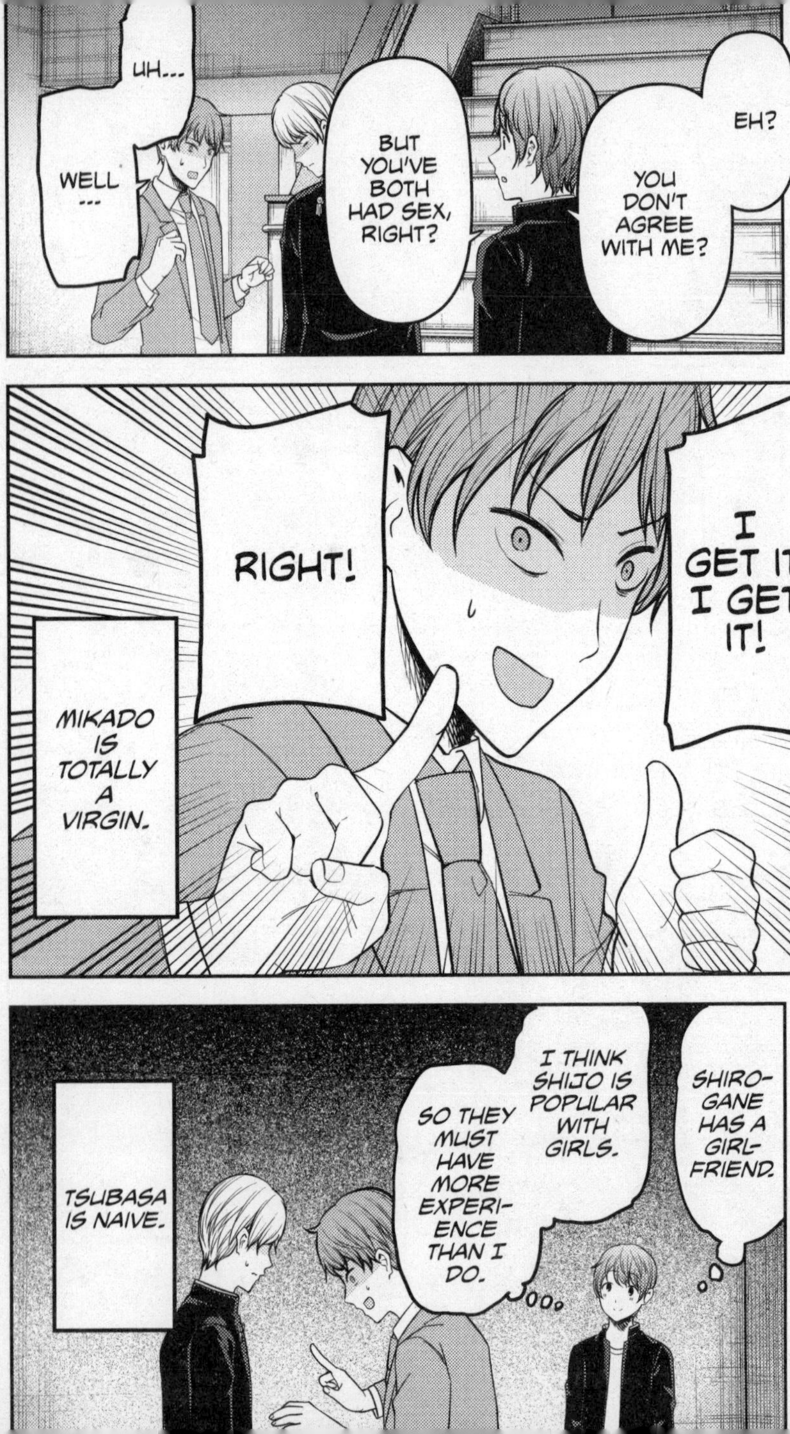
EH?
YOU DON'T AGREE WITH ME?
BUT YOU'VE BOTH HAD SEX, RIGHT?
UH...
WELL...
I GET IT, I GET IT!
RIGHT!
MIKADO IS TOTALLY A VIRGIN.
SHIROGANE HAS A GIRLFRIEND.
I THINK SHIJO IS POPULAR WITH GIRLS.
SO THEY MUST HAVE MORE EXPERIENCE THAN I DO.
TSUBASA IS NAIVE.

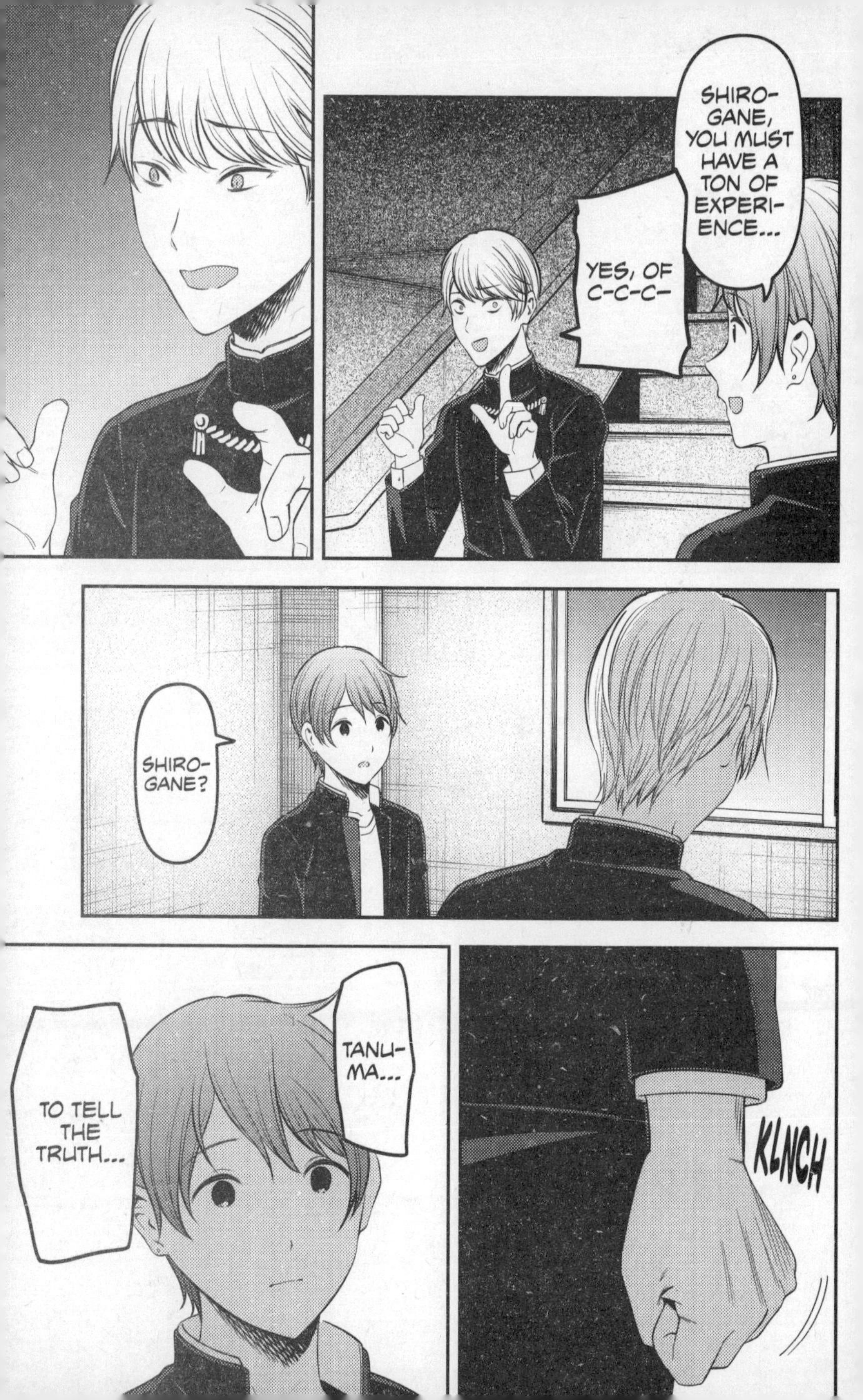
SHIRO-GANE, YOU MUST HAVE A TON OF EXPERI-ENCE...
YES, OF C-C-C-
SHIRO-GANE?
KLNCH
TANU-MA...
TO TELL THE TRUTH...

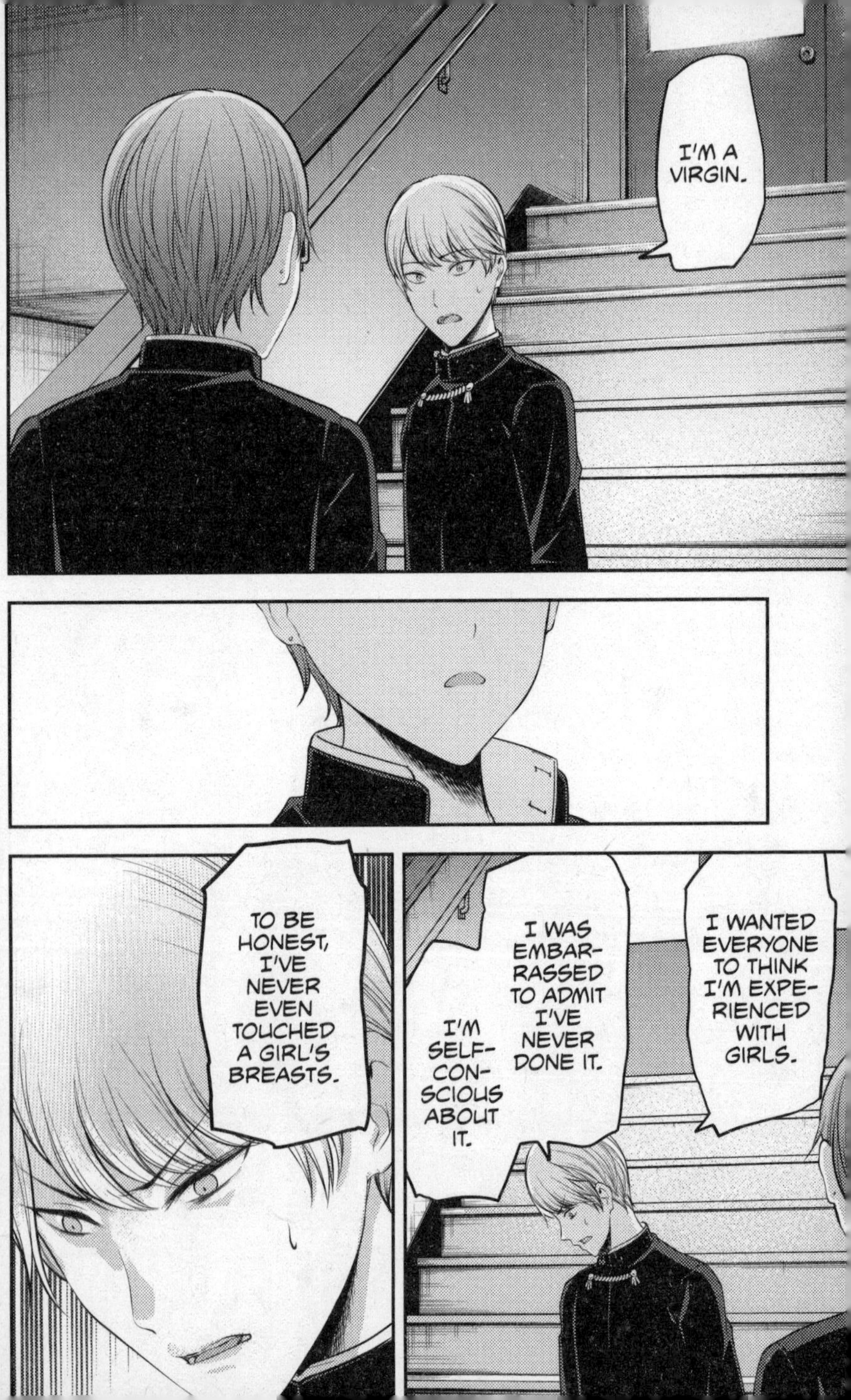
I'M A VIRGIN.
I WANTED EVERYONE TO THINK I'M EXPE-RIENCED WITH GIRLS.
I WAS EMBAR-RASSED TO ADMIT I'VE NEVER DONE IT.
I'M SELF-CON-SCIOUS ABOUT IT.
TO BE HONEST, I'VE NEVER EVEN TOUCHED A GIRL'S BREASTS.

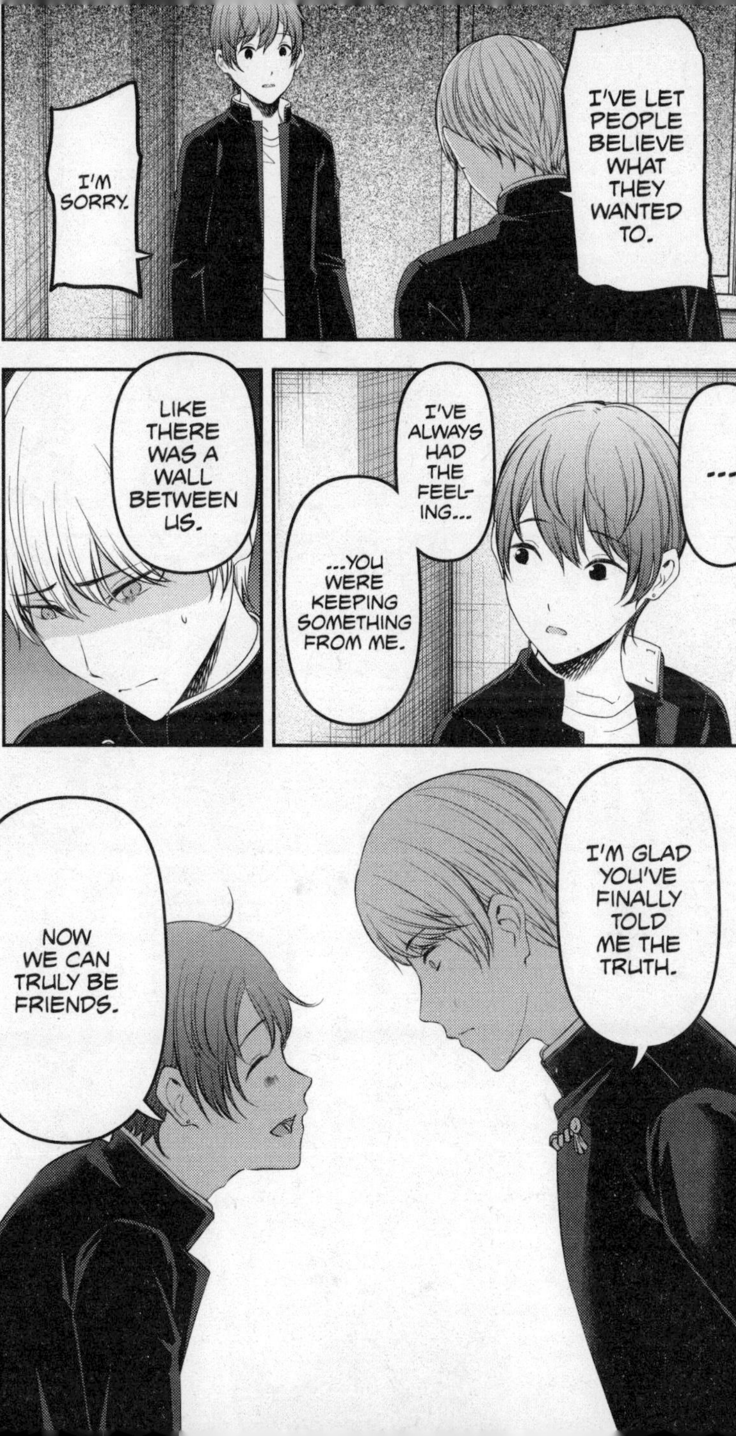
I'VE LET PEOPLE BELIEVE WHAT THEY WANTED TO.
I'M SORRY.
...
I'VE ALWAYS HAD THE FEELING...
...YOU WERE KEEPING SOMETHING FROM ME.
LIKE THERE WAS A WALL BETWEEN US.
I'M GLAD YOU'VE FINALLY TOLD ME THE TRUTH.
NOW WE CAN TRULY BE FRIENDS.

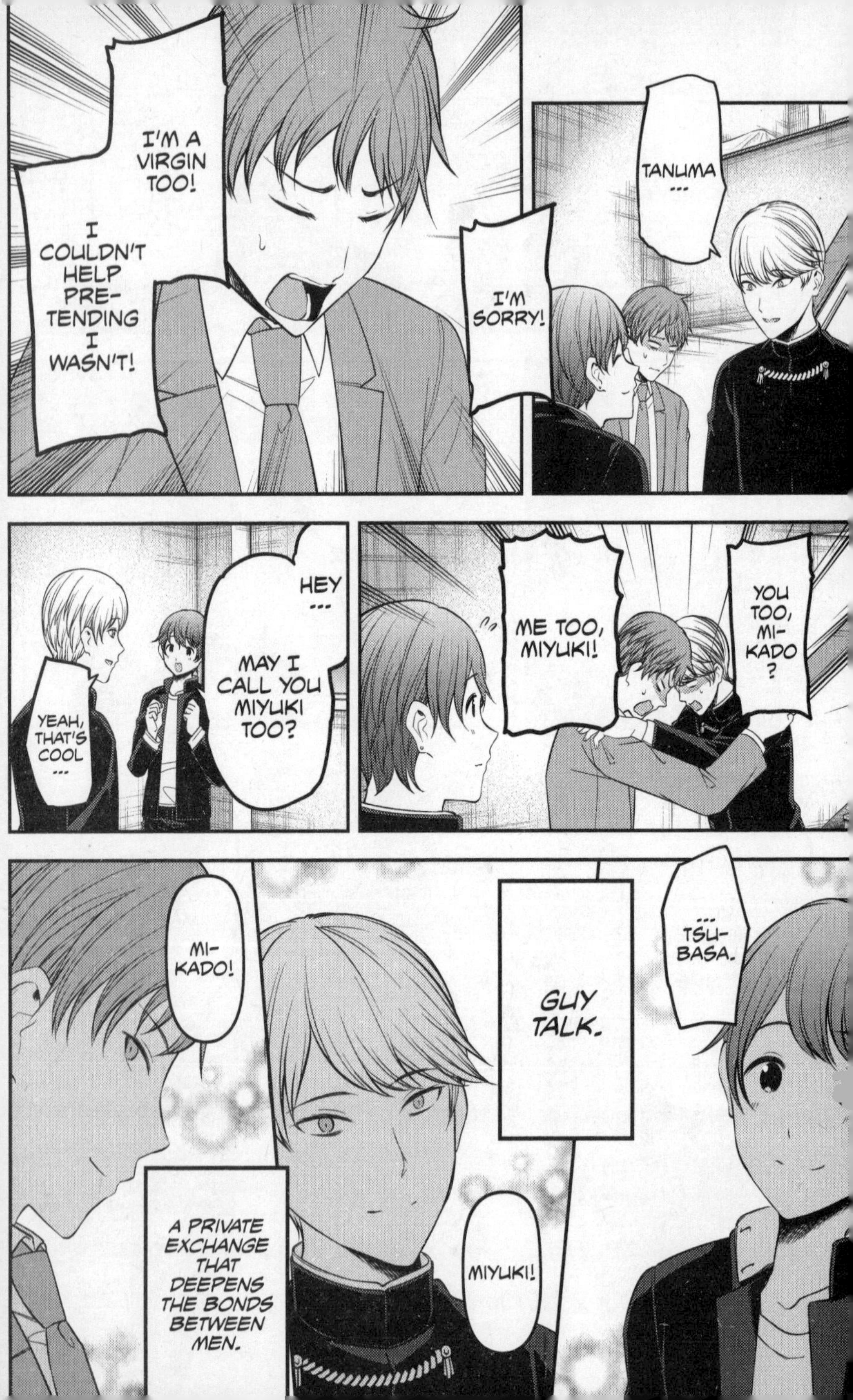
TANUMA ...
I'M SORRY!
I'M A VIRGIN TOO!
I COULDN'T HELP PRE-TENDING I WASN'T!
YOU TOO, MI-KADO?
ME TOO, MIYUKI!
HEY ...
MAY I CALL YOU MIYUKI TOO?
YEAH, THAT'S COOL ...
... TSU-BASA.
GUY TALK.
MIYUKI!
MI-KADO!
A PRIVATE EXCHANGE THAT DEEPENS THE BONDS BETWEEN MEN.

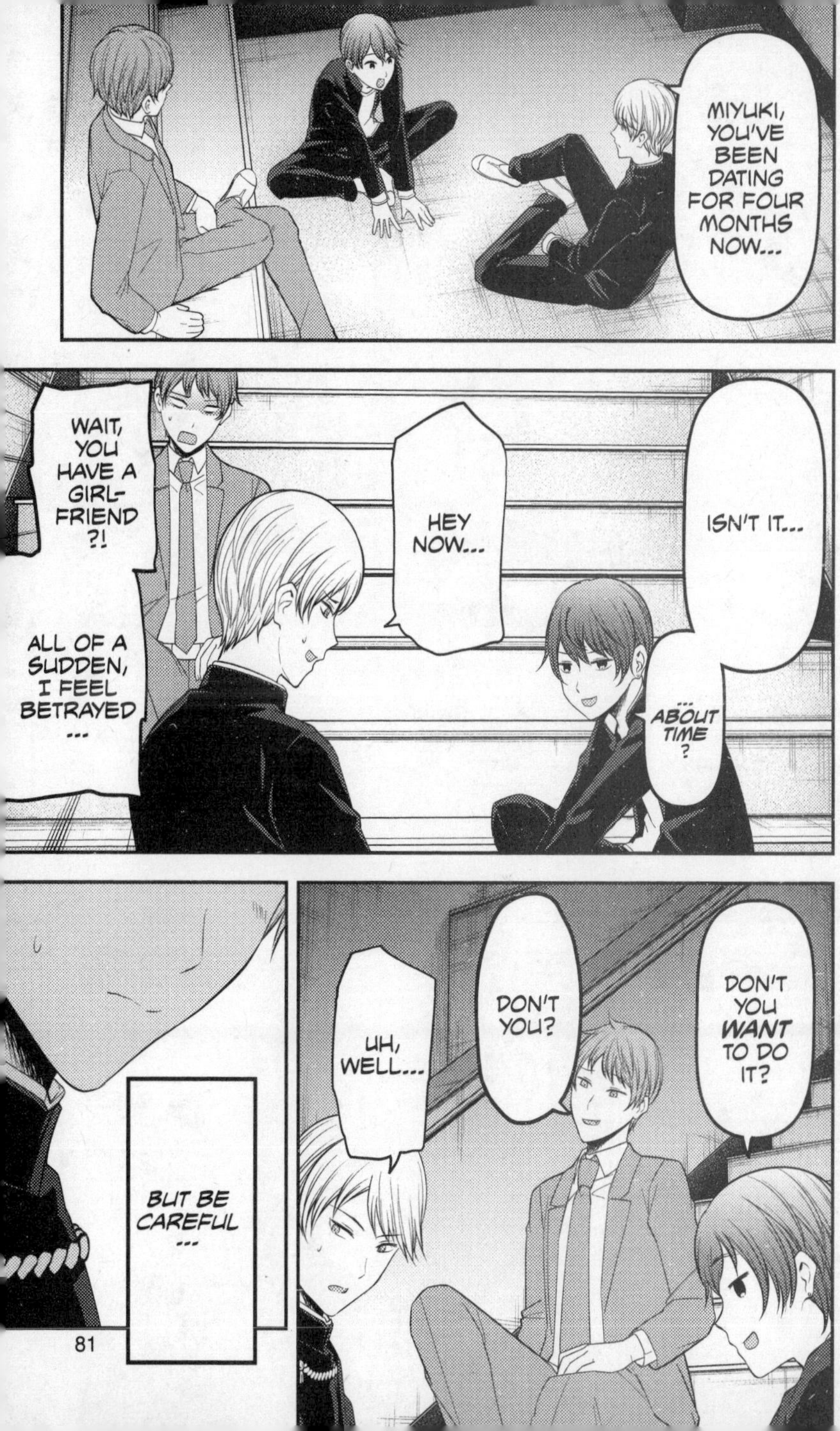
MIYUKI, YOU'VE BEEN DATING FOR FOUR MONTHS NOW...
ISN'T IT...
...ABOUT TIME?
HEY NOW...
WAIT, YOU HAVE A GIRL-FRIEND?!
ALL OF A SUDDEN, I FEEL BETRAYED...
DON'T YOU *WANT* TO DO IT?
DON'T YOU?
UH, WELL...
BUT BE CAREFUL...

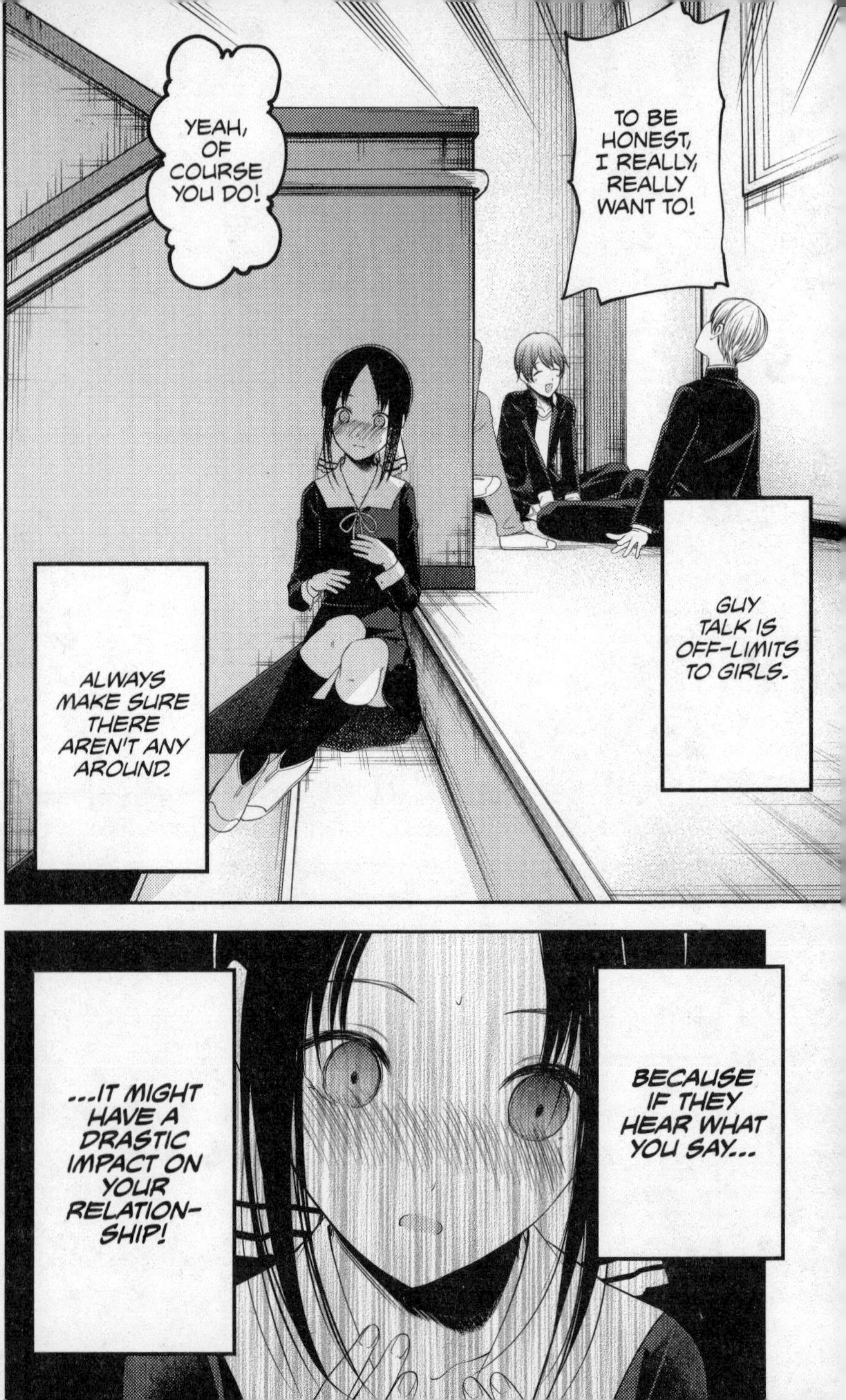
TO BE HONEST, I REALLY, REALLY WANT TO!
YEAH, OF COURSE YOU DO!
GUY TALK IS OFF-LIMITS TO GIRLS.
ALWAYS MAKE SURE THERE AREN'T ANY AROUND.
BECAUSE IF THEY HEAR WHAT YOU SAY...
...IT MIGHT HAVE A DRASTIC IMPACT ON YOUR RELATION-SHIP!

No girl-
friend, but
plenty of
unrequited
feelings →

KAGUYA-SAMA
LOVE IS WAR

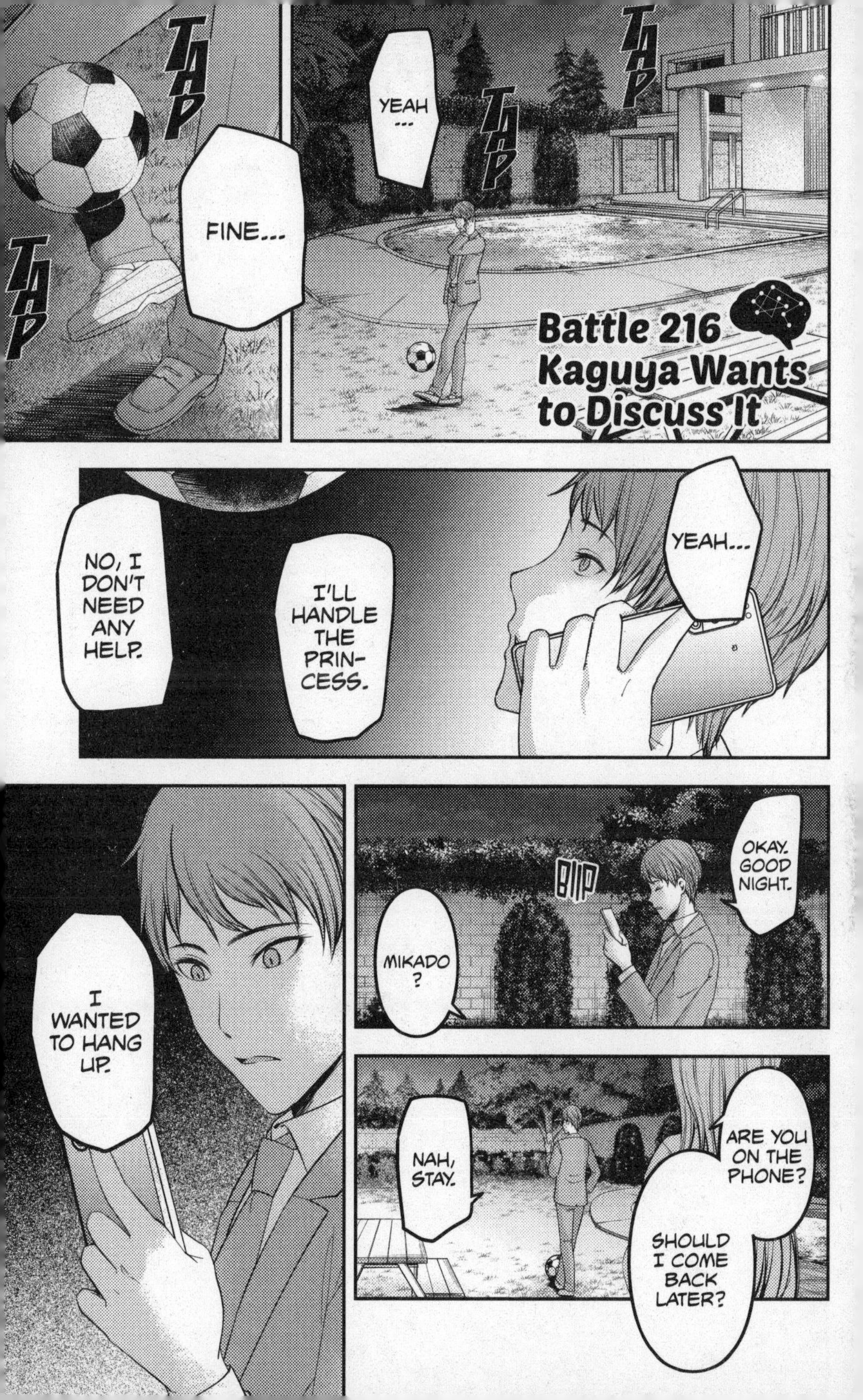
TAP
TAP
TAP
YEAH ...
Battle 216 Kaguya Wants to Discuss It
FINE...
TAP
TAP
YEAH...
I'LL HANDLE THE PRIN-CESS.
NO, I DON'T NEED ANY HELP.
OKAY. GOOD NIGHT.
BLIP
MIKADO?
ARE YOU ON THE PHONE?
SHOULD I COME BACK LATER?
NAH, STAY.
I WANTED TO HANG UP.

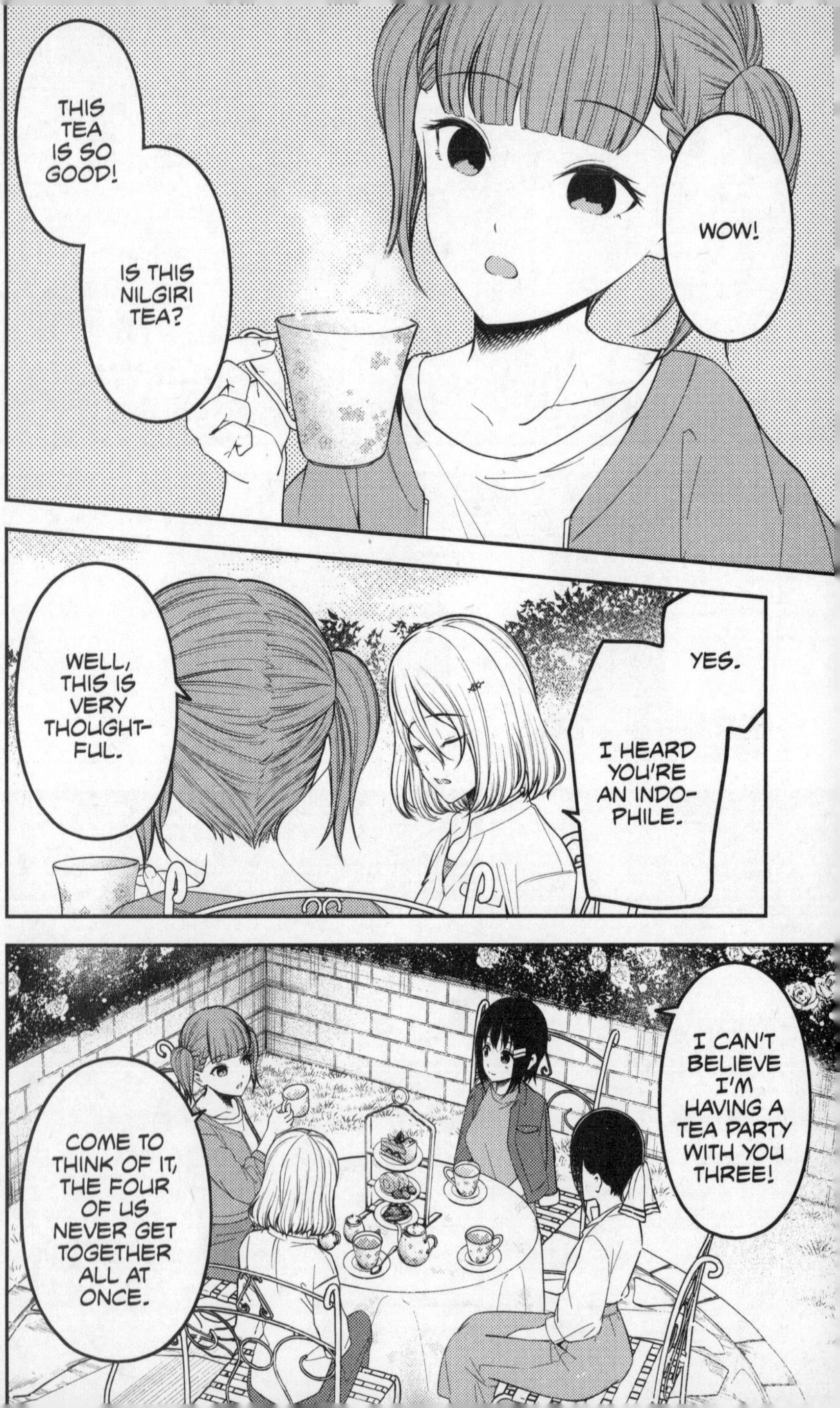
WOW!
THIS TEA IS SO GOOD!
IS THIS NILGIRI TEA?
YES.
I HEARD YOU'RE AN INDO-PHILE.
WELL, THIS IS VERY THOUGHT-FUL.
I CAN'T BELIEVE I'M HAVING A TEA PARTY WITH YOU THREE!
COME TO THINK OF IT, THE FOUR OF US NEVER GET TOGETHER ALL AT ONCE.

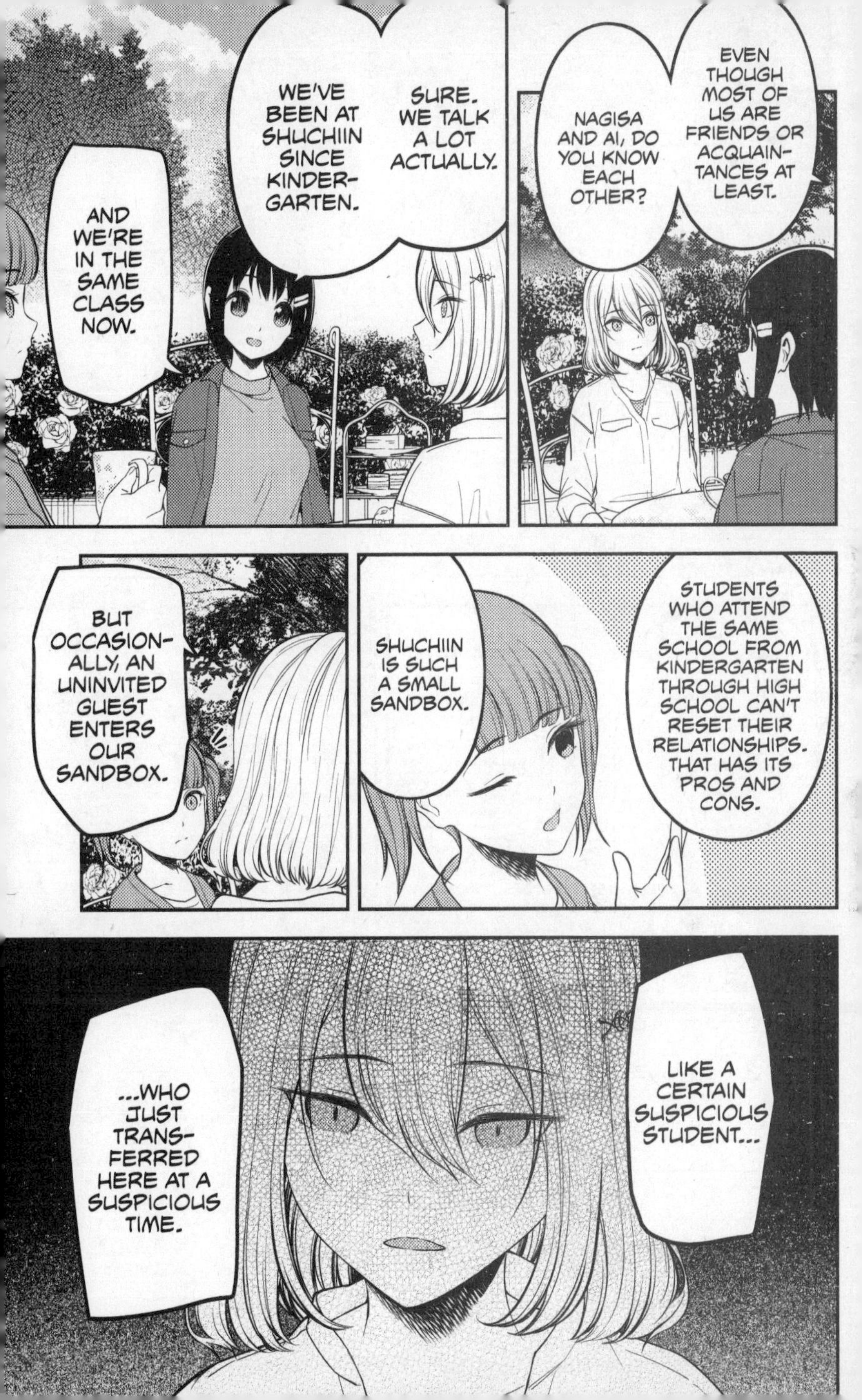
EVEN THOUGH MOST OF US ARE FRIENDS OR ACQUAINTANCES AT LEAST.
NAGISA AND AI, DO YOU KNOW EACH OTHER?
SURE. WE TALK A LOT ACTUALLY.
WE'VE BEEN AT SHUCHIIN SINCE KINDERGARTEN.
AND WE'RE IN THE SAME CLASS NOW.
STUDENTS WHO ATTEND THE SAME SCHOOL FROM KINDERGARTEN THROUGH HIGH SCHOOL CAN'T RESET THEIR RELATIONSHIPS. THAT HAS ITS PROS AND CONS.
SHUCHIIN IS SUCH A SMALL SANDBOX.
BUT OCCASIONALLY, AN UNINVITED GUEST ENTERS OUR SANDBOX.
LIKE A CERTAIN SUSPICIOUS STUDENT...
...WHO JUST TRANSFERRED HERE AT A SUSPICIOUS TIME.

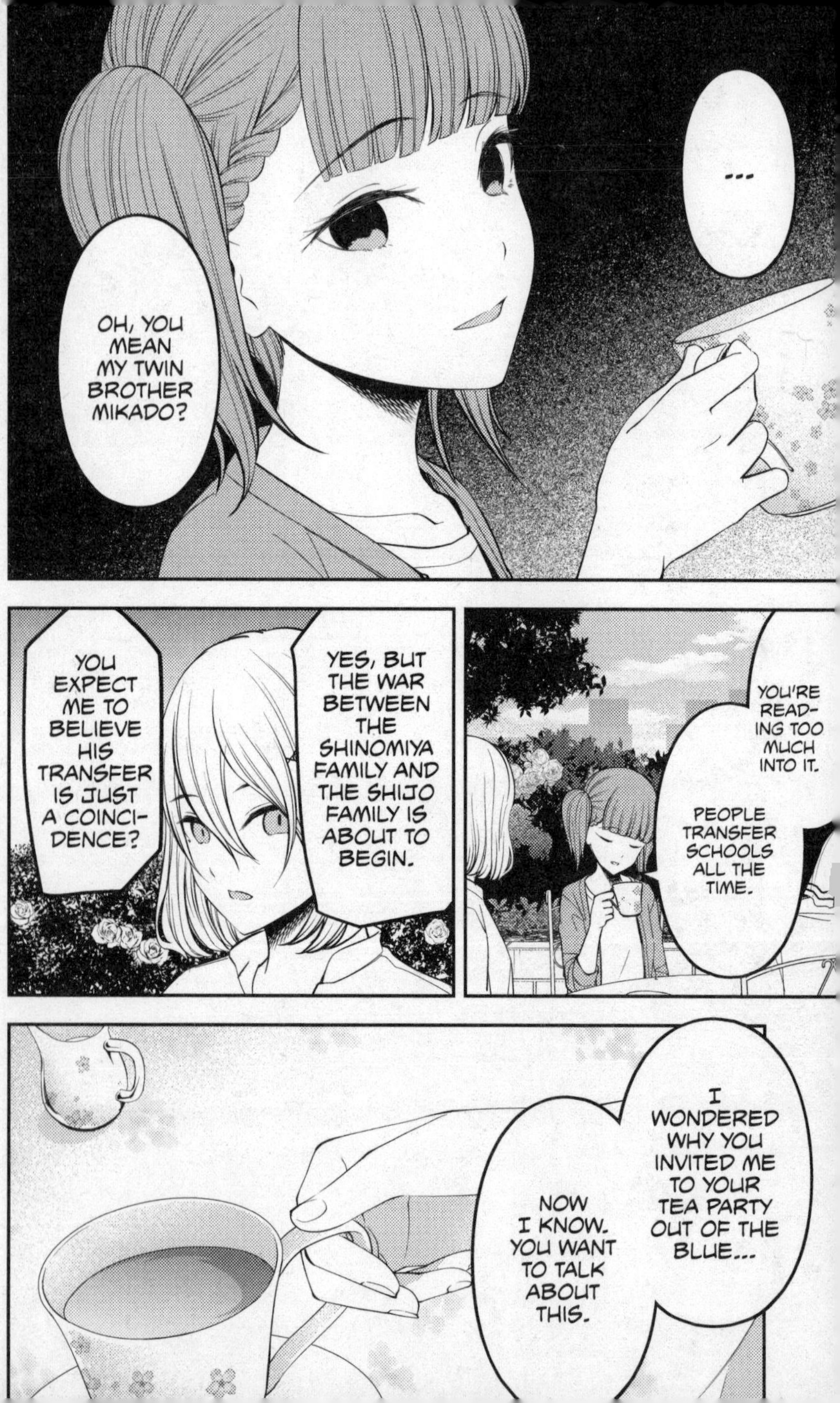
...
OH, YOU MEAN MY TWIN BROTHER MIKADO?
YOU'RE READING TOO MUCH INTO IT.
PEOPLE TRANSFER SCHOOLS ALL THE TIME.
YES, BUT THE WAR BETWEEN THE SHINOMIYA FAMILY AND THE SHIJO FAMILY IS ABOUT TO BEGIN.
YOU EXPECT ME TO BELIEVE HIS TRANSFER IS JUST A COINCIDENCE?
I WONDERED WHY YOU INVITED ME TO YOUR TEA PARTY OUT OF THE BLUE...
NOW I KNOW. YOU WANT TO TALK ABOUT THIS.

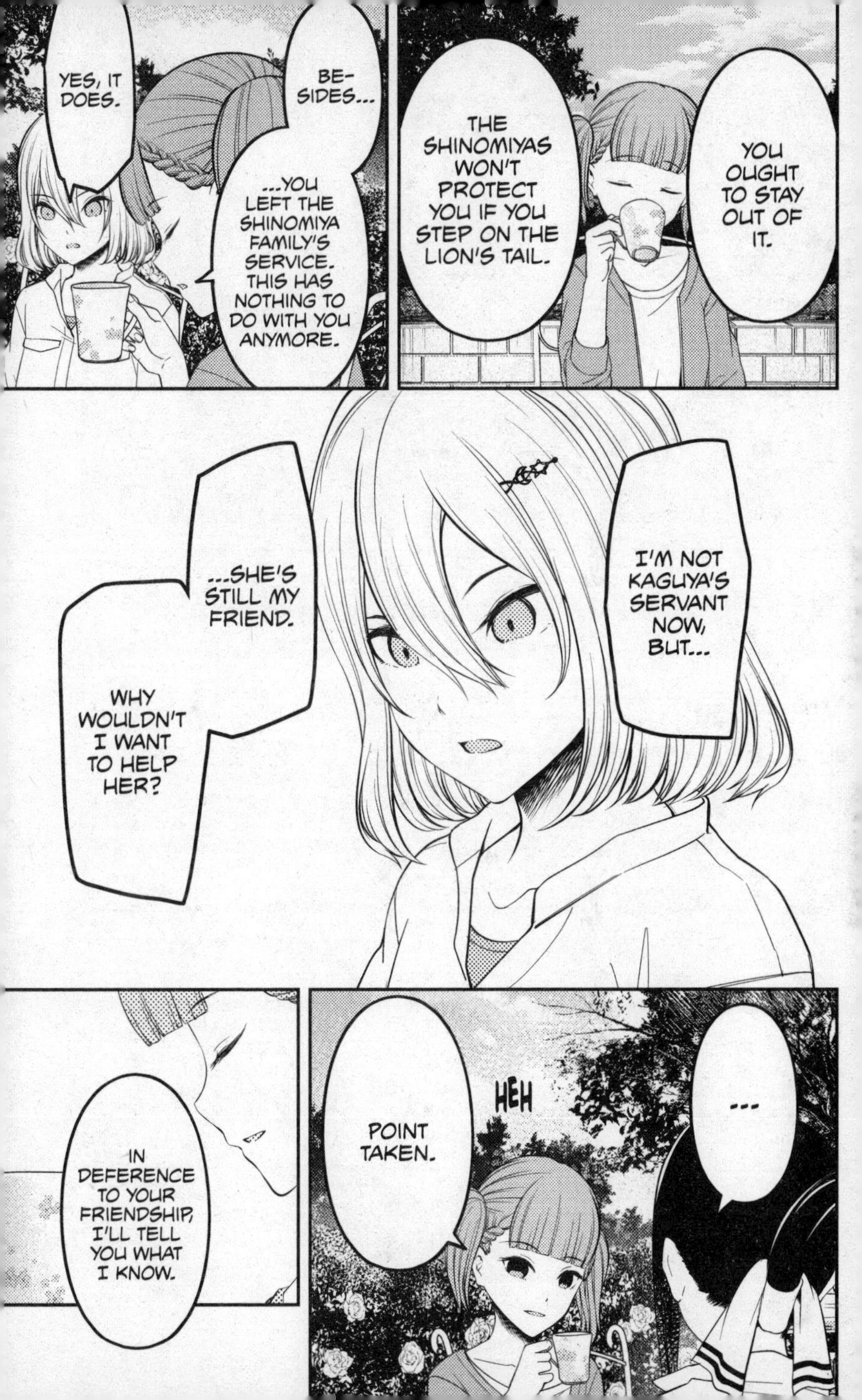
YOU OUGHT TO STAY OUT OF IT.
THE SHINOMIYAS WON'T PROTECT YOU IF YOU STEP ON THE LION'S TAIL.
BE-SIDES...
...YOU LEFT THE SHINOMIYA FAMILY'S SERVICE. THIS HAS NOTHING TO DO WITH YOU ANYMORE.
YES, IT DOES.
I'M NOT KAGUYA'S SERVANT NOW, BUT...
...SHE'S STILL MY FRIEND.
WHY WOULDN'T I WANT TO HELP HER?
...
HEH
POINT TAKEN.
IN DEFERENCE TO YOUR FRIENDSHIP, I'LL TELL YOU WHAT I KNOW.

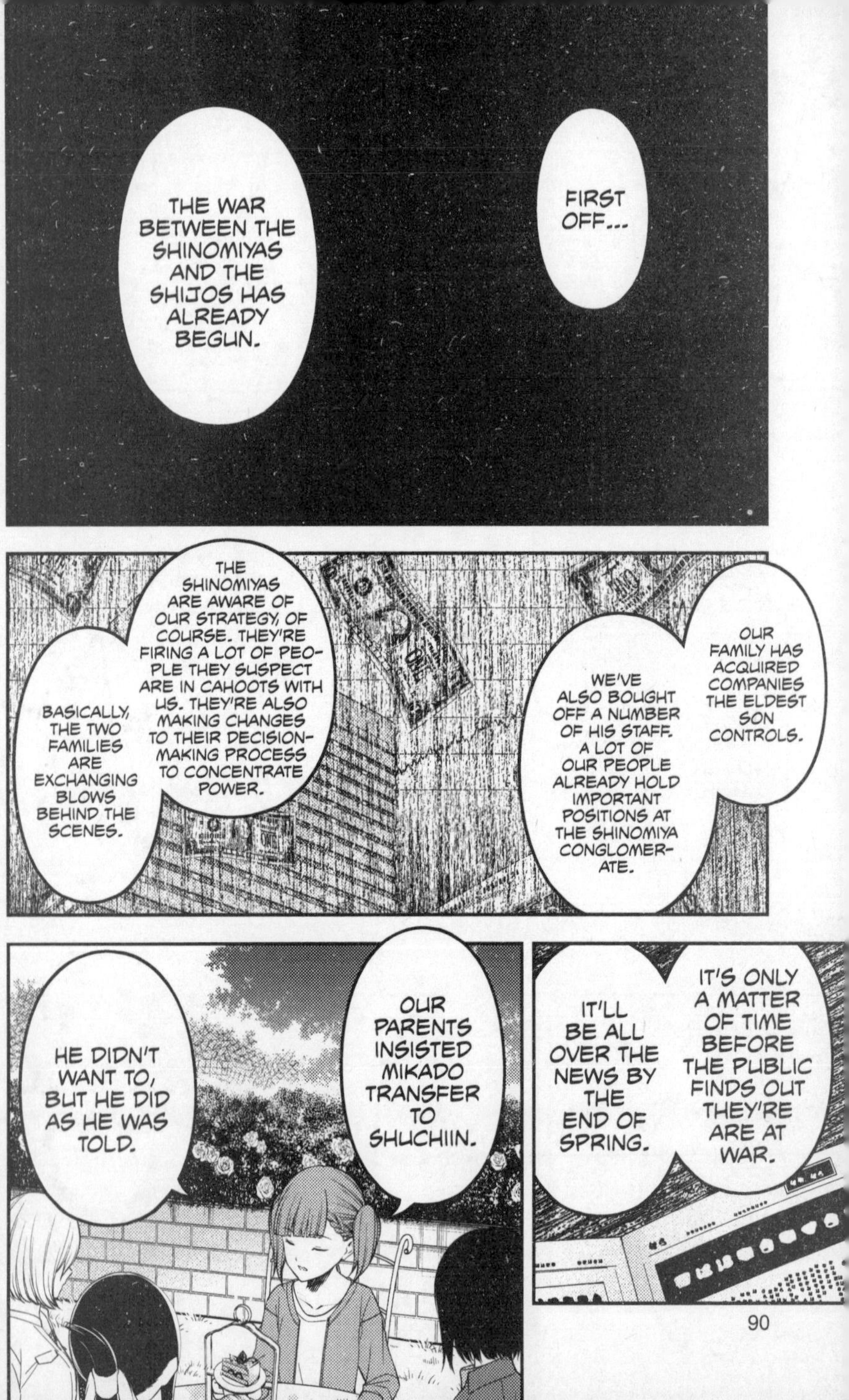

FIRST OFF...
THE WAR BETWEEN THE SHINOMIYAS AND THE SHIJOS HAS ALREADY BEGUN.
OUR FAMILY HAS ACQUIRED COMPANIES THE ELDEST SON CONTROLS.
WE'VE ALSO BOUGHT OFF A NUMBER OF HIS STAFF. A LOT OF OUR PEOPLE ALREADY HOLD IMPORTANT POSITIONS AT THE SHINOMIYA CONGLOMER-ATE.
THE SHINOMIYAS ARE AWARE OF OUR STRATEGY, OF COURSE. THEY'RE FIRING A LOT OF PEO-PLE THEY SUSPECT ARE IN CAHOOTS WITH US. THEY'RE ALSO MAKING CHANGES TO THEIR DECISION-MAKING PROCESS TO CONCENTRATE POWER.
BASICALLY, THE TWO FAMILIES ARE EXCHANGING BLOWS BEHIND THE SCENES.
IT'S ONLY A MATTER OF TIME BEFORE THE PUBLIC FINDS OUT THEY'RE ARE AT WAR.
IT'LL BE ALL OVER THE NEWS BY THE END OF SPRING.
OUR PARENTS INSISTED MIKADO TRANSFER TO SHUCHIIN.
HE DIDN'T WANT TO, BUT HE DID AS HE WAS TOLD.

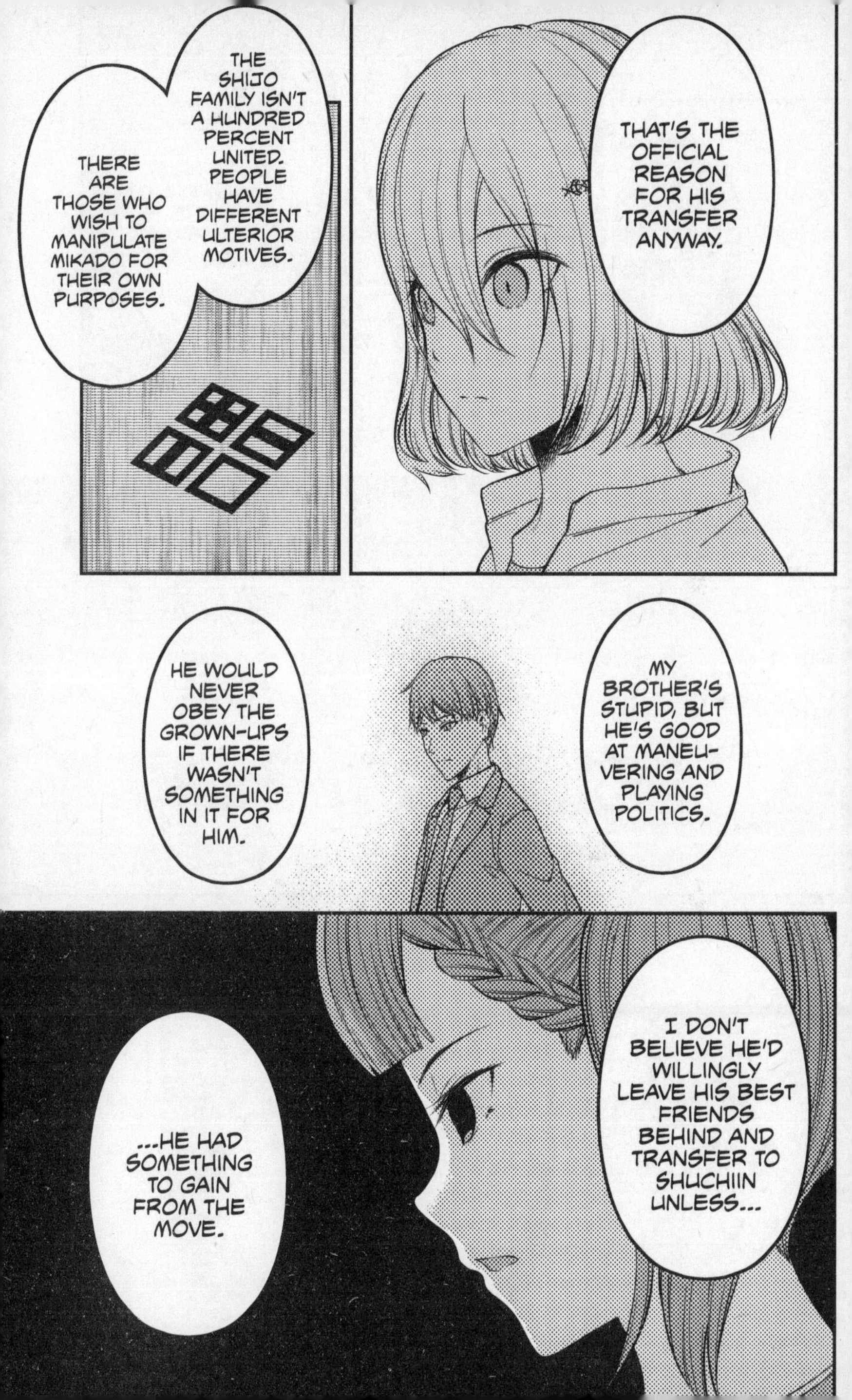
THAT'S THE OFFICIAL REASON FOR HIS TRANSFER ANYWAY.
THE SHIJO FAMILY ISN'T A HUNDRED PERCENT UNITED. PEOPLE HAVE DIFFERENT ULTERIOR MOTIVES.
THERE ARE THOSE WHO WISH TO MANIPULATE MIKADO FOR THEIR OWN PURPOSES.
MY BROTHER'S STUPID, BUT HE'S GOOD AT MANEU-VERING AND PLAYING POLITICS.
HE WOULD NEVER OBEY THE GROWN-UPS IF THERE WASN'T SOMETHING IN IT FOR HIM.
I DON'T BELIEVE HE'D WILLINGLY LEAVE HIS BEST FRIENDS BEHIND AND TRANSFER TO SHUCHIIN UNLESS...
...HE HAD SOMETHING TO GAIN FROM THE MOVE.

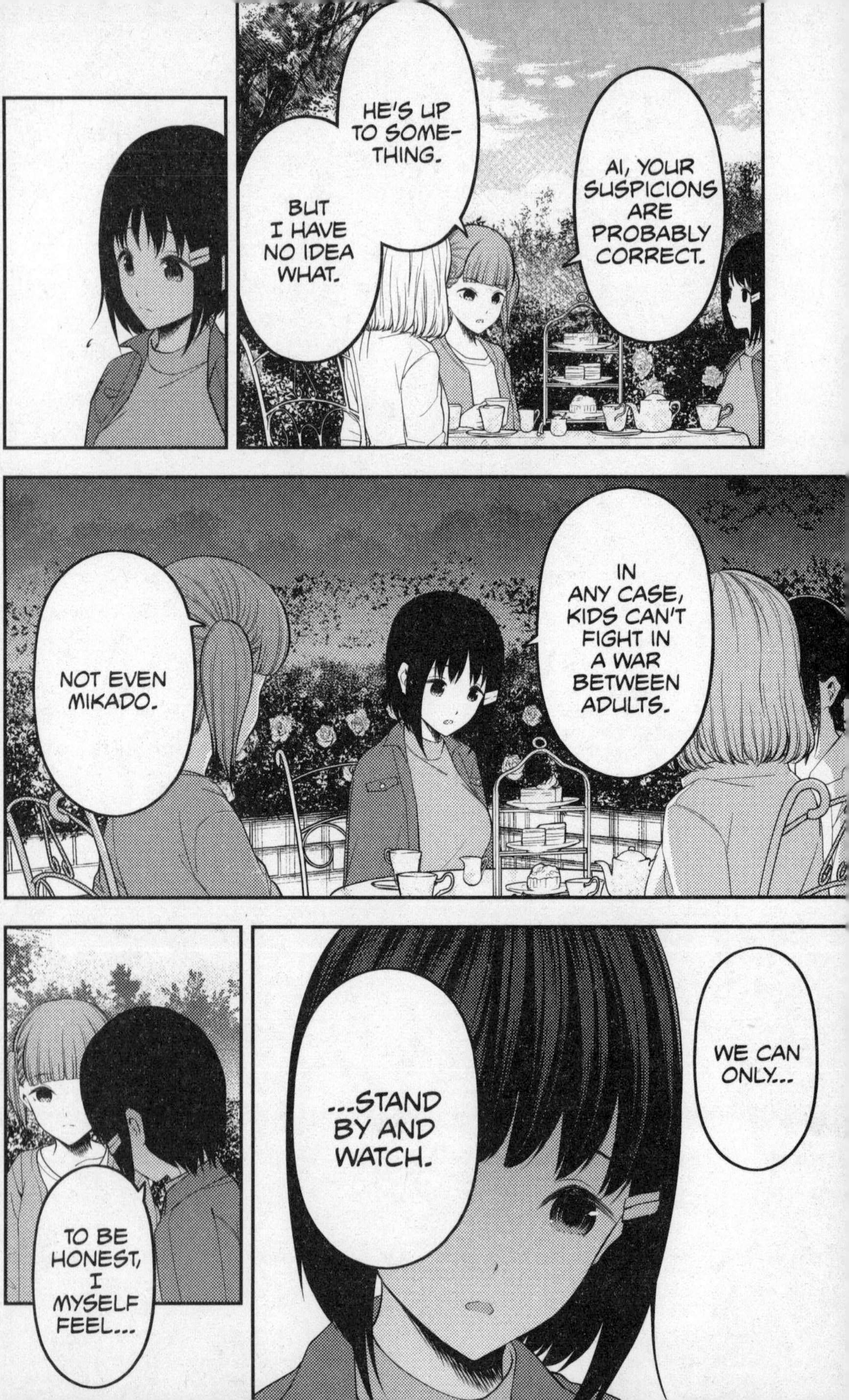
AI, YOUR SUSPICIONS ARE PROBABLY CORRECT.
HE'S UP TO SOME-THING.
BUT I HAVE NO IDEA WHAT.
IN ANY CASE, KIDS CAN'T FIGHT IN A WAR BETWEEN ADULTS.
NOT EVEN MIKADO.
WE CAN ONLY...
...STAND BY AND WATCH.
TO BE HONEST, I MYSELF FEEL...

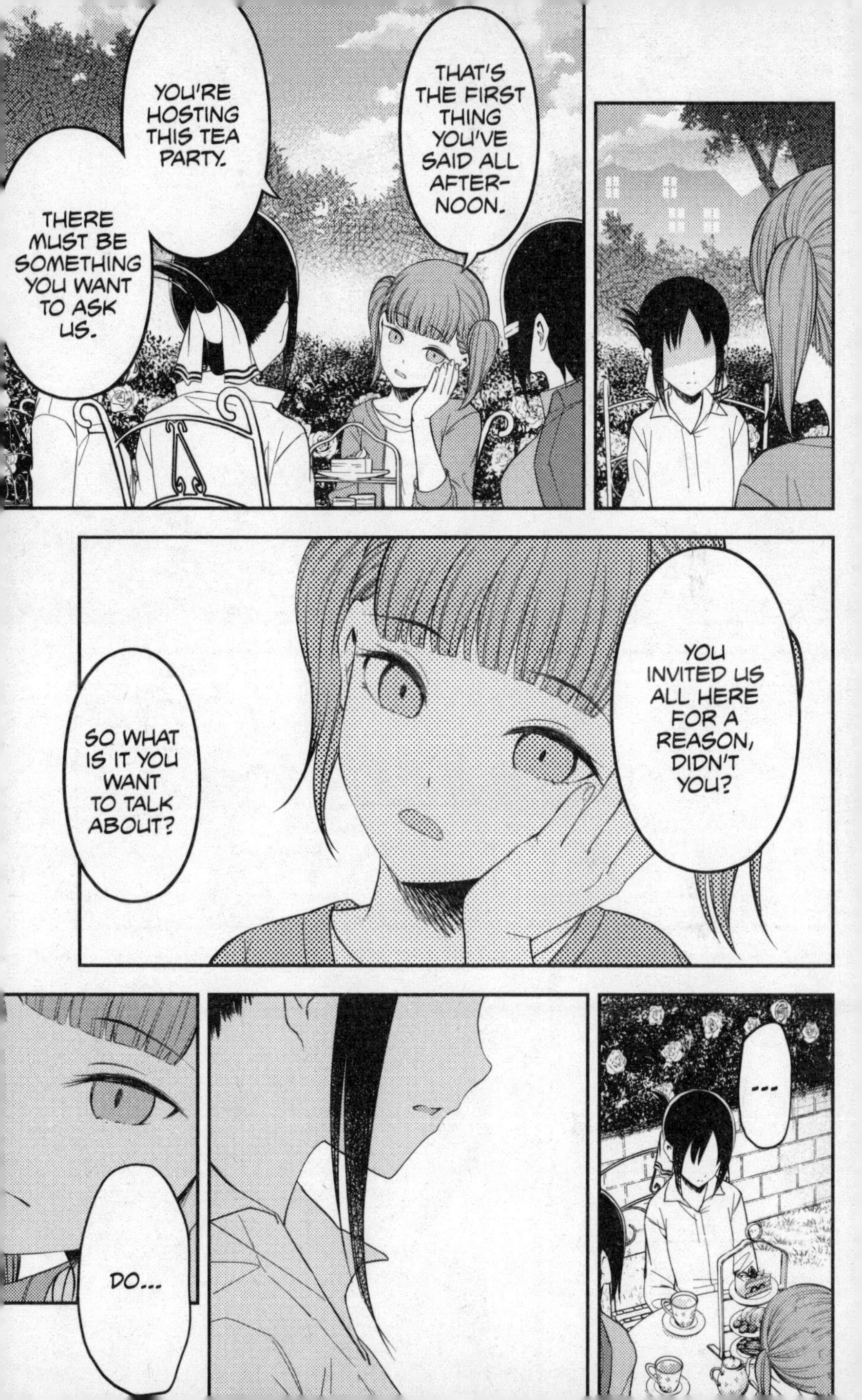
THAT'S THE FIRST THING YOU'VE SAID ALL AFTER-NOON.
YOU'RE HOSTING THIS TEA PARTY.
THERE MUST BE SOMETHING YOU WANT TO ASK US.
YOU INVITED US ALL HERE FOR A REASON, DIDN'T YOU?
SO WHAT IS IT YOU WANT TO TALK ABOUT?
...
DO...

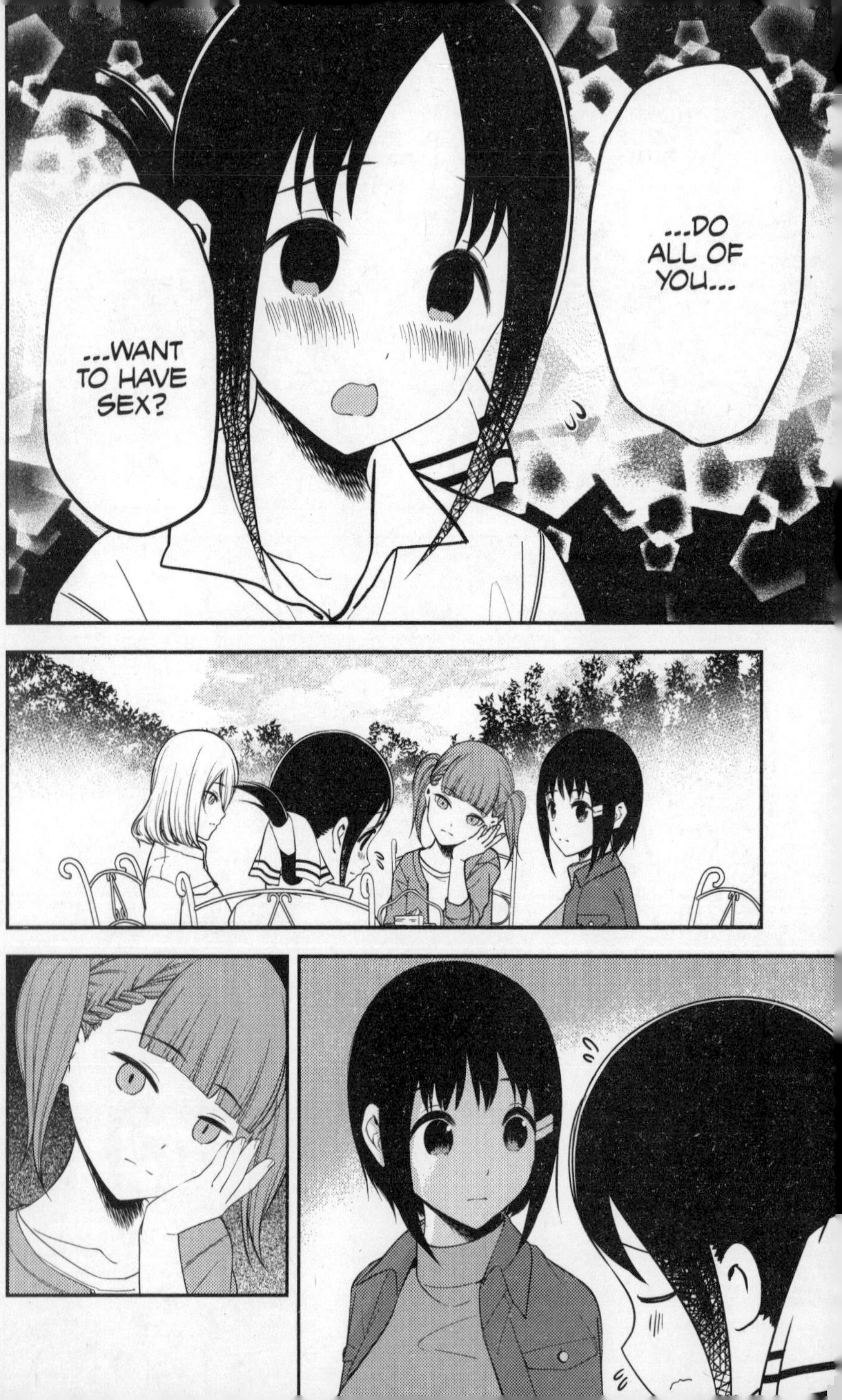
...DO ALL OF YOU...
...WANT TO HAVE SEX?

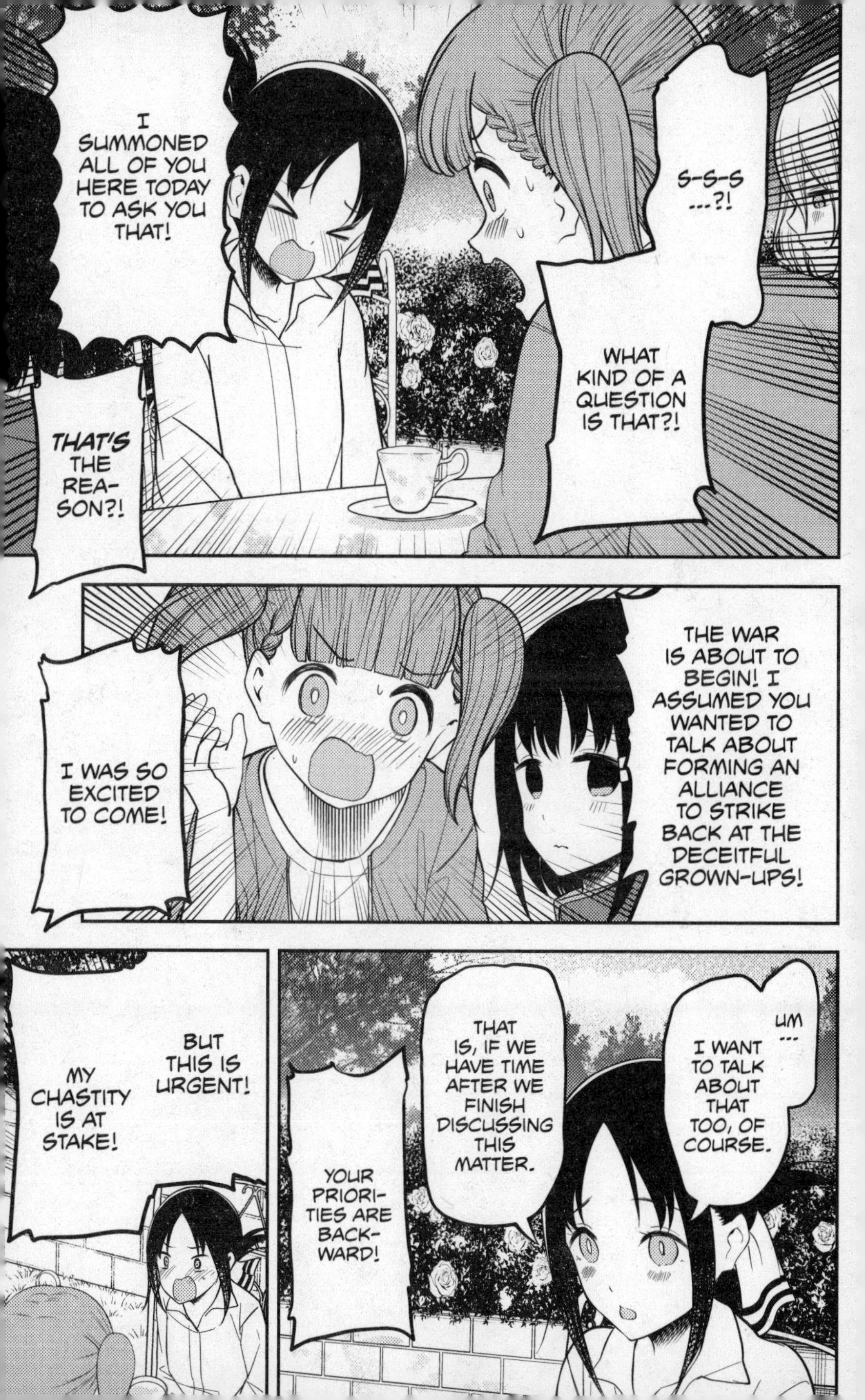
I SUMMONED ALL OF YOU HERE TODAY TO ASK YOU THAT!
S-S-S ...?!
WHAT KIND OF A QUESTION IS THAT?!
THAT'S THE REA-SON?!
THE WAR IS ABOUT TO BEGIN! I ASSUMED YOU WANTED TO TALK ABOUT FORMING AN ALLIANCE TO STRIKE BACK AT THE DECEITFUL GROWN-UPS!
I WAS SO EXCITED TO COME!
UM ...
I WANT TO TALK ABOUT THAT TOO, OF COURSE.
THAT IS, IF WE HAVE TIME AFTER WE FINISH DISCUSSING THIS MATTER.
YOUR PRIORI-TIES ARE BACK-WARD!
BUT THIS IS URGENT!
MY CHASTITY IS AT STAKE!

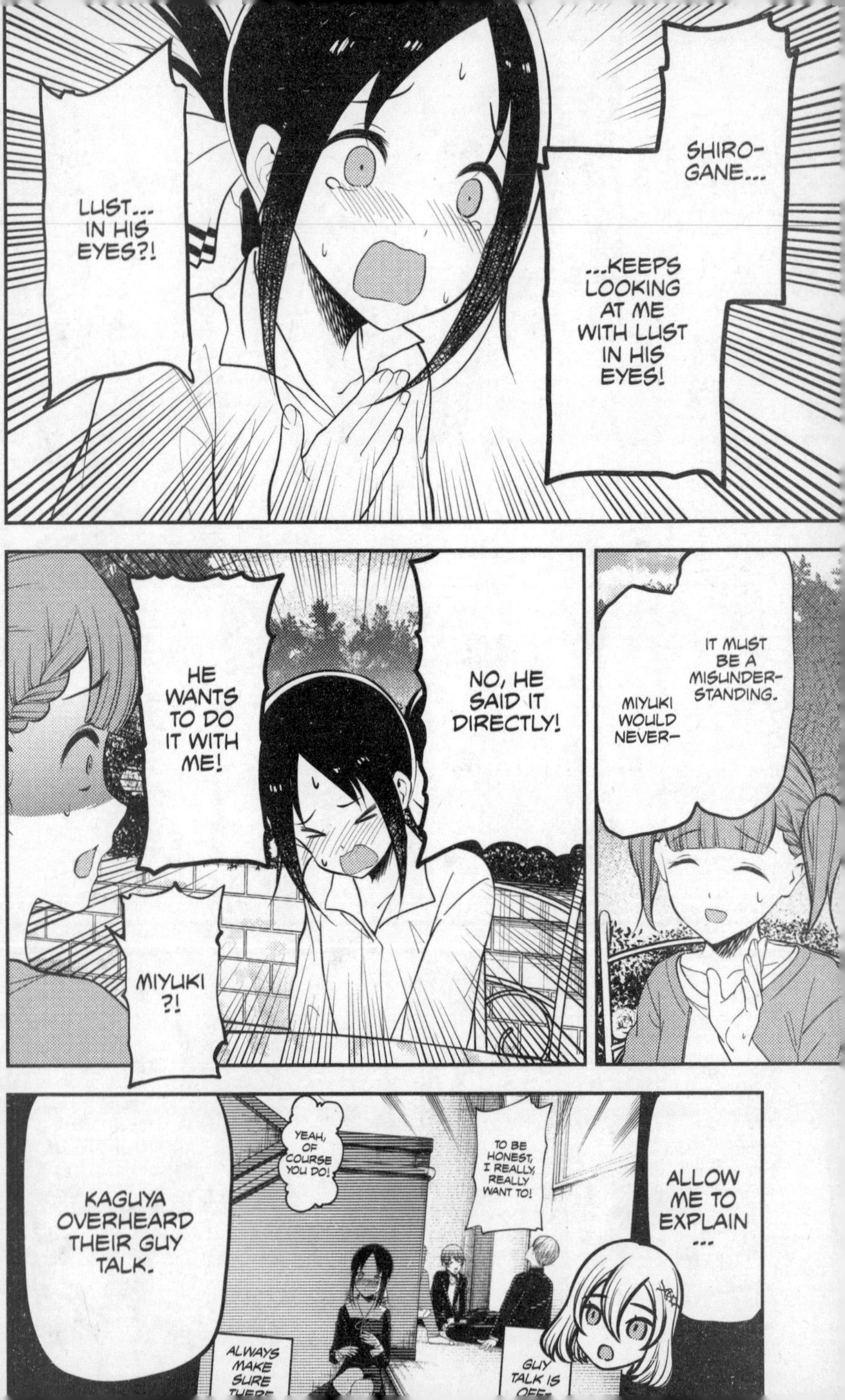
SHIRO-GANE...
...KEEPS LOOKING AT ME WITH LUST IN HIS EYES!
LUST... IN HIS EYES?!
IT MUST BE A MISUNDER-STANDING.
MIYUKI WOULD NEVER—
NO, HE SAID IT DIRECTLY!
HE WANTS TO DO IT WITH ME!
MIYUKI ?!
ALLOW ME TO EXPLAIN ...
TO BE HONEST, I REALLY, REALLY WANT TO!
YEAH, OF COURSE YOU DO!
KAGUYA OVERHEARD THEIR GUY TALK.
GUY TALK IS
ALWAYS MAKE SURE

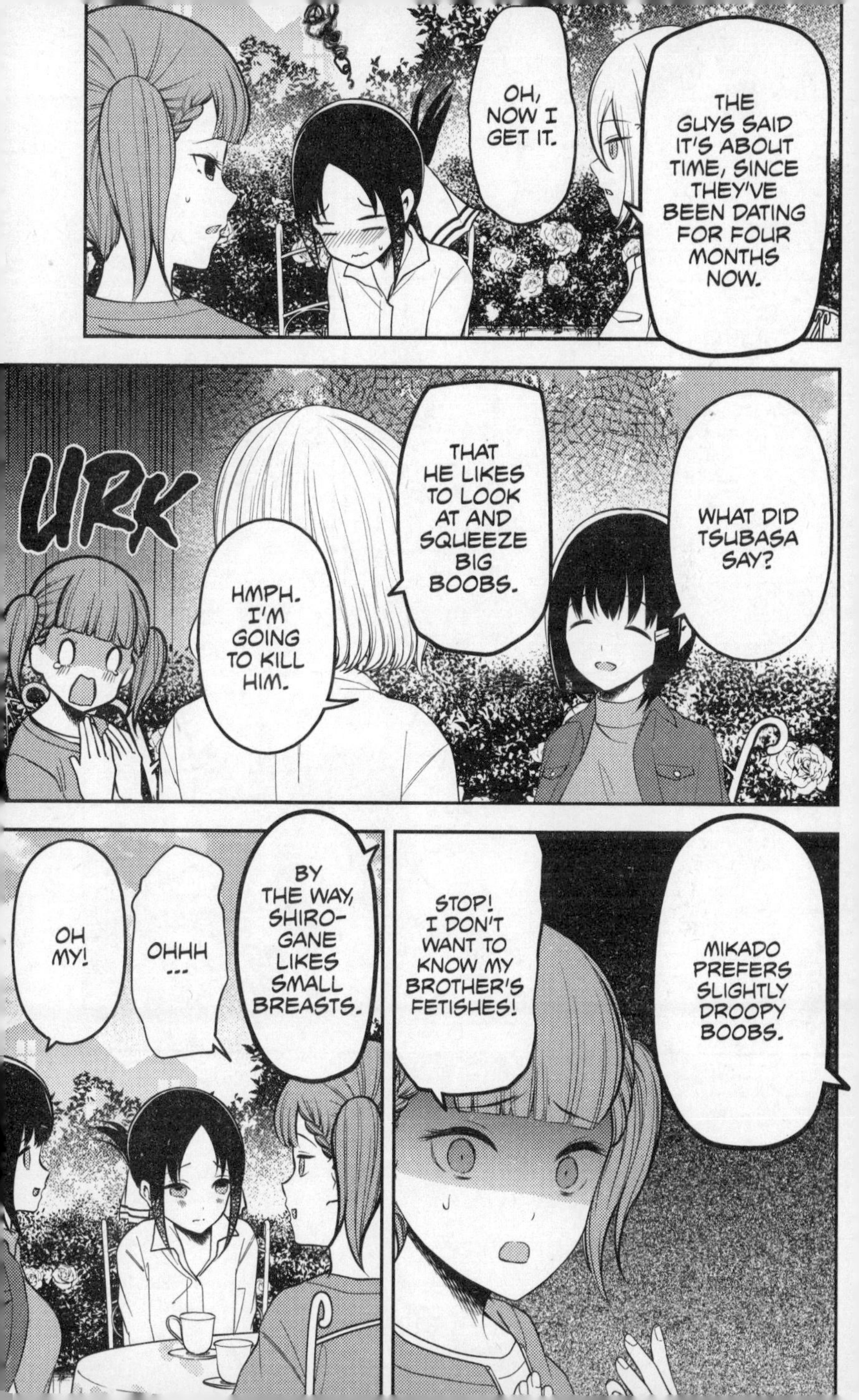
THE GUYS SAID IT'S ABOUT TIME, SINCE THEY'VE BEEN DATING FOR FOUR MONTHS NOW.
OH, NOW I GET IT.
WHAT DID TSUBASA SAY?
THAT HE LIKES TO LOOK AT AND SQUEEZE BIG BOOBS.
HMPH. I'M GOING TO KILL HIM.
URK
MIKADO PREFERS SLIGHTLY DROOPY BOOBS.
STOP! I DON'T WANT TO KNOW MY BROTHER'S FETISHES!
BY THE WAY, SHIRO-GANE LIKES SMALL BREASTS.
OHHH ...
OH MY!

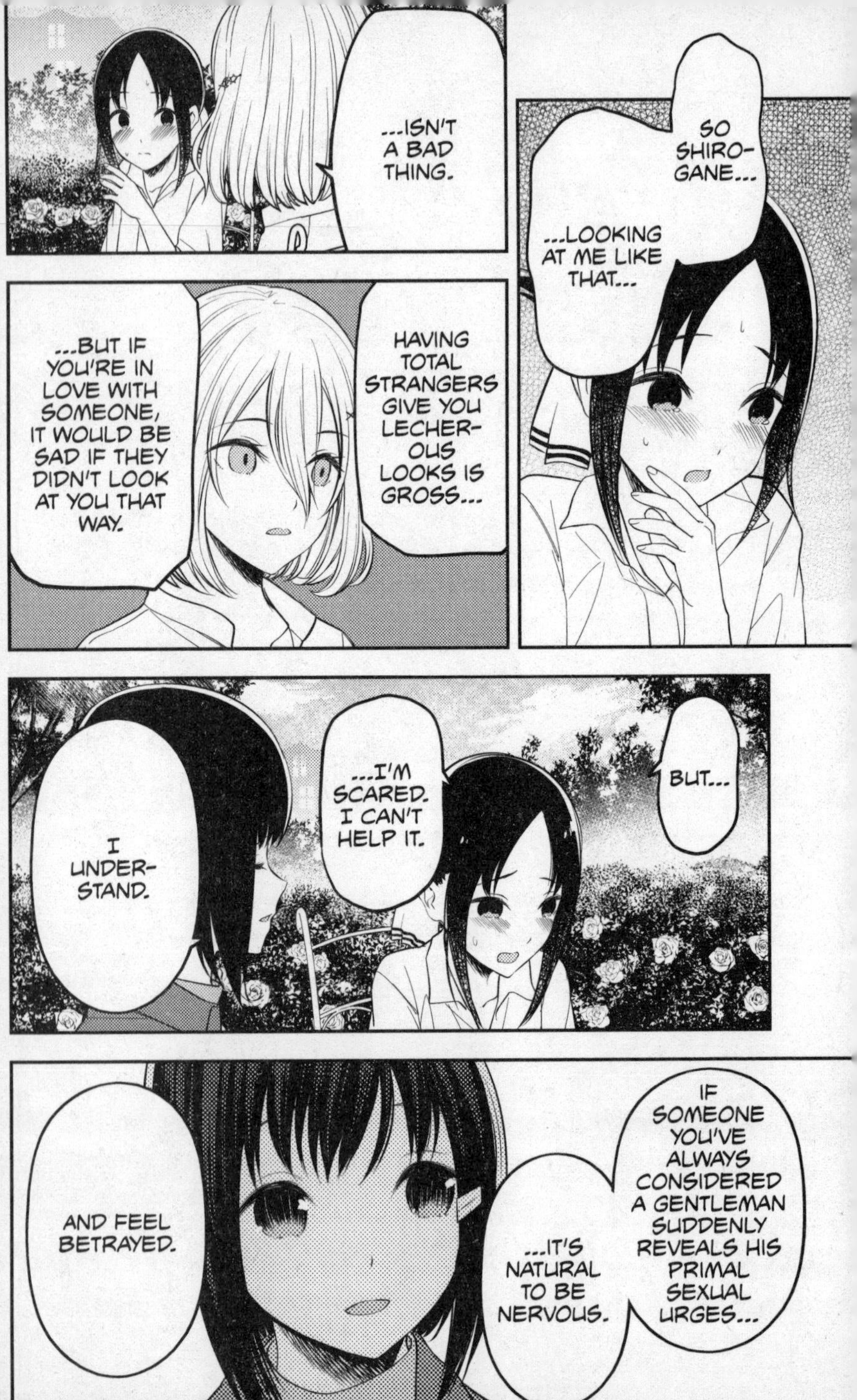
SO SHIRO-GANE...
...LOOKING AT ME LIKE THAT...
...ISN'T A BAD THING.
HAVING TOTAL STRANGERS GIVE YOU LECHER-OUS LOOKS IS GROSS...
...BUT IF YOU'RE IN LOVE WITH SOMEONE, IT WOULD BE SAD IF THEY DIDN'T LOOK AT YOU THAT WAY.
BUT...
...I'M SCARED. I CAN'T HELP IT.
I UNDER-STAND.
IF SOMEONE YOU'VE ALWAYS CONSIDERED A GENTLEMAN SUDDENLY REVEALS HIS PRIMAL SEXUAL URGES...
...IT'S NATURAL TO BE NERVOUS.
AND FEEL BETRAYED.

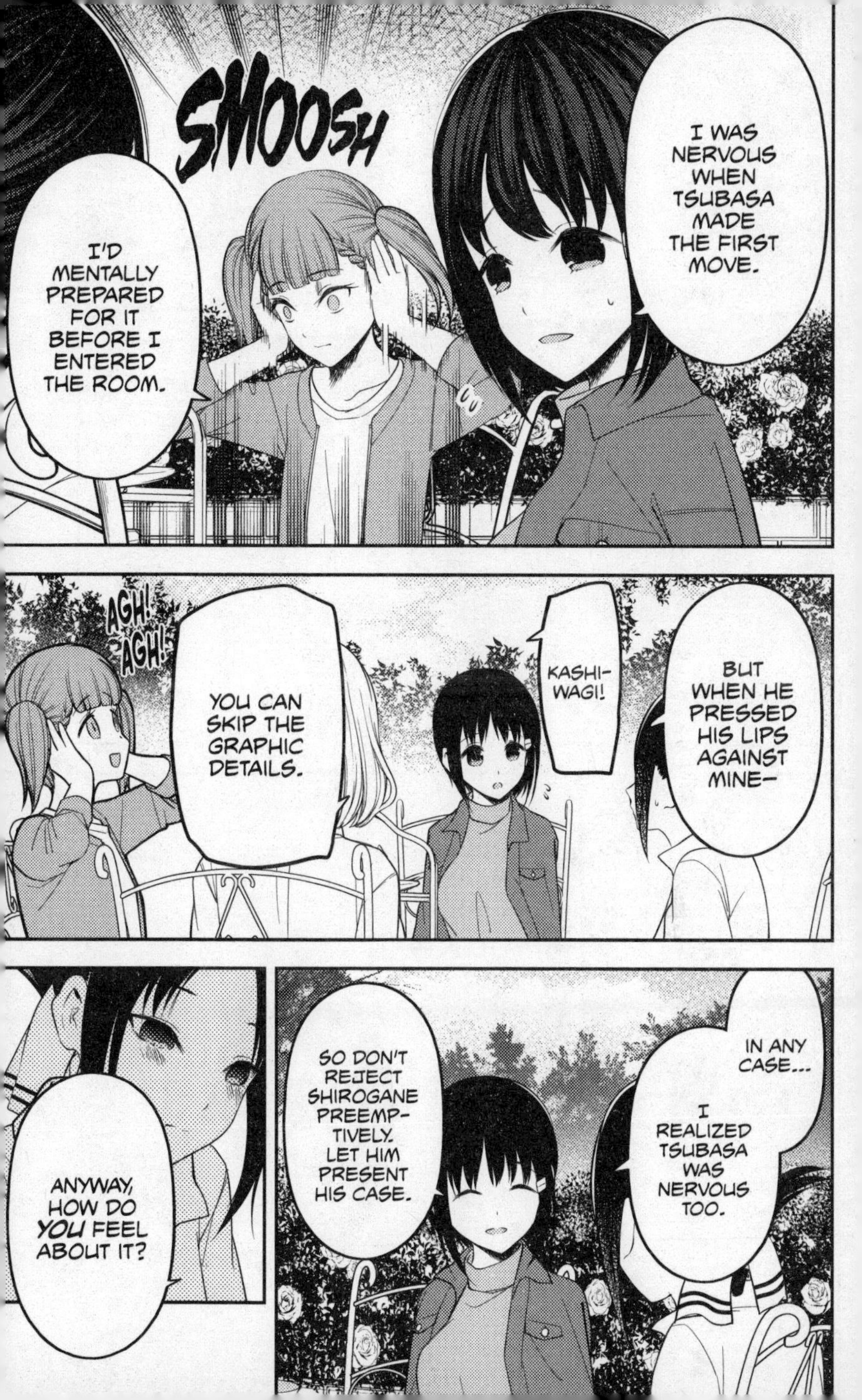
I WAS NERVOUS WHEN TSUBASA MADE THE FIRST MOVE.
SHOOSH
I'D MENTALLY PREPARED FOR IT BEFORE I ENTERED THE ROOM.
BUT WHEN HE PRESSED HIS LIPS AGAINST MINE–
KASHI-WAGI!
YOU CAN SKIP THE GRAPHIC DETAILS.
AGH! AGH!
IN ANY CASE...
I REALIZED TSUBASA WAS NERVOUS TOO.
SO DON'T REJECT SHIROGANE PREEMP-TIVELY. LET HIM PRESENT HIS CASE.
ANYWAY, HOW DO *YOU* FEEL ABOUT IT?

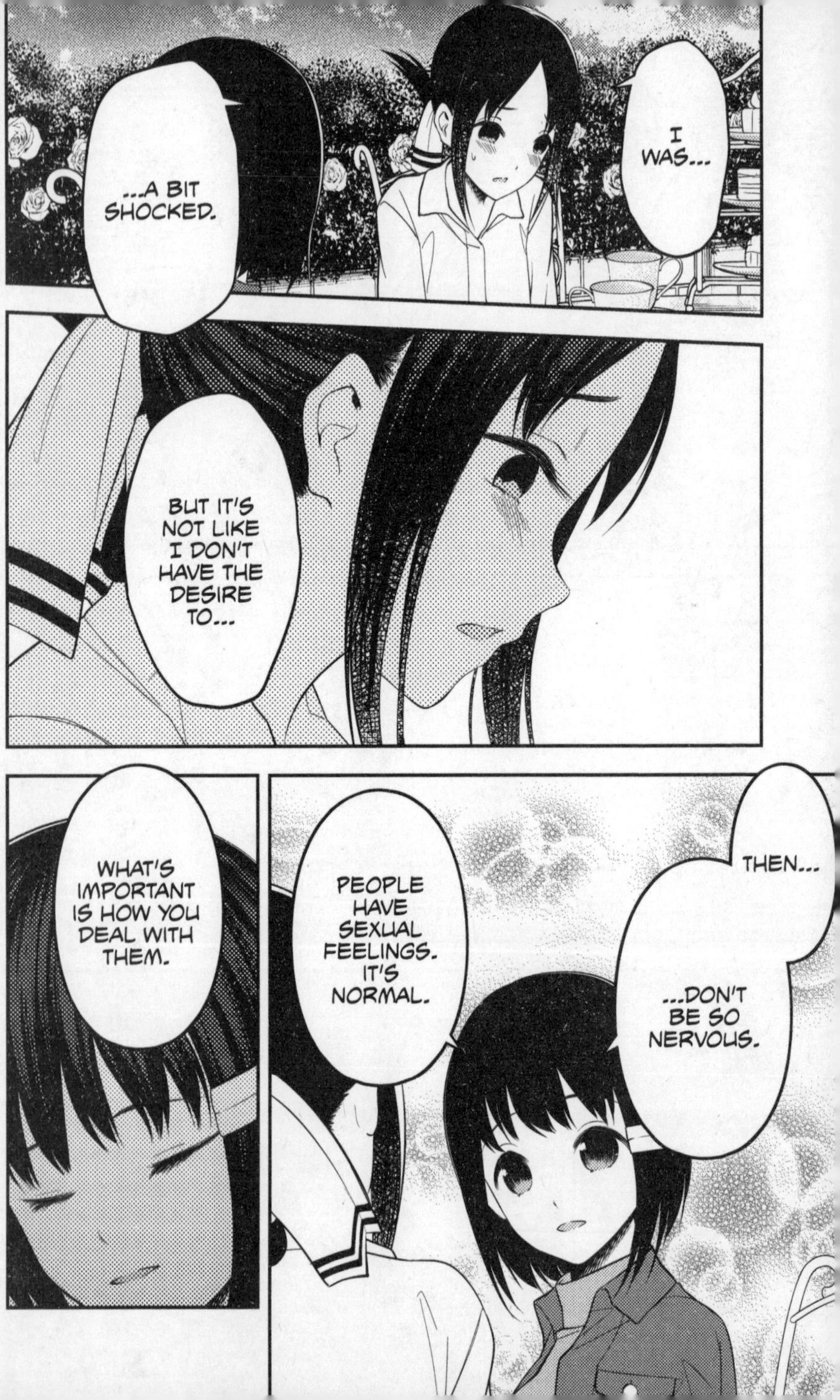
I WAS...
...A BIT SHOCKED.
BUT IT'S NOT LIKE I DON'T HAVE THE DESIRE TO...
THEN...
...DON'T BE SO NERVOUS.
PEOPLE HAVE SEXUAL FEELINGS. IT'S NORMAL.
WHAT'S IMPORTANT IS HOW YOU DEAL WITH THEM.

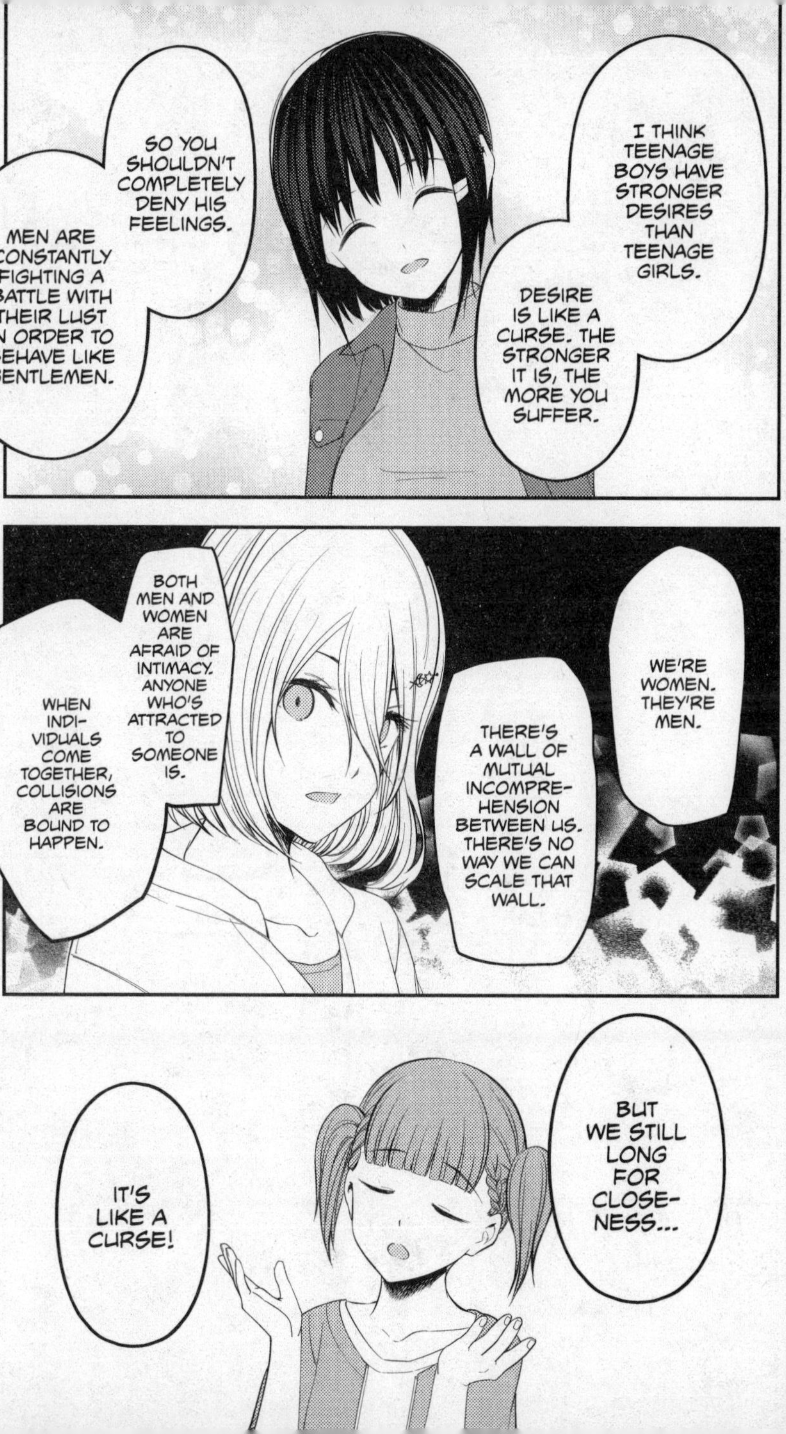
I THINK TEENAGE BOYS HAVE STRONGER DESIRES THAN TEENAGE GIRLS.
DESIRE IS LIKE A CURSE. THE STRONGER IT IS, THE MORE YOU SUFFER.
SO YOU SHOULDN'T COMPLETELY DENY HIS FEELINGS.
MEN ARE CONSTANTLY FIGHTING A BATTLE WITH THEIR LUST IN ORDER TO BEHAVE LIKE GENTLEMEN.
WE'RE WOMEN. THEY'RE MEN.
THERE'S A WALL OF MUTUAL INCOMPRE-HENSION BETWEEN US. THERE'S NO WAY WE CAN SCALE THAT WALL.
BOTH MEN AND WOMEN ARE AFRAID OF INTIMACY. ANYONE WHO'S ATTRACTED TO SOMEONE IS.
WHEN INDI-VIDUALS COME TOGETHER, COLLISIONS ARE BOUND TO HAPPEN.
BUT WE STILL LONG FOR CLOSE-NESS...
IT'S LIKE A CURSE!

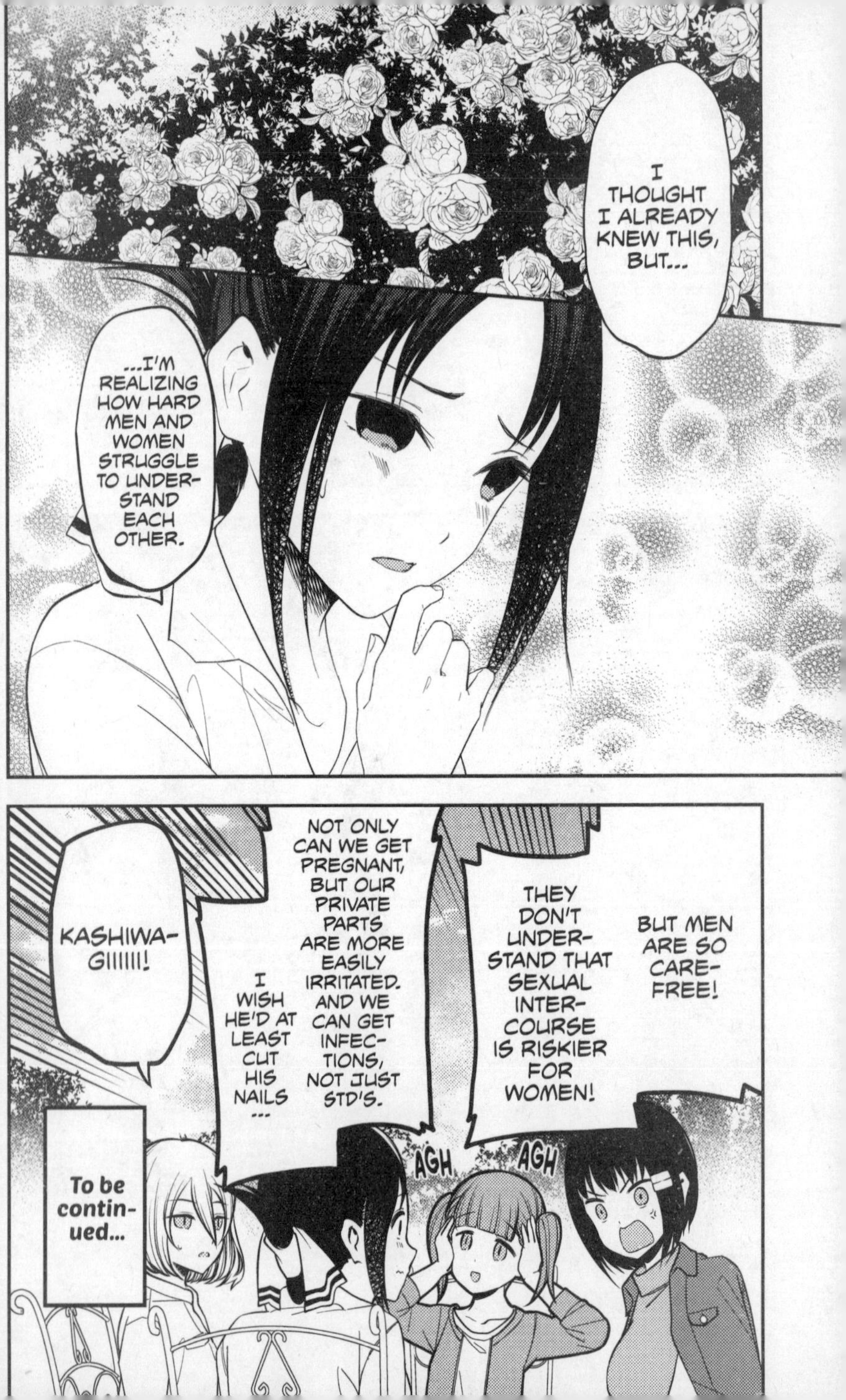
I THOUGHT I ALREADY KNEW THIS, BUT...
...I'M REALIZING HOW HARD MEN AND WOMEN STRUGGLE TO UNDER-STAND EACH OTHER.
BUT MEN ARE SO CARE-FREE!
THEY DON'T UNDER-STAND THAT SEXUAL INTER-COURSE IS RISKIER FOR WOMEN!
NOT ONLY CAN WE GET PREGNANT, BUT OUR PRIVATE PARTS ARE MORE EASILY IRRITATED. AND WE CAN GET INFEC-TIONS, NOT JUST STD'S.
I WISH HE'D AT LEAST CUT HIS NAILS ...
AGH
AGH
KASHIWA-GIIIIIII!
To be contin-ued...

Doesn't have a boyfriend because she's so accustomed to unrequited feelings →

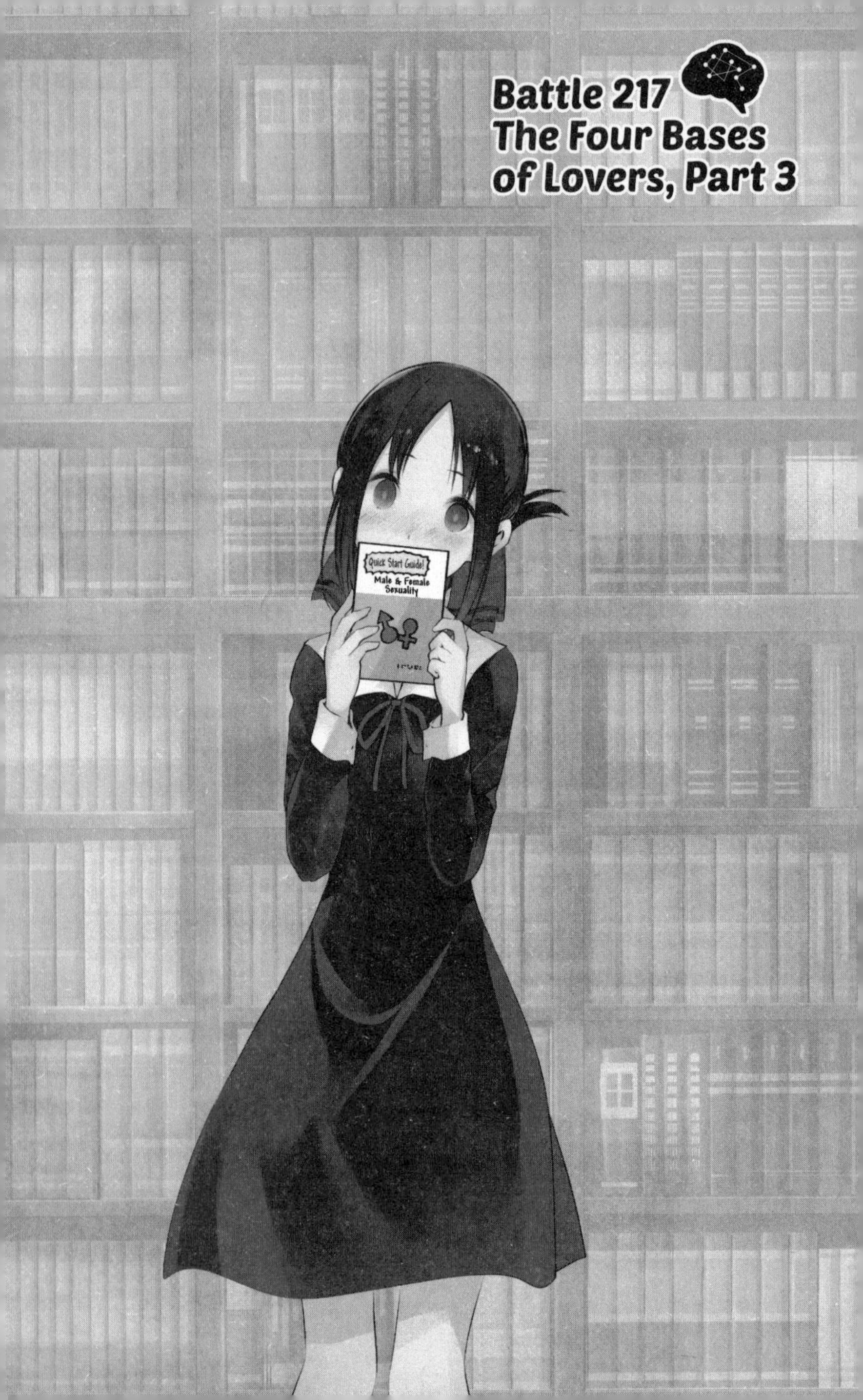
Battle 217
The Four Bases of Lovers, Part 3
Quick Start Guide!
Male & Female Sexuality

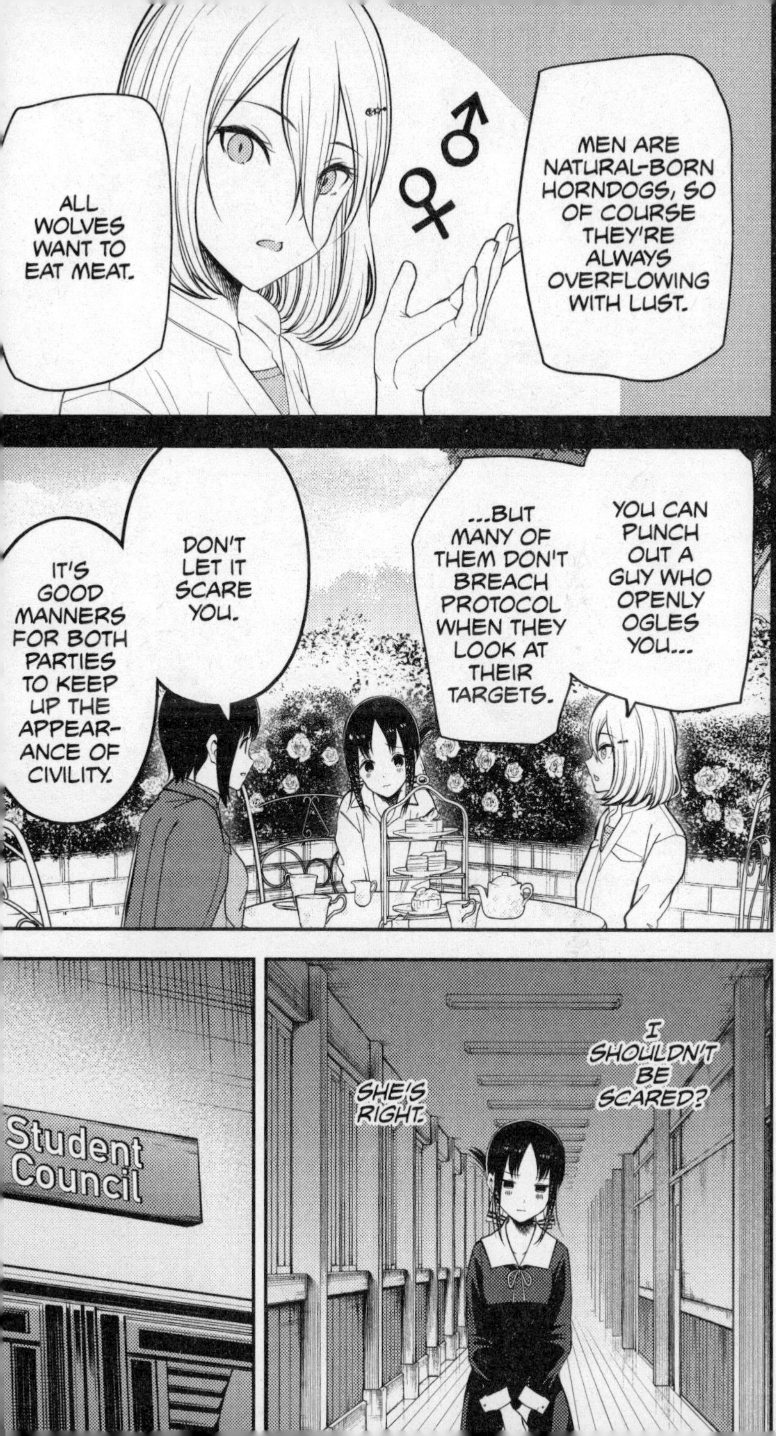
MEN ARE NATURAL-BORN HORNDOGS, SO OF COURSE THEY'RE ALWAYS OVERFLOWING WITH LUST.
ALL WOLVES WANT TO EAT MEAT.
YOU CAN PUNCH OUT A GUY WHO OPENLY OGLES YOU...
...BUT MANY OF THEM DON'T BREACH PROTOCOL WHEN THEY LOOK AT THEIR TARGETS.
DON'T LET IT SCARE YOU.
IT'S GOOD MANNERS FOR BOTH PARTIES TO KEEP UP THE APPEAR-ANCE OF CIVILITY.
I SHOULDN'T BE SCARED?
SHE'S RIGHT.
Student Council

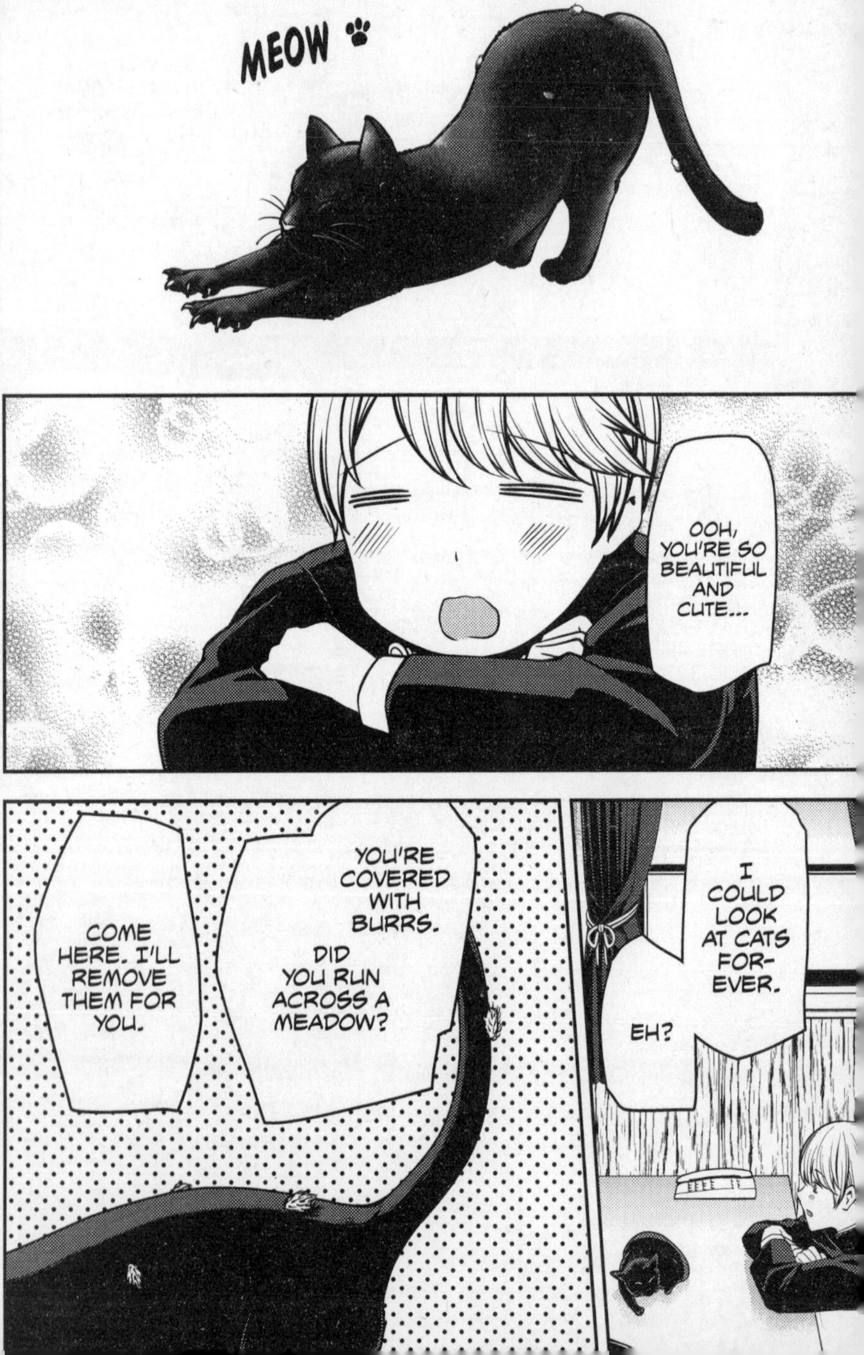
MEOW
OOH, YOU'RE SO BEAUTIFUL AND CUTE...
I COULD LOOK AT CATS FOREVER.
EH?
YOU'RE COVERED WITH BURRS.
DID YOU RUN ACROSS A MEADOW?
COME HERE. I'LL REMOVE THEM FOR YOU.

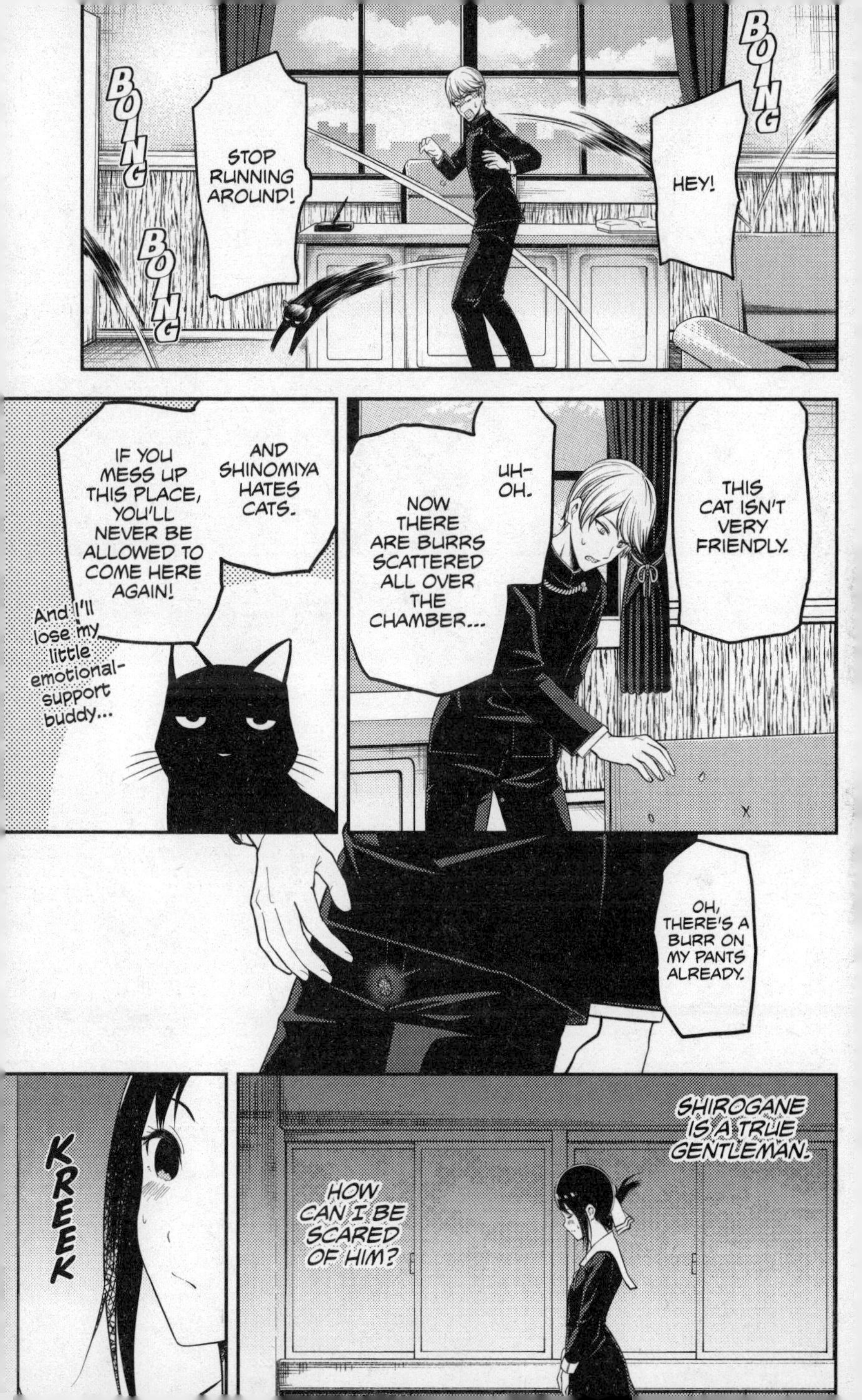
BOING
HEY!
STOP RUNNING AROUND!
BOING
BOING
THIS CAT ISN'T VERY FRIENDLY.
UH-OH.
NOW THERE ARE BURRS SCATTERED ALL OVER THE CHAMBER...
AND SHINOMIYA HATES CATS.
IF YOU MESS UP THIS PLACE, YOU'LL NEVER BE ALLOWED TO COME HERE AGAIN!
And I'll lose my little emotional-support buddy...
OH, THERE'S A BURR ON MY PANTS ALREADY.
SHIROGANE IS A TRUE GENTLEMAN.
HOW CAN I BE SCARED OF HIM?
KREEK

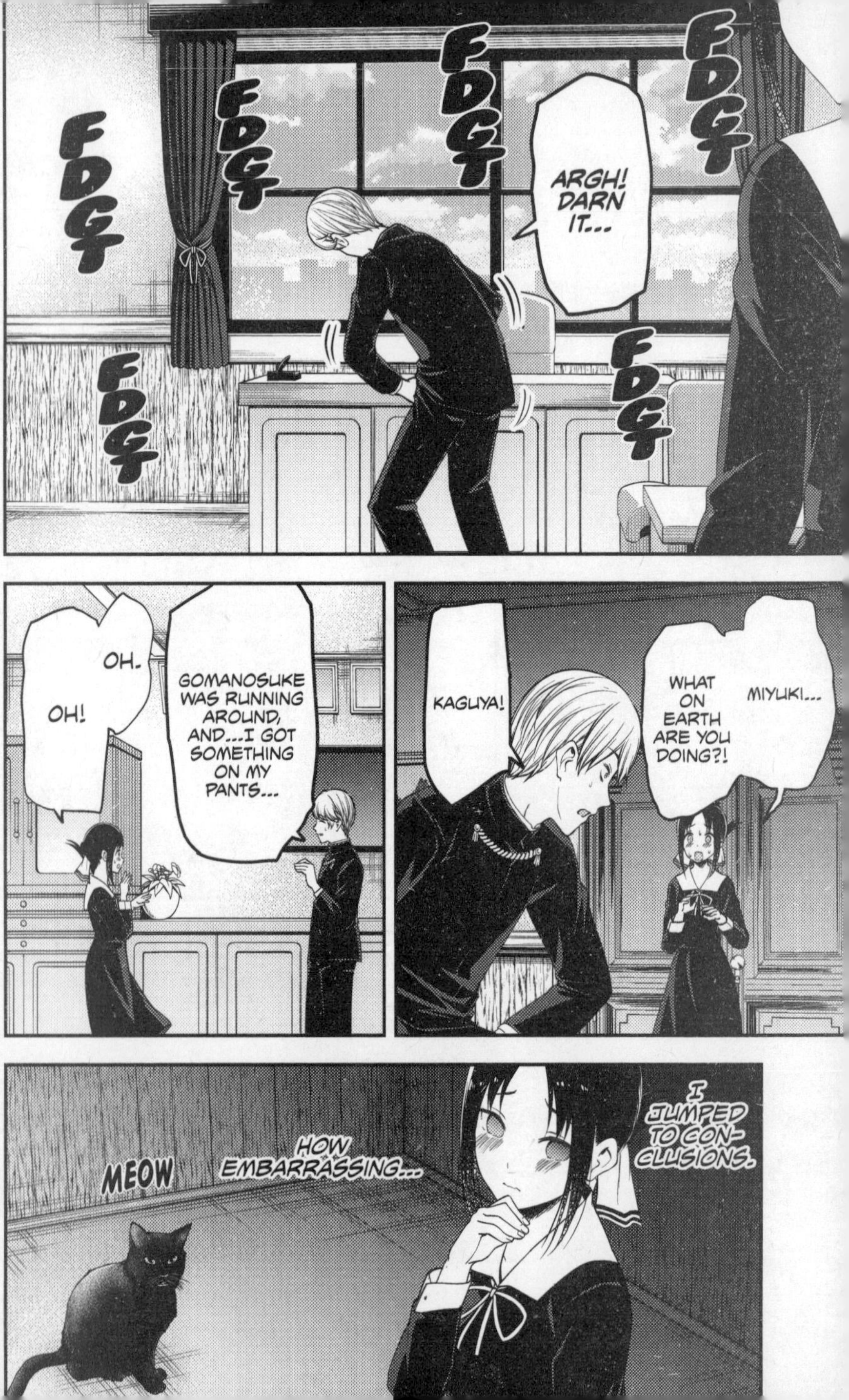
FDG
FDG
ARGH! DARN IT...
FDG
FDG
FDG
FDG
MIYUKI...
WHAT ON EARTH ARE YOU DOING?!
KAGUYA!
GOMANOSUKE WAS RUNNING AROUND, AND...I GOT SOMETHING ON MY PANTS...
OH.
OH!
I JUMPED TO CON-CLUSIONS.
HOW EMBARRASSING...
MEOW

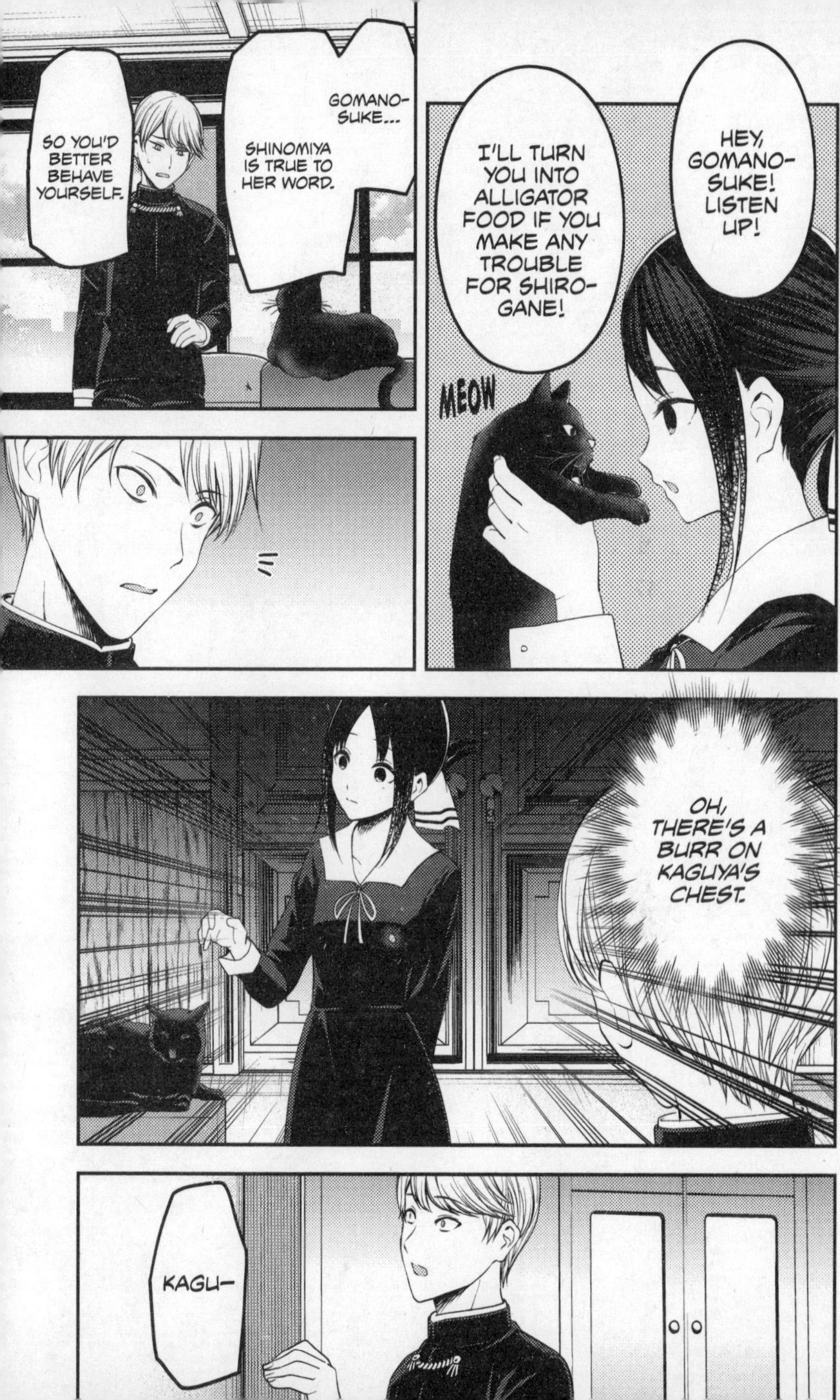
HEY, GOMANO-SUKE! LISTEN UP!
I'LL TURN YOU INTO ALLIGATOR FOOD IF YOU MAKE ANY TROUBLE FOR SHIRO-GANE!
MEOW
GOMANO-SUKE...
SHINOMIYA IS TRUE TO HER WORD.
SO YOU'D BETTER BEHAVE YOURSELF.
OH, THERE'S A BURR ON KAGUYA'S CHEST.
KAGU—

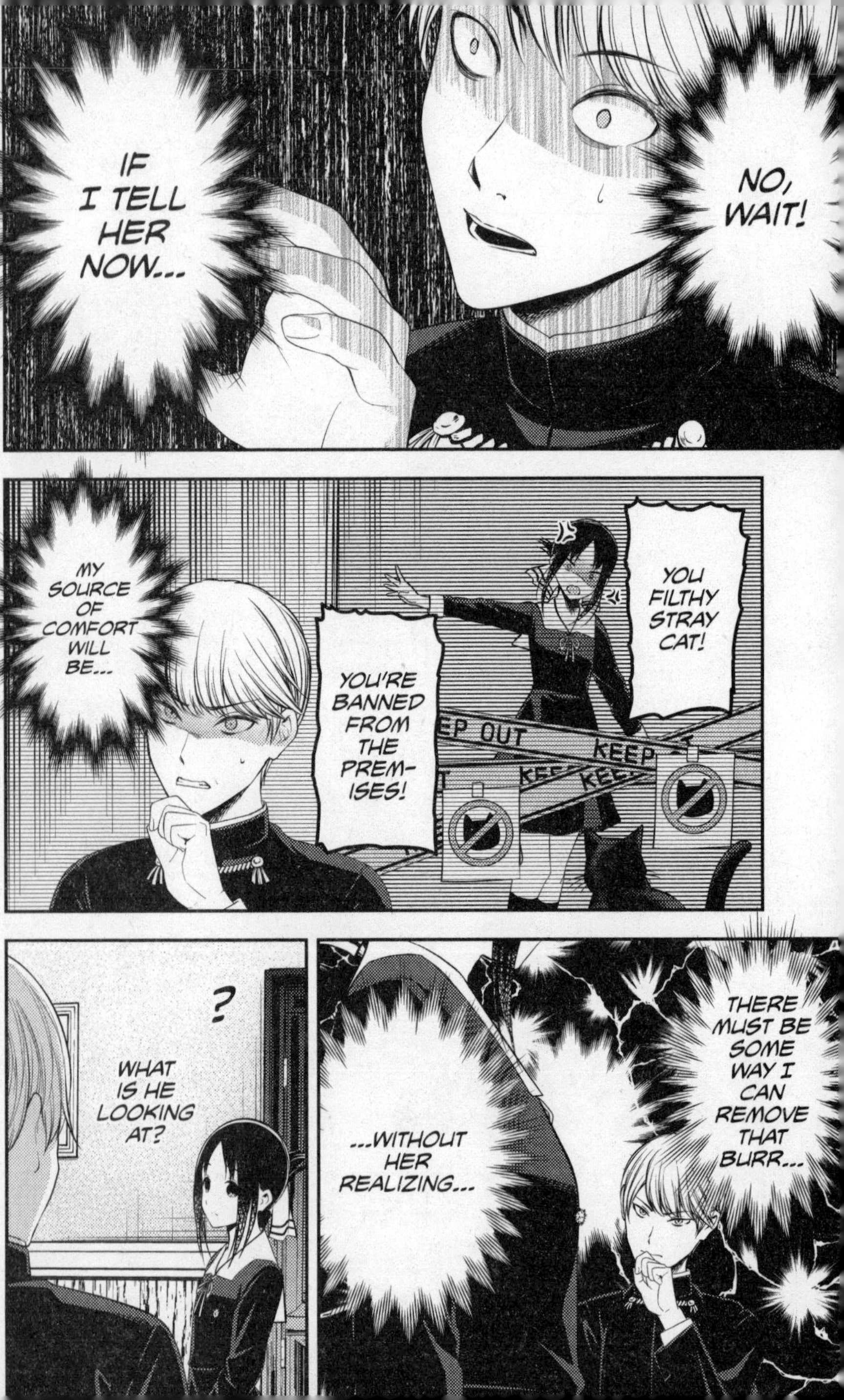
NO, WAIT!
IF I TELL HER NOW...
YOU FILTHY STRAY CAT!
YOU'RE BANNED FROM THE PREMISES!
MY SOURCE OF COMFORT WILL BE...
KEEP OUT
THERE MUST BE SOME WAY I CAN REMOVE THAT BURR...
...WITHOUT HER REALIZING...
?
WHAT IS HE LOOKING AT?

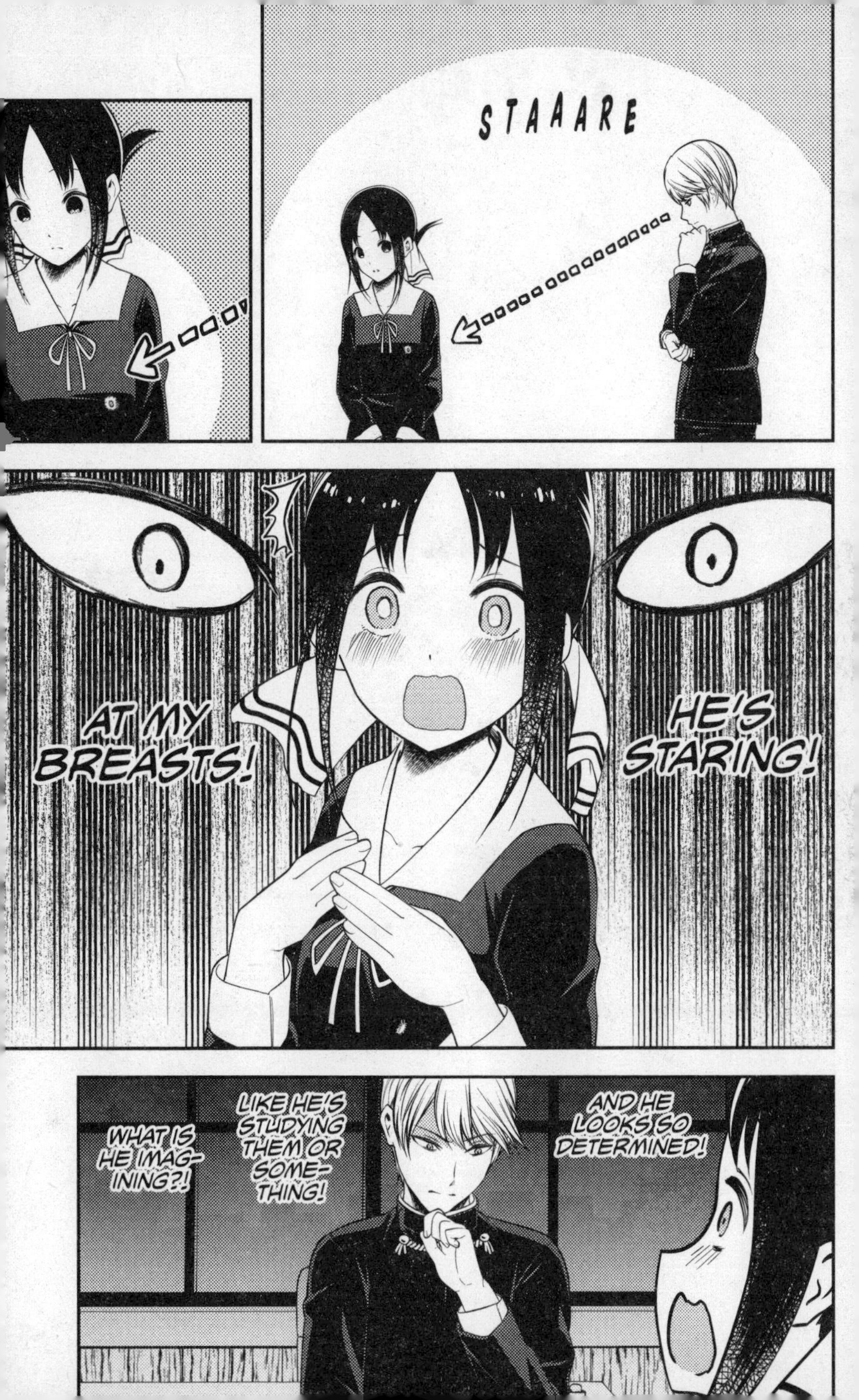
STAAARE
HE'S STARING!
AT MY BREASTS!
AND HE LOOKS SO DETERMINED!
LIKE HE'S STUDYING THEM OR SOMETHING!
WHAT IS HE IMAGINING?!

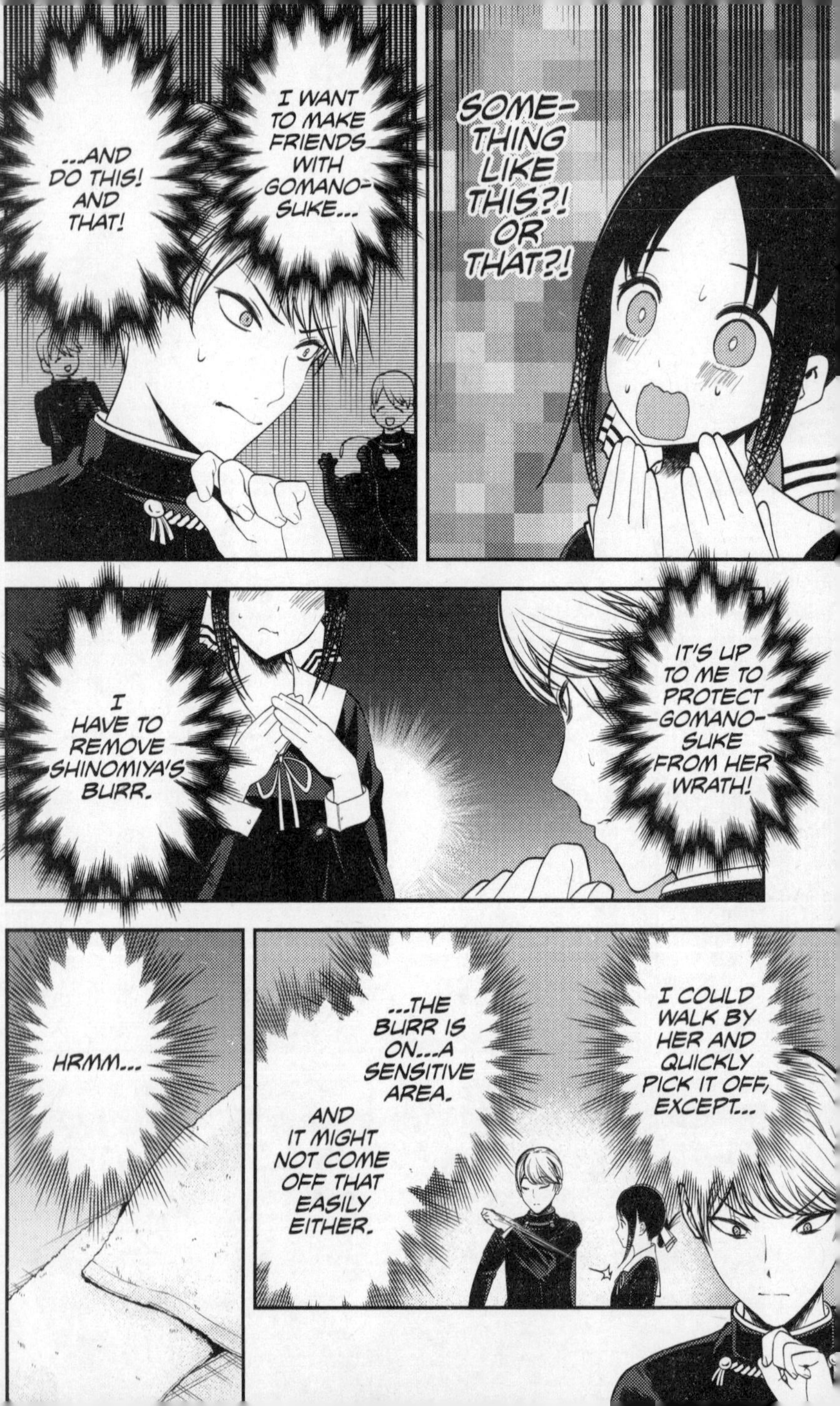
SOMETHING LIKE THIS?! OR THAT?!
I WANT TO MAKE FRIENDS WITH GOMANOSUKE...
...AND DO THIS! AND THAT!
IT'S UP TO ME TO PROTECT GOMANOSUKE FROM HER WRATH!
I HAVE TO REMOVE SHINOMIYA'S BURR.
I COULD WALK BY HER AND QUICKLY PICK IT OFF, EXCEPT...
...THE BURR IS ON...A SENSITIVE AREA.
AND IT MIGHT NOT COME OFF THAT EASILY EITHER.
HRMM...

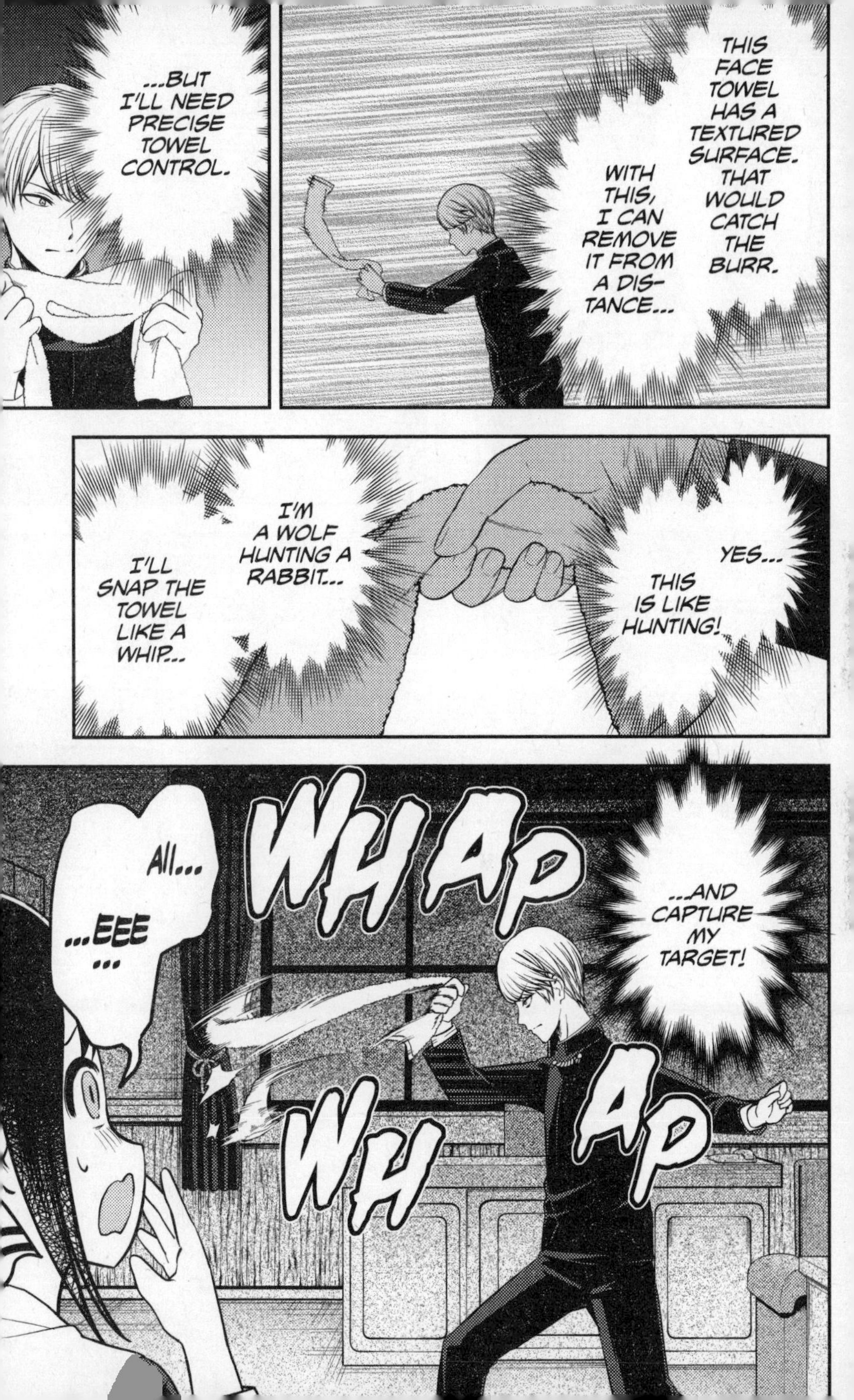
THIS FACE TOWEL HAS A TEXTURED SURFACE. THAT WOULD CATCH THE BURR.
WITH THIS, I CAN REMOVE IT FROM A DISTANCE...
...BUT I'LL NEED PRECISE TOWEL CONTROL.
YES...
THIS IS LIKE HUNTING!
I'M A WOLF HUNTING A RABBIT...
I'LL SNAP THE TOWEL LIKE A WHIP...
...AND CAPTURE MY TARGET!
WHAP
WHAP
AII...
...EEE...

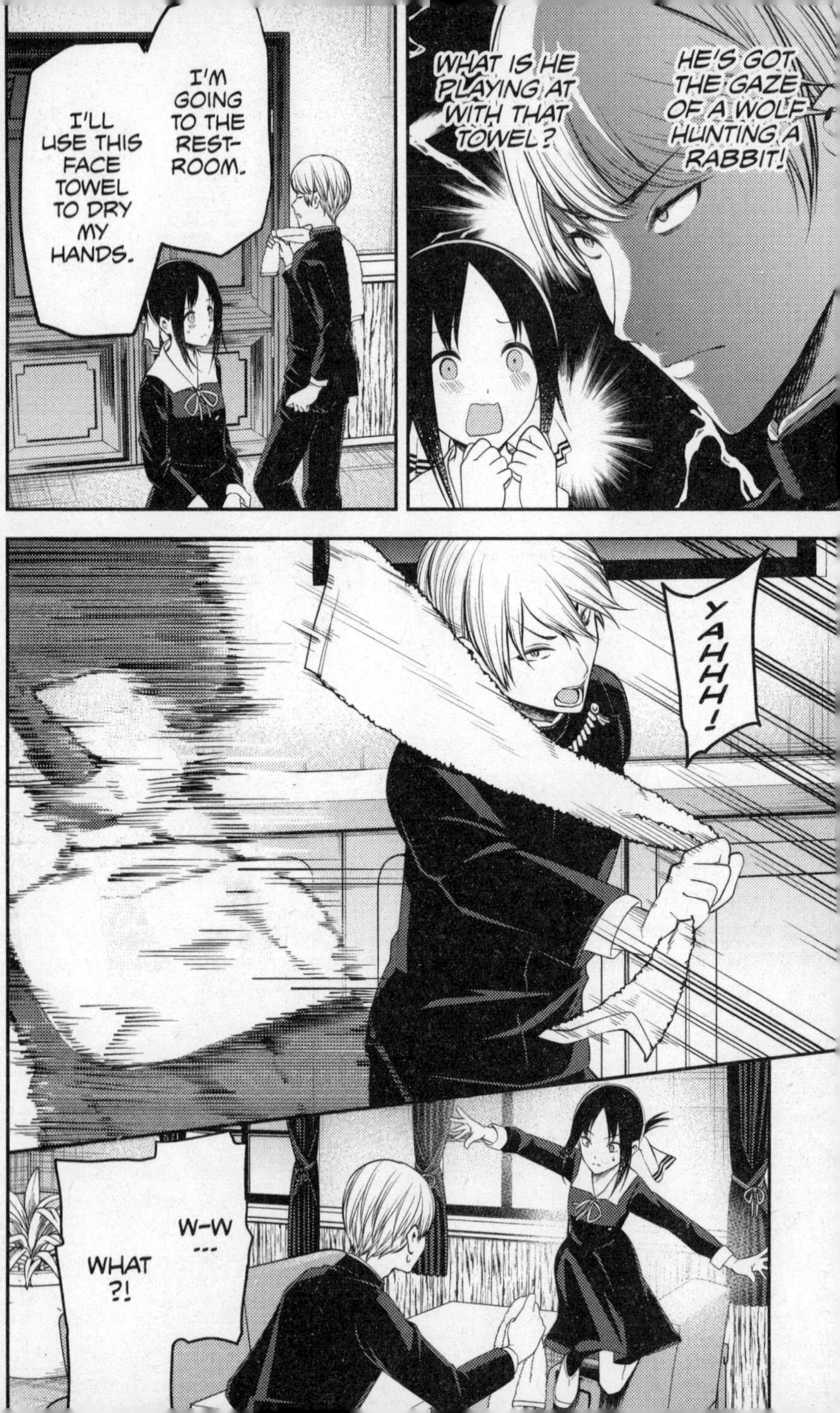
HE'S GOT THE GAZE OF A WOLF HUNTING A RABBIT!
WHAT IS HE PLAYING AT WITH THAT TOWEL?
I'M GOING TO THE REST-ROOM.
I'LL USE THIS FACE TOWEL TO DRY MY HANDS.
YAHHH!
W-W...
WHAT?!

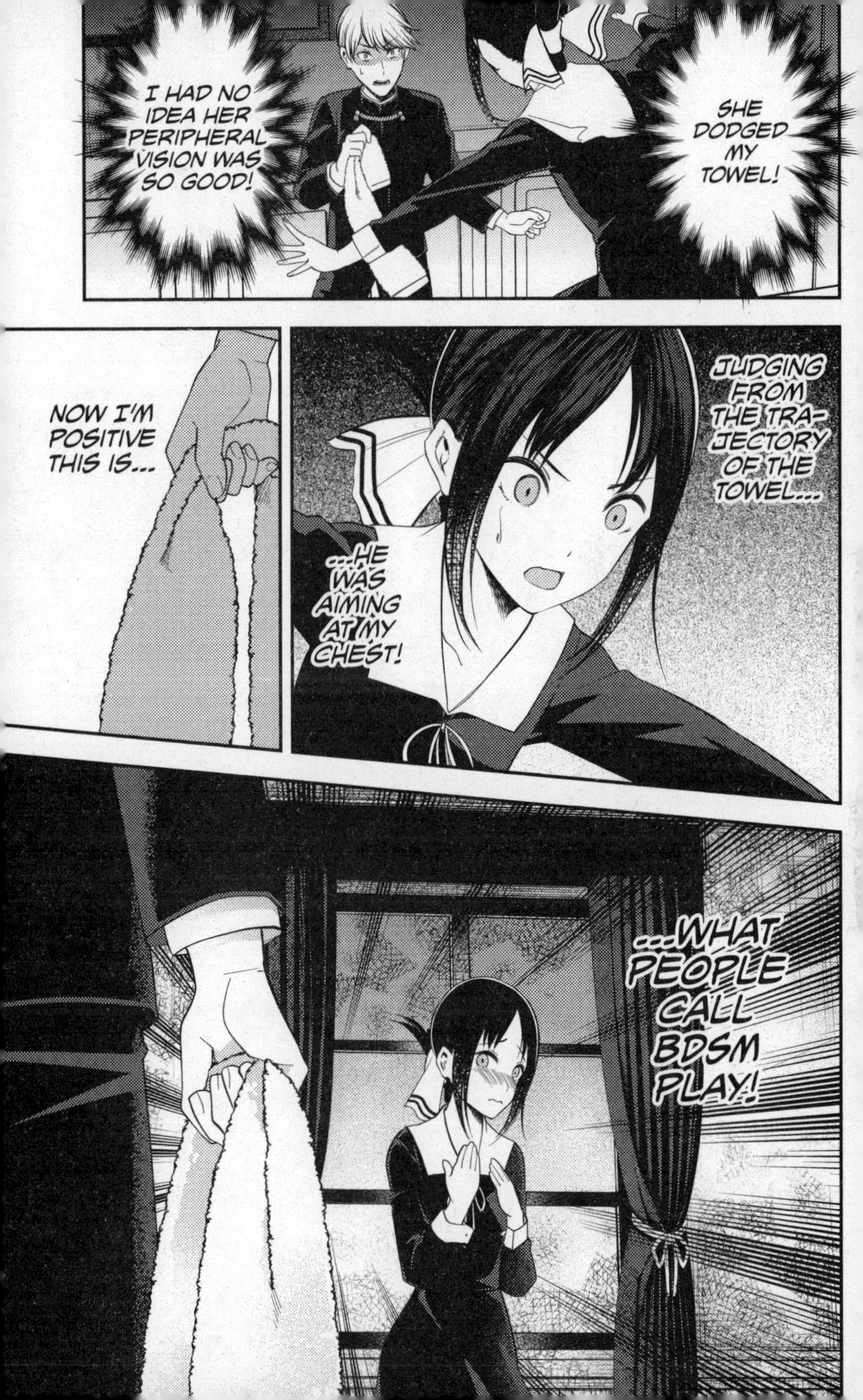
SHE DODGED MY TOWEL!
I HAD NO IDEA HER PERIPHERAL VISION WAS SO GOOD!
JUDGING FROM THE TRA-JECTORY OF THE TOWEL...
...HE WAS AIMING AT MY CHEST!
NOW I'M POSITIVE THIS IS...
...WHAT PEOPLE CALL BDSM PLAY!

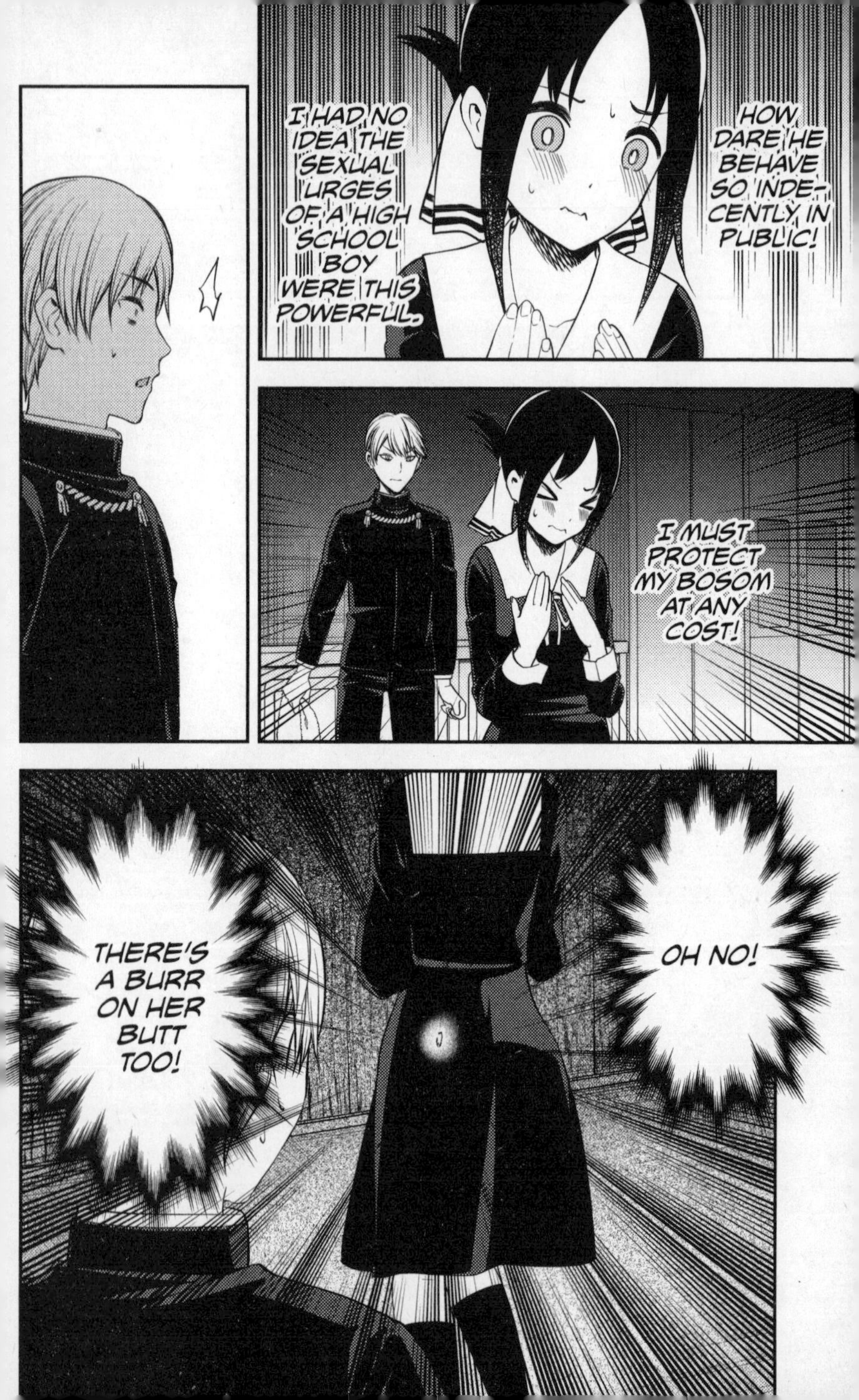
HOW DARE HE BEHAVE SO INDE-CENTLY IN PUBLIC!
I HAD NO IDEA THE SEXUAL URGES OF A HIGH SCHOOL BOY WERE THIS POWERFUL.
I MUST PROTECT MY BOSOM AT ANY COST!
OH NO!
THERE'S A BURR ON HER BUTT TOO!

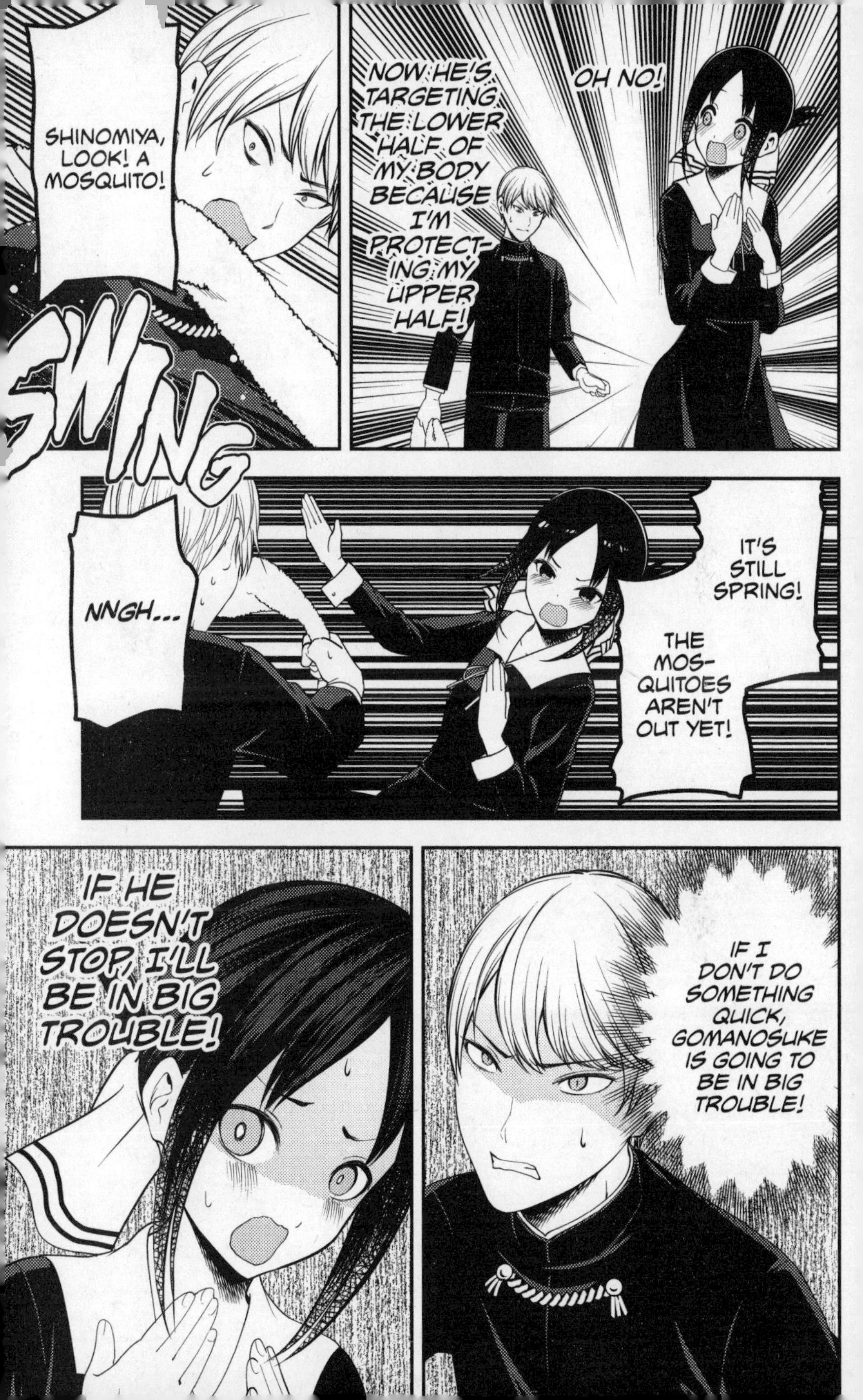
OH NO!
NOW HE'S TARGETING THE LOWER HALF OF MY BODY BECAUSE I'M PROTECTING MY UPPER HALF!
SHINOMIYA, LOOK! A MOSQUITO!
SWING
IT'S STILL SPRING!
THE MOSQUITOES AREN'T OUT YET!
NNGH...
IF I DON'T DO SOMETHING QUICK, GOMANOSUKE IS GOING TO BE IN BIG TROUBLE!
IF HE DOESN'T STOP, I'LL BE IN BIG TROUBLE!

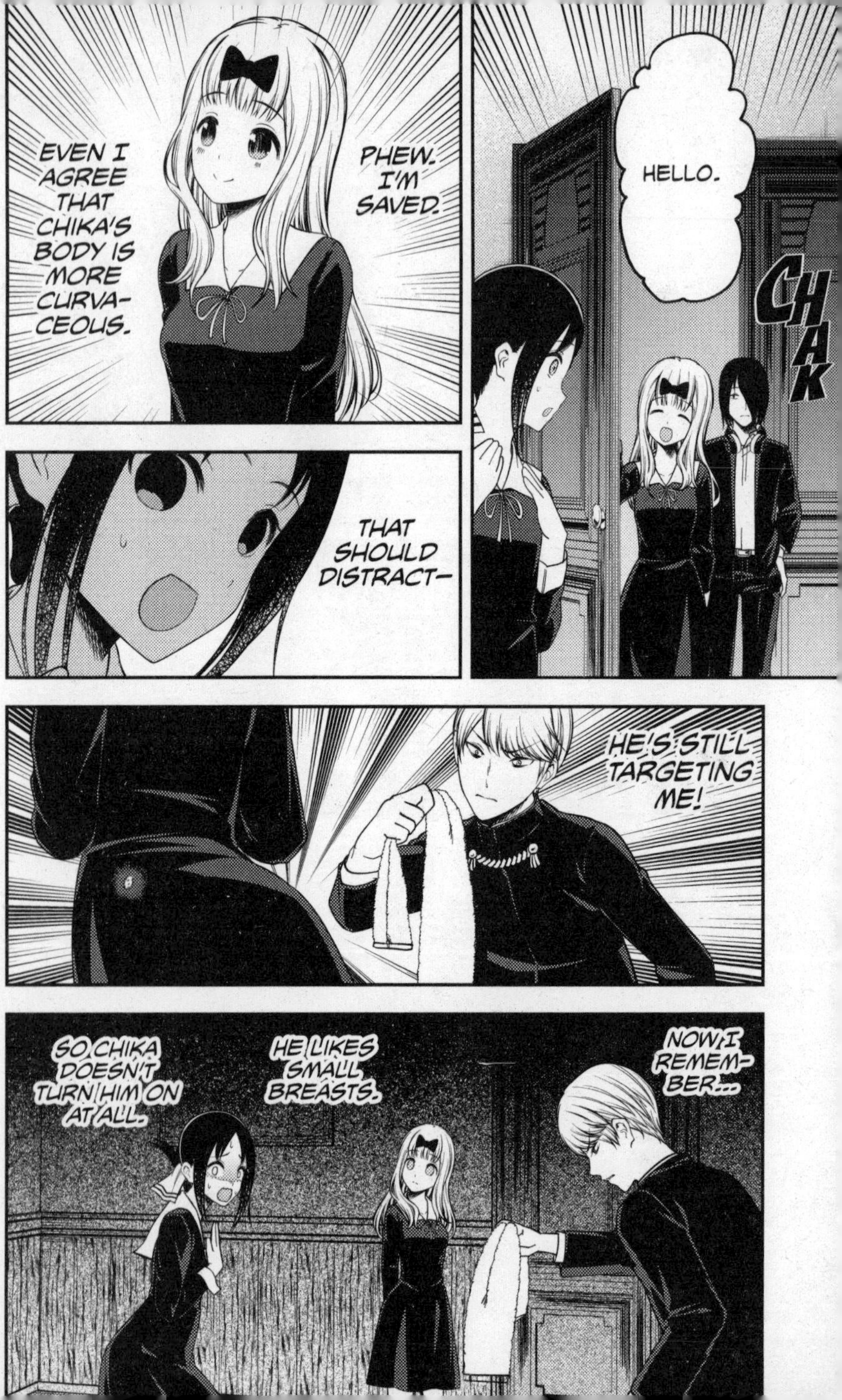
HELLO.
CHAK
PHEW. I'M SAVED.
EVEN I AGREE THAT CHIKA'S BODY IS MORE CURVACEOUS.
THAT SHOULD DISTRACT—
HE'S STILL TARGETING ME!
NOW I REMEMBER...
HE LIKES SMALL BREASTS.
SO CHIKA DOESN'T TURN HIM ON AT ALL.

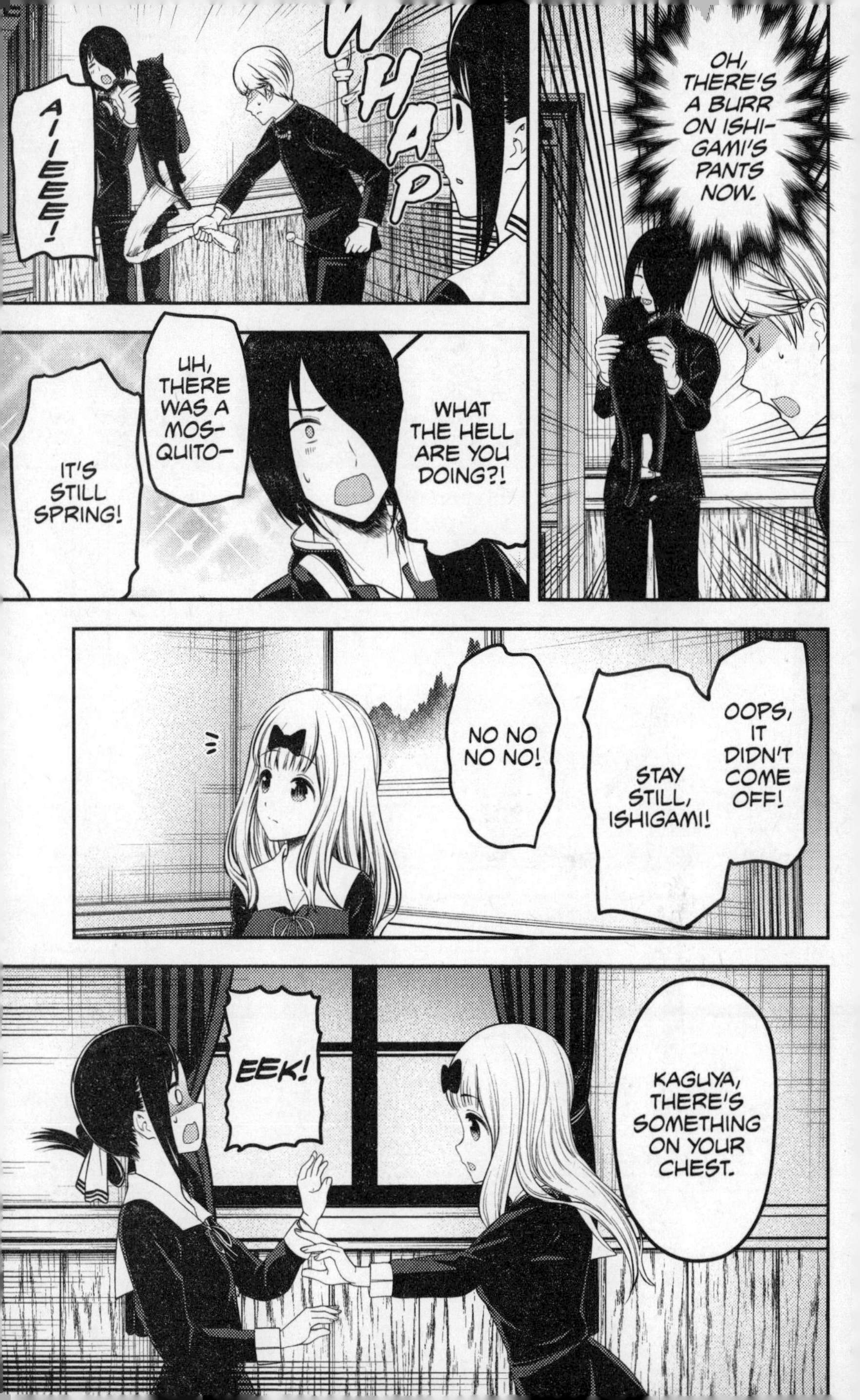
OH, THERE'S A BURR ON ISHIGAMI'S PANTS NOW.
WHAP
AIIEEE!
WHAT THE HELL ARE YOU DOING?!
UH, THERE WAS A MOSQUITO—
IT'S STILL SPRING!
OOPS, IT DIDN'T COME OFF!
STAY STILL, ISHIGAMI!
NO NO NO NO!
KAGUYA, THERE'S SOMETHING ON YOUR CHEST.
EEK!

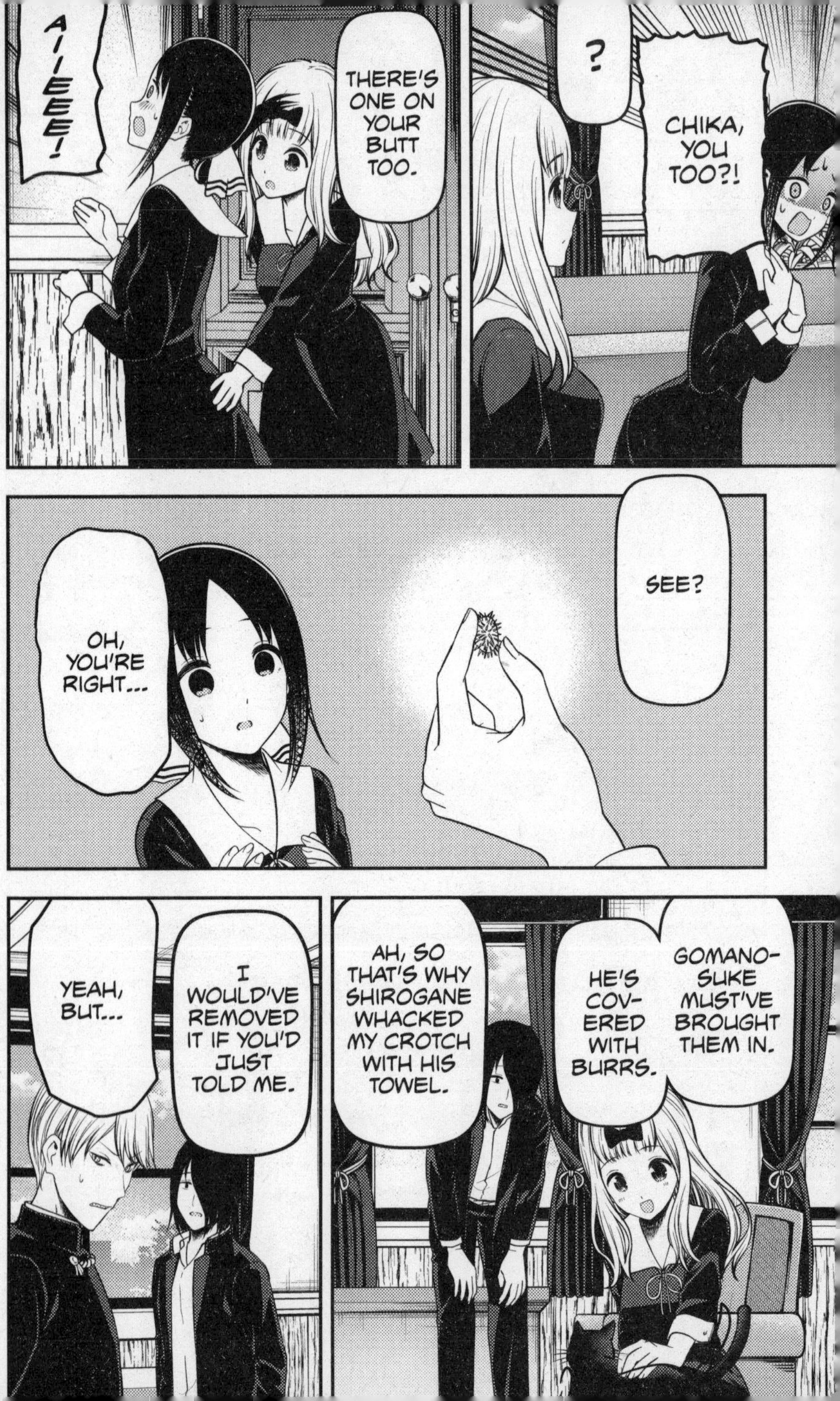
CHIKA, YOU TOO?!
?
THERE'S ONE ON YOUR BUTT TOO.
AIIEEE!
SEE?
OH, YOU'RE RIGHT...
GOMANOSUKE MUST'VE BROUGHT THEM IN.
HE'S COVERED WITH BURRS.
AH, SO THAT'S WHY SHIROGANE WHACKED MY CROTCH WITH HIS TOWEL.
I WOULD'VE REMOVED IT IF YOU'D JUST TOLD ME.
YEAH, BUT...

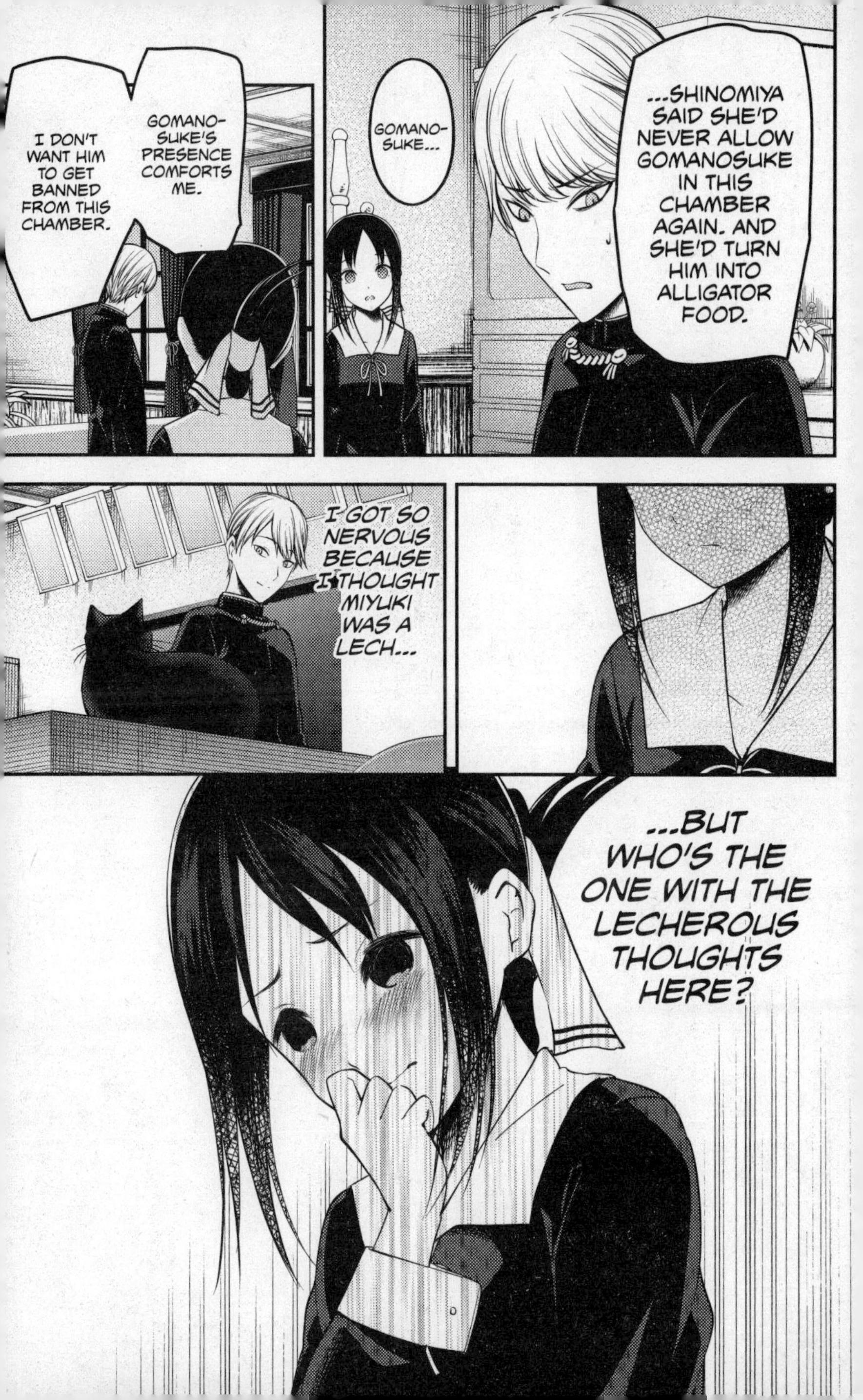
...SHINOMIYA SAID SHE'D NEVER ALLOW GOMANOSUKE IN THIS CHAMBER AGAIN. AND SHE'D TURN HIM INTO ALLIGATOR FOOD.
GOMANO-SUKE...
GOMANO-SUKE'S PRESENCE COMFORTS ME.
I DON'T WANT HIM TO GET BANNED FROM THIS CHAMBER.
I GOT SO NERVOUS BECAUSE I THOUGHT MIYUKI WAS A LECH...
...BUT WHO'S THE ONE WITH THE LECHEROUS THOUGHTS HERE?

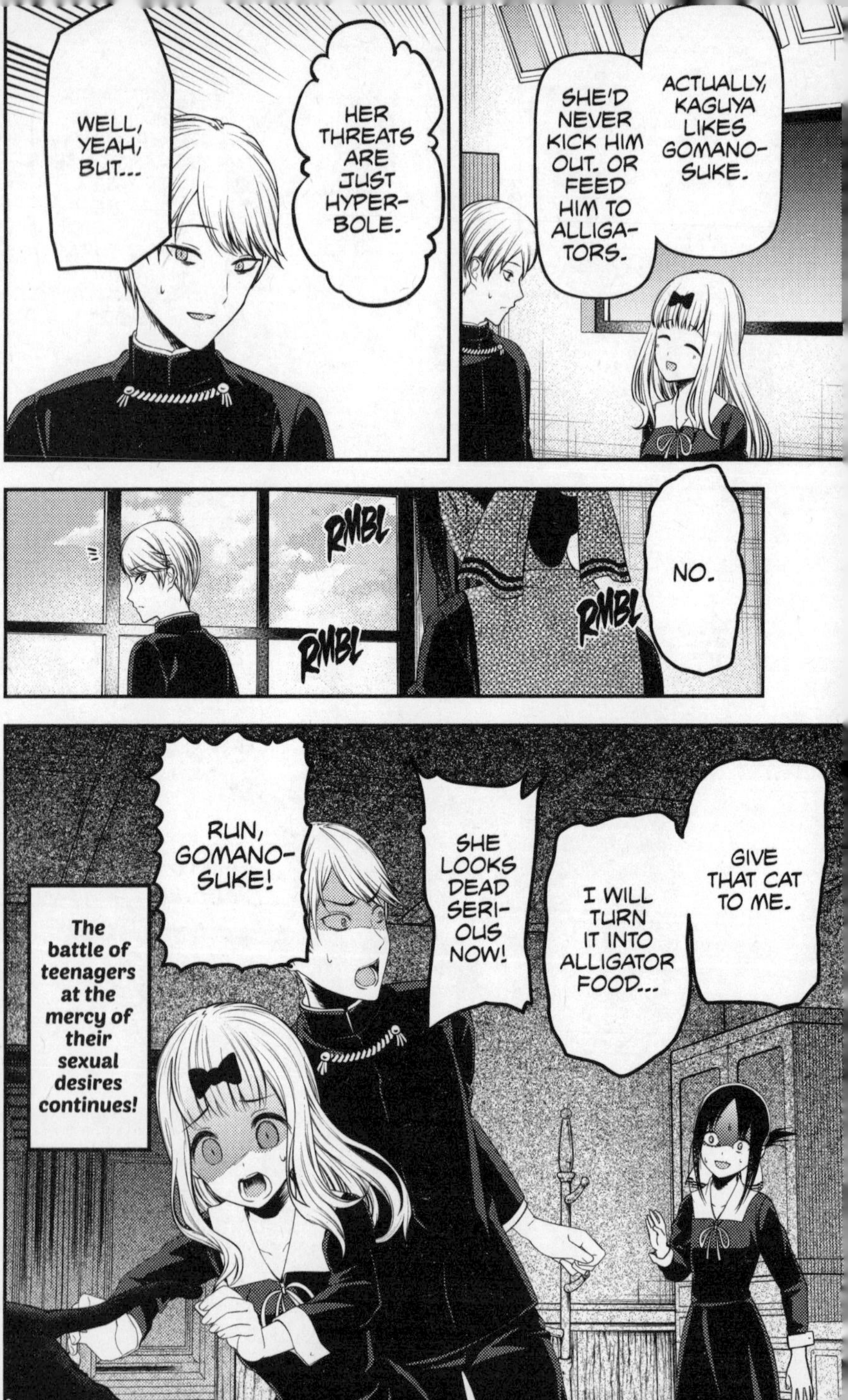
ACTUALLY, KAGUYA LIKES GOMANO-SUKE.
SHE'D NEVER KICK HIM OUT. OR FEED HIM TO ALLIGA-TORS.
HER THREATS ARE JUST HYPER-BOLE.
WELL, YEAH, BUT...
NO.
RMBL
RMBL
RMBL
GIVE THAT CAT TO ME.
I WILL TURN IT INTO ALLIGATOR FOOD...
SHE LOOKS DEAD SERI-OUS NOW!
RUN, GOMANO-SUKE!
The battle of teenagers at the mercy of their sexual desires continues!

URK

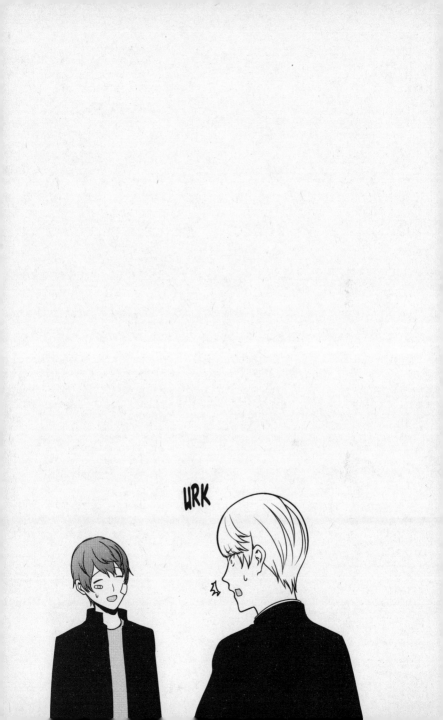

KAGUYA-SAMA

LOVE IS WAR

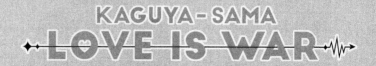

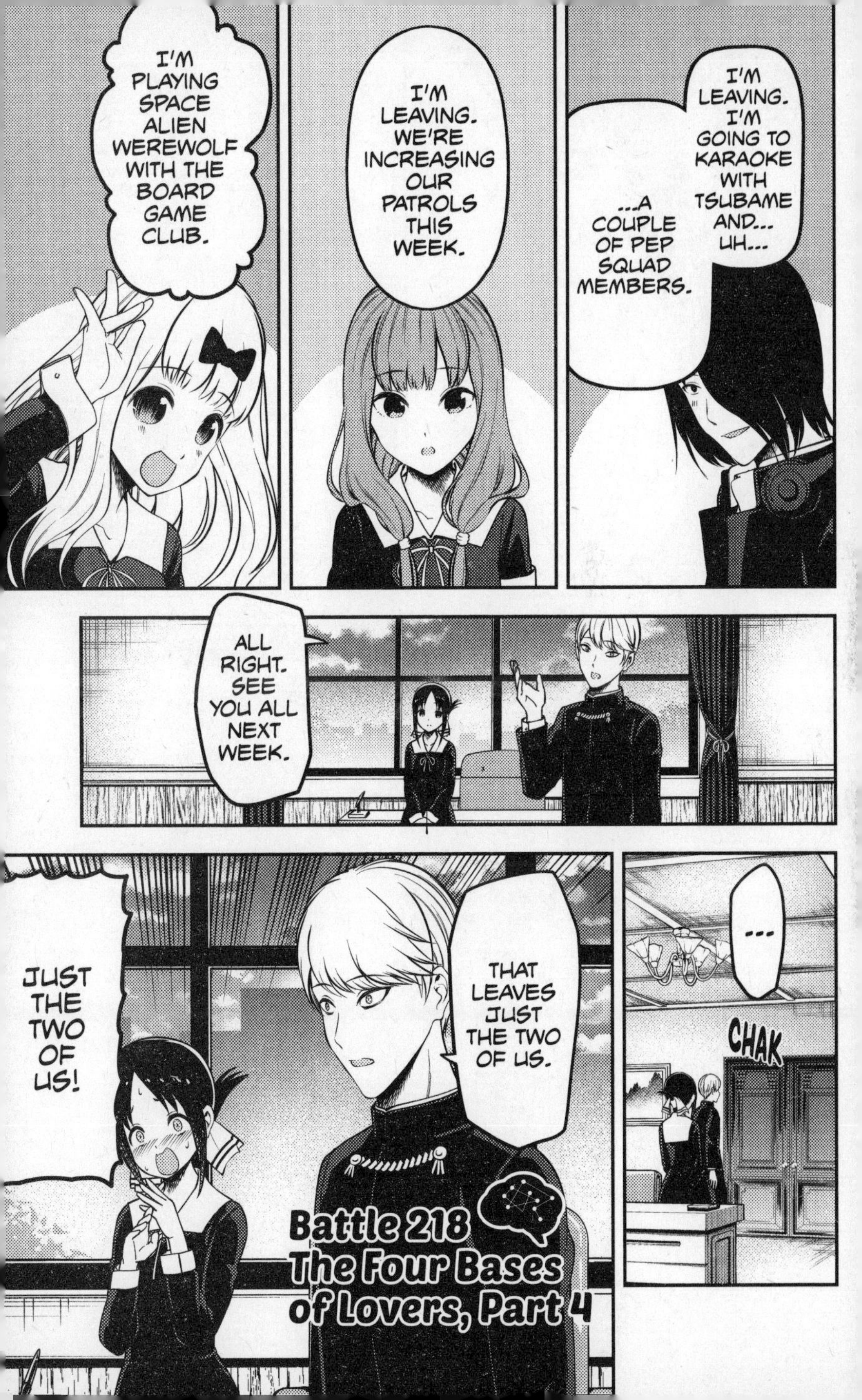
I'M LEAVING. I'M GOING TO KARAOKE WITH TSUBAME AND... UH...
...A COUPLE OF PEP SQUAD MEMBERS.
I'M LEAVING. WE'RE INCREASING OUR PATROLS THIS WEEK.
I'M PLAYING SPACE ALIEN WEREWOLF WITH THE BOARD GAME CLUB.
ALL RIGHT. SEE YOU ALL NEXT WEEK.
...
CHAK
THAT LEAVES JUST THE TWO OF US.
JUST THE TWO OF US!
Battle 218
The Four Bases of Lovers, Part 4

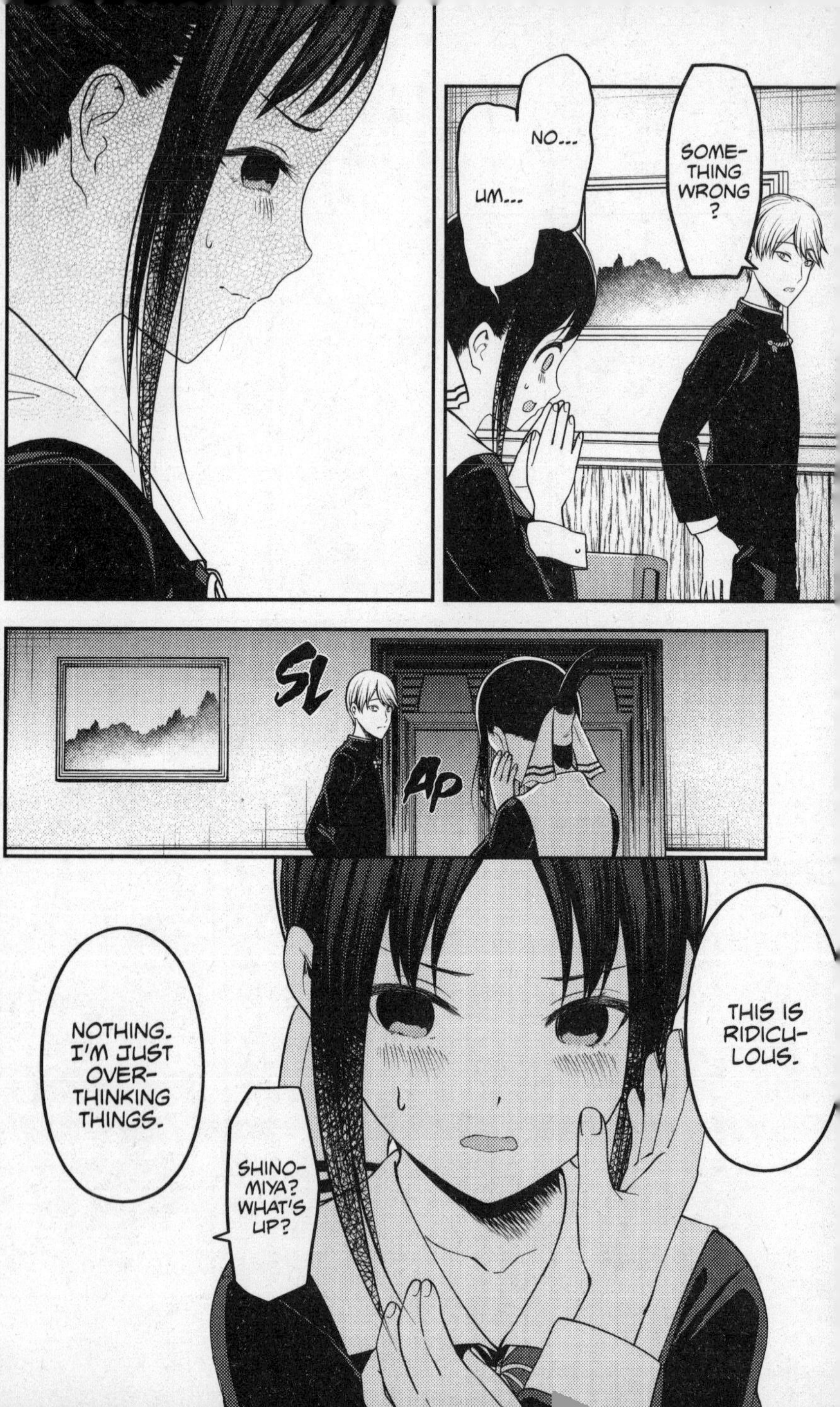
SOME-
THING
WRONG
?
NO...
UM...
SL
AP
THIS IS
RIDICU-
LOUS.
SHINO-
MIYA?
WHAT'S
UP?
NOTHING.
I'M JUST
OVER-
THINKING
THINGS.

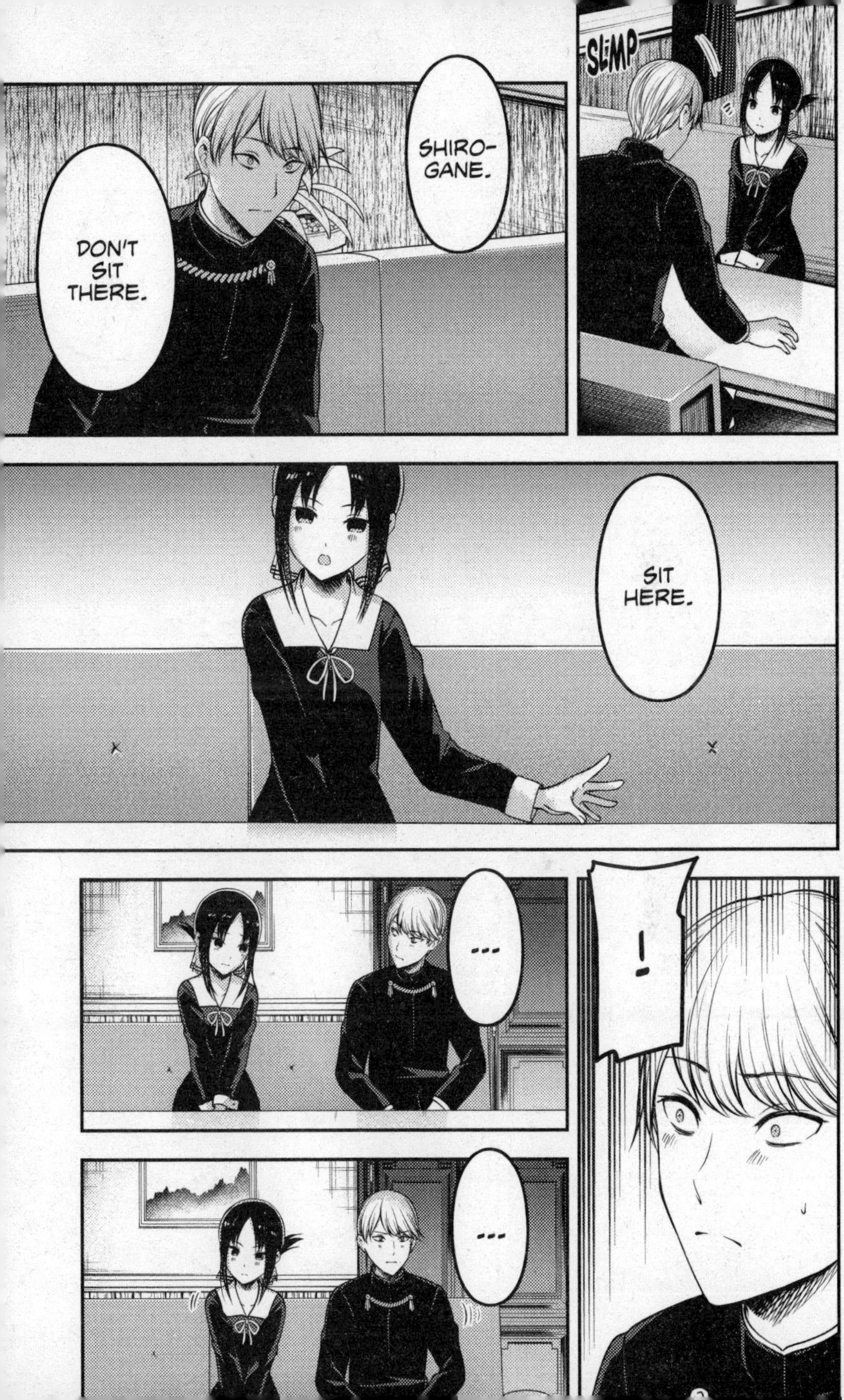
SLIMP
SHIRO-GANE.
DON'T SIT THERE.
SIT HERE.
!
...
...

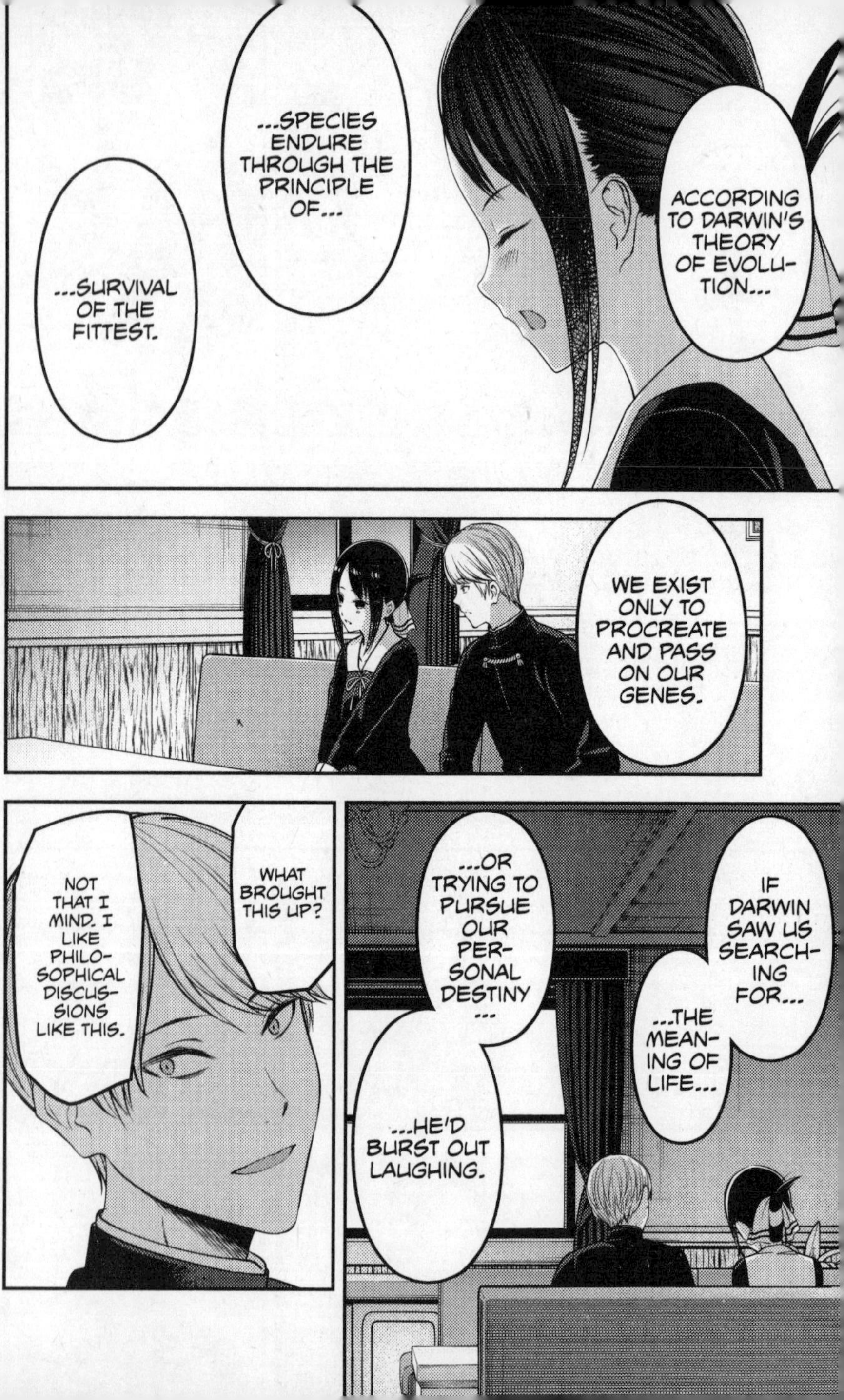
ACCORDING TO DARWIN'S THEORY OF EVOLUTION...
...SPECIES ENDURE THROUGH THE PRINCIPLE OF...
...SURVIVAL OF THE FITTEST.
WE EXIST ONLY TO PROCREATE AND PASS ON OUR GENES.
IF DARWIN SAW US SEARCHING FOR...
...THE MEANING OF LIFE...
...OR TRYING TO PURSUE OUR PERSONAL DESTINY...
...HE'D BURST OUT LAUGHING.
WHAT BROUGHT THIS UP?
NOT THAT I MIND. I LIKE PHILOSOPHICAL DISCUSSIONS LIKE THIS.

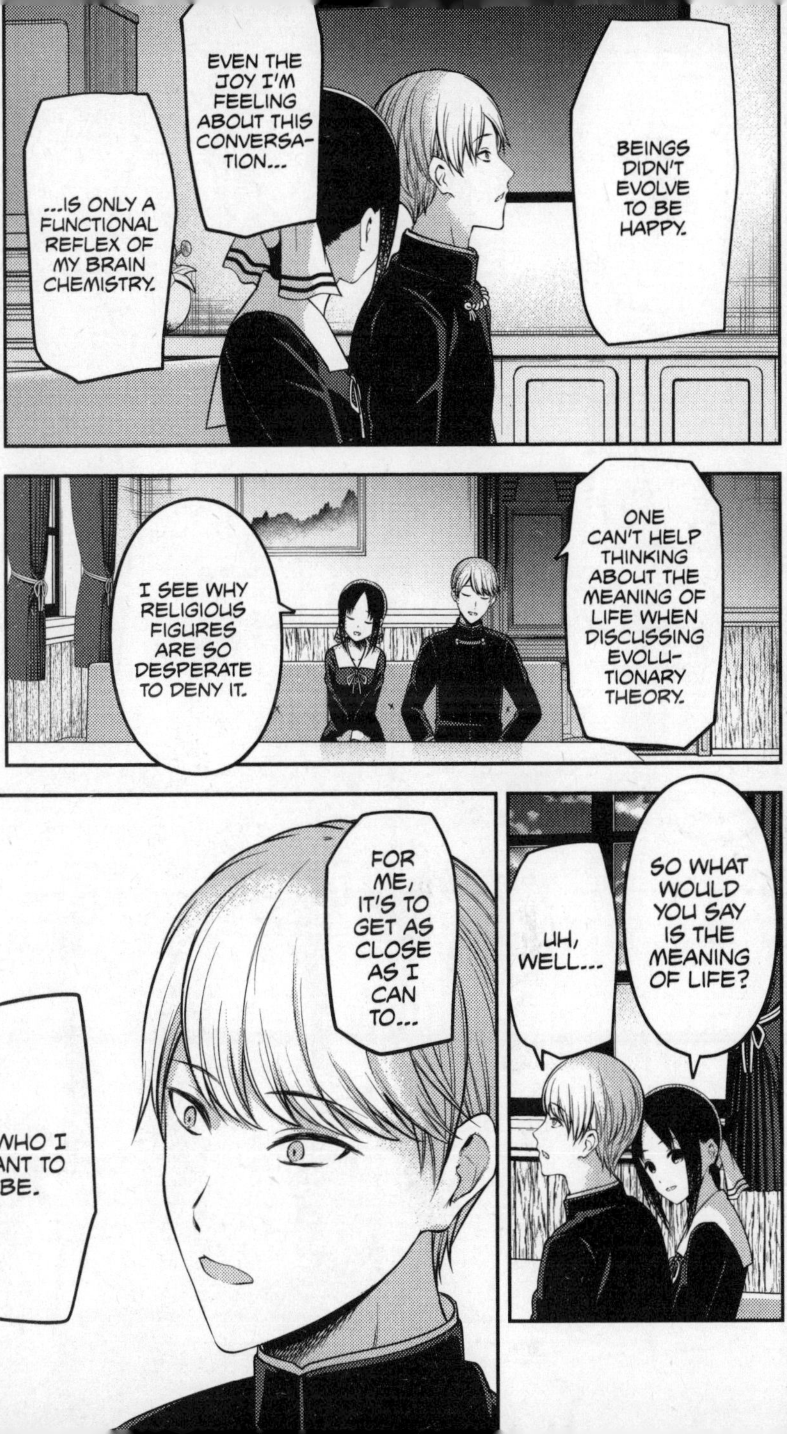
BEINGS DIDN'T EVOLVE TO BE HAPPY.
EVEN THE JOY I'M FEELING ABOUT THIS CONVERSATION...
...IS ONLY A FUNCTIONAL REFLEX OF MY BRAIN CHEMISTRY.
ONE CAN'T HELP THINKING ABOUT THE MEANING OF LIFE WHEN DISCUSSING EVOLUTIONARY THEORY.
I SEE WHY RELIGIOUS FIGURES ARE SO DESPERATE TO DENY IT.
SO WHAT WOULD YOU SAY IS THE MEANING OF LIFE?
UH, WELL...
FOR ME, IT'S TO GET AS CLOSE AS I CAN TO...
...WHO I WANT TO BE.

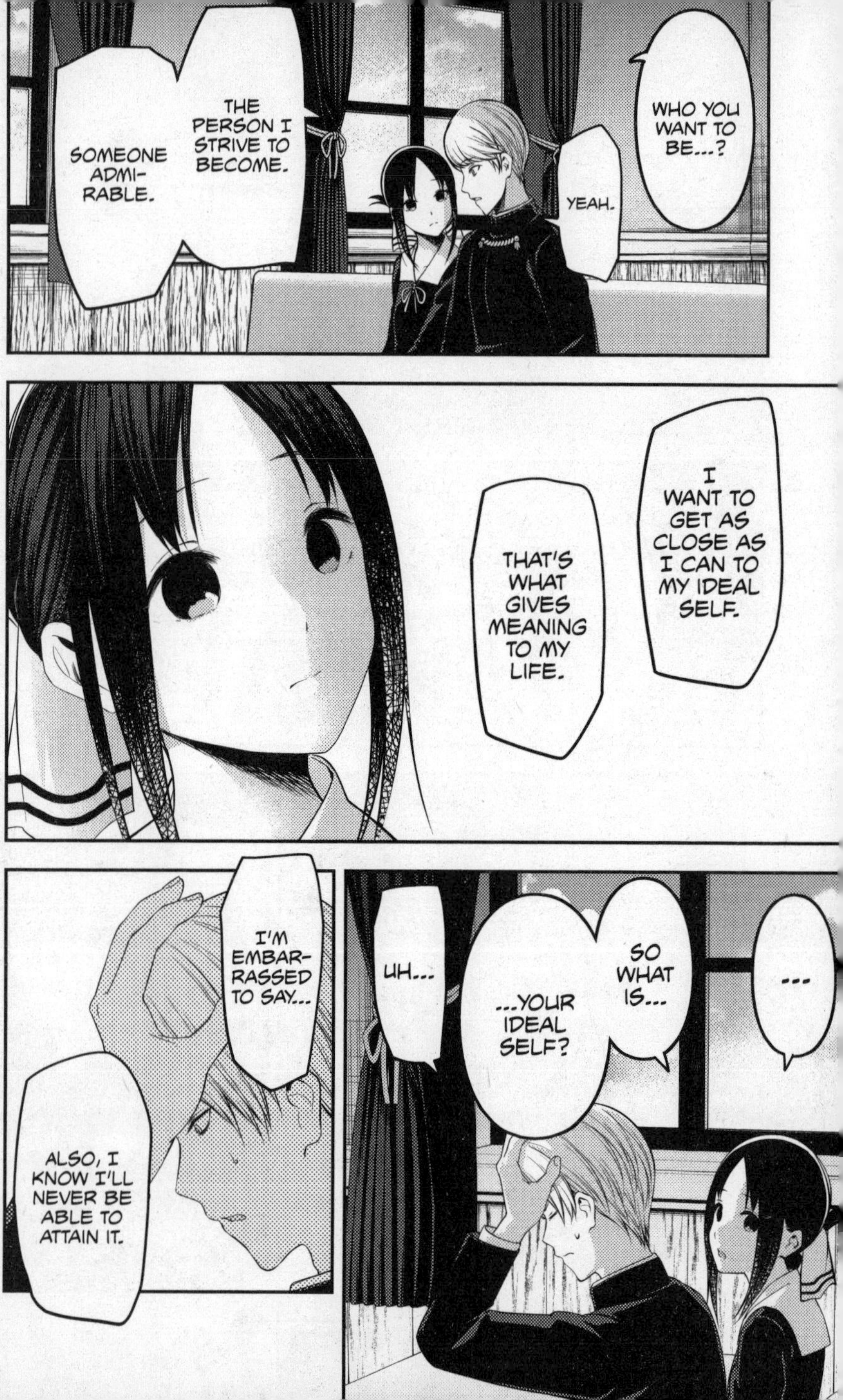
WHO YOU WANT TO BE...?
YEAH.
THE PERSON I STRIVE TO BECOME.
SOMEONE ADMI-RABLE.
I WANT TO GET AS CLOSE AS I CAN TO MY IDEAL SELF.
THAT'S WHAT GIVES MEANING TO MY LIFE.
...
SO WHAT IS...
...YOUR IDEAL SELF?
UH...
I'M EMBAR-RASSED TO SAY...
ALSO, I KNOW I'LL NEVER BE ABLE TO ATTAIN IT.

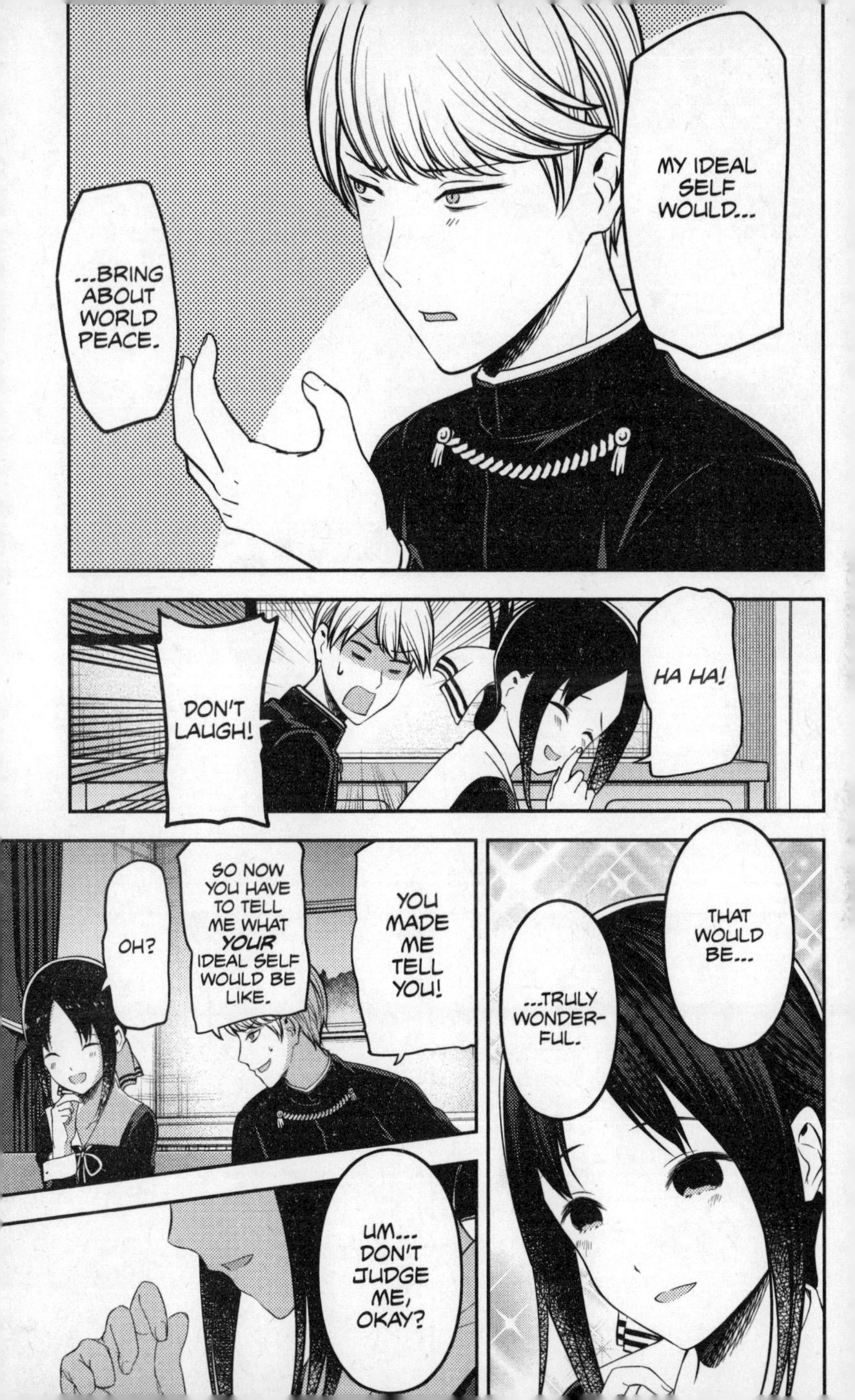
MY IDEAL SELF WOULD...
...BRING ABOUT WORLD PEACE.
HA HA!
DON'T LAUGH!
THAT WOULD BE...
...TRULY WONDERFUL.
YOU MADE ME TELL YOU!
SO NOW YOU HAVE TO TELL ME WHAT *YOUR* IDEAL SELF WOULD BE LIKE.
OH?
UM... DON'T JUDGE ME, OKAY?

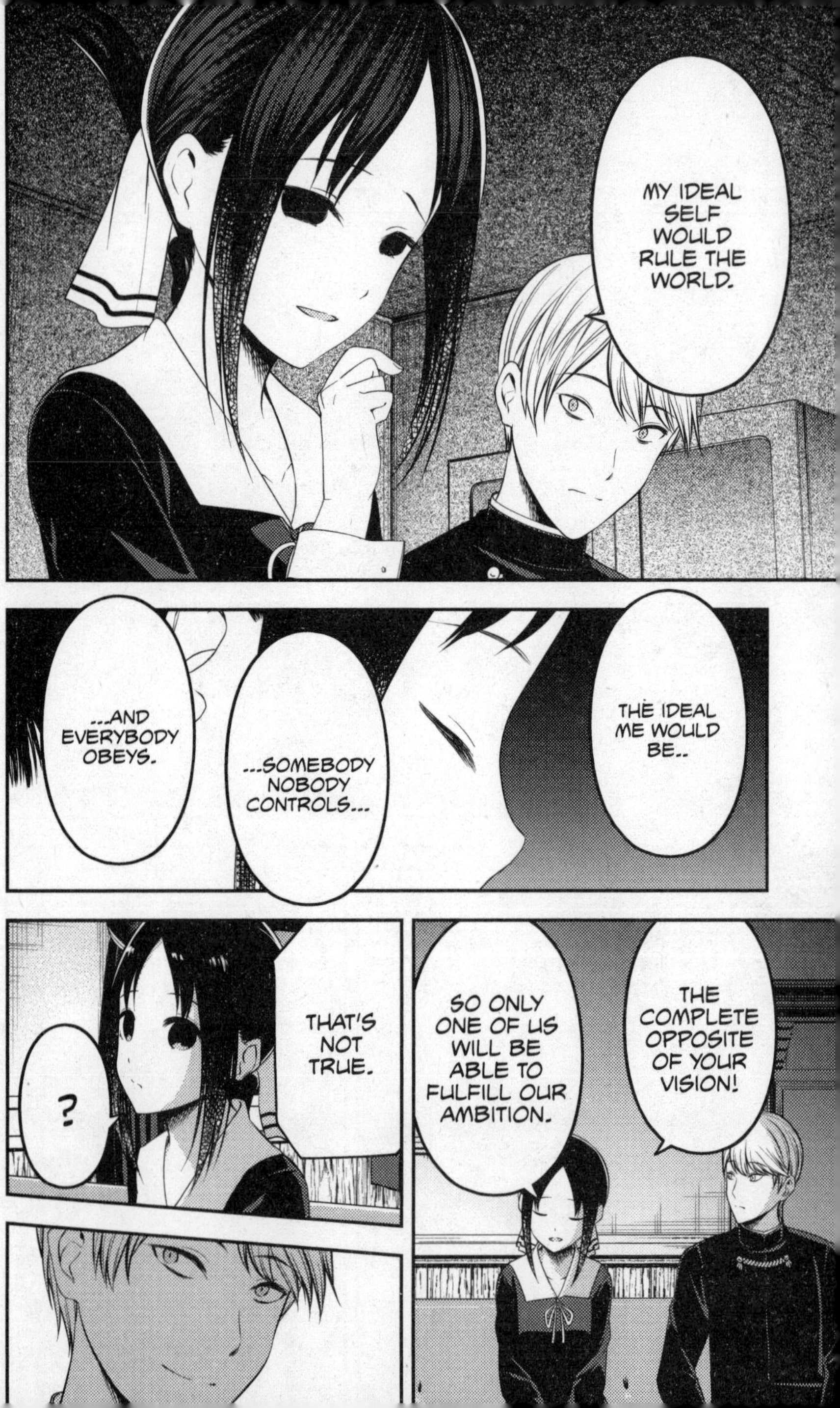
MY IDEAL SELF WOULD RULE THE WORLD.
THE IDEAL ME WOULD BE..
...SOMEBODY NOBODY CONTROLS...
...AND EVERYBODY OBEYS.
THE COMPLETE OPPOSITE OF YOUR VISION!
SO ONLY ONE OF US WILL BE ABLE TO FULFILL OUR AMBITION.
THAT'S NOT TRUE.
?

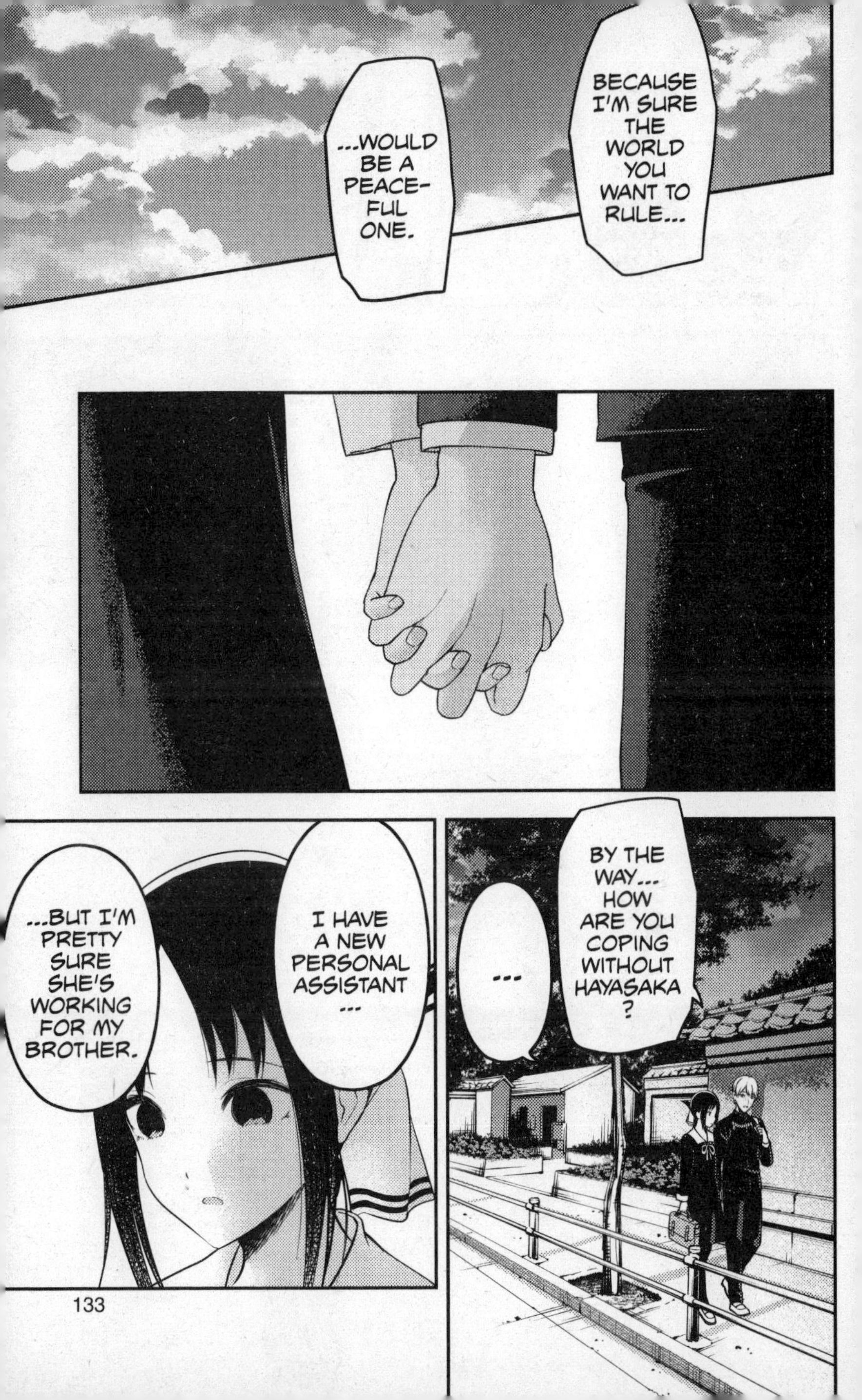
BECAUSE I'M SURE THE WORLD YOU WANT TO RULE...
...WOULD BE A PEACE-FUL ONE.
BY THE WAY... HOW ARE YOU COPING WITHOUT HAYASAKA?
...
I HAVE A NEW PERSONAL ASSISTANT...
...BUT I'M PRETTY SURE SHE'S WORKING FOR MY BROTHER.

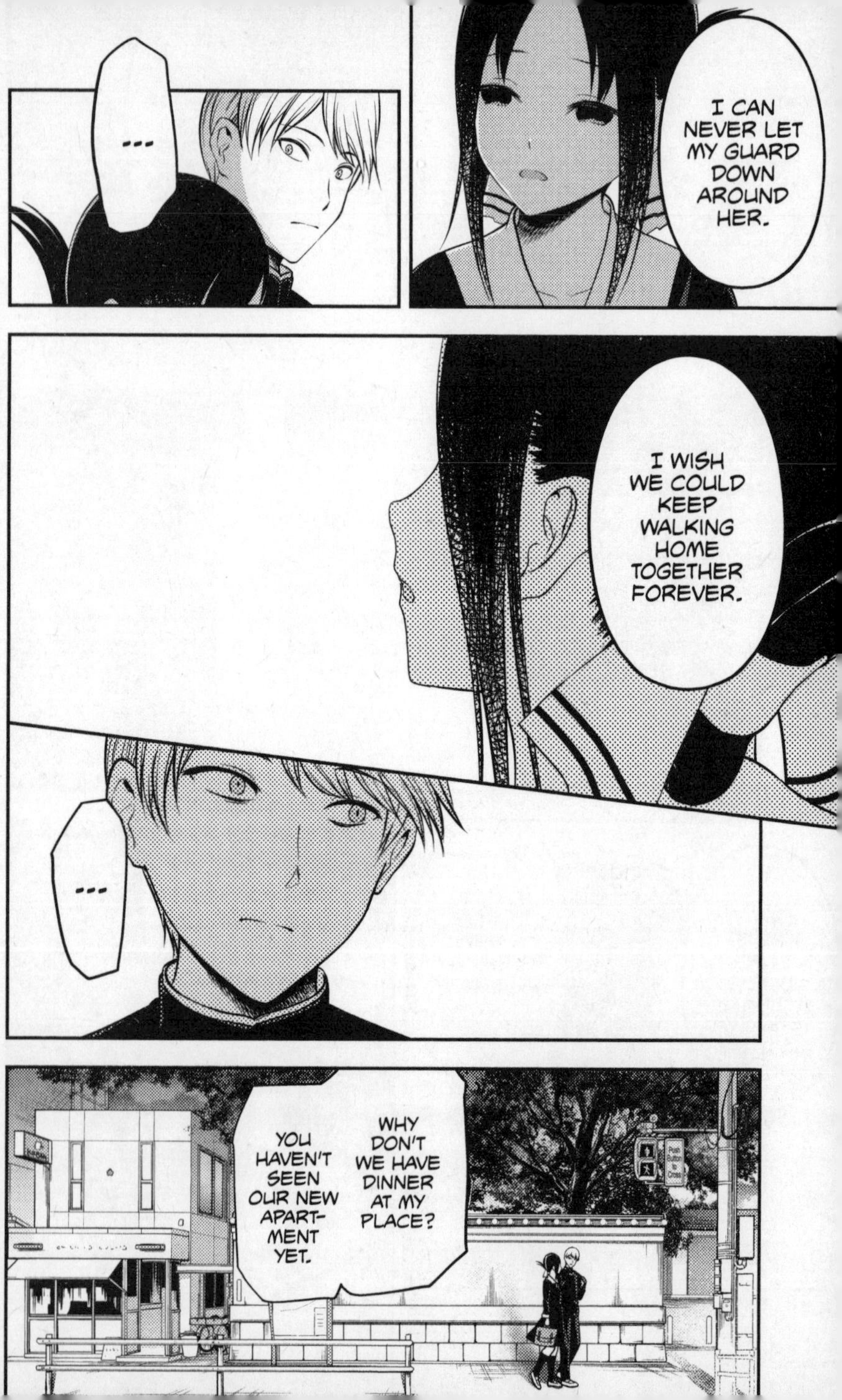
I CAN NEVER LET MY GUARD DOWN AROUND HER.
...
I WISH WE COULD KEEP WALKING HOME TOGETHER FOREVER.
...
WHY DON'T WE HAVE DINNER AT MY PLACE?
YOU HAVEN'T SEEN OUR NEW APART-MENT YET.

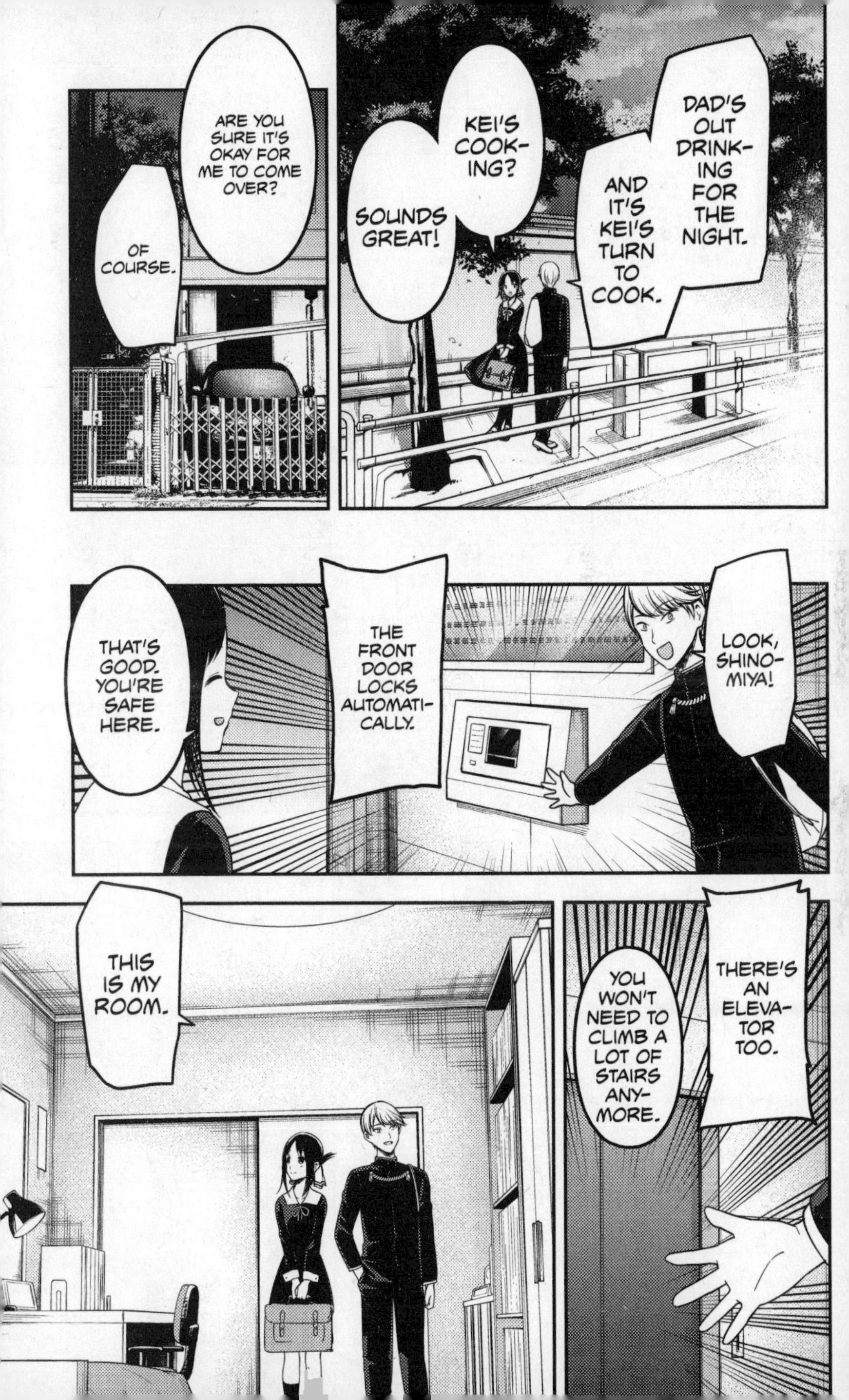
DAD'S OUT DRINKING FOR THE NIGHT.
AND IT'S KEI'S TURN TO COOK.
KEI'S COOKING?
SOUNDS GREAT!
ARE YOU SURE IT'S OKAY FOR ME TO COME OVER?
OF COURSE.
LOOK, SHINOMIYA!
THE FRONT DOOR LOCKS AUTOMATICALLY.
THAT'S GOOD. YOU'RE SAFE HERE.
THERE'S AN ELEVATOR TOO.
YOU WON'T NEED TO CLIMB A LOT OF STAIRS ANYMORE.
THIS IS MY ROOM.

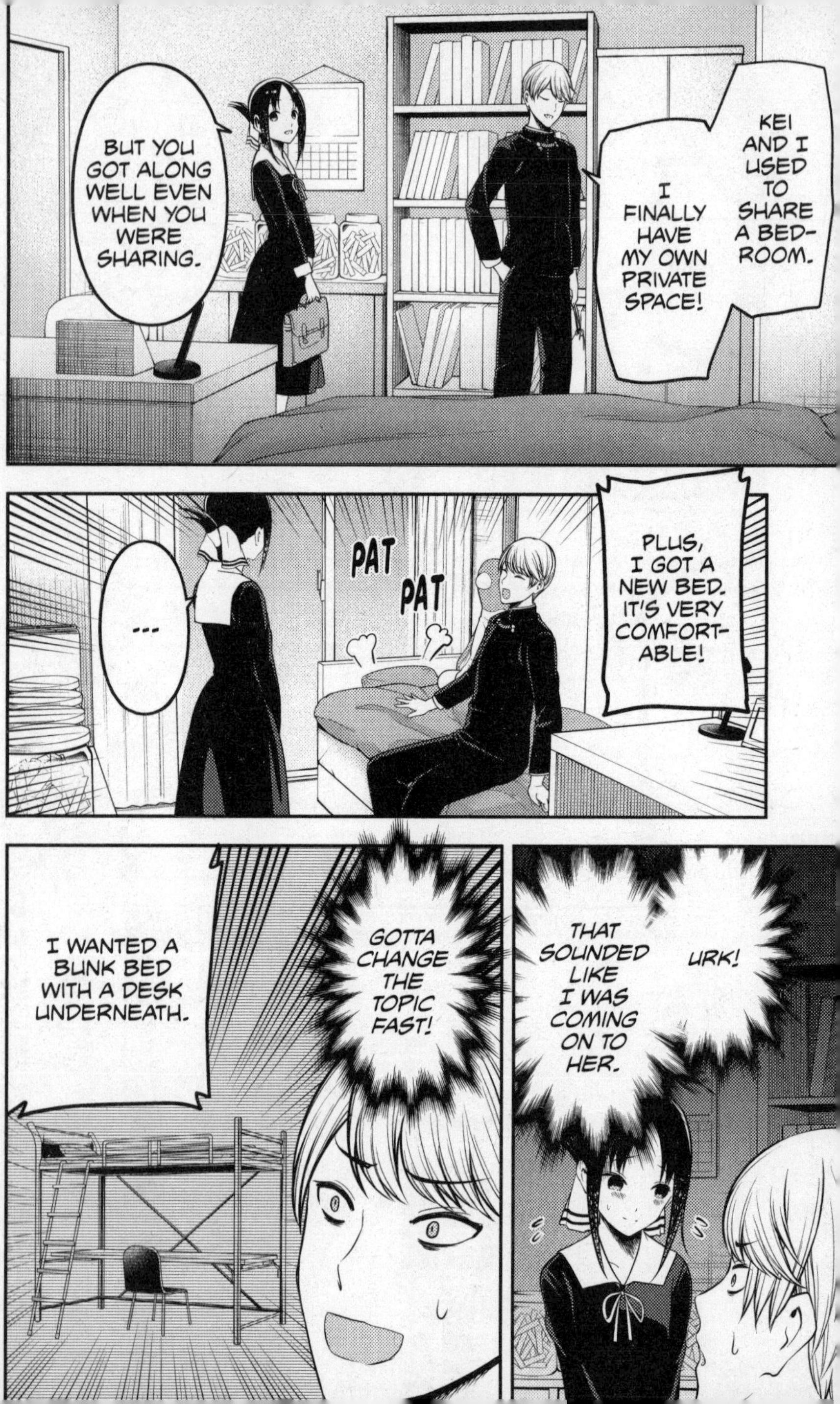
KEI AND I USED TO SHARE A BEDROOM.
I FINALLY HAVE MY OWN PRIVATE SPACE!
BUT YOU GOT ALONG WELL EVEN WHEN YOU WERE SHARING.
PLUS, I GOT A NEW BED. IT'S VERY COMFORTABLE!
PAT PAT
...
URK!
THAT SOUNDED LIKE I WAS COMING ON TO HER.
GOTTA CHANGE THE TOPIC FAST!
I WANTED A BUNK BED WITH A DESK UNDERNEATH.

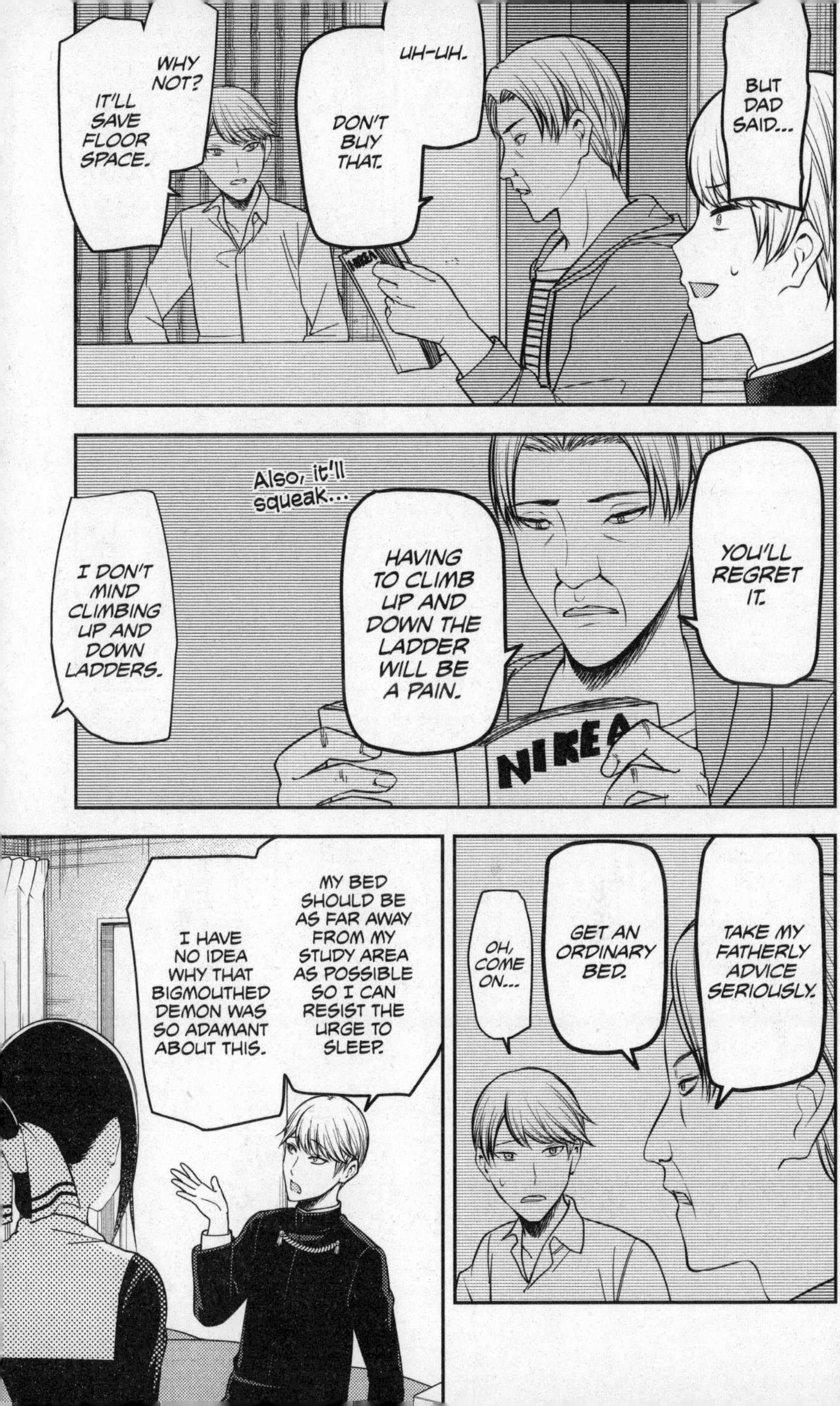
BUT DAD SAID...
UH-UH. DON'T BUY THAT.
WHY NOT? IT'LL SAVE FLOOR SPACE.
YOU'LL REGRET IT.
HAVING TO CLIMB UP AND DOWN THE LADDER WILL BE A PAIN.
Also, it'll squeak...
I DON'T MIND CLIMBING UP AND DOWN LADDERS.
NIKEA
TAKE MY FATHERLY ADVICE SERIOUSLY.
GET AN ORDINARY BED.
OH, COME ON...
MY BED SHOULD BE AS FAR AWAY FROM MY STUDY AREA AS POSSIBLE SO I CAN RESIST THE URGE TO SLEEP.
I HAVE NO IDEA WHY THAT BIGMOUTHED DEMON WAS SO ADAMANT ABOUT THIS.

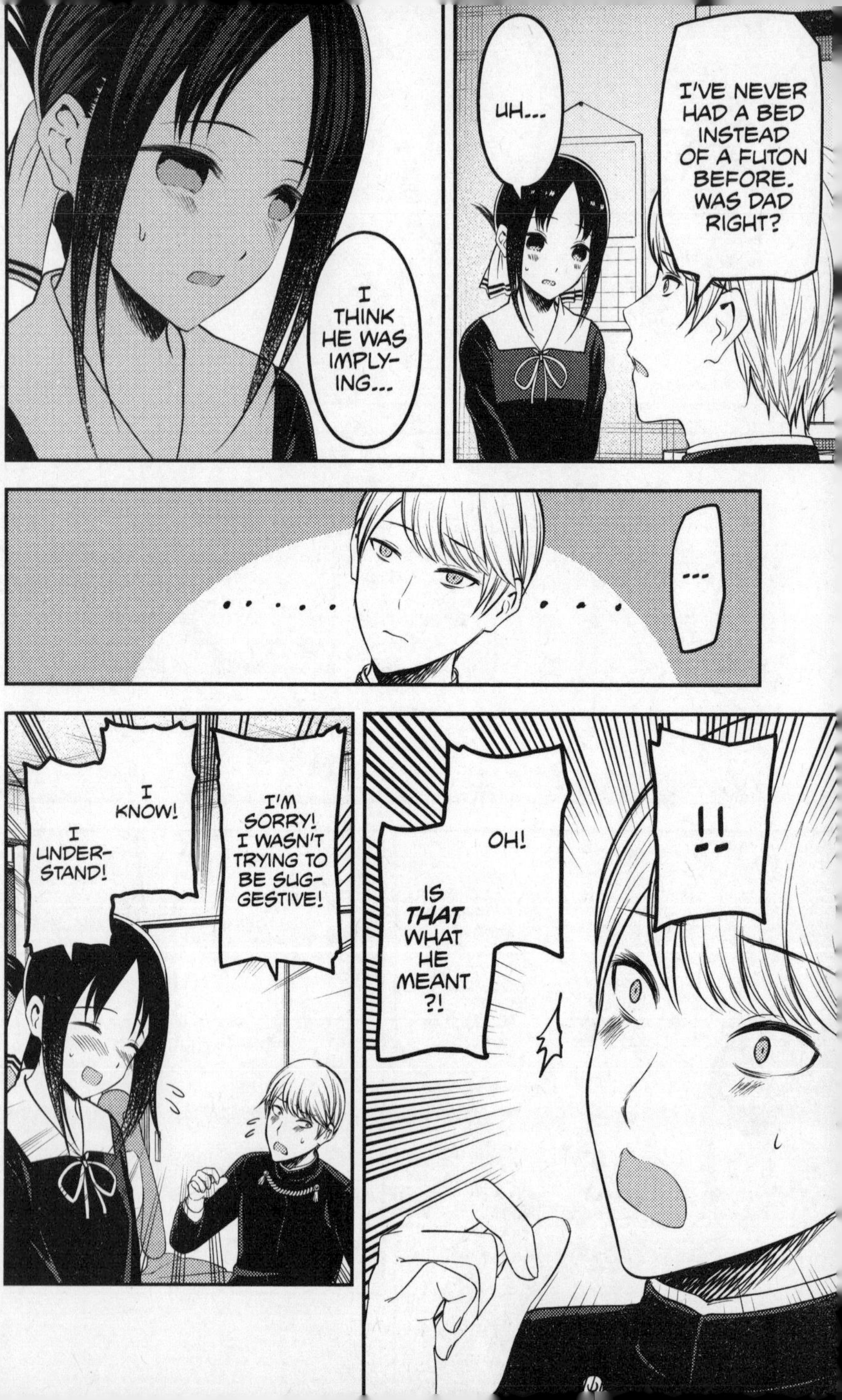

I'VE NEVER HAD A BED INSTEAD OF A FUTON BEFORE. WAS DAD RIGHT?
UH...
I THINK HE WAS IMPLY-ING...
...
OH!
IS THAT WHAT HE MEANT?!
I'M SORRY! I WASN'T TRYING TO BE SUG-GESTIVE!
I KNOW!
I UNDER-STAND!

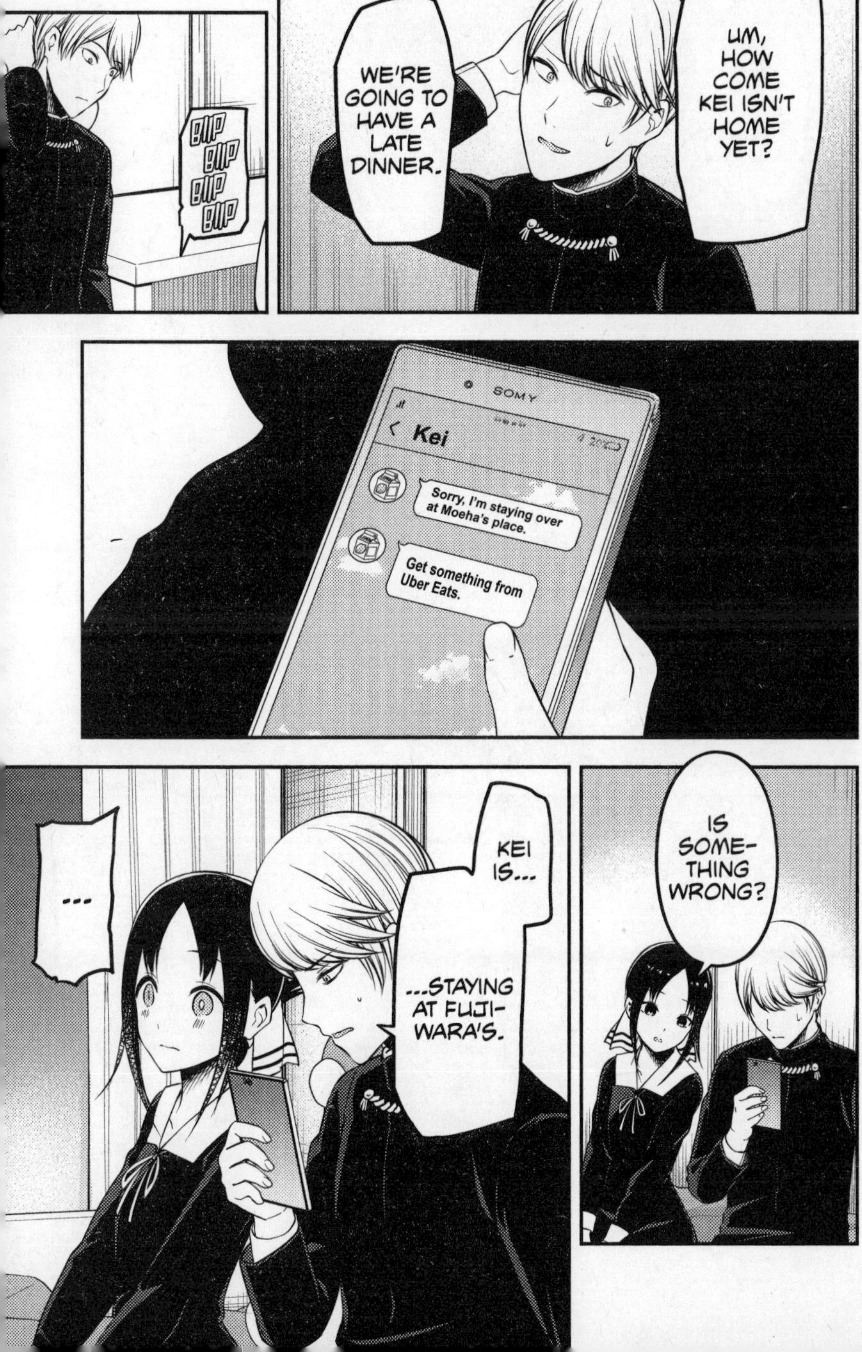
UM, HOW COME KEI ISN'T HOME YET?
WE'RE GOING TO HAVE A LATE DINNER.
BIIP BIIP BIIP BIIP
SOMY
Kei
Sorry, I'm staying over at Moeha's place.
Get something from Uber Eats.
IS SOME-THING WRONG?
KEI IS...
...STAYING AT FUJI-WARA'S.
...

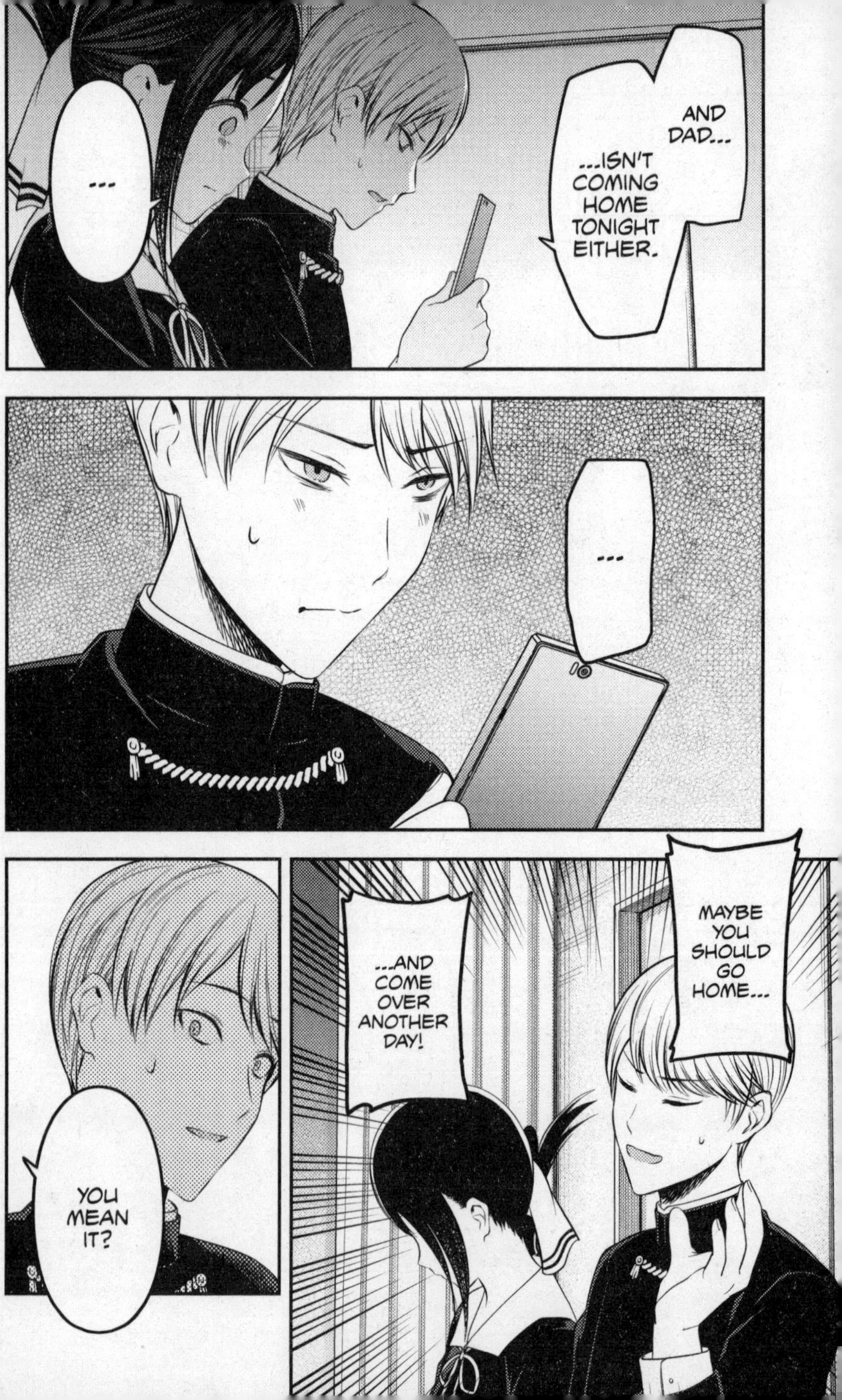
AND DAD...
...ISN'T COMING HOME TONIGHT EITHER.
...
...
MAYBE YOU SHOULD GO HOME...
...AND COME OVER ANOTHER DAY!
YOU MEAN IT?

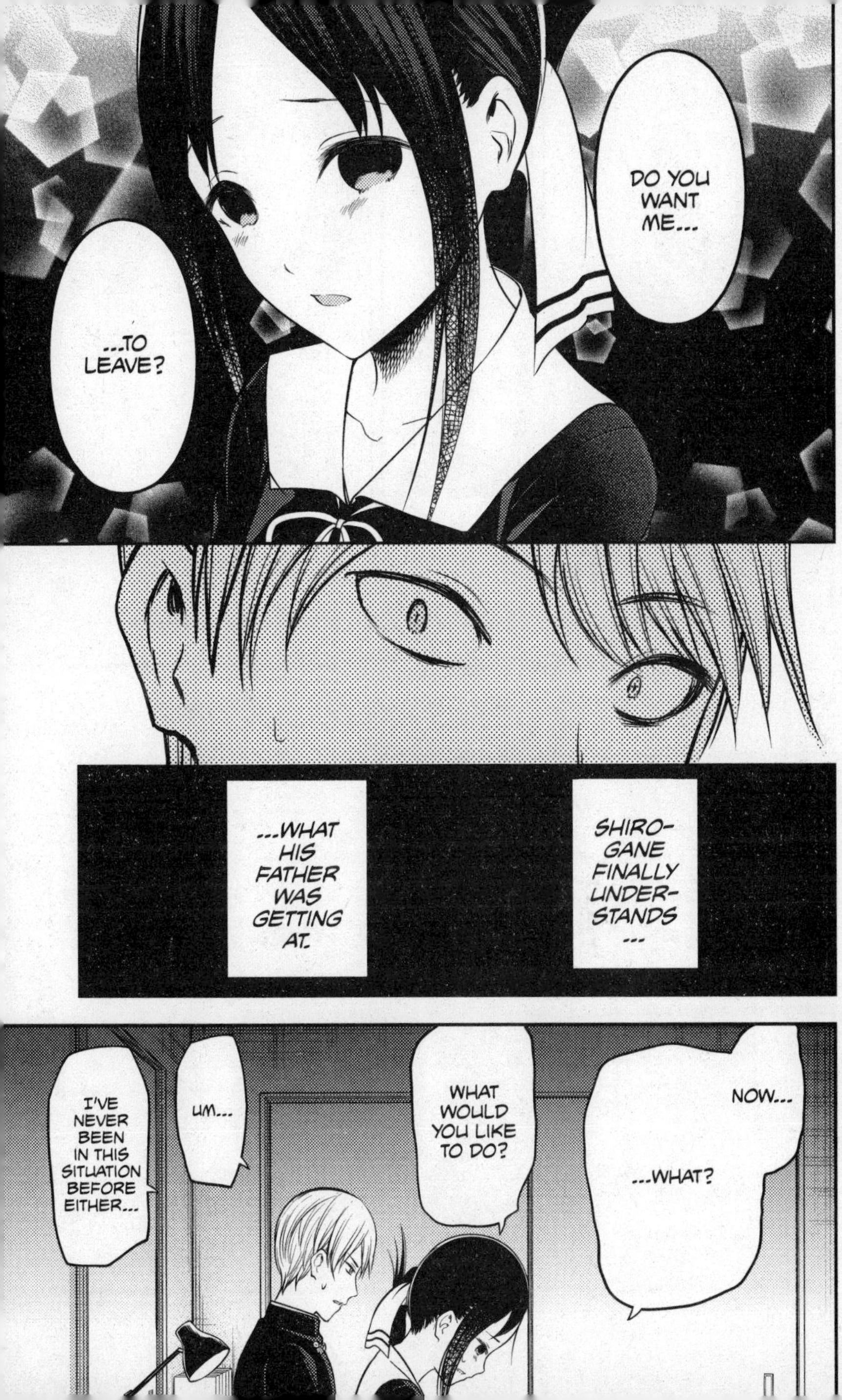
DO YOU WANT ME...
...TO LEAVE?
SHIRO-GANE FINALLY UNDER-STANDS...
...WHAT HIS FATHER WAS GETTING AT.
NOW...
...WHAT?
WHAT WOULD YOU LIKE TO DO?
UM...
I'VE NEVER BEEN IN THIS SITUATION BEFORE EITHER...

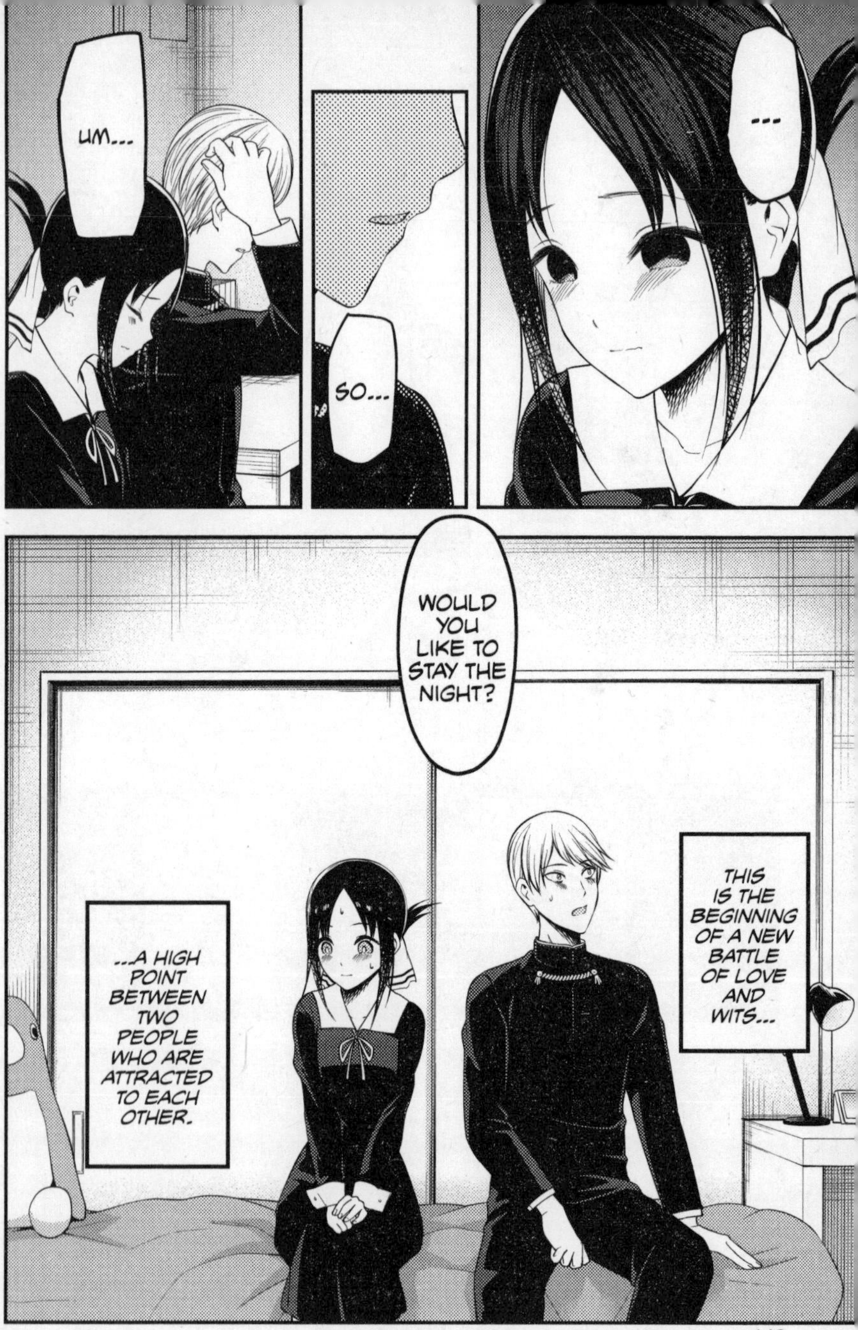
...
SO...
UM...
WOULD YOU LIKE TO STAY THE NIGHT?
THIS IS THE BEGINNING OF A NEW BATTLE OF LOVE AND WITS...
...A HIGH POINT BETWEEN TWO PEOPLE WHO ARE ATTRACTED TO EACH OTHER.

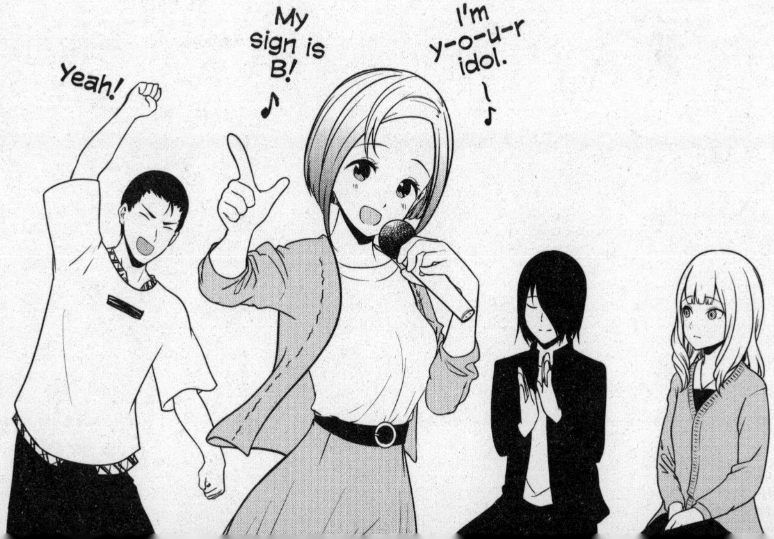

I'm y-o-u-r idol. ~ ♪
My sign is B! ♪
Yeah!

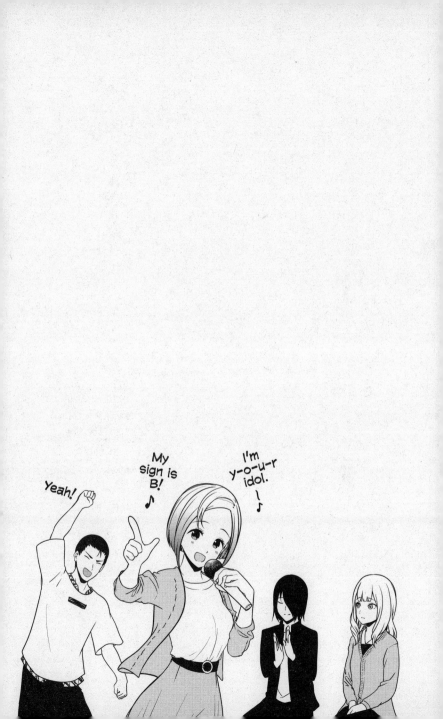

KAGUYA-SAMA

LOVE IS WAR

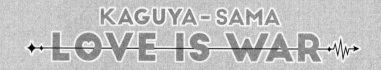

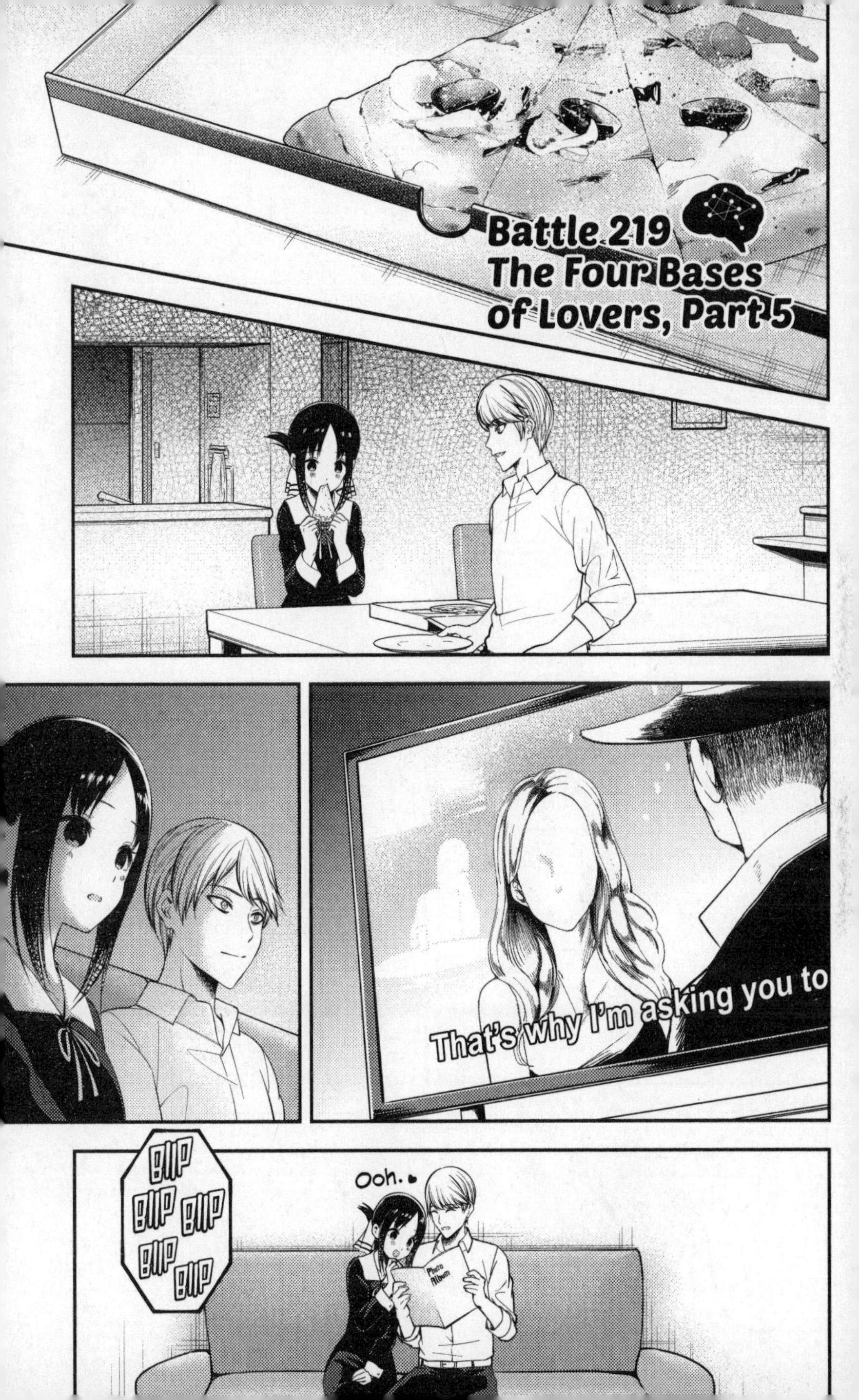
Battle 219
The Four Bases of Lovers, Part 5
That's why I'm asking you to
BLIP
BLIP BLIP
BLIP
BLIP
Ooh.
Photo Album

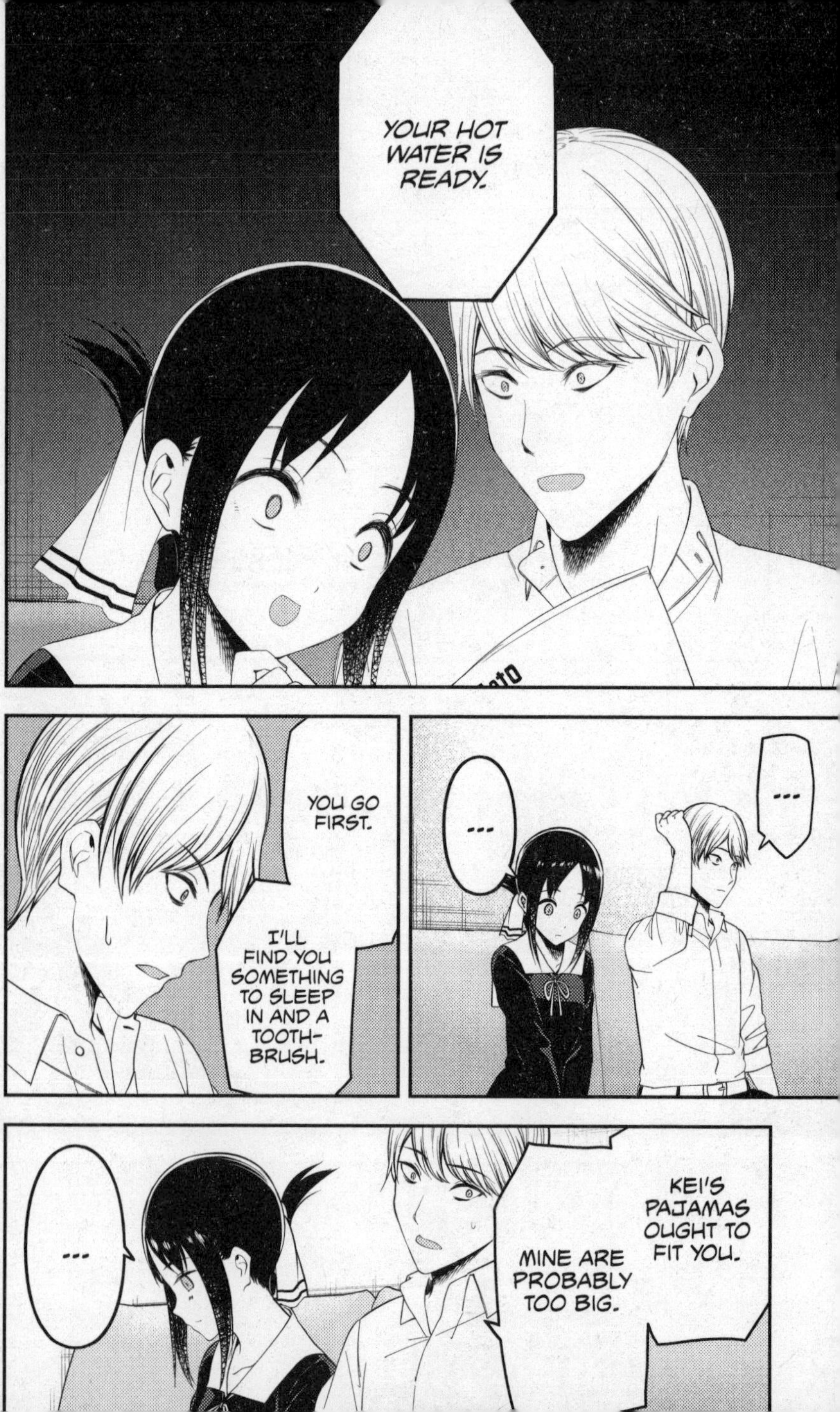
YOUR HOT WATER IS READY.
...
...
YOU GO FIRST.
I'LL FIND YOU SOMETHING TO SLEEP IN AND A TOOTH-BRUSH.
KEI'S PAJAMAS OUGHT TO FIT YOU.
MINE ARE PROBABLY TOO BIG.
...

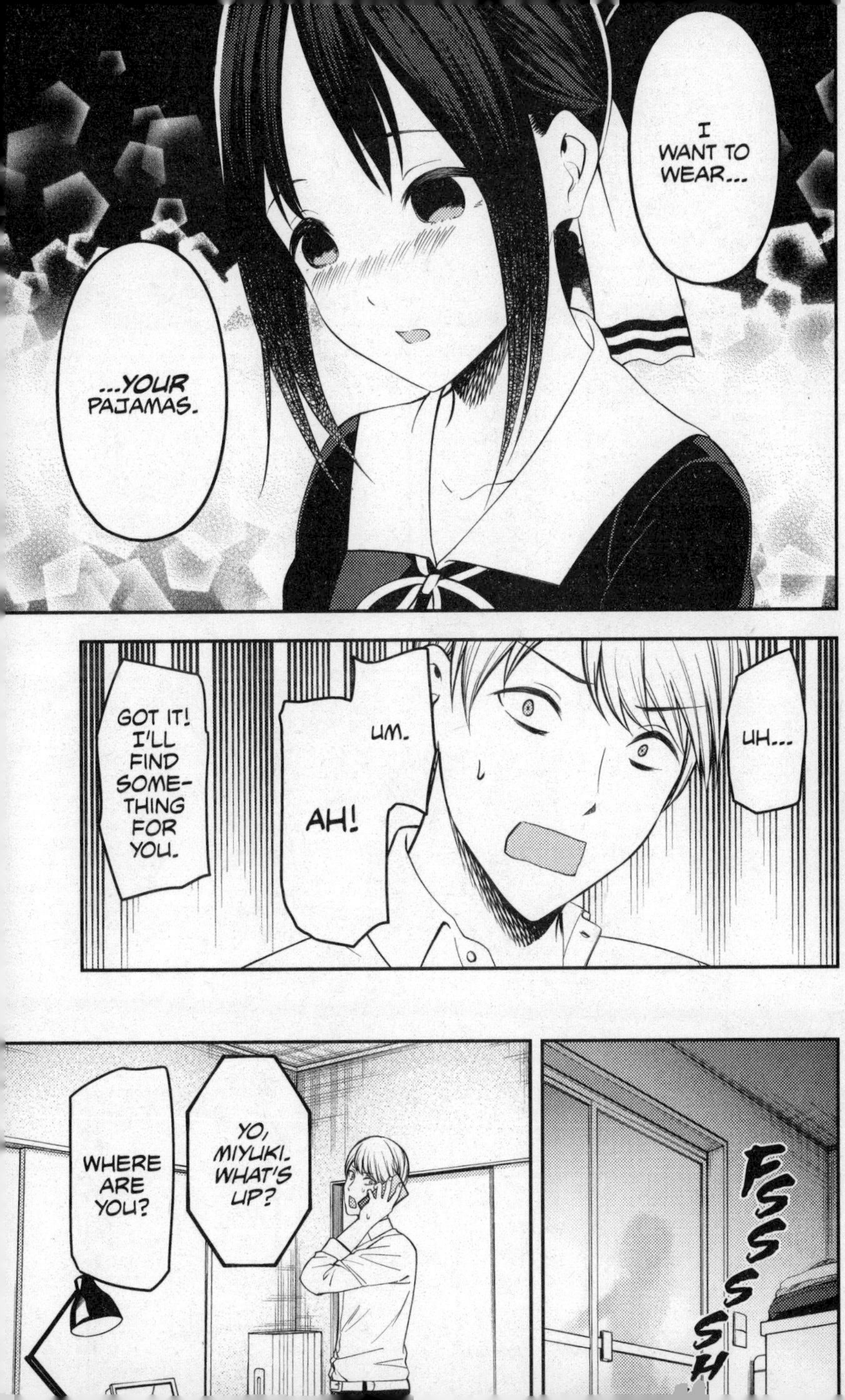
I WANT TO WEAR...
...YOUR PAJAMAS.
UH...
UM.
AH!
GOT IT! I'LL FIND SOME-THING FOR YOU.
FSSSSH
YO, MIYUKI. WHAT'S UP?
WHERE ARE YOU?

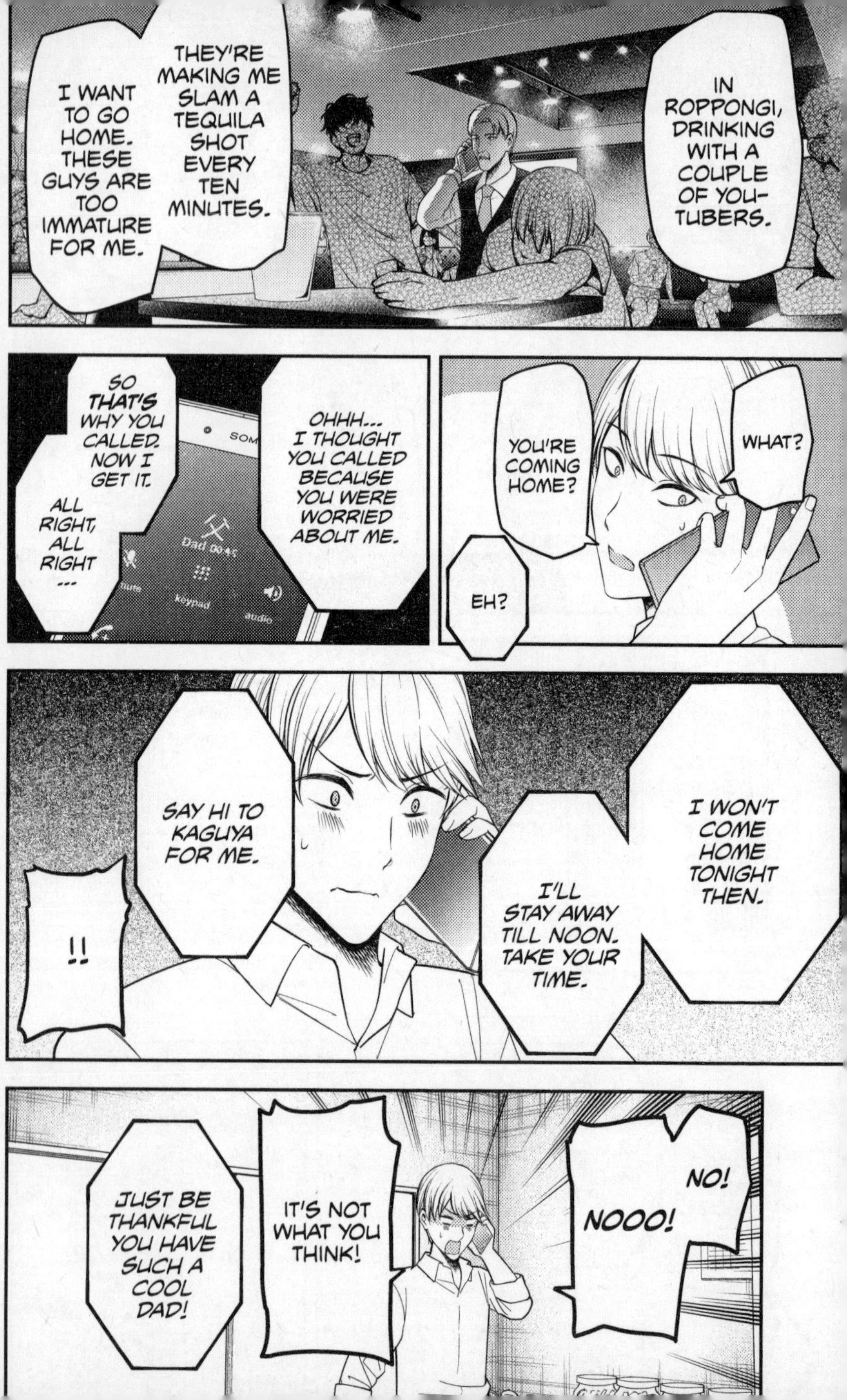
IN ROPPONGI, DRINKING WITH A COUPLE OF YOU-TUBERS.
THEY'RE MAKING ME SLAM A TEQUILA SHOT EVERY TEN MINUTES.
I WANT TO GO HOME. THESE GUYS ARE TOO IMMATURE FOR ME.
WHAT?
YOU'RE COMING HOME?
EH?
OHHH... I THOUGHT YOU CALLED BECAUSE YOU WERE WORRIED ABOUT ME.
SO **THAT'S** WHY YOU CALLED. NOW I GET IT.
ALL RIGHT, ALL RIGHT...
Dad 00:45
keypad
audio
I WON'T COME HOME TONIGHT THEN.
I'LL STAY AWAY TILL NOON. TAKE YOUR TIME.
SAY HI TO KAGUYA FOR ME.
!!
NO!
NOOO!
IT'S NOT WHAT YOU THINK!
JUST BE THANKFUL YOU HAVE SUCH A COOL DAD!

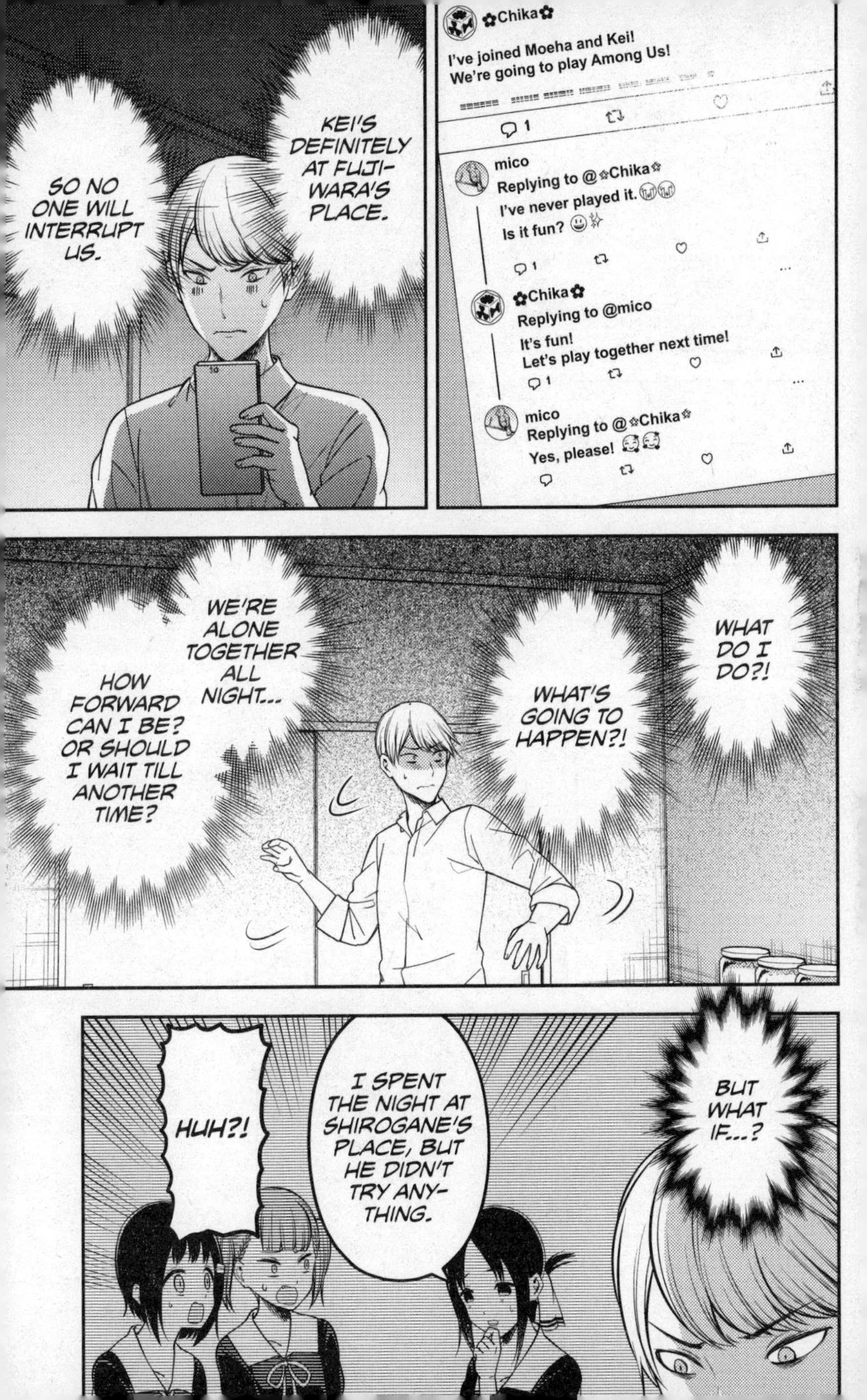
✿Chika✿
I've joined Moeha and Kei!
We're going to play Among Us!
1
mico
Replying to @✿Chika✿
I've never played it.
Is it fun?
1
✿Chika✿
Replying to @mico
It's fun!
Let's play together next time!
1
mico
Replying to @✿Chika✿
Yes, please!
KEI'S DEFINITELY AT FUJI-WARA'S PLACE.
SO NO ONE WILL INTERRUPT US.
WHAT DO I DO?!
WHAT'S GOING TO HAPPEN?!
WE'RE ALONE TOGETHER ALL NIGHT...
HOW FORWARD CAN I BE? OR SHOULD I WAIT TILL ANOTHER TIME?
BUT WHAT IF...?
I SPENT THE NIGHT AT SHIROGANE'S PLACE, BUT HE DIDN'T TRY ANY-THING.
HUH?!

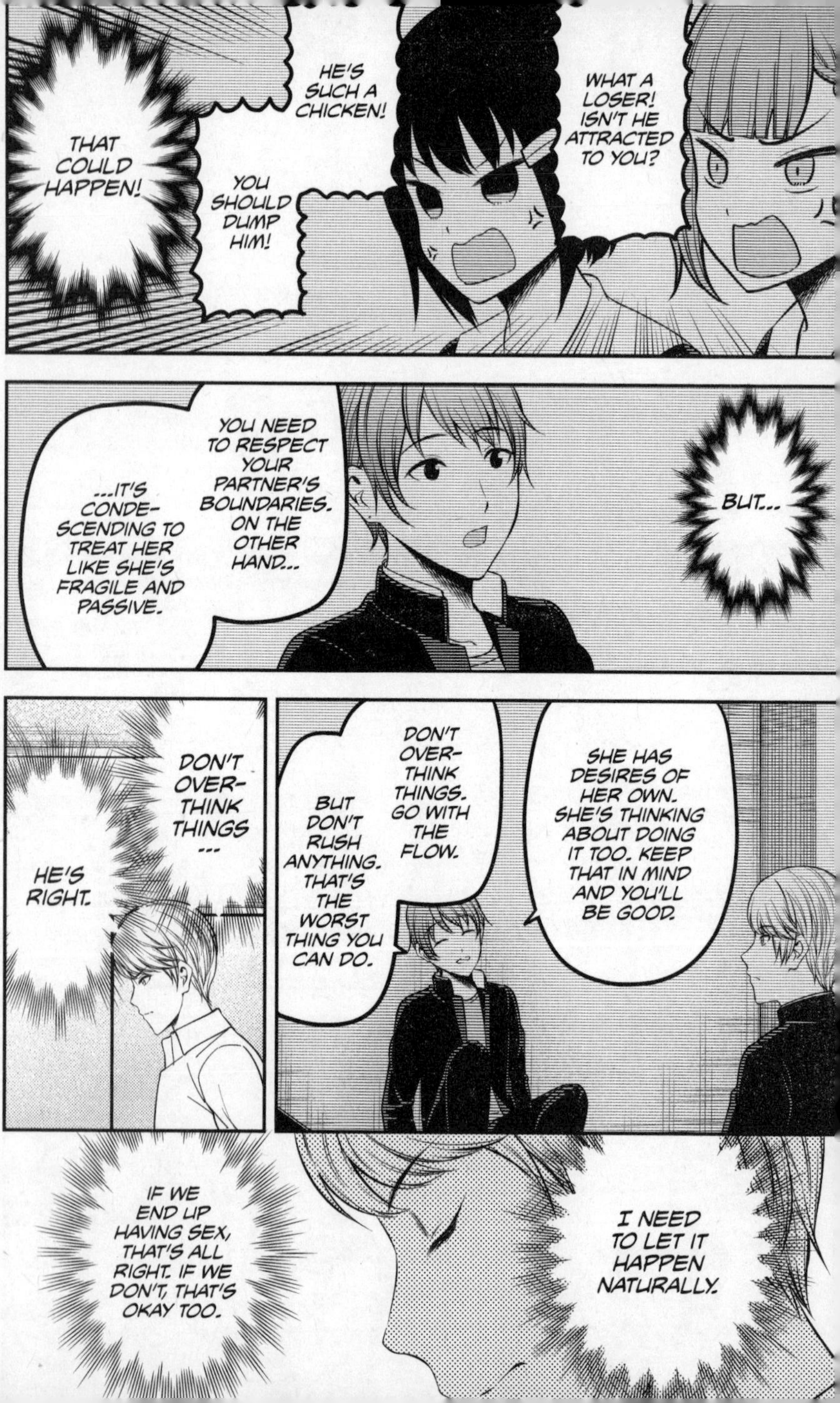
WHAT A LOSER! ISN'T HE ATTRACTED TO YOU?
HE'S SUCH A CHICKEN!
YOU SHOULD DUMP HIM!
THAT COULD HAPPEN!
BUT...
YOU NEED TO RESPECT YOUR PARTNER'S BOUNDARIES. ON THE OTHER HAND...
...IT'S CONDE-SCENDING TO TREAT HER LIKE SHE'S FRAGILE AND PASSIVE.
SHE HAS DESIRES OF HER OWN. SHE'S THINKING ABOUT DOING IT TOO. KEEP THAT IN MIND AND YOU'LL BE GOOD.
DON'T OVER-THINK THINGS. GO WITH THE FLOW.
BUT DON'T RUSH ANYTHING. THAT'S THE WORST THING YOU CAN DO.
DON'T OVER-THINK THINGS...
HE'S RIGHT.
I NEED TO LET IT HAPPEN NATURALLY.
IF WE END UP HAVING SEX, THAT'S ALL RIGHT. IF WE DON'T, THAT'S OKAY TOO.

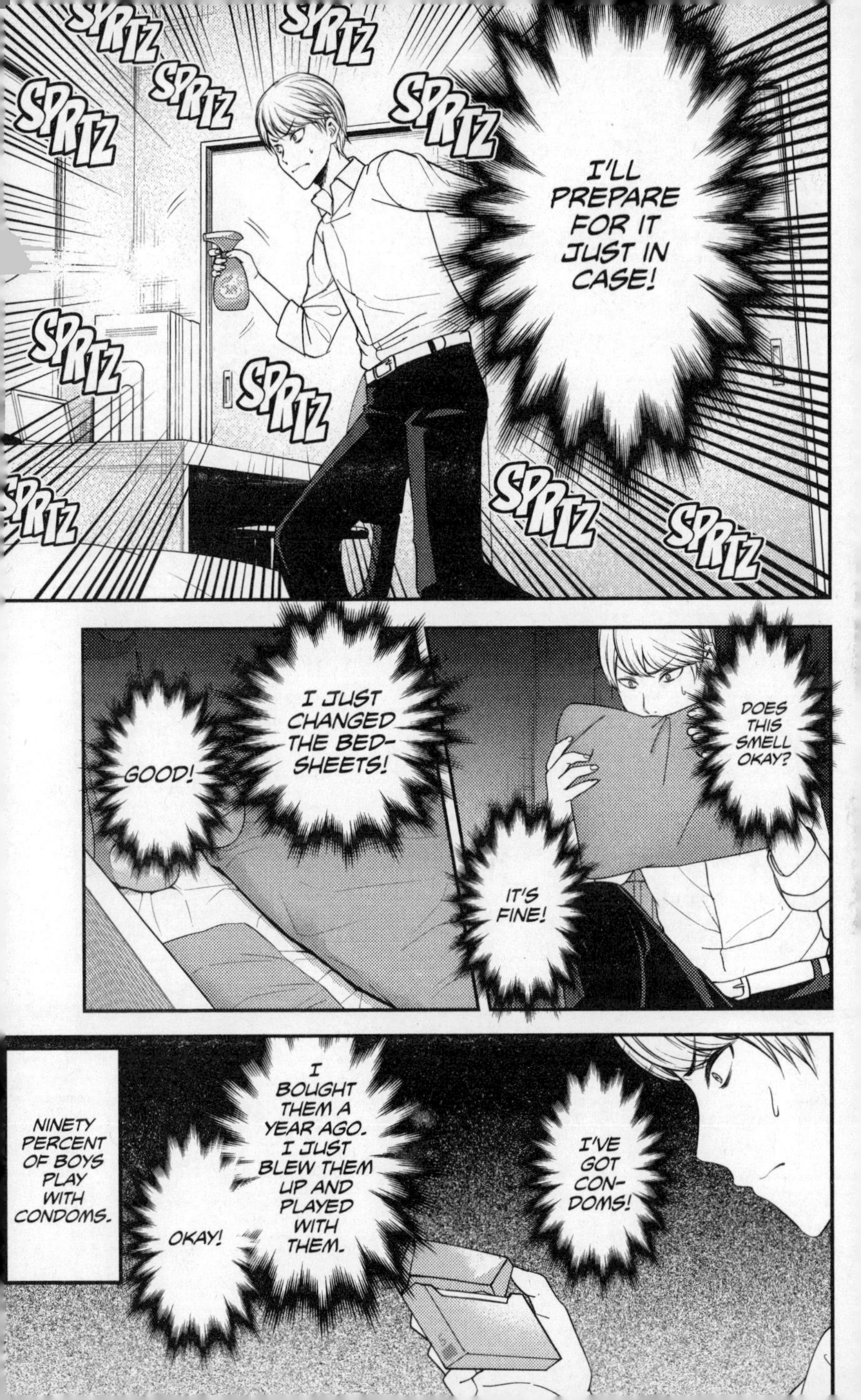

SPRTZ
SPRTZ
I'LL PREPARE FOR IT JUST IN CASE!
SPRTZ
SPRTZ
SPRTZ
SPRTZ
SPRTZ
SPRTZ
SPRTZ
SPRTZ
DOES THIS SMELL OKAY?
IT'S FINE!
I JUST CHANGED THE BED-SHEETS!
GOOD!
I'VE GOT CON-DOMS!
I BOUGHT THEM A YEAR AGO. I JUST BLEW THEM UP AND PLAYED WITH THEM.
OKAY!
NINETY PERCENT OF BOYS PLAY WITH CONDOMS.

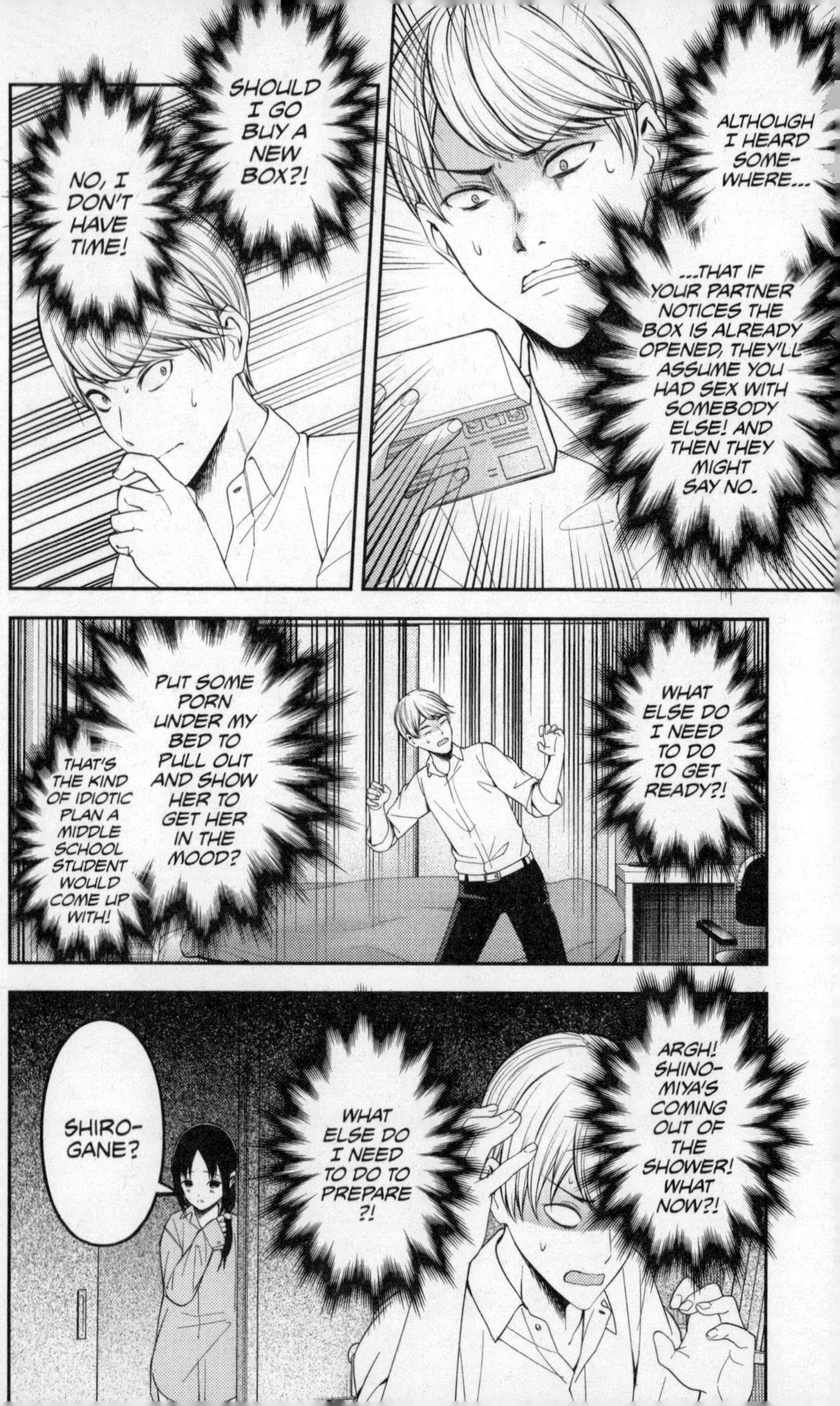
ALTHOUGH I HEARD SOME-WHERE...
...THAT IF YOUR PARTNER NOTICES THE BOX IS ALREADY OPENED, THEY'LL ASSUME YOU HAD SEX WITH SOMEBODY ELSE! AND THEN THEY MIGHT SAY NO.
SHOULD I GO BUY A NEW BOX?!
NO, I DON'T HAVE TIME!
WHAT ELSE DO I NEED TO DO TO GET READY?!
PUT SOME PORN UNDER MY BED TO PULL OUT AND SHOW HER TO GET HER IN THE MOOD?
THAT'S THE KIND OF IDIOTIC PLAN A MIDDLE SCHOOL STUDENT WOULD COME UP WITH!
ARGH! SHINO-MIYA'S COMING OUT OF THE SHOWER! WHAT NOW?!
WHAT ELSE DO I NEED TO DO TO PREPARE ?!
SHIRO-GANE?

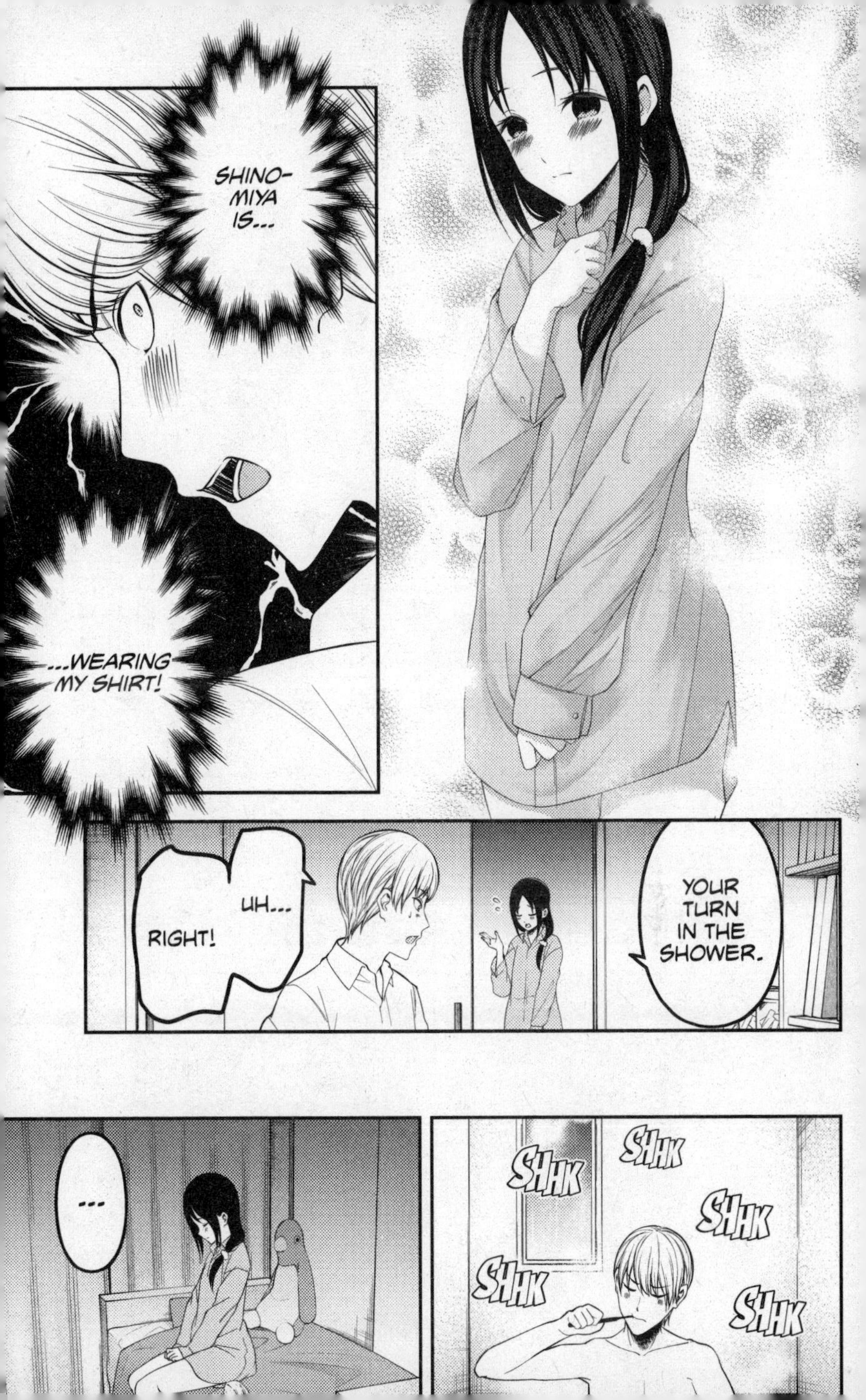
SHINO-MIYA IS...
...WEARING MY SHIRT!
YOUR TURN IN THE SHOWER.
UH... RIGHT!
SHHK
SHHK
SHHK
SHHK
...

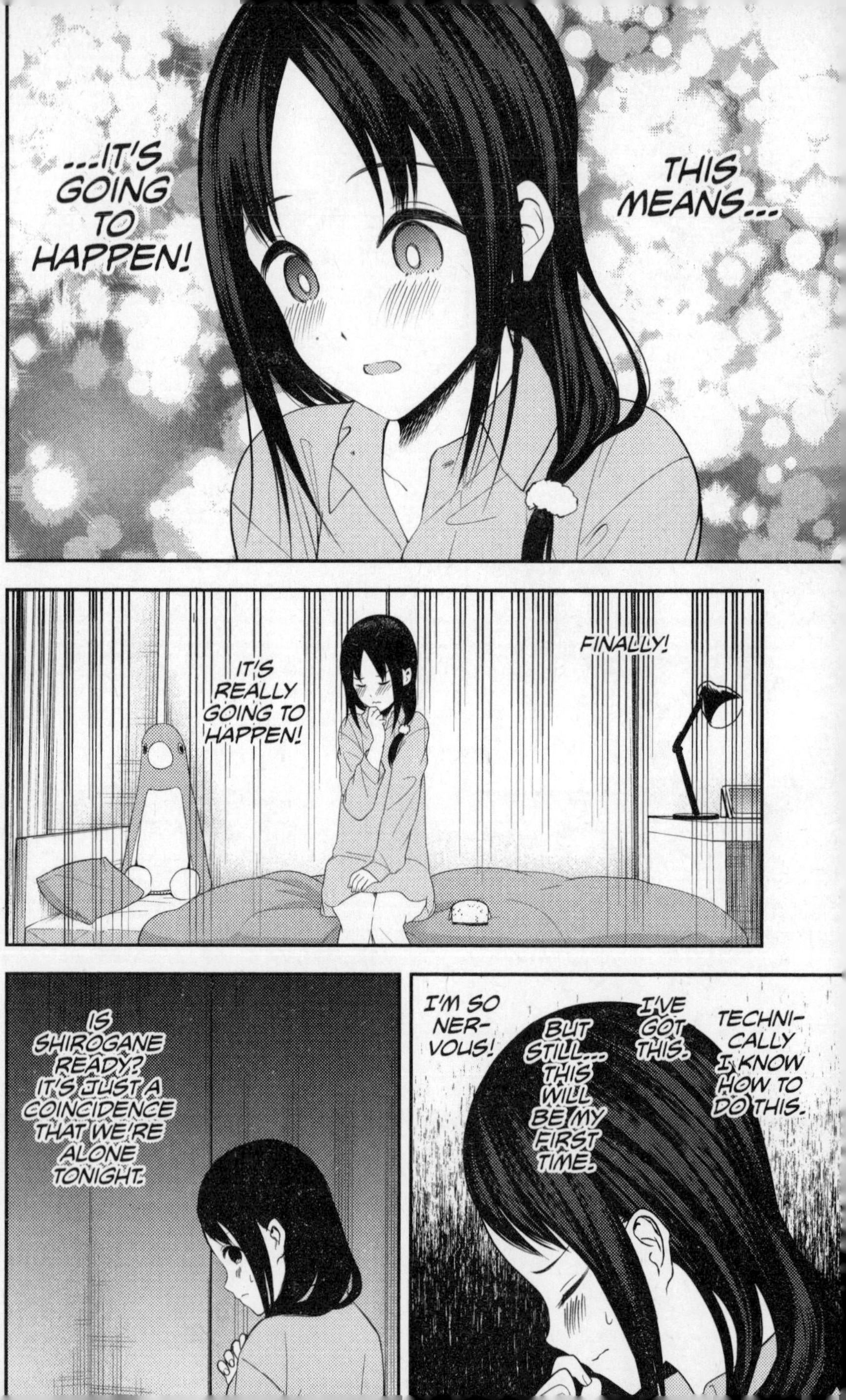
THIS MEANS...
...IT'S GOING TO HAPPEN!
FINALLY!
IT'S REALLY GOING TO HAPPEN!
TECHNI-CALLY I KNOW HOW TO DO THIS.
I'VE GOT THIS.
BUT STILL... THIS WILL BE MY FIRST TIME.
I'M SO NER-VOUS!
IS SHIROGANE READY? IT'S JUST A COINCIDENCE THAT WE'RE ALONE TONIGHT.

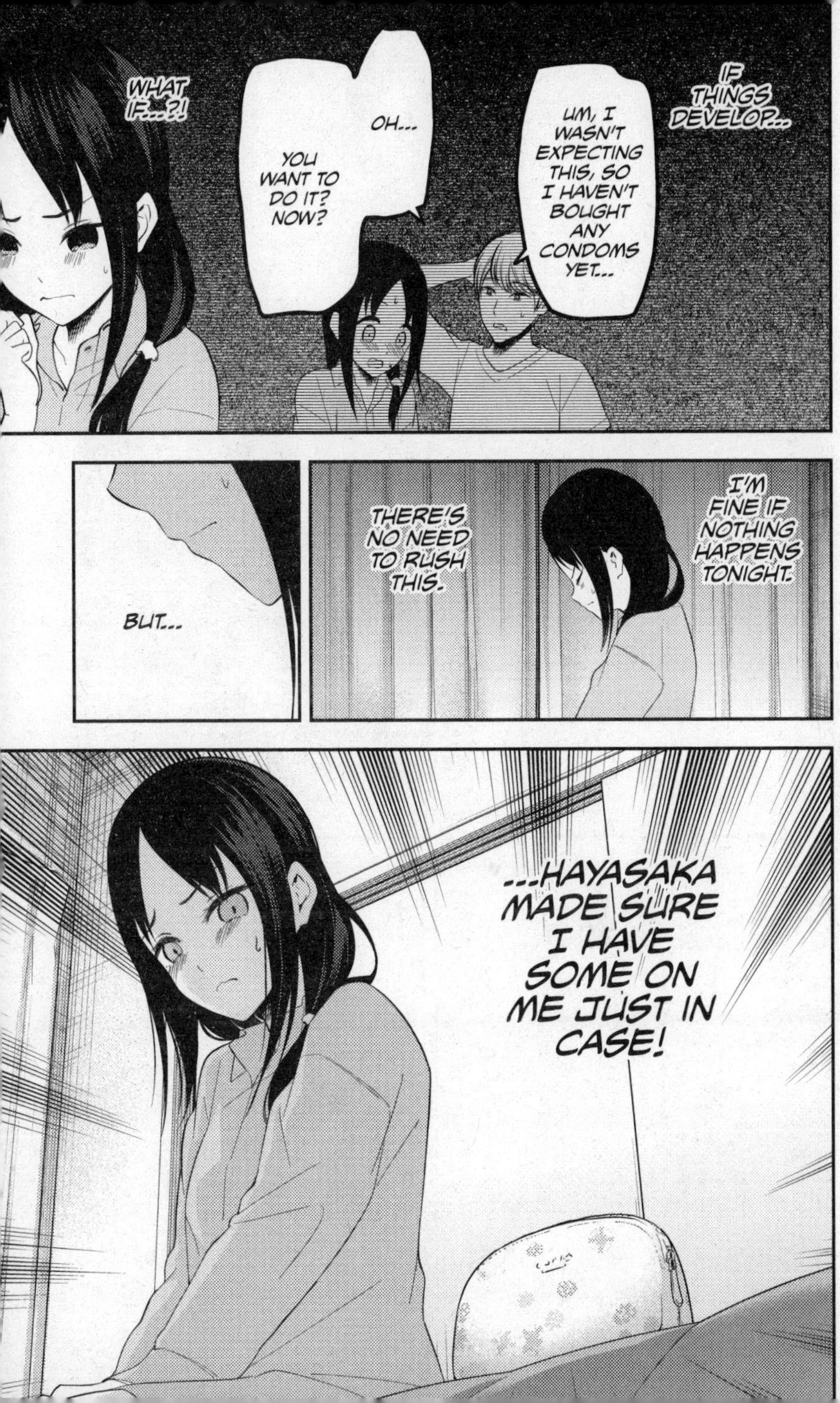
IF THINGS DEVELOP...
UM, I WASN'T EXPECTING THIS, SO I HAVEN'T BOUGHT ANY CONDOMS YET...
OH...
YOU WANT TO DO IT? NOW?
WHAT IF...?!
I'M FINE IF NOTHING HAPPENS TONIGHT.
THERE'S NO NEED TO RUSH THIS.
BUT...
...HAYASAKA MADE SURE I HAVE SOME ON ME JUST IN CASE!

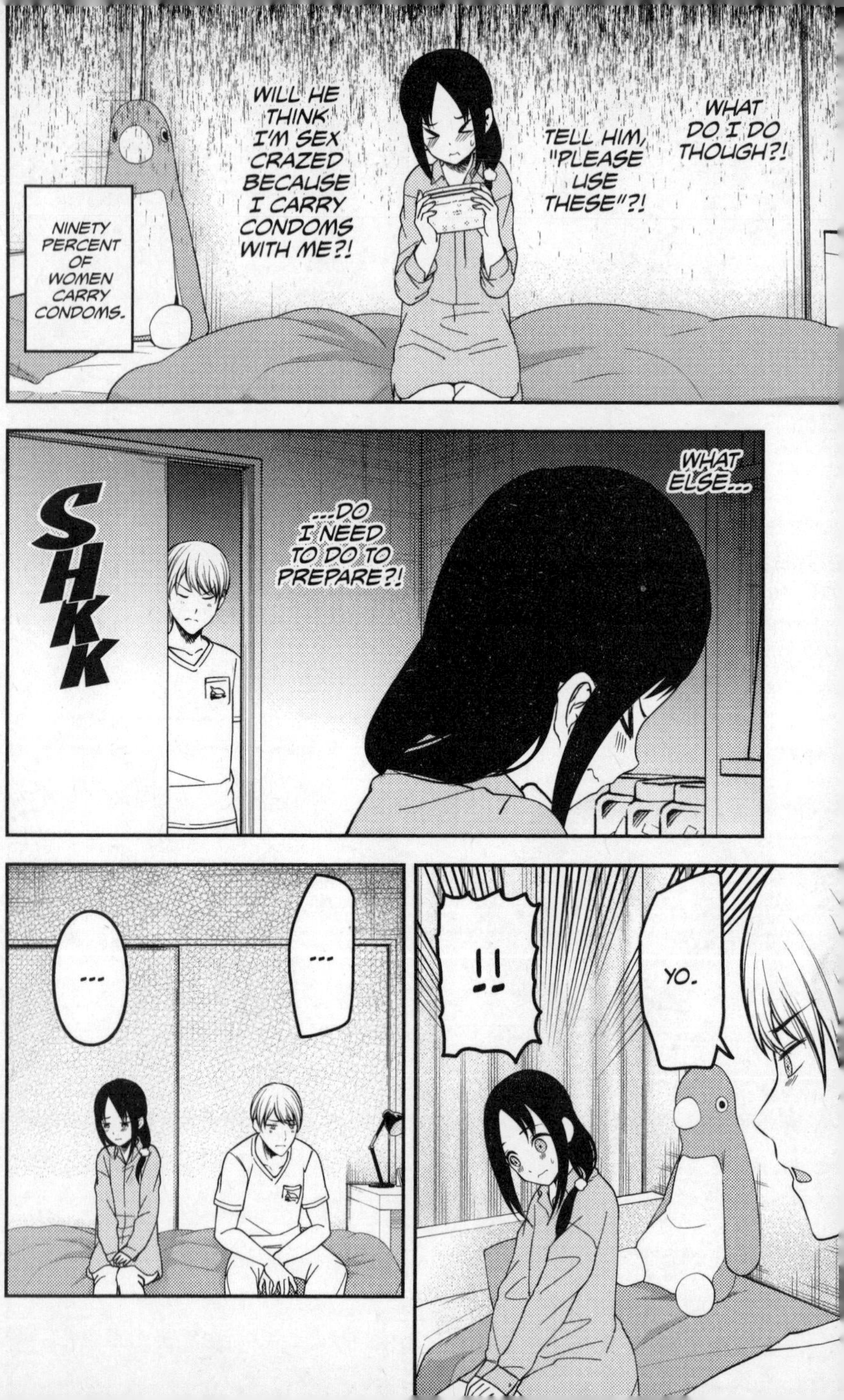
WHAT DO I DO THOUGH?!
TELL HIM, "PLEASE USE THESE"?!
WILL HE THINK I'M SEX CRAZED BECAUSE I CARRY CONDOMS WITH ME?!
NINETY PERCENT OF WOMEN CARRY CONDOMS.
WHAT ELSE...
...DO I NEED TO DO TO PREPARE?!
SHKK
YO.
!!
...
...

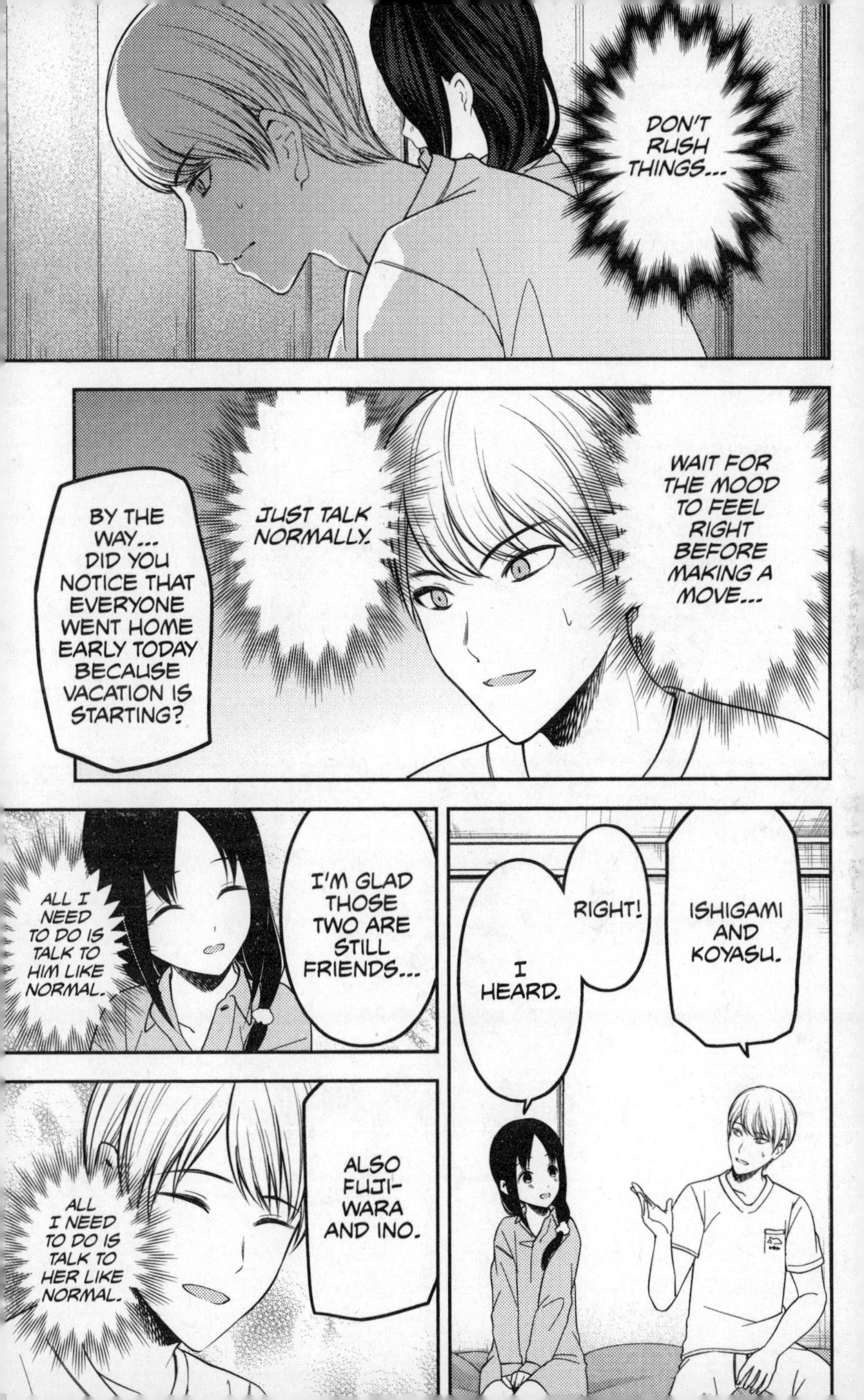
DON'T RUSH THINGS...
WAIT FOR THE MOOD TO FEEL RIGHT BEFORE MAKING A MOVE...
JUST TALK NORMALLY.
BY THE WAY... DID YOU NOTICE THAT EVERYONE WENT HOME EARLY TODAY BECAUSE VACATION IS STARTING?
ISHIGAMI AND KOYASU.
RIGHT!
I HEARD.
I'M GLAD THOSE TWO ARE STILL FRIENDS...
ALL I NEED TO DO IS TALK TO HIM LIKE NORMAL.
ALSO FUJI-WARA AND INO.
ALL I NEED TO DO IS TALK TO HER LIKE NORMAL.

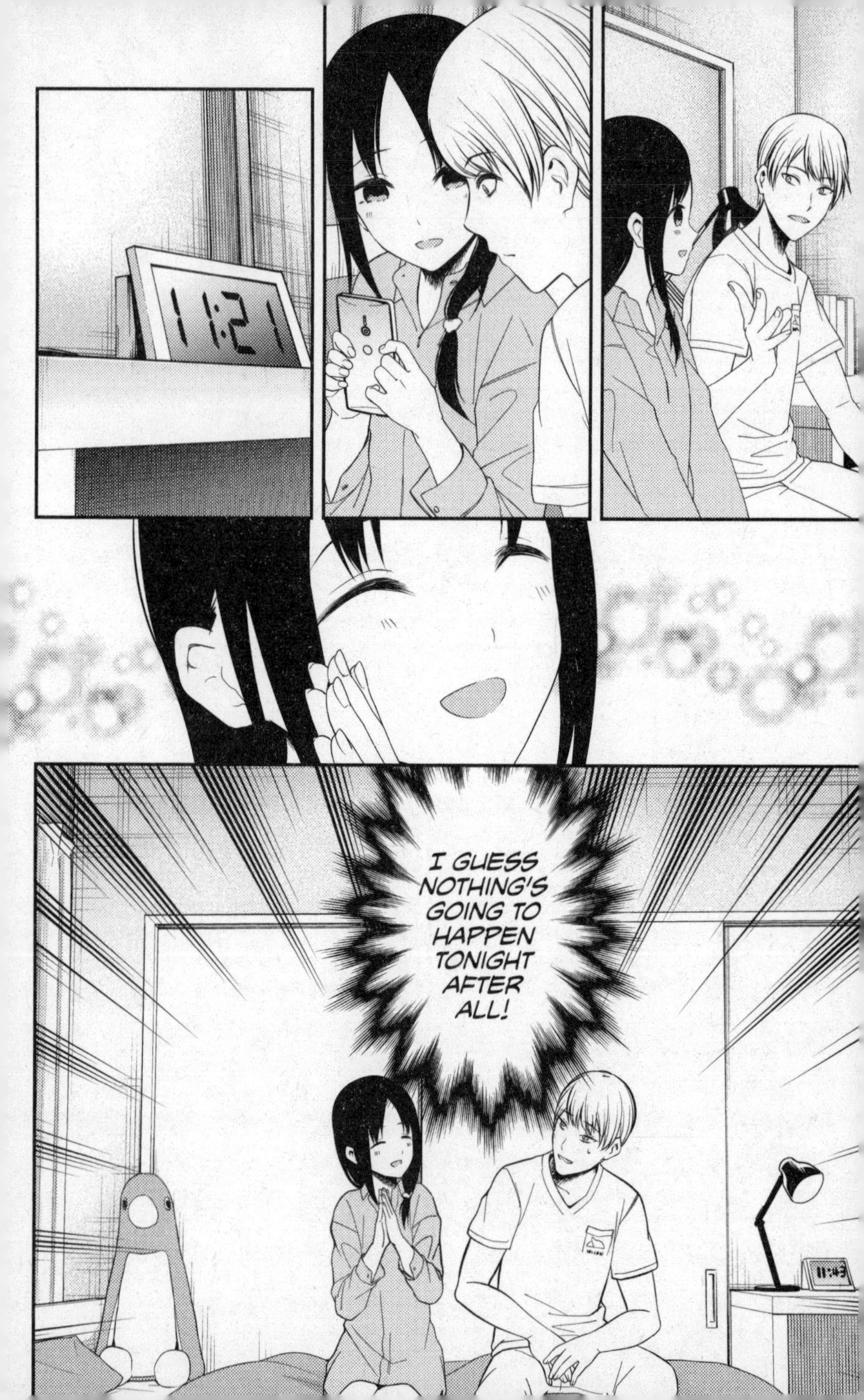
I GUESS NOTHING'S GOING TO HAPPEN TONIGHT AFTER ALL!

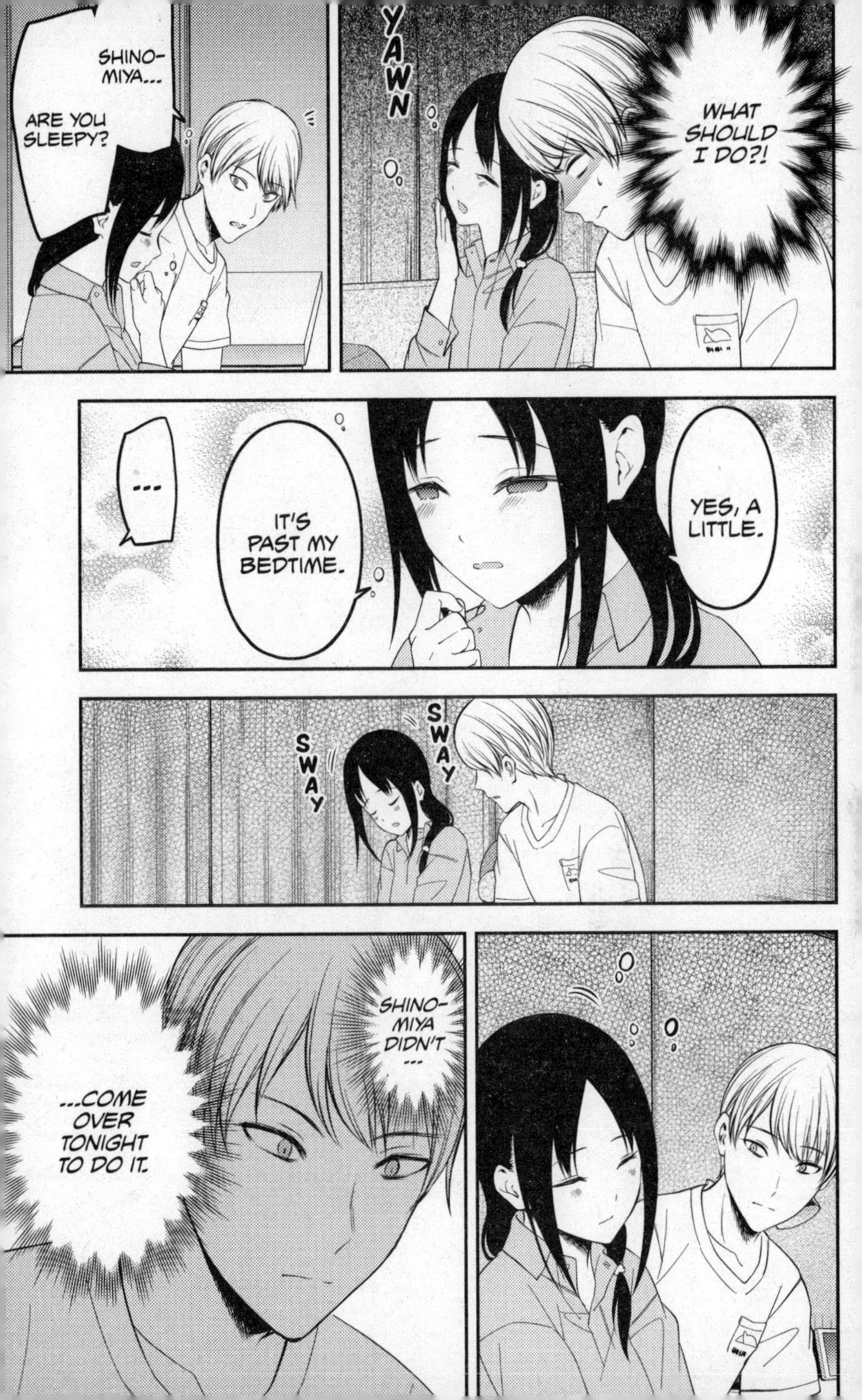
WHAT SHOULD I DO?!
YAWN
SHINO-MIYA...
ARE YOU SLEEPY?
YES, A LITTLE.
IT'S PAST MY BEDTIME.
...
SWAY
SWAY
SHINO-MIYA DIDN'T...
...COME OVER TONIGHT TO DO IT.

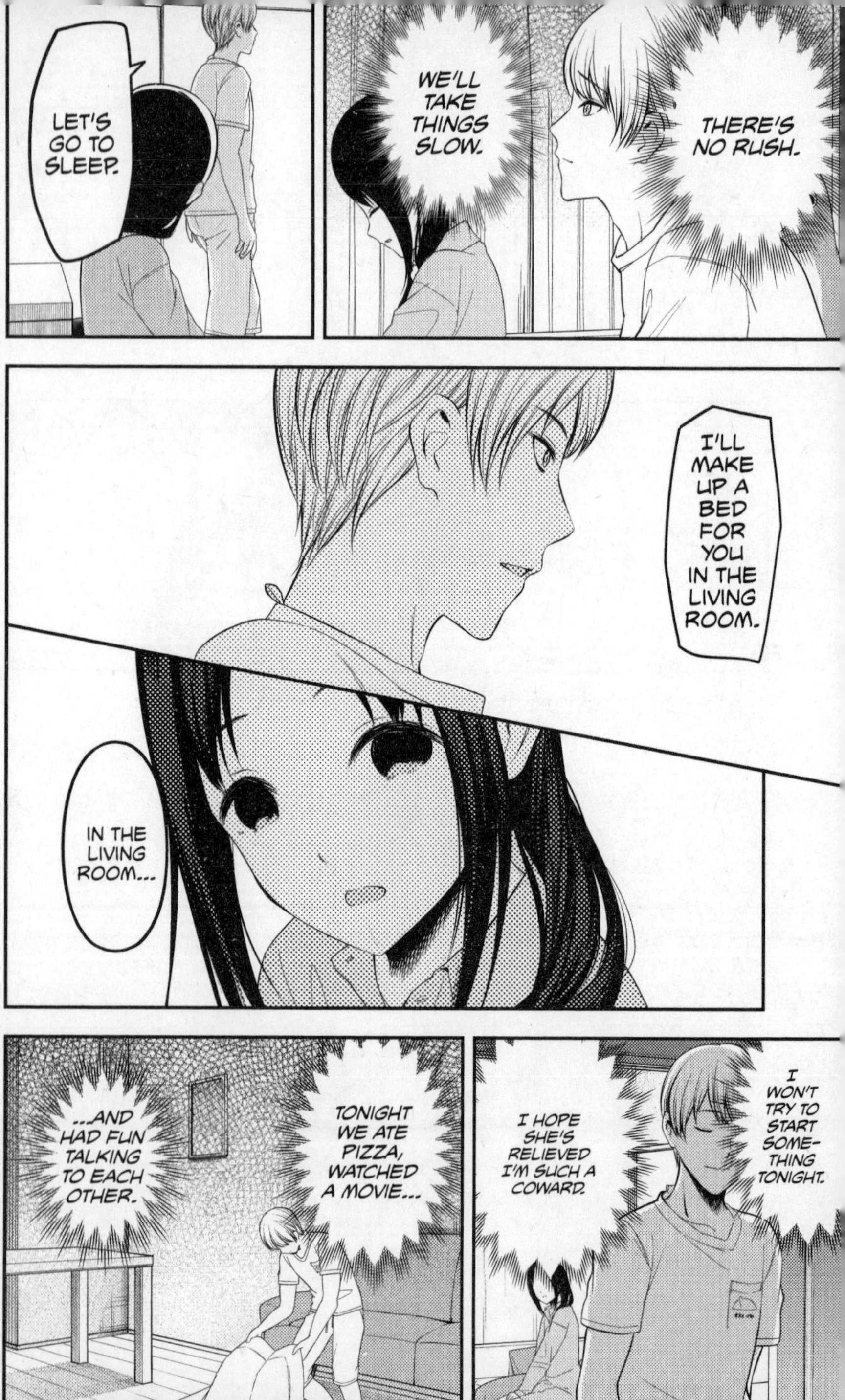
THERE'S NO RUSH.
WE'LL TAKE THINGS SLOW.
LET'S GO TO SLEEP.
I'LL MAKE UP A BED FOR YOU IN THE LIVING ROOM.
IN THE LIVING ROOM...
I WON'T TRY TO START SOME-THING TONIGHT.
I HOPE SHE'S RELIEVED I'M SUCH A COWARD.
TONIGHT WE ATE PIZZA, WATCHED A MOVIE...
...AND HAD FUN TALKING TO EACH OTHER.

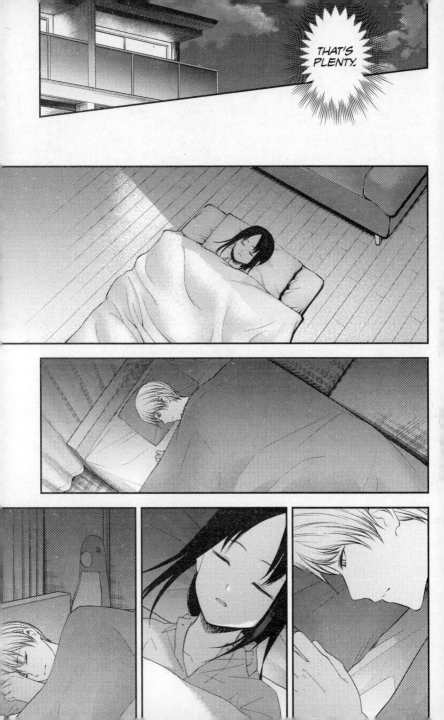

THAT'S
PLENTY.

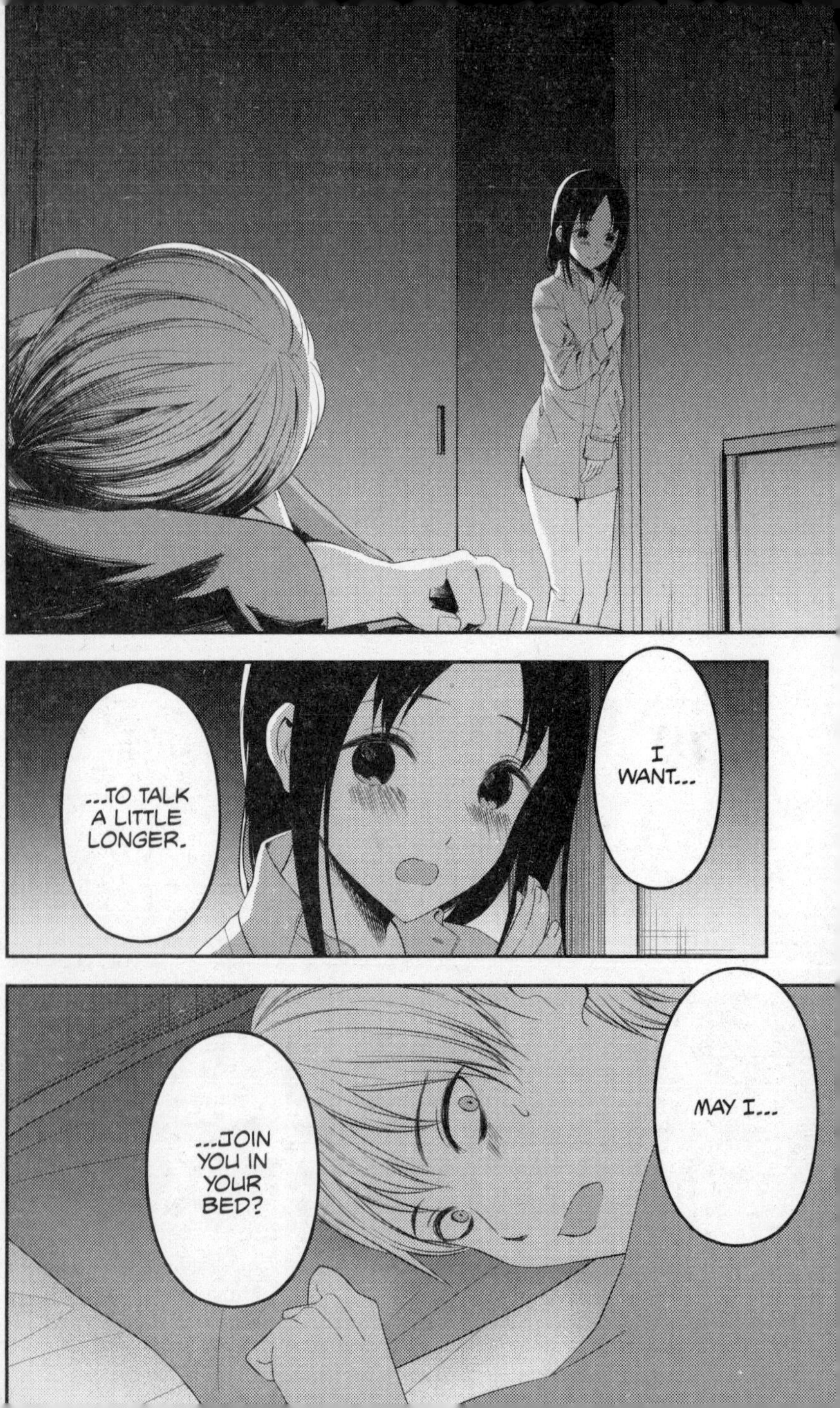
I WANT...
...TO TALK A LITTLE LONGER.
MAY I...
...JOIN YOU IN YOUR BED?

I WAS WATCHING THE SECURITY CAMS. ONLY GIGAKO AND KEI ENTERED ADMIN.
Toyomi
I WAS IN STORAGE WITH GIGAKO BEFORE SHE LEFT, SO SHE MUST HAVE JUST GOTTEN KILLED.
Makky
N-NO!
GIGAKO WAS ALREADY DEAD WHEN I ENTERED ADMIN!
...
Gigako
KEI, YOU WERE ON TOP OF THE VENT.
Chika
SO WHY DIDN'T YOU REPORT HER DEAD BODY RIGHT AWAY?
Mom
YOU KILLED HER, KEI.
Moeha
MOM AND DAD ARE INNOCENT! WE WERE IN THE REACTOR PERFORMING AN EMERGENCY TASK.
Dad

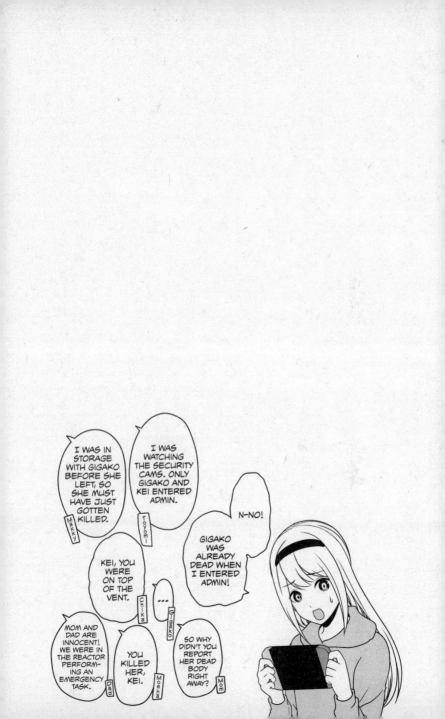

KAGUYA-SAMA

LOVE IS WAR

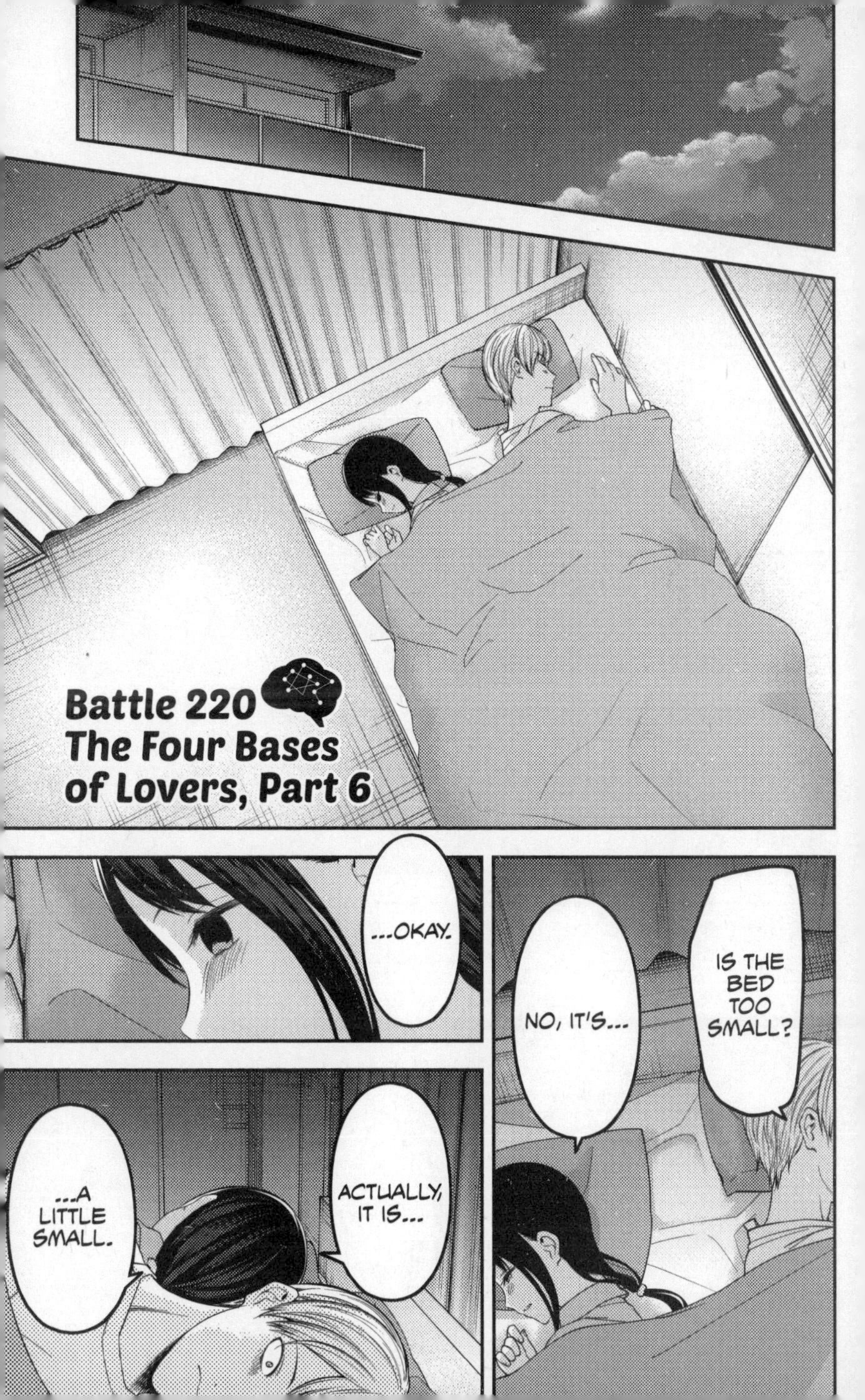
Battle 220
The Four Bases of Lovers, Part 6
IS THE BED TOO SMALL?
NO, IT'S...
...OKAY.
ACTUALLY, IT IS...
...A LITTLE SMALL.

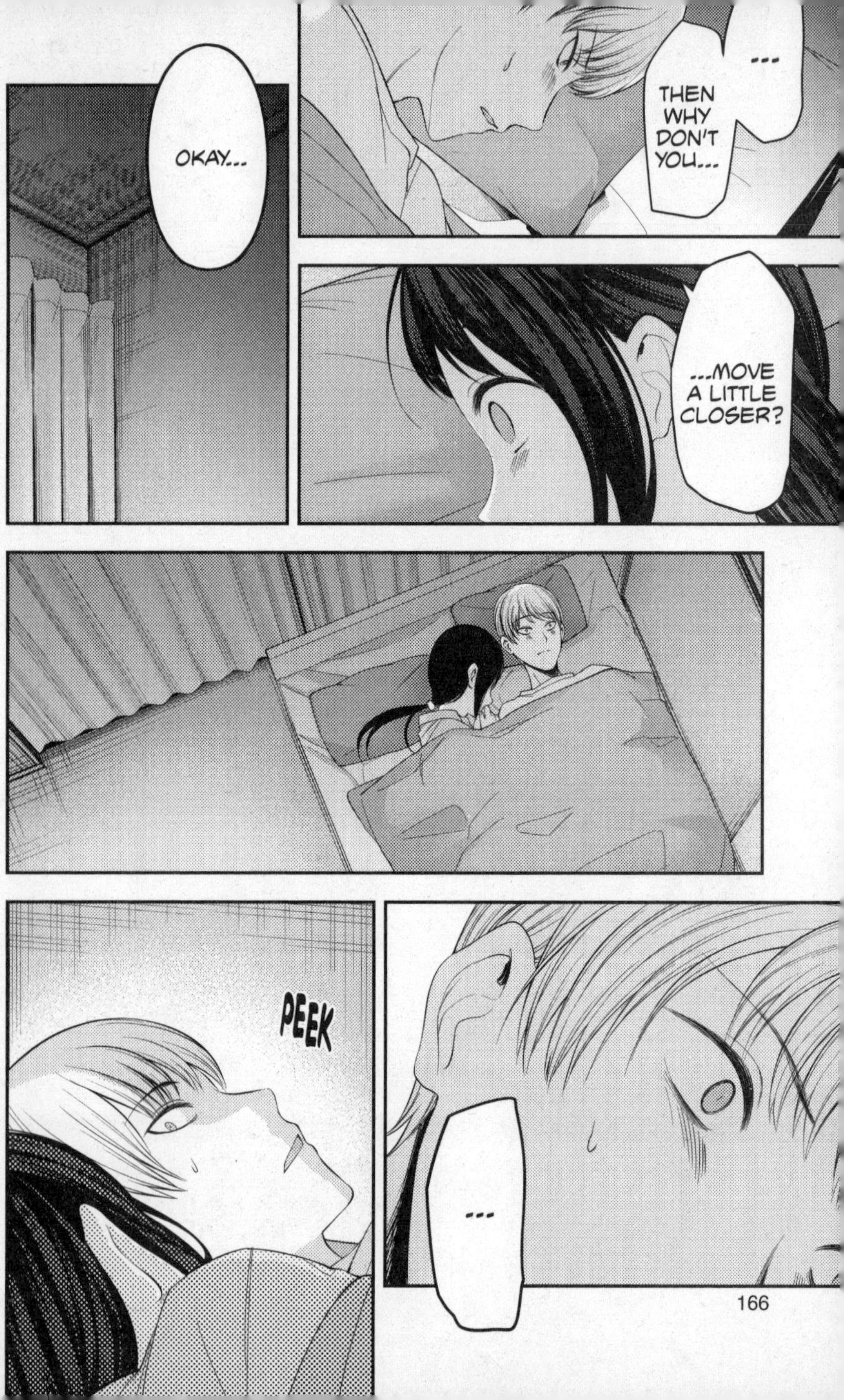
...
THEN WHY DON'T YOU...
...MOVE A LITTLE CLOSER?
OKAY...
...
PEEK

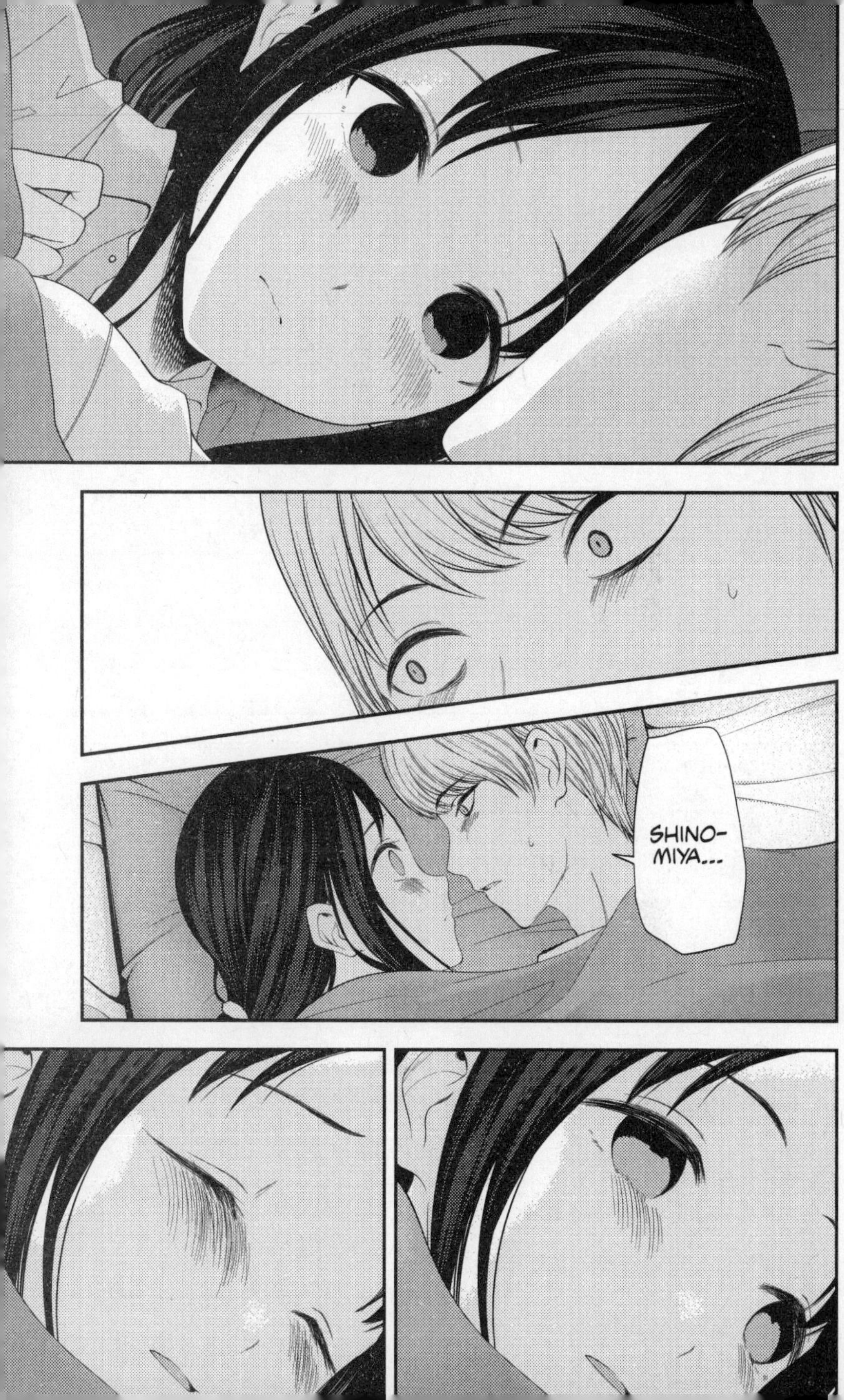
SHINO-
MIYA...

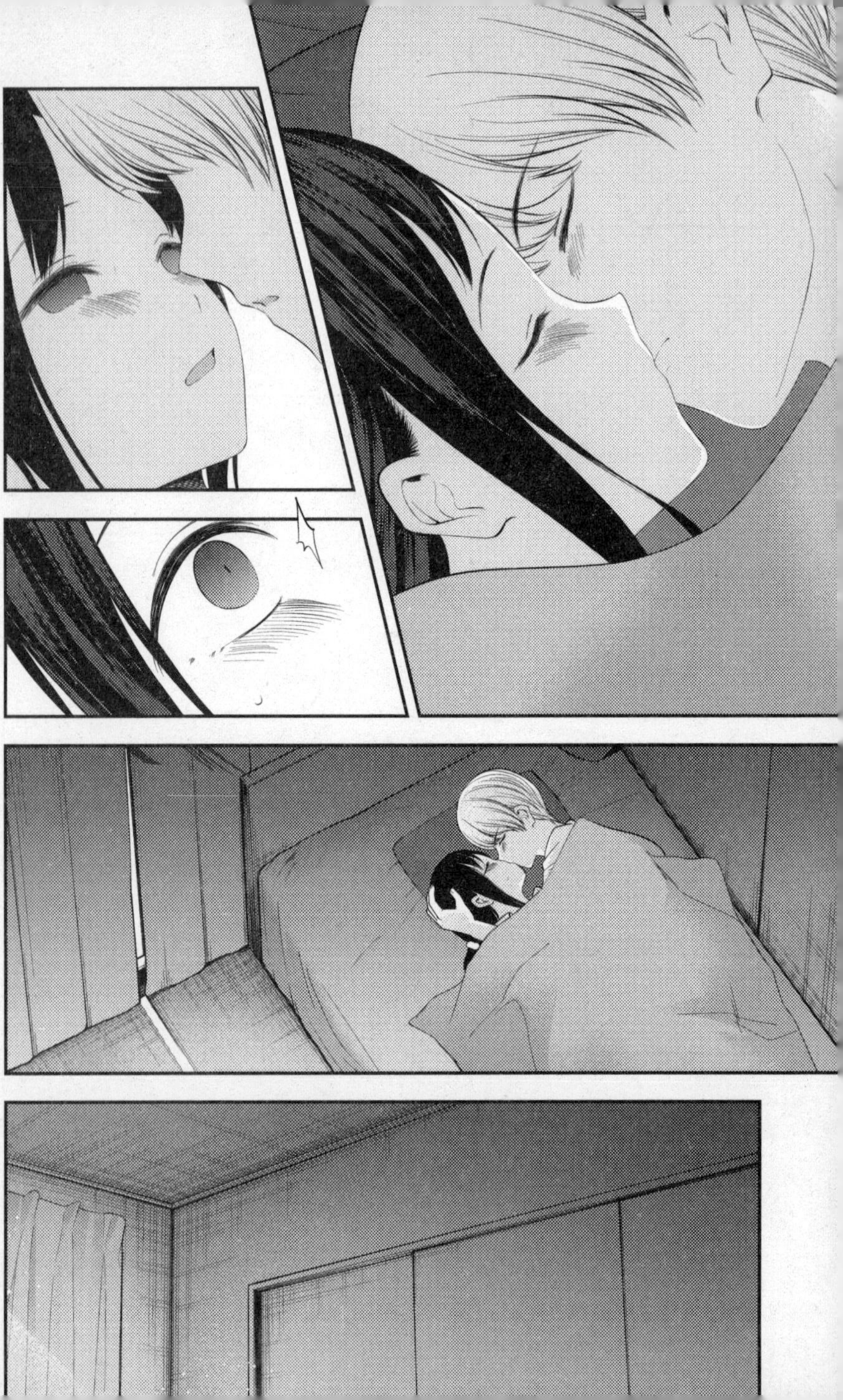

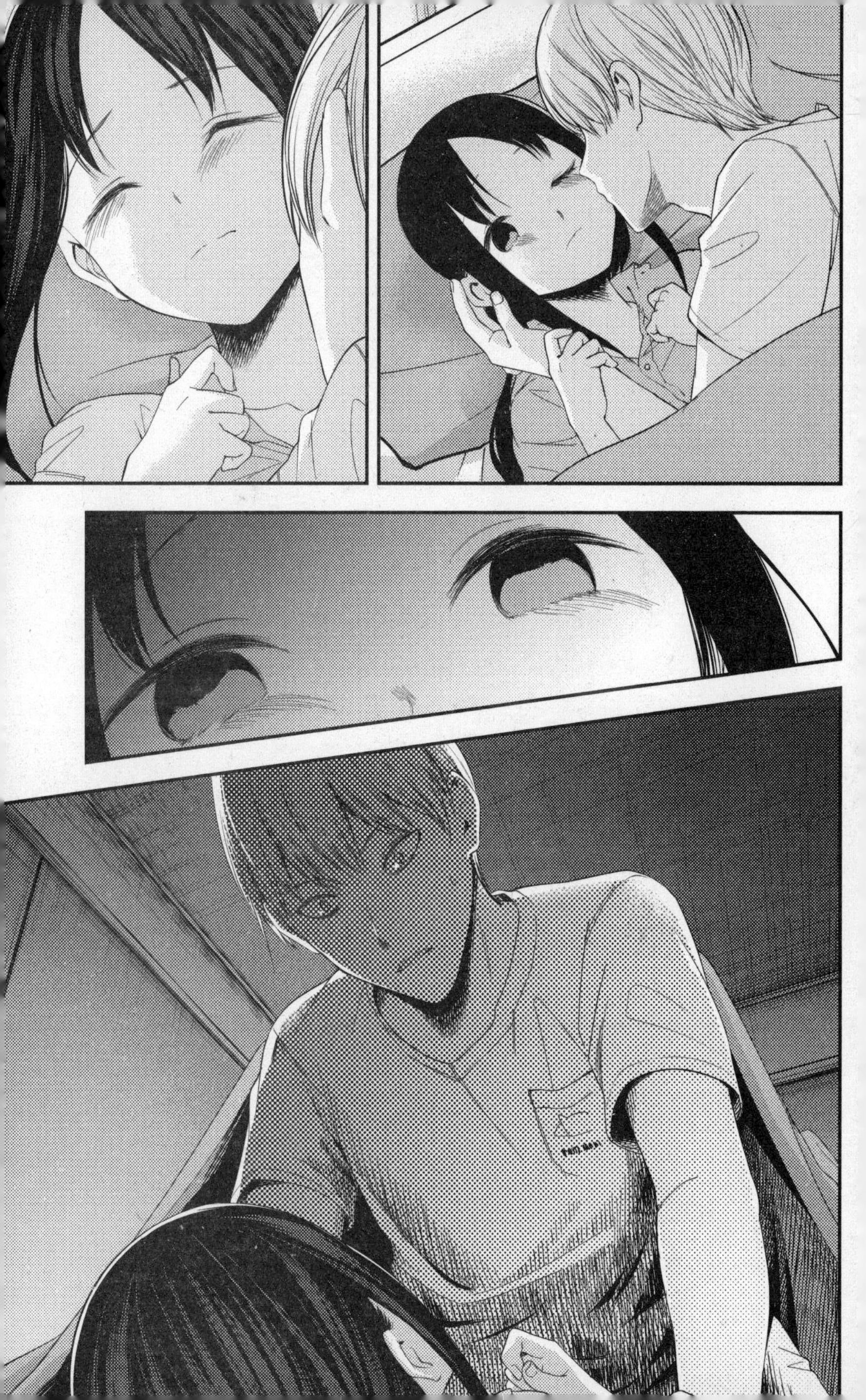

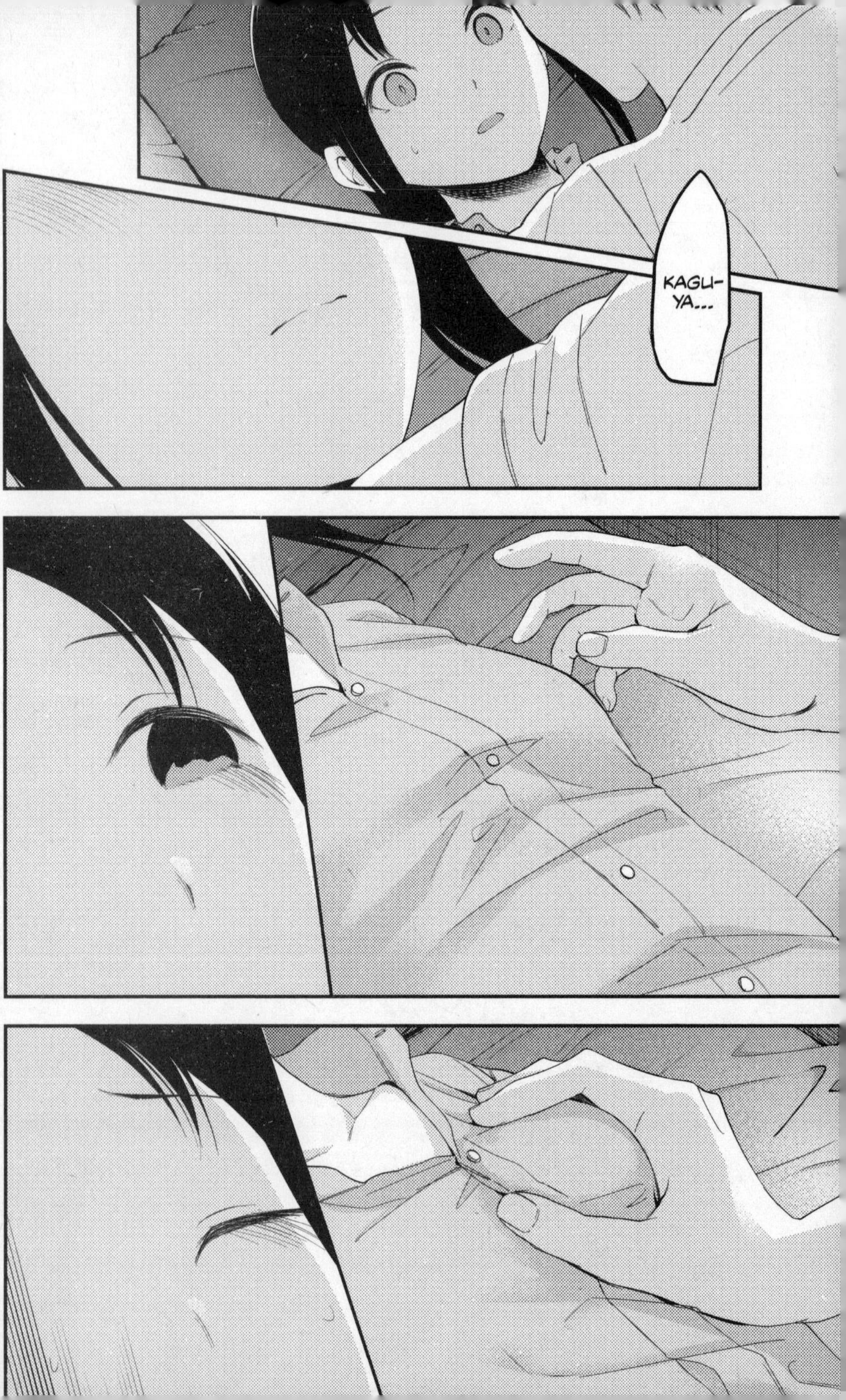
KAGU-
YA...

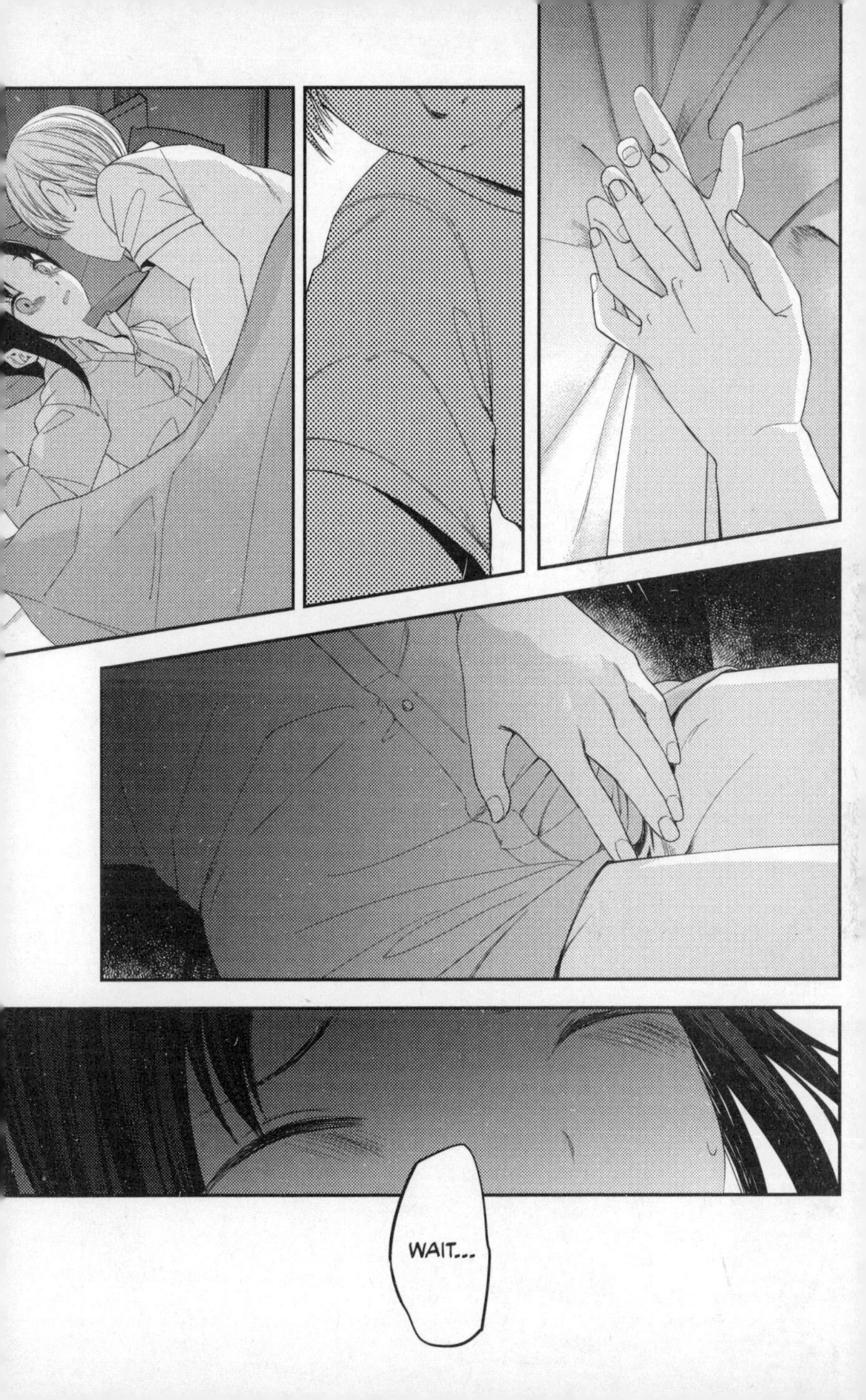
WAIT...

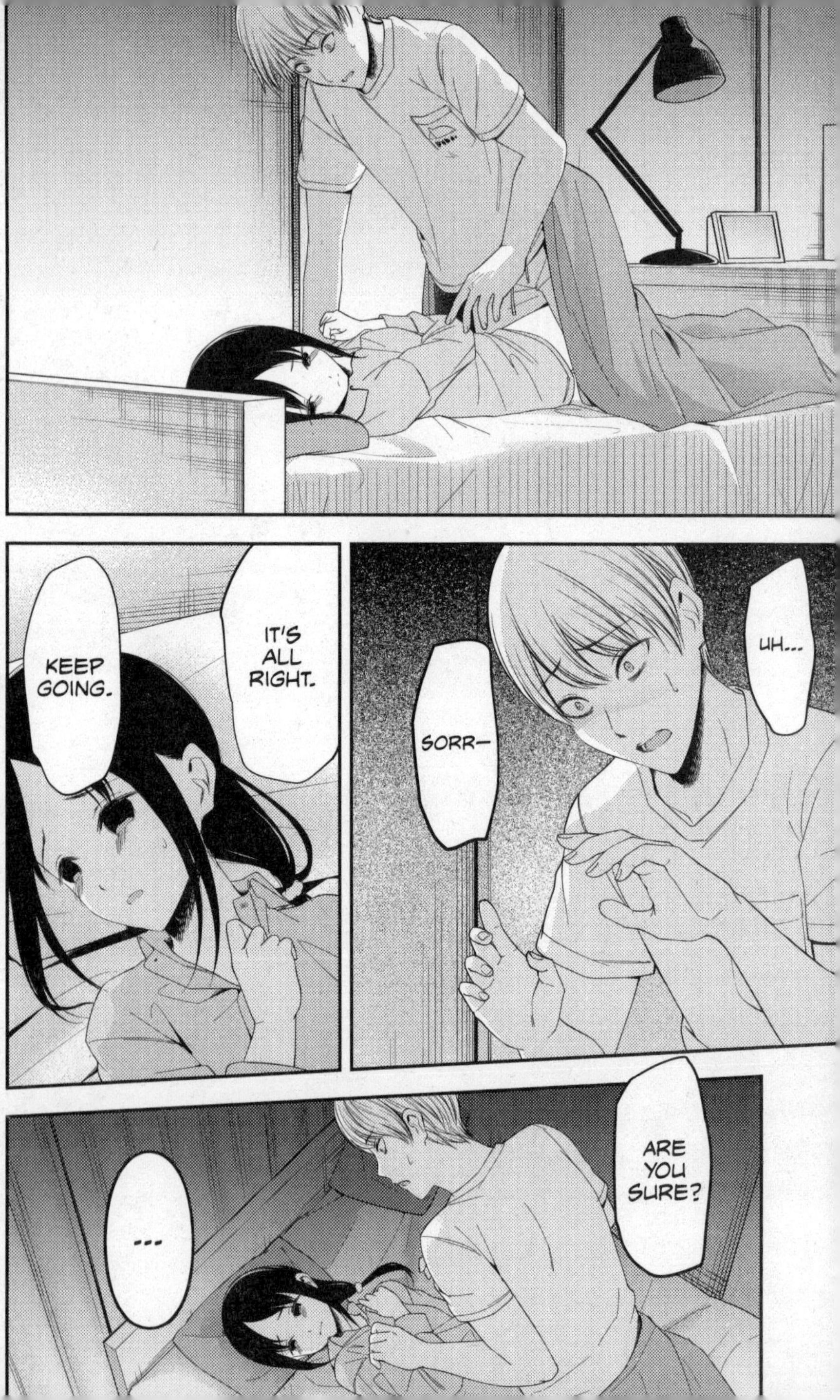
UH...
SORR—
IT'S ALL RIGHT.
KEEP GOING.
ARE YOU SURE?
...

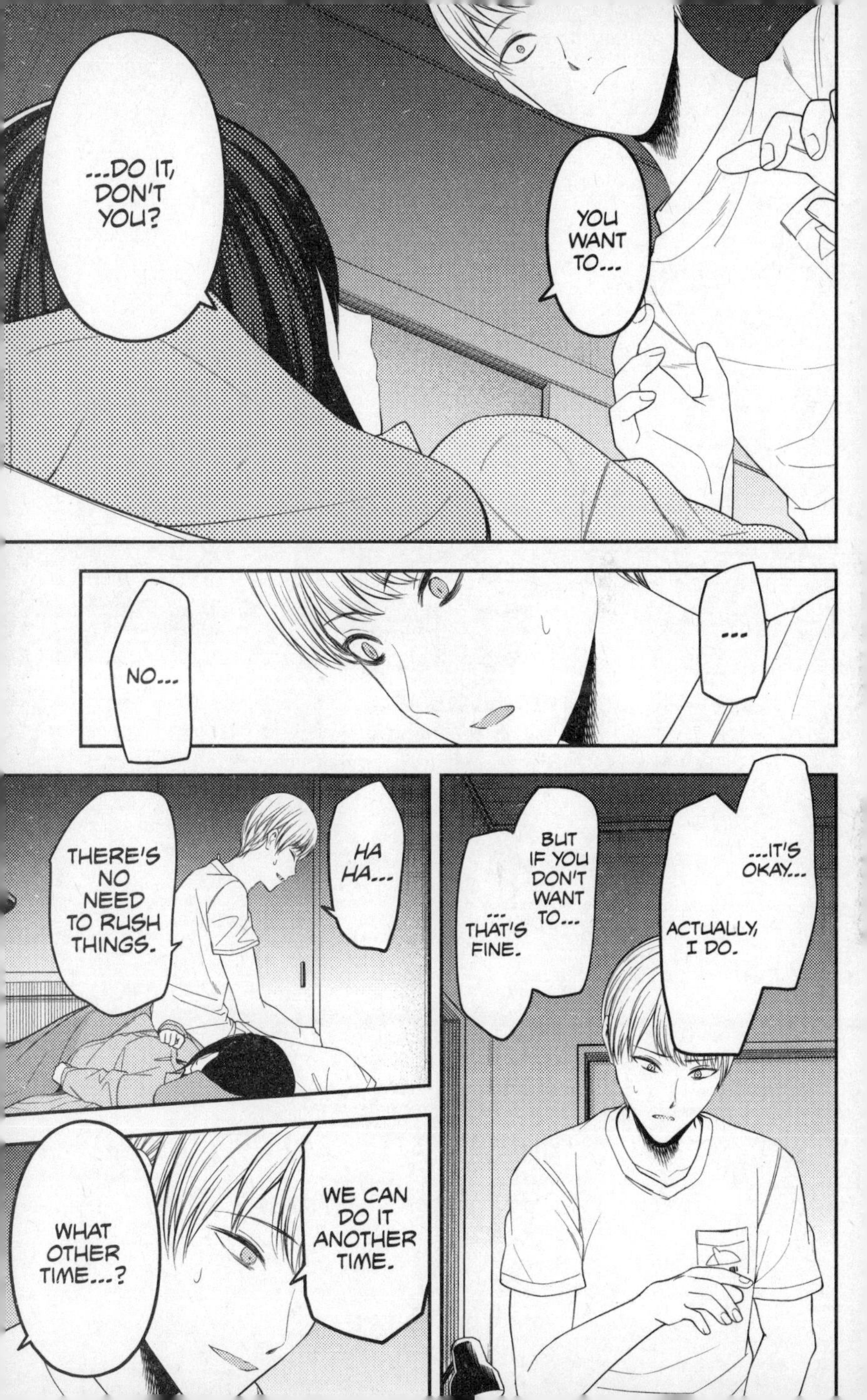
YOU WANT TO...
...DO IT, DON'T YOU?
...
NO...
...IT'S OKAY... ACTUALLY, I DO.
BUT IF YOU DON'T WANT TO... ...THAT'S FINE.
HA HA...
THERE'S NO NEED TO RUSH THINGS.
WE CAN DO IT ANOTHER TIME.
WHAT OTHER TIME...?

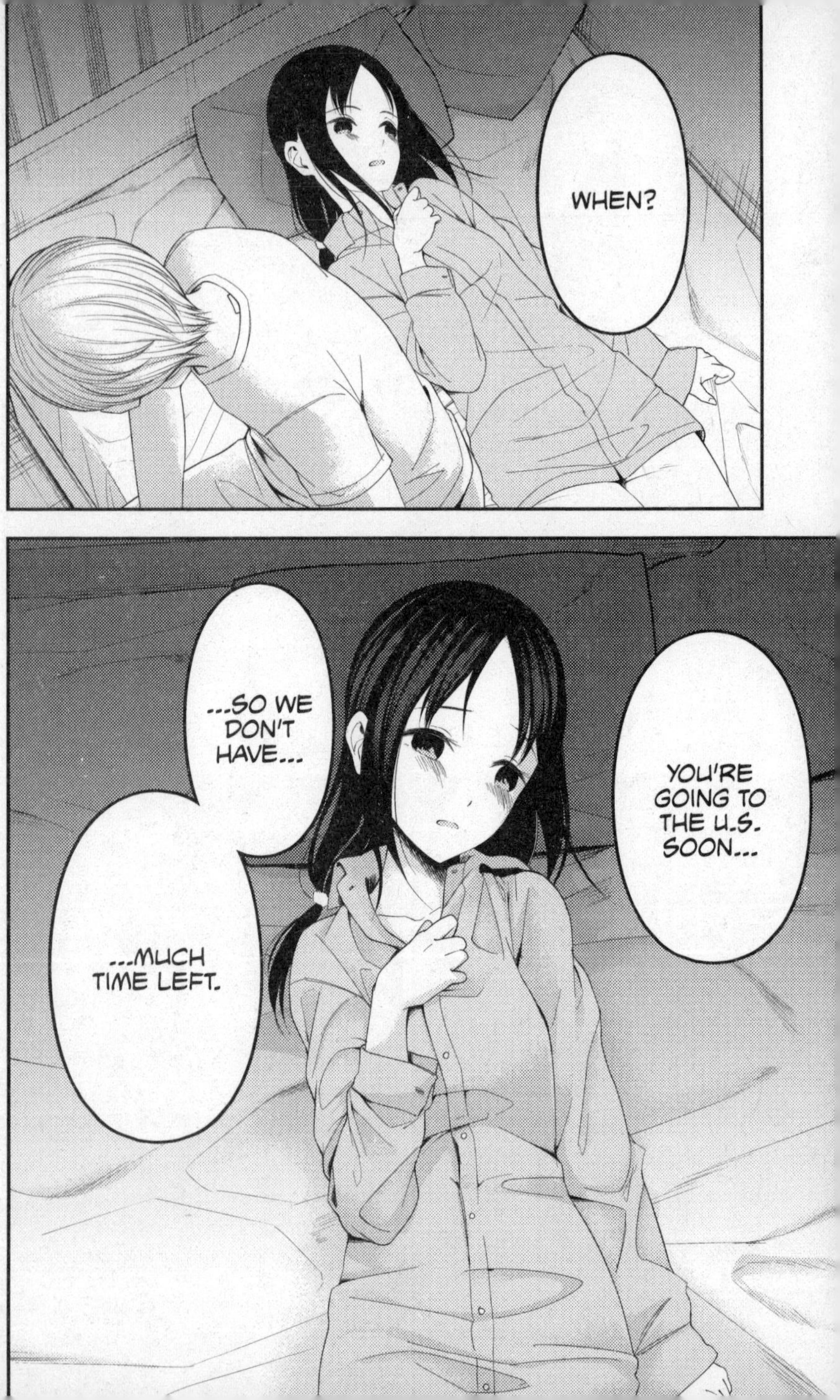
WHEN?
YOU'RE GOING TO THE U.S. SOON...
...SO WE DON'T HAVE...
...MUCH TIME LEFT.

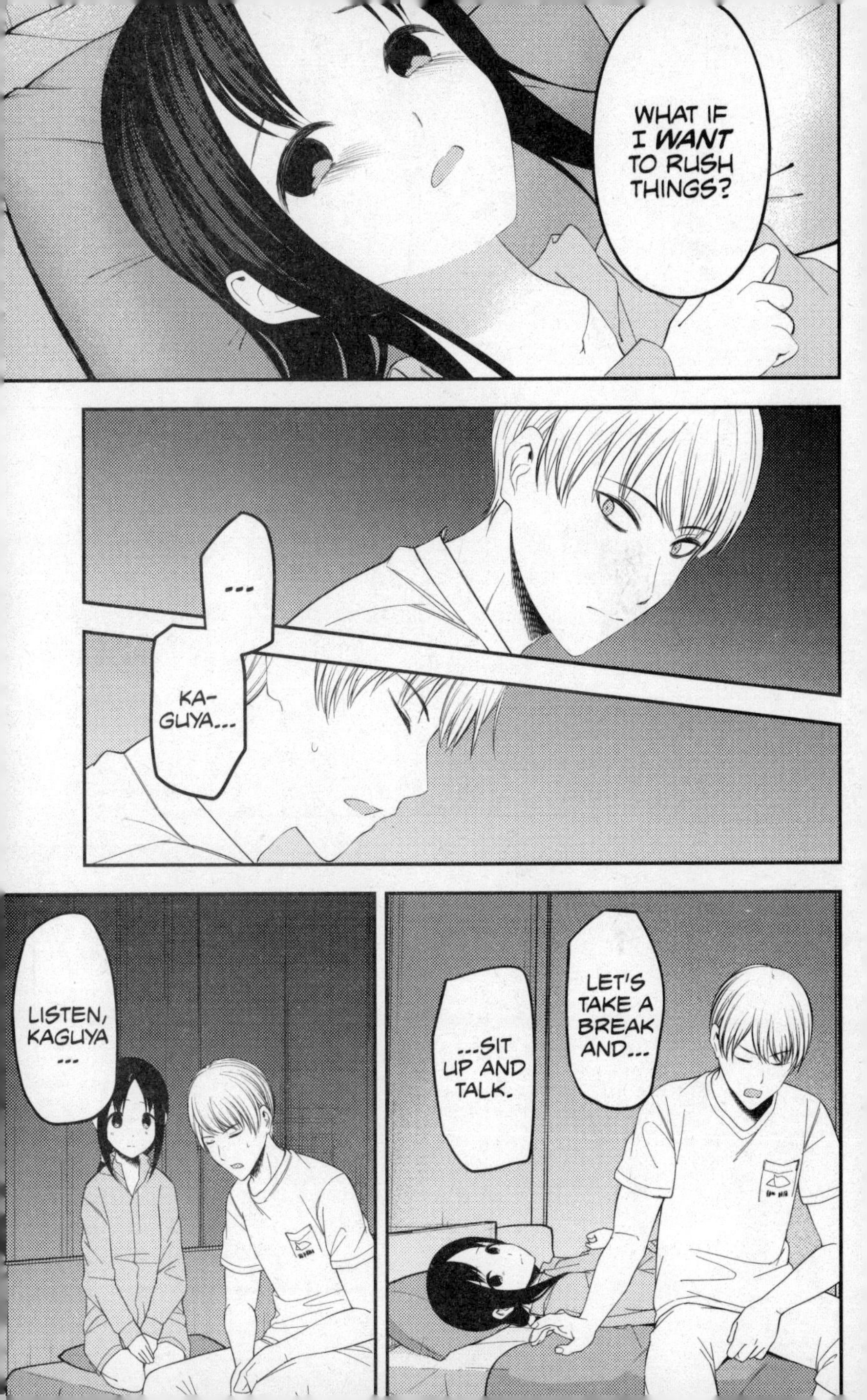
WHAT IF I ***WANT*** TO RUSH THINGS?
...
KA-GUYA...
LET'S TAKE A BREAK AND...
...SIT UP AND TALK.
LISTEN, KAGUYA...

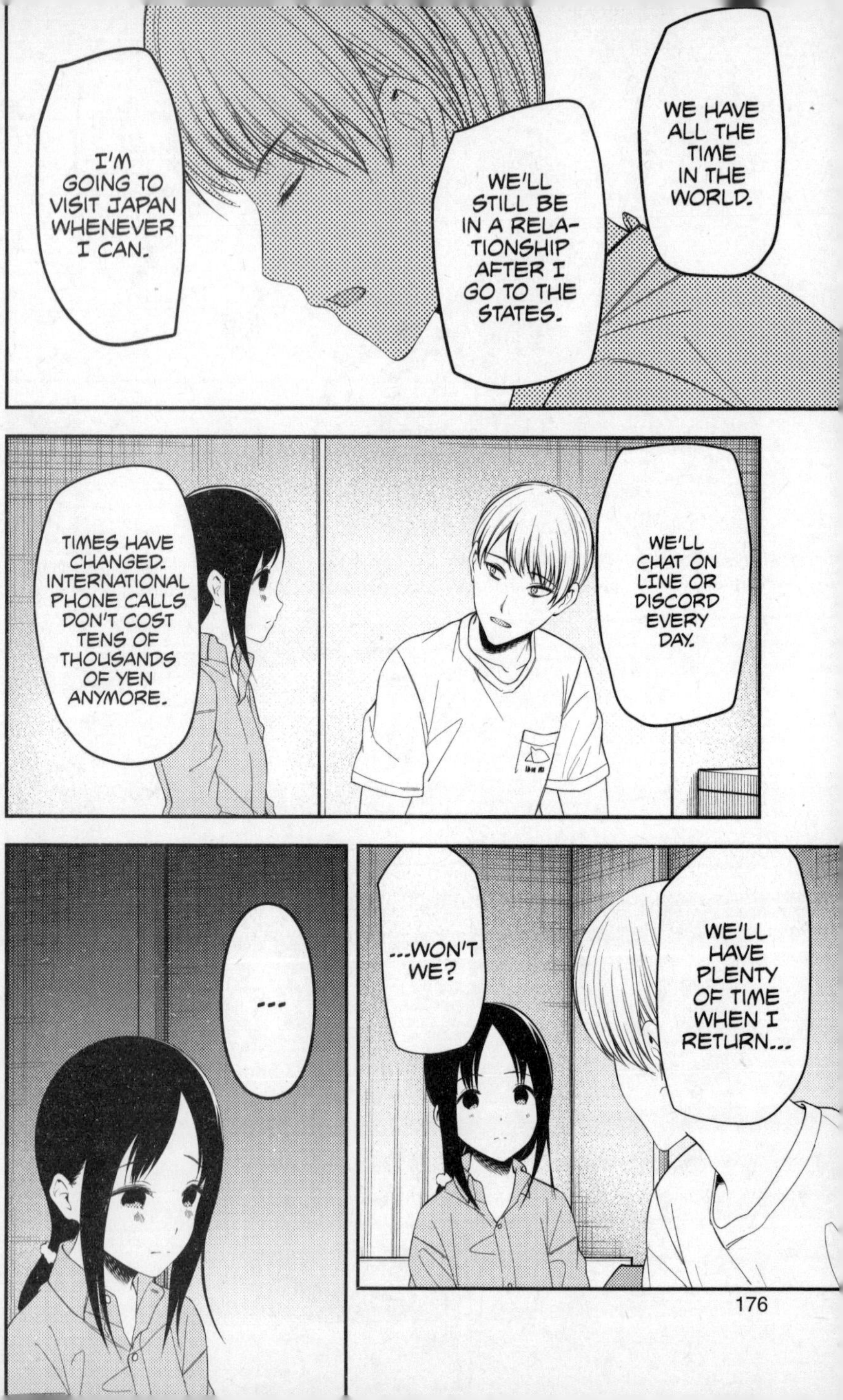
WE HAVE ALL THE TIME IN THE WORLD.
WE'LL STILL BE IN A RELA-TIONSHIP AFTER I GO TO THE STATES.
I'M GOING TO VISIT JAPAN WHENEVER I CAN.
WE'LL CHAT ON LINE OR DISCORD EVERY DAY.
TIMES HAVE CHANGED. INTERNATIONAL PHONE CALLS DON'T COST TENS OF THOUSANDS OF YEN ANYMORE.
WE'LL HAVE PLENTY OF TIME WHEN I RETURN...
...WON'T WE?
...

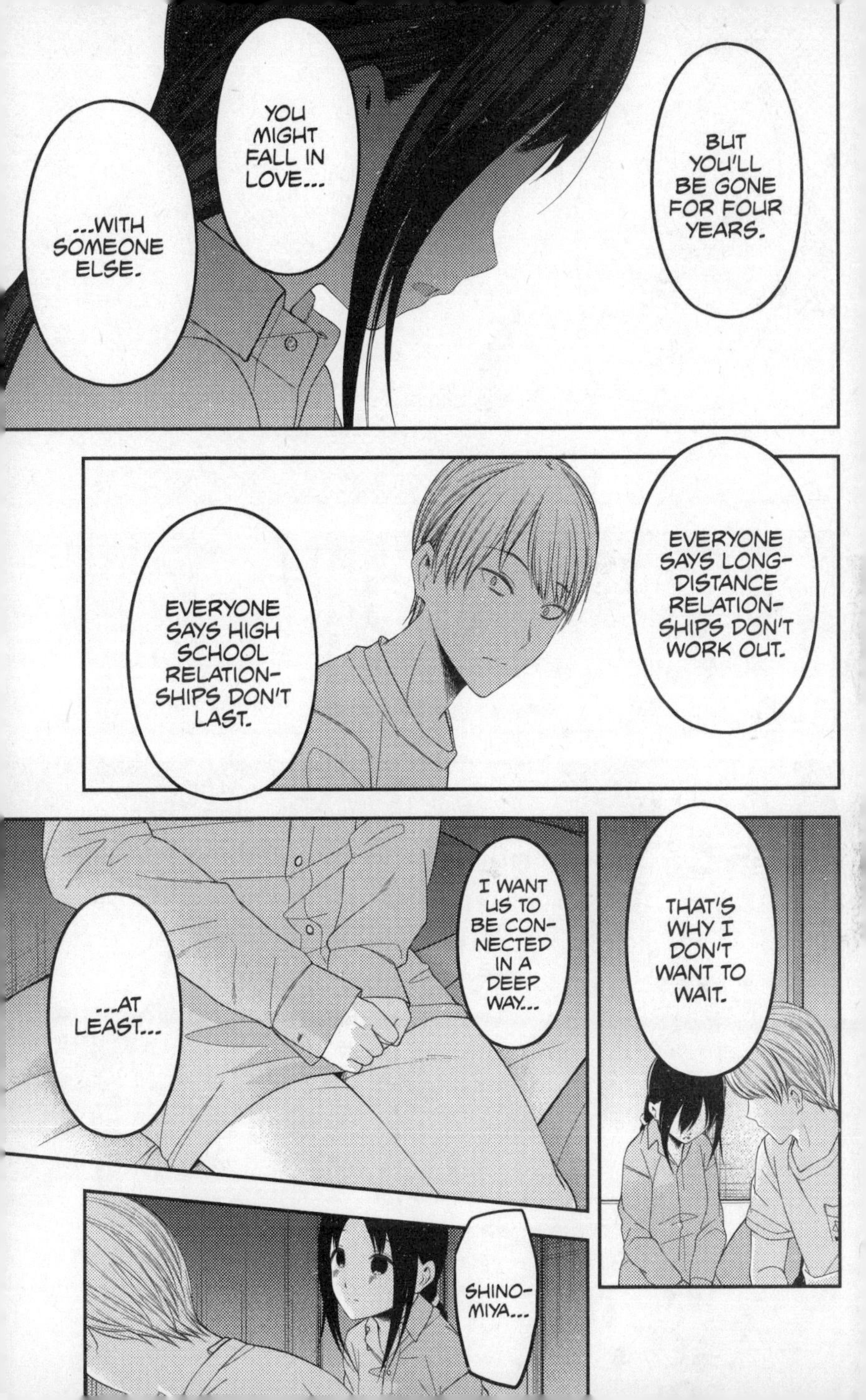
BUT YOU'LL BE GONE FOR FOUR YEARS.
YOU MIGHT FALL IN LOVE...
...WITH SOMEONE ELSE.
EVERYONE SAYS LONG-DISTANCE RELATION-SHIPS DON'T WORK OUT.
EVERYONE SAYS HIGH SCHOOL RELATION-SHIPS DON'T LAST.
THAT'S WHY I DON'T WANT TO WAIT.
I WANT US TO BE CON-NECTED IN A DEEP WAY...
...AT LEAST...
SHINO-MIYA...

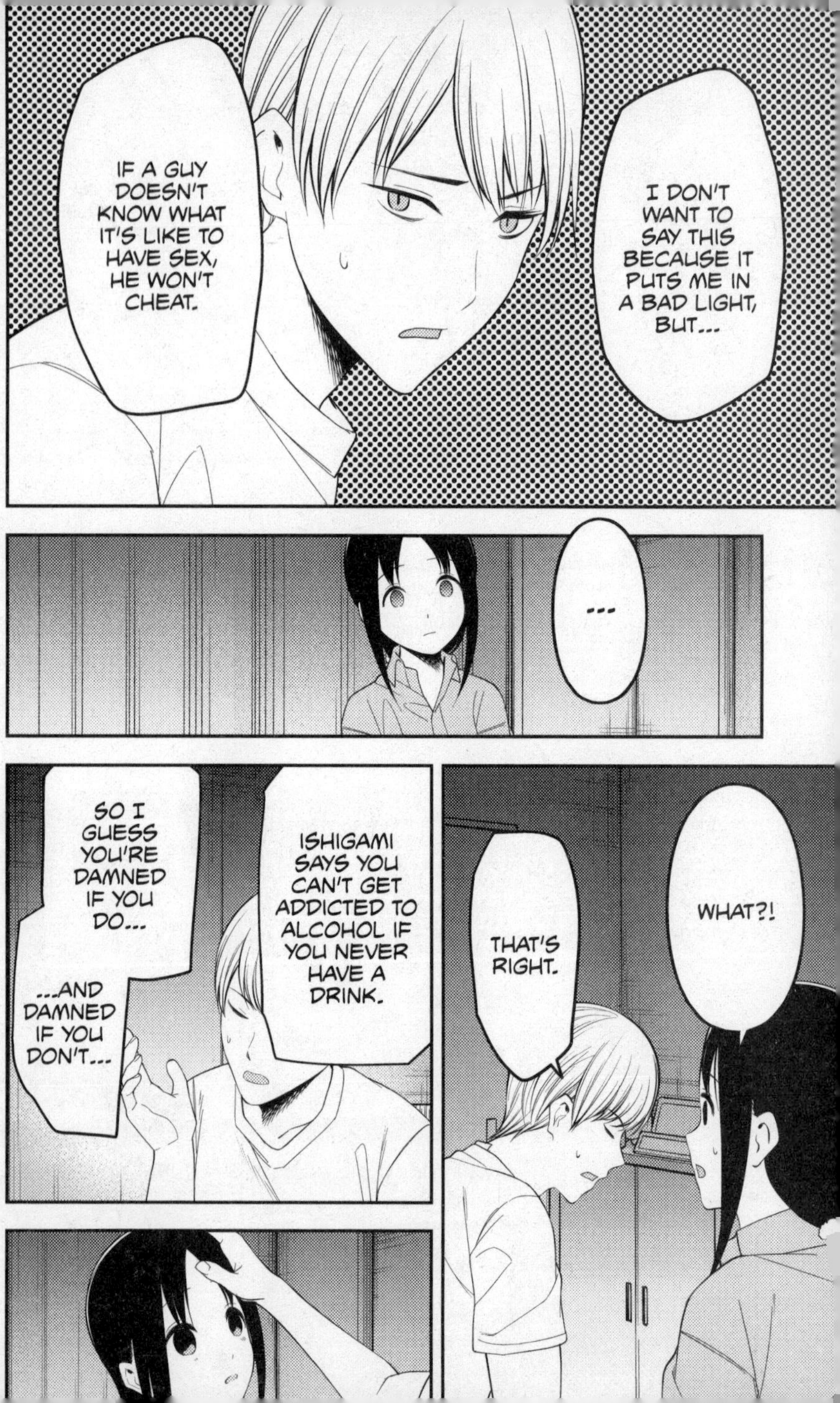
I DON'T WANT TO SAY THIS BECAUSE IT PUTS ME IN A BAD LIGHT, BUT...
IF A GUY DOESN'T KNOW WHAT IT'S LIKE TO HAVE SEX, HE WON'T CHEAT.
...
WHAT?!
THAT'S RIGHT.
ISHIGAMI SAYS YOU CAN'T GET ADDICTED TO ALCOHOL IF YOU NEVER HAVE A DRINK.
SO I GUESS YOU'RE DAMNED IF YOU DO...
...AND DAMNED IF YOU DON'T...

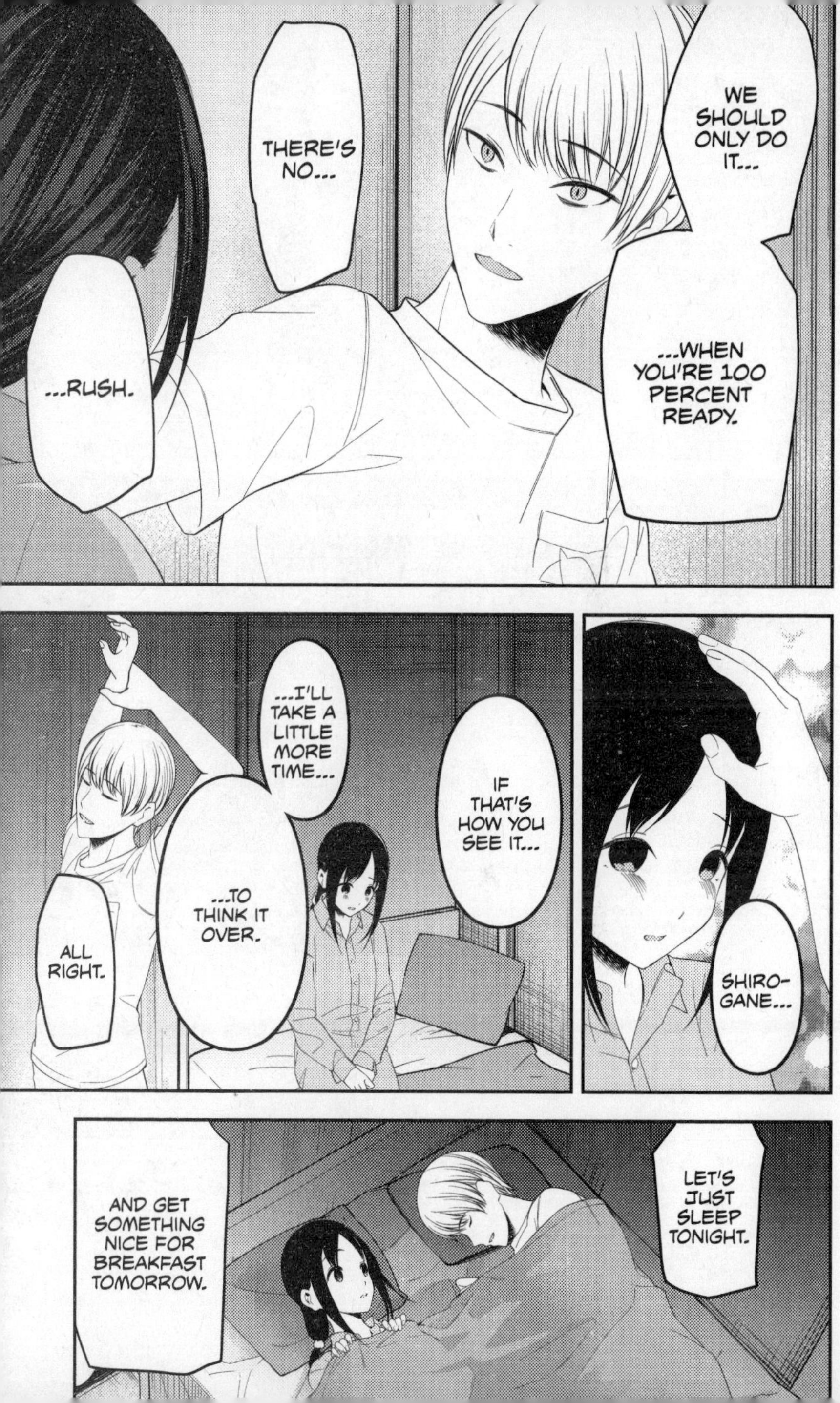
WE SHOULD ONLY DO IT...
...WHEN YOU'RE 100 PERCENT READY.
THERE'S NO...
...RUSH.
SHIRO-GANE...
IF THAT'S HOW YOU SEE IT...
...I'LL TAKE A LITTLE MORE TIME...
...TO THINK IT OVER.
ALL RIGHT.
LET'S JUST SLEEP TONIGHT.
AND GET SOMETHING NICE FOR BREAKFAST TOMORROW.

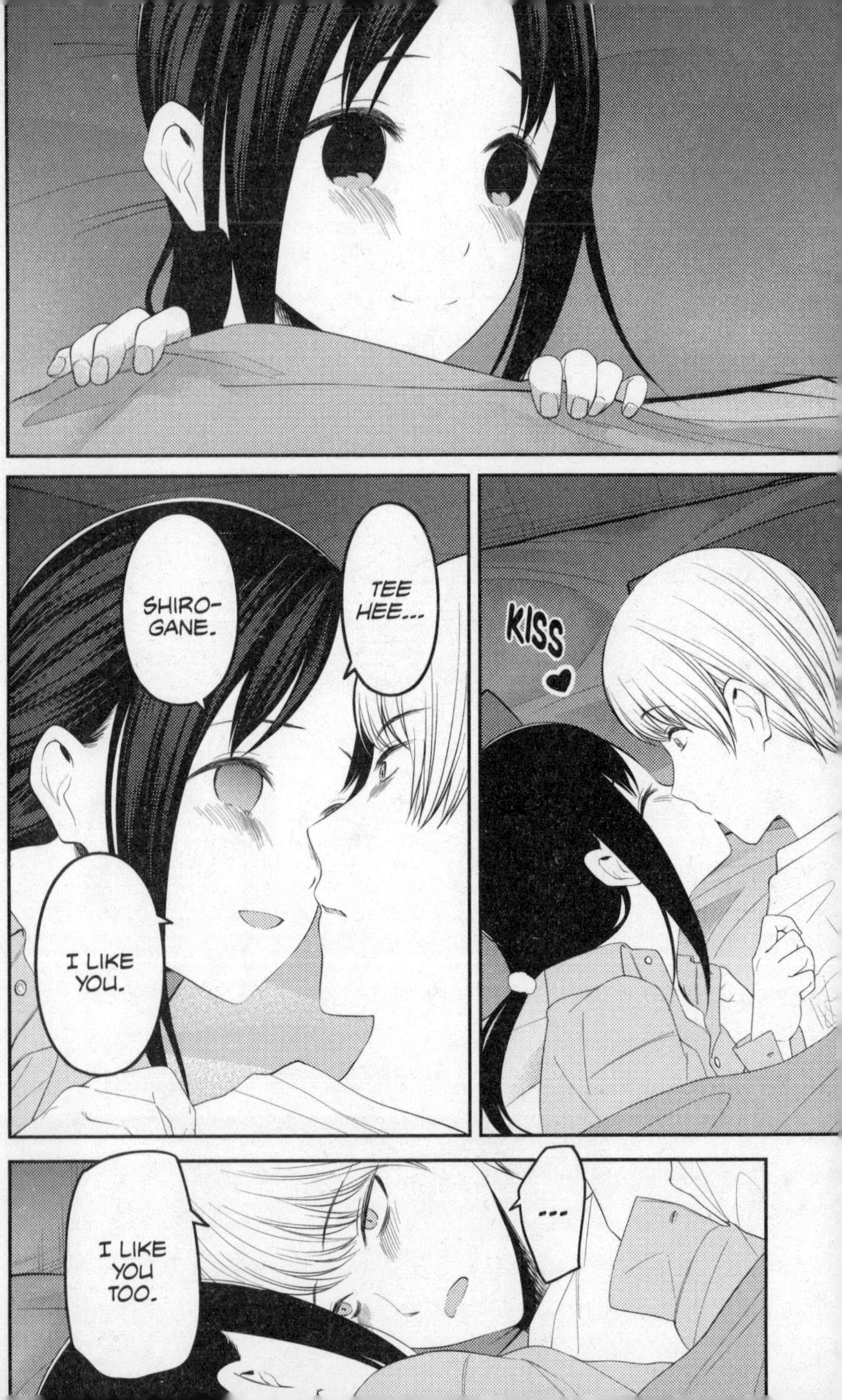
KISS
♥
TEE HEE...
SHIRO-GANE.
I LIKE YOU.
...
I LIKE YOU TOO.

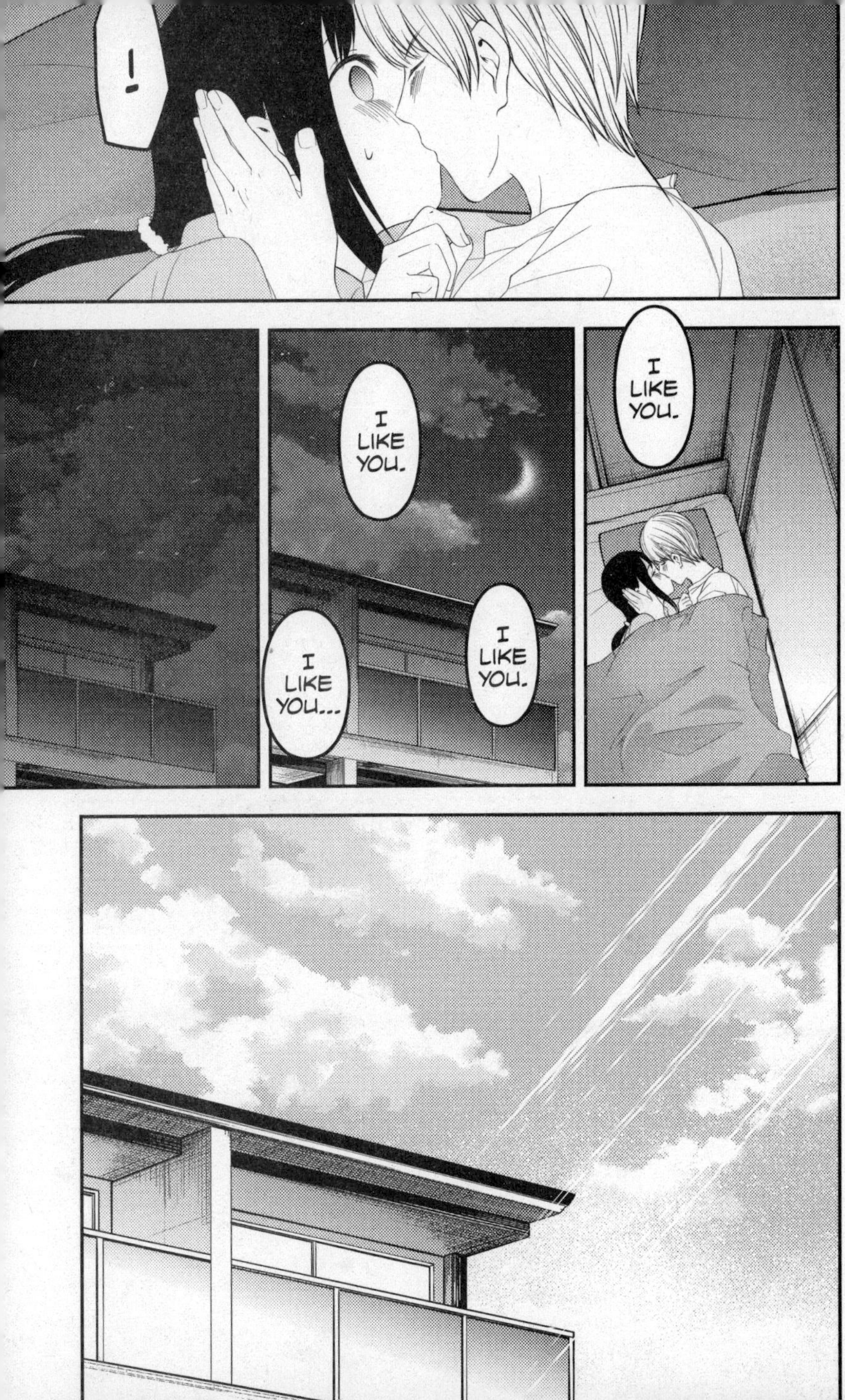
!
I LIKE YOU.
I LIKE YOU.
I LIKE YOU.
I LIKE YOU...

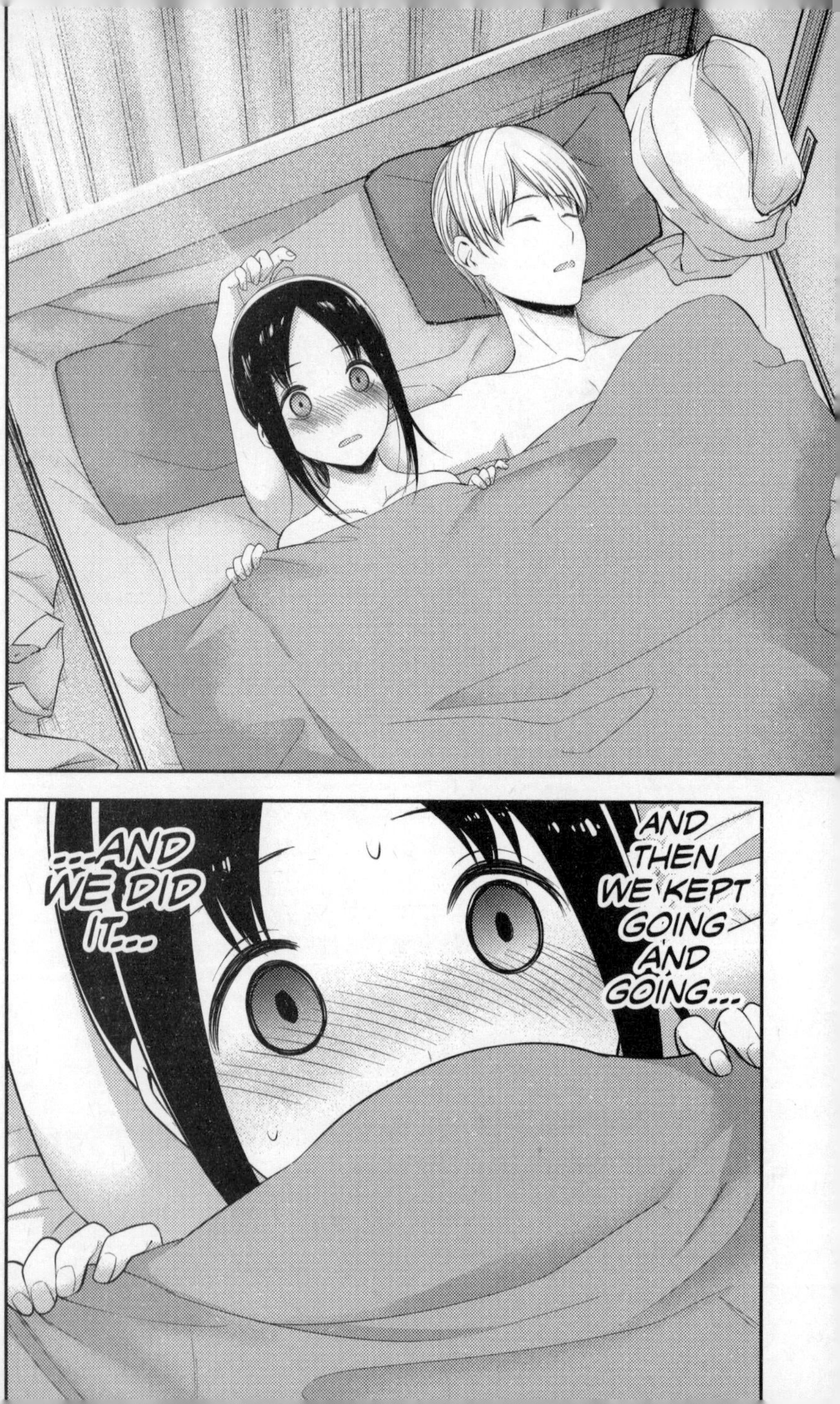
AND THEN WE KEPT GOING AND GOING...
...AND WE DID IT...

KAGUYA-SAMA
LOVE IS WAR

Battle 221 Kaguya Wants to Talk

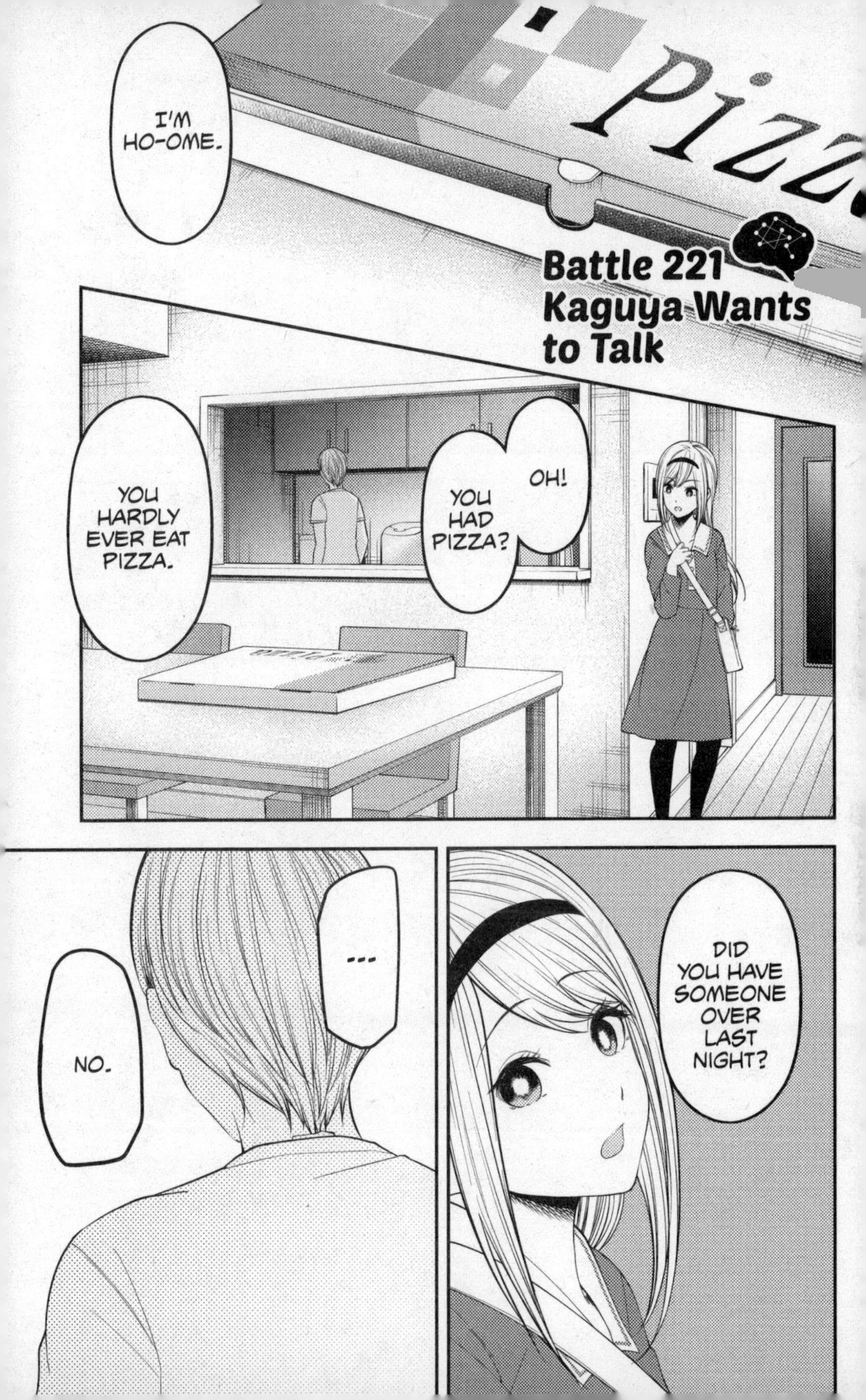
I'M HO-OME.
OH!
YOU HAD PIZZA?
YOU HARDLY EVER EAT PIZZA.
DID YOU HAVE SOMEONE OVER LAST NIGHT?
...
NO.

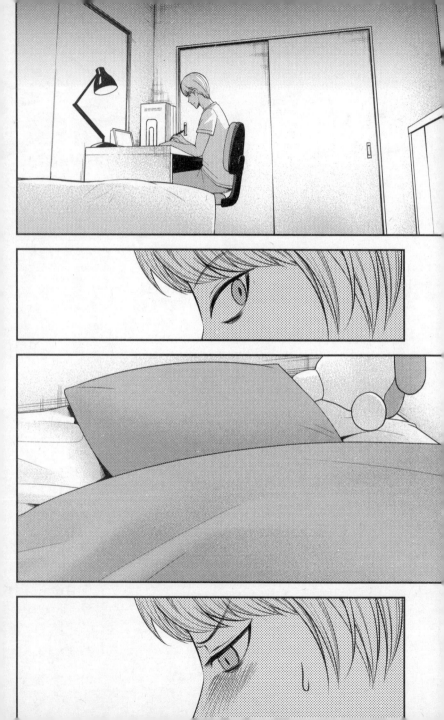

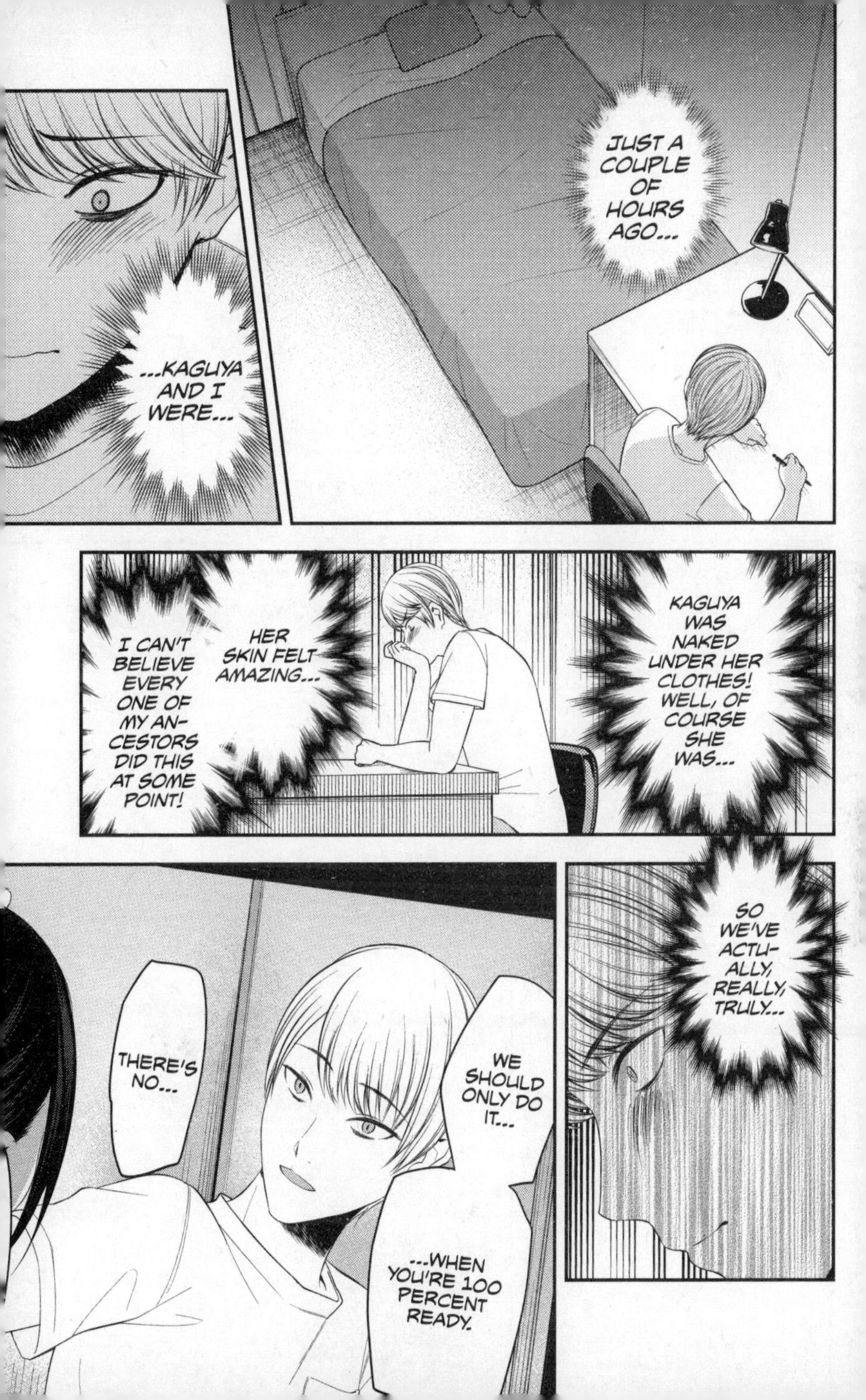
JUST A COUPLE OF HOURS AGO...
...KAGUYA AND I WERE...
KAGUYA WAS NAKED UNDER HER CLOTHES! WELL, OF COURSE SHE WAS...
HER SKIN FELT AMAZING...
I CAN'T BELIEVE EVERY ONE OF MY AN-CESTORS DID THIS AT SOME POINT!
SO WE'VE ACTU-ALLY, REALLY, TRULY...
THERE'S NO...
WE SHOULD ONLY DO IT...
...WHEN YOU'RE 100 PERCENT READY.

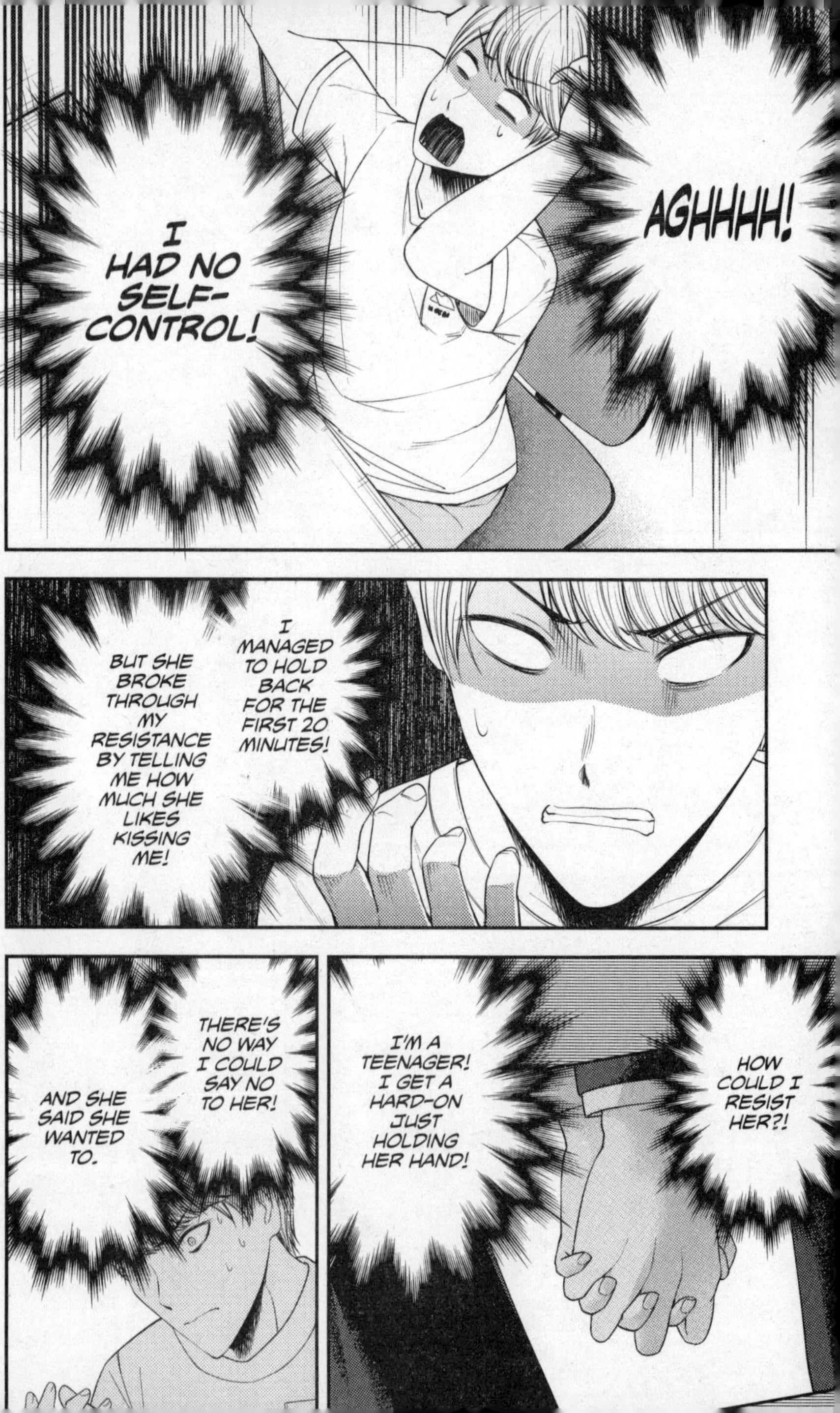
AGHHHH!
I HAD NO SELF-CONTROL!
I MANAGED TO HOLD BACK FOR THE FIRST 20 MINUTES!
BUT SHE BROKE THROUGH MY RESISTANCE BY TELLING ME HOW MUCH SHE LIKES KISSING ME!
HOW COULD I RESIST HER?!
I'M A TEENAGER! I GET A HARD-ON JUST HOLDING HER HAND!
THERE'S NO WAY I COULD SAY NO TO HER!
AND SHE SAID SHE WANTED TO.

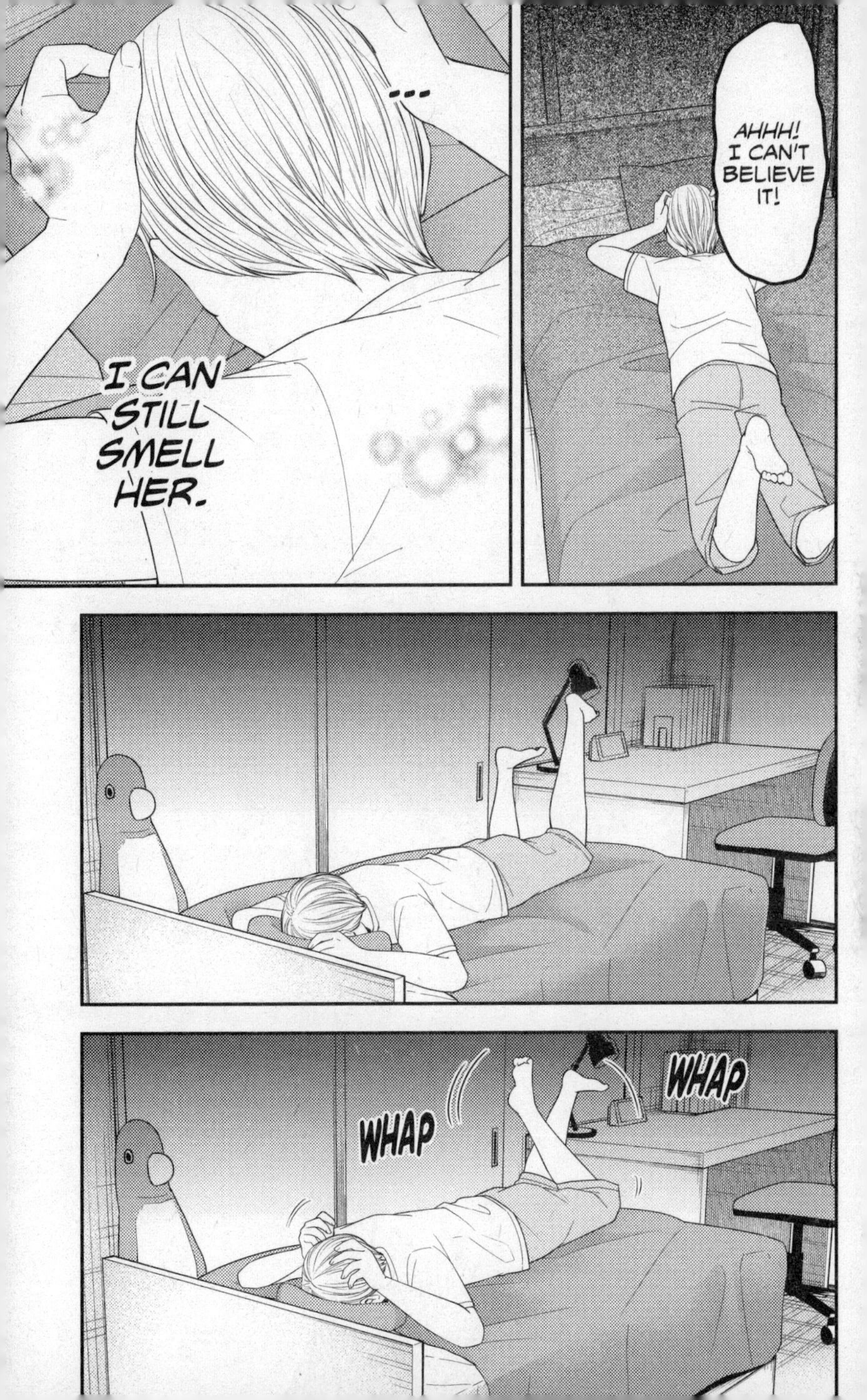
AHHH! I CAN'T BELIEVE IT!
...
I CAN STILL SMELL HER.
WHAP
WHAP

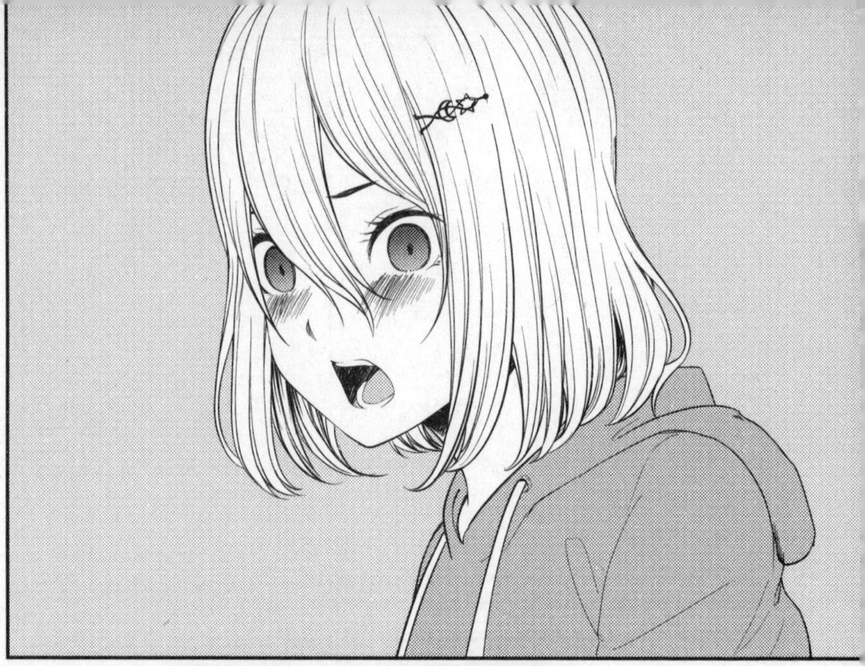
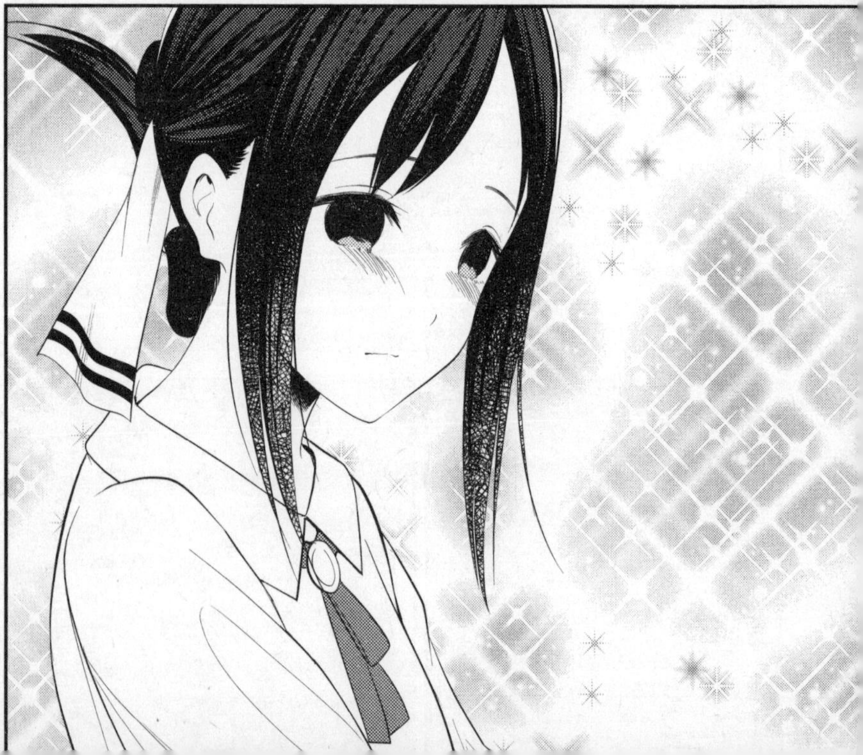

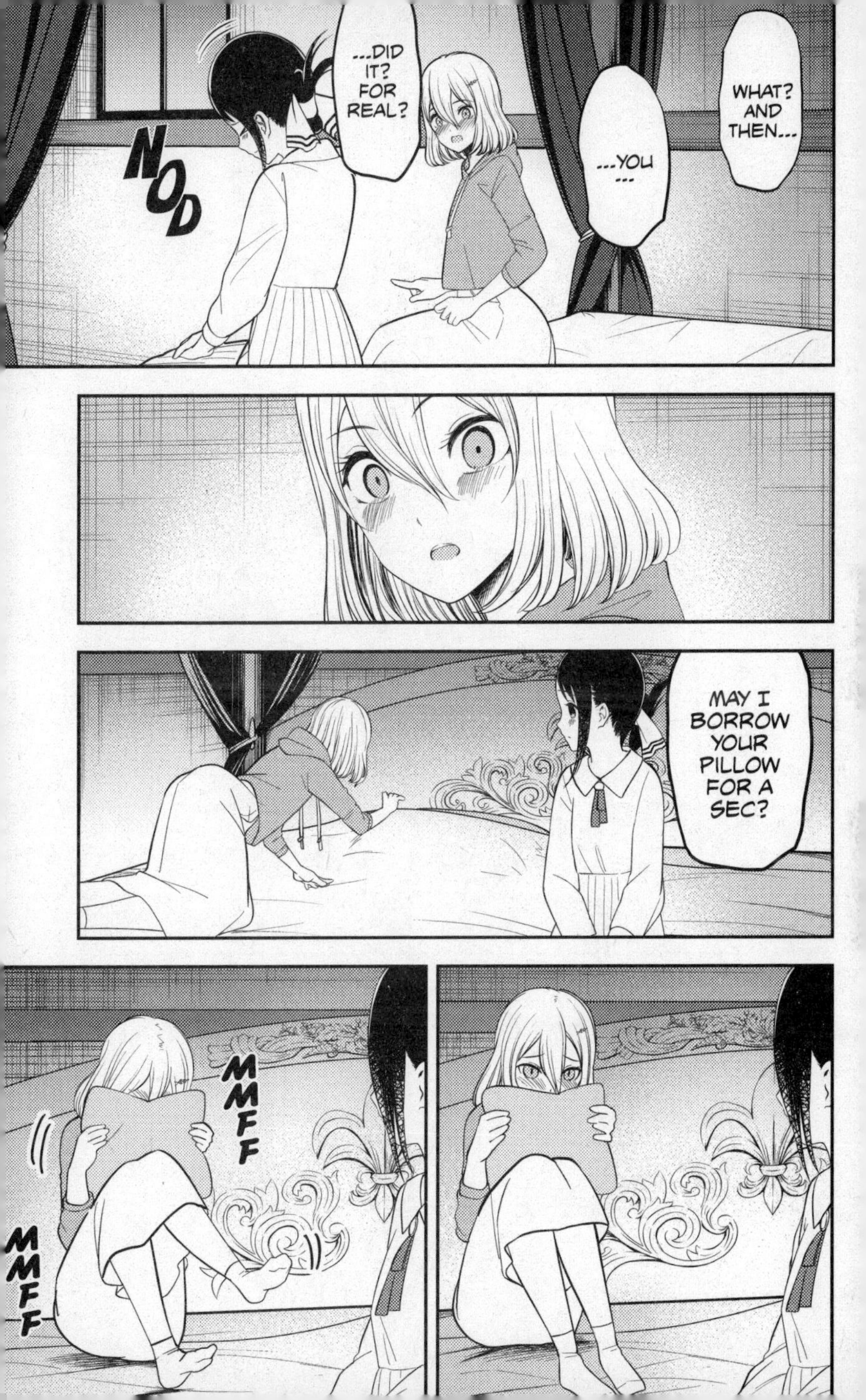
WHAT? AND THEN...
...YOU ...
...DID IT? FOR REAL?
NOD
MAY I BORROW YOUR PILLOW FOR A SEC?
MMFF
MMFF

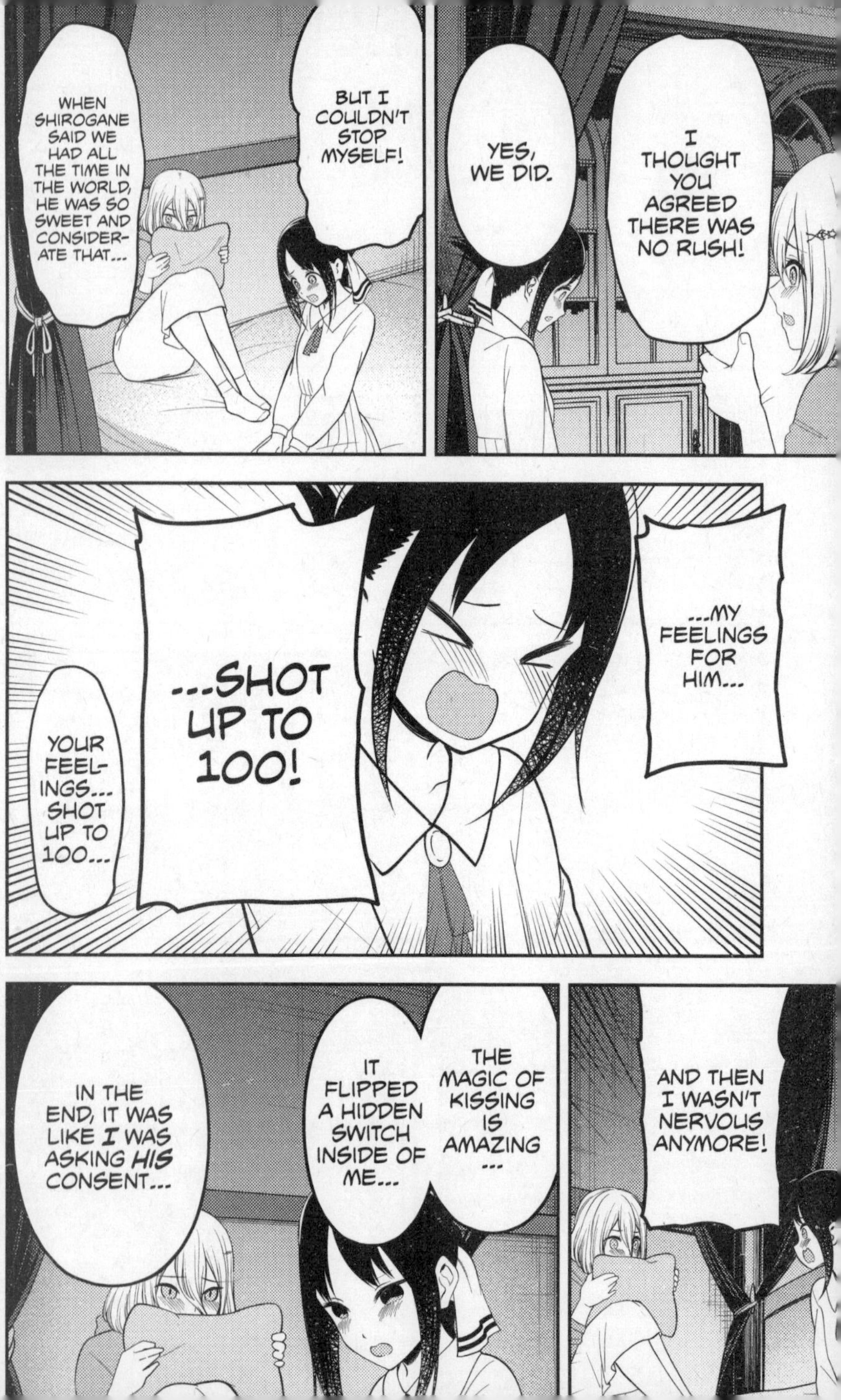
I THOUGHT YOU AGREED THERE WAS NO RUSH!
YES, WE DID.
BUT I COULDN'T STOP MYSELF!
WHEN SHIROGANE SAID WE HAD ALL THE TIME IN THE WORLD, HE WAS SO SWEET AND CONSIDER-ATE THAT...
...MY FEELINGS FOR HIM...
...SHOT UP TO 100!
YOUR FEEL-INGS... SHOT UP TO 100...
AND THEN I WASN'T NERVOUS ANYMORE!
THE MAGIC OF KISSING IS AMAZING...
IT FLIPPED A HIDDEN SWITCH INSIDE OF ME...
IN THE END, IT WAS LIKE I WAS ASKING HIS CONSENT...

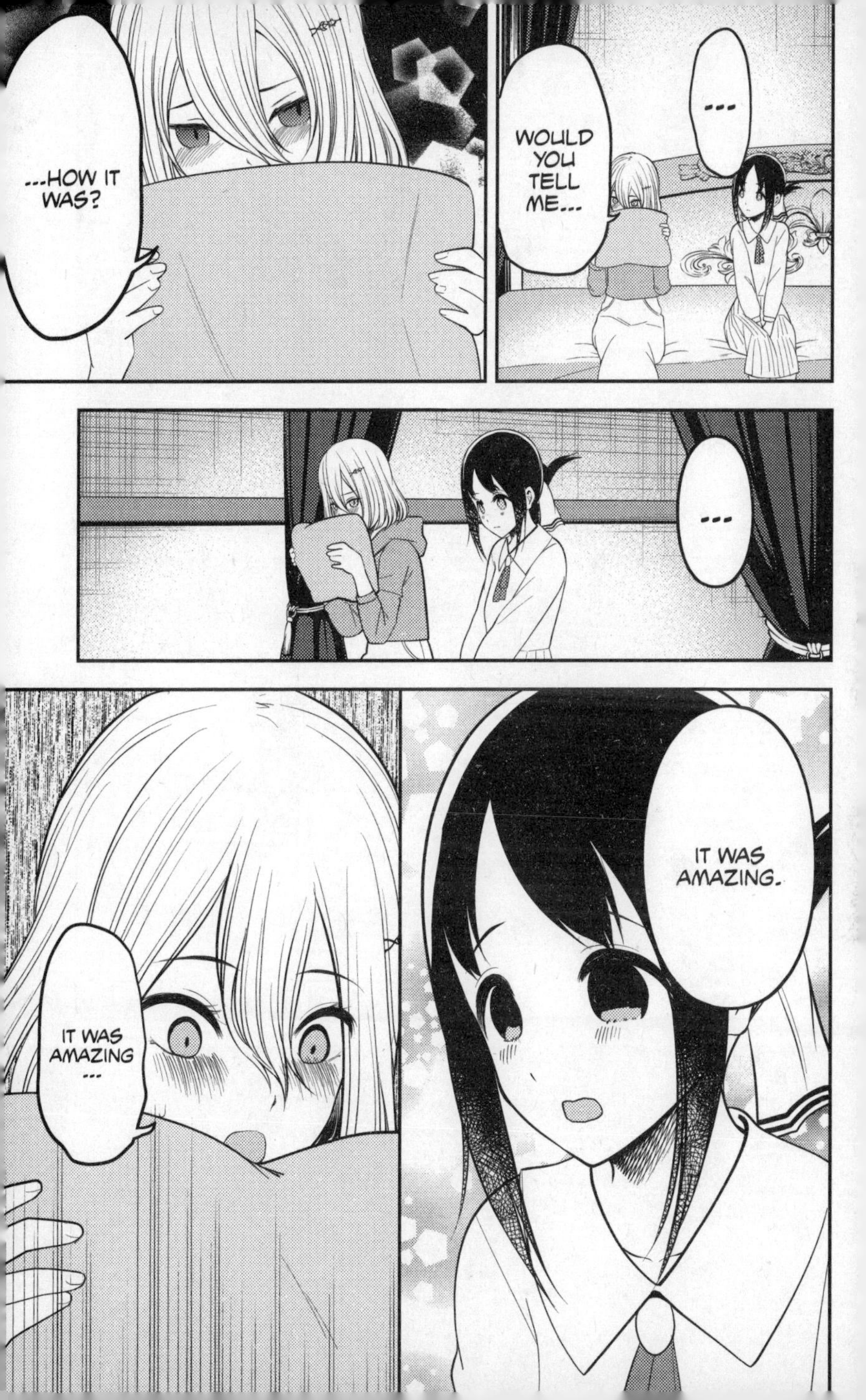
...
WOULD YOU TELL ME...
...HOW IT WAS?
...
IT WAS AMAZING.
IT WAS AMAZING ...

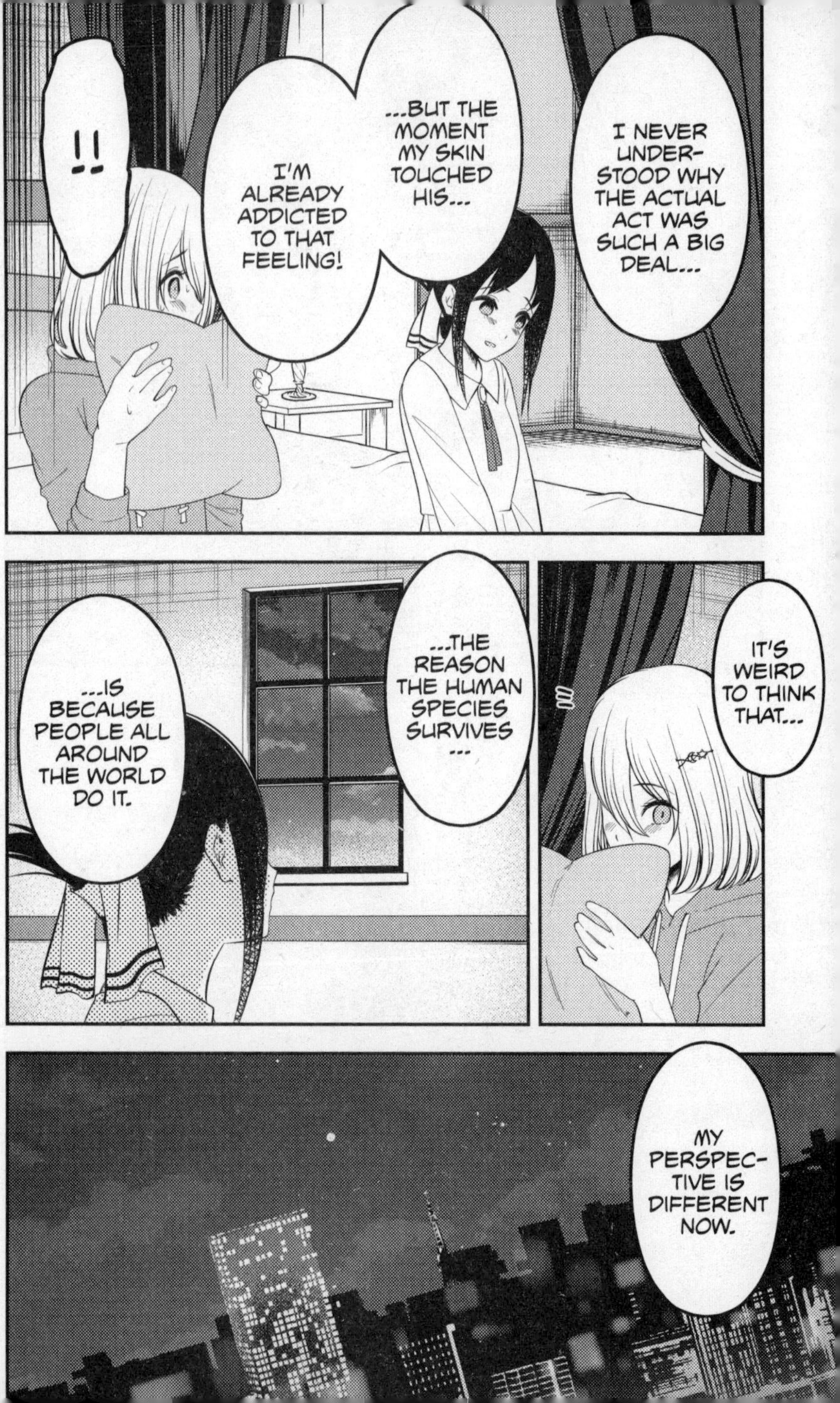
I NEVER UNDER-STOOD WHY THE ACTUAL ACT WAS SUCH A BIG DEAL...
...BUT THE MOMENT MY SKIN TOUCHED HIS...
I'M ALREADY ADDICTED TO THAT FEELING!
!!
IT'S WEIRD TO THINK THAT...
...THE REASON THE HUMAN SPECIES SURVIVES...
...IS BECAUSE PEOPLE ALL AROUND THE WORLD DO IT.
MY PERSPEC-TIVE IS DIFFERENT NOW.

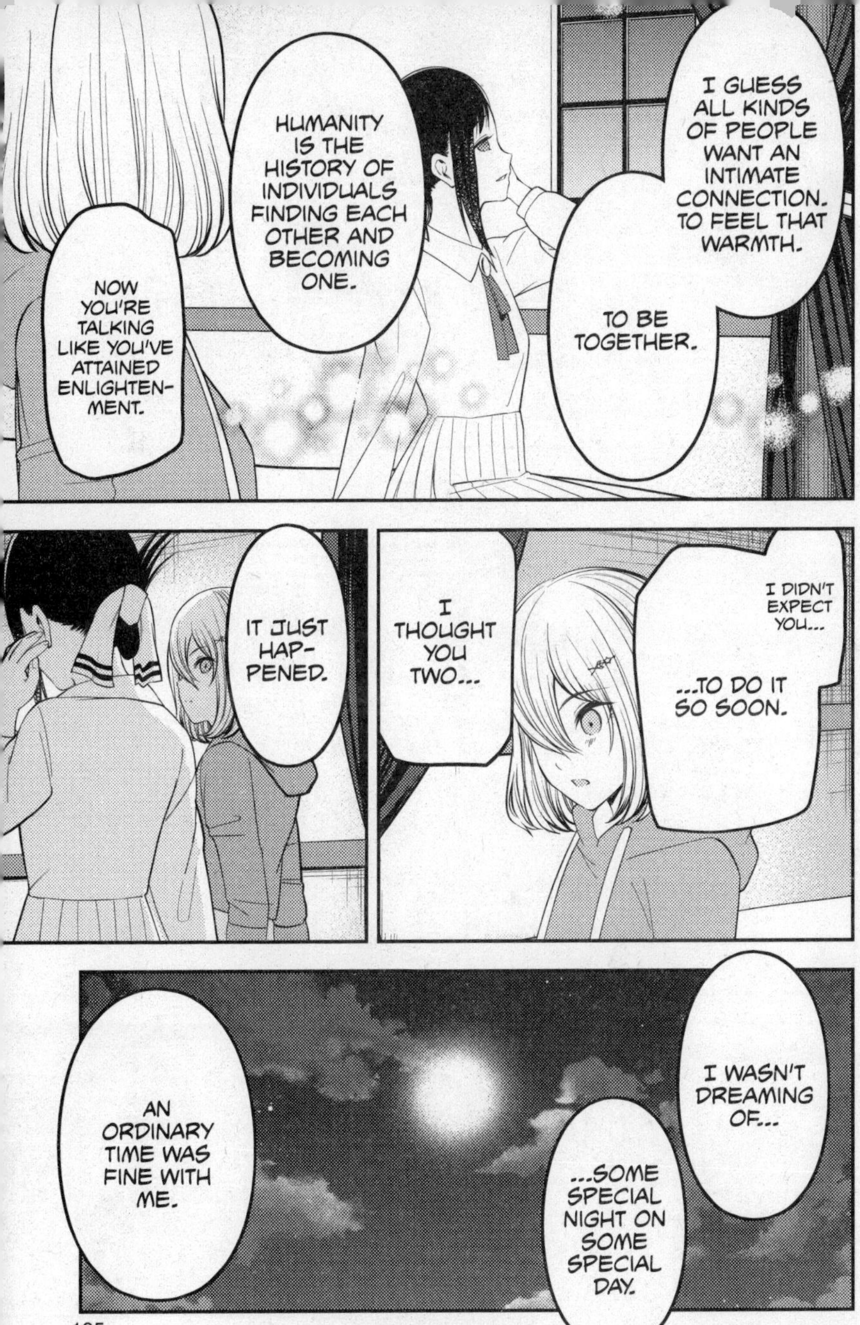
I GUESS ALL KINDS OF PEOPLE WANT AN INTIMATE CONNECTION. TO FEEL THAT WARMTH.
TO BE TOGETHER.
HUMANITY IS THE HISTORY OF INDIVIDUALS FINDING EACH OTHER AND BECOMING ONE.
NOW YOU'RE TALKING LIKE YOU'VE ATTAINED ENLIGHTEN-MENT.
I DIDN'T EXPECT YOU...
...TO DO IT SO SOON.
I THOUGHT YOU TWO...
IT JUST HAP-PENED.
I WASN'T DREAMING OF...
...SOME SPECIAL NIGHT ON SOME SPECIAL DAY.
AN ORDINARY TIME WAS FINE WITH ME.

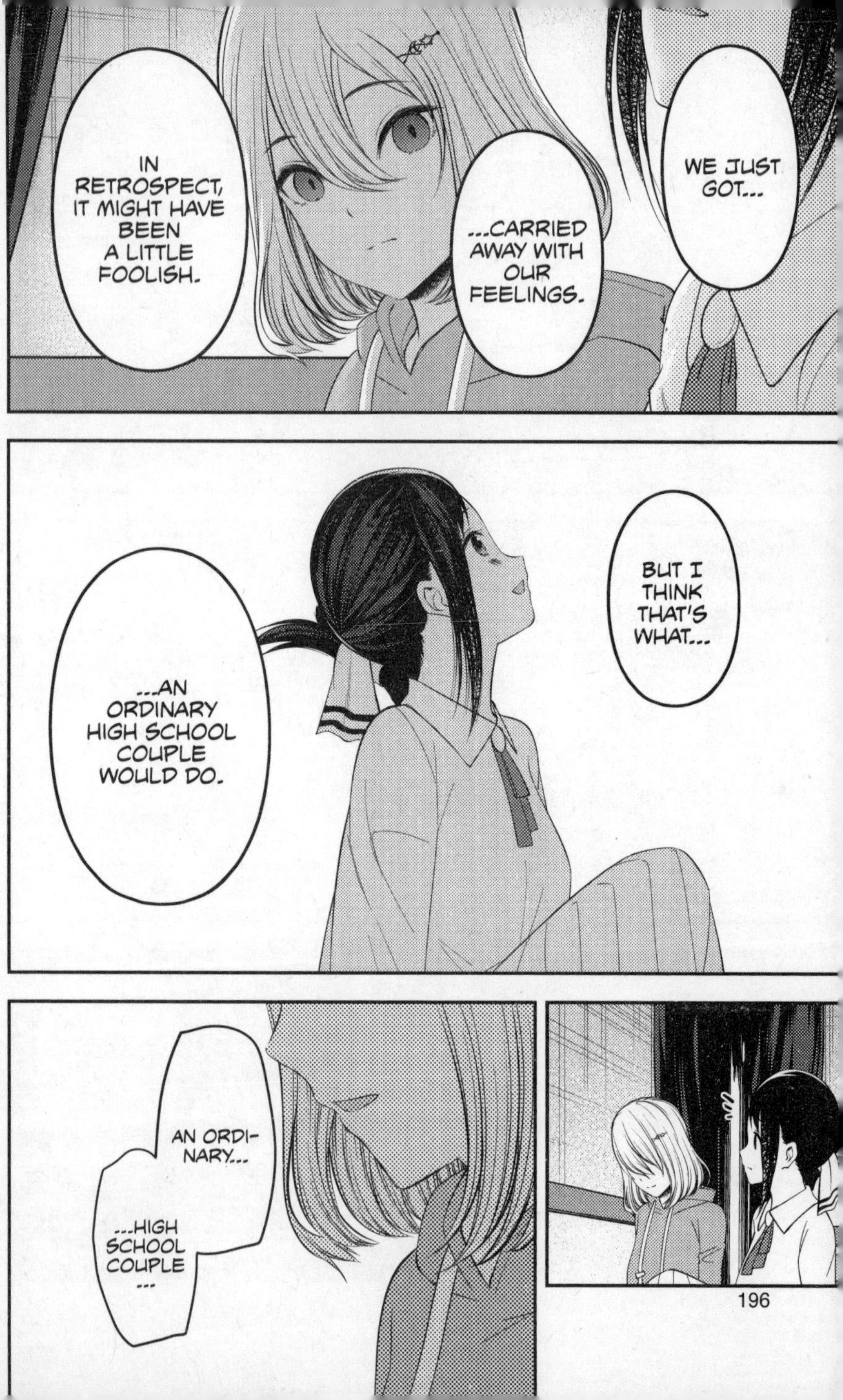
WE JUST GOT...
...CARRIED AWAY WITH OUR FEELINGS.
IN RETROSPECT, IT MIGHT HAVE BEEN A LITTLE FOOLISH.
BUT I THINK THAT'S WHAT...
...AN ORDINARY HIGH SCHOOL COUPLE WOULD DO.
AN ORDINARY...
...HIGH SCHOOL COUPLE...

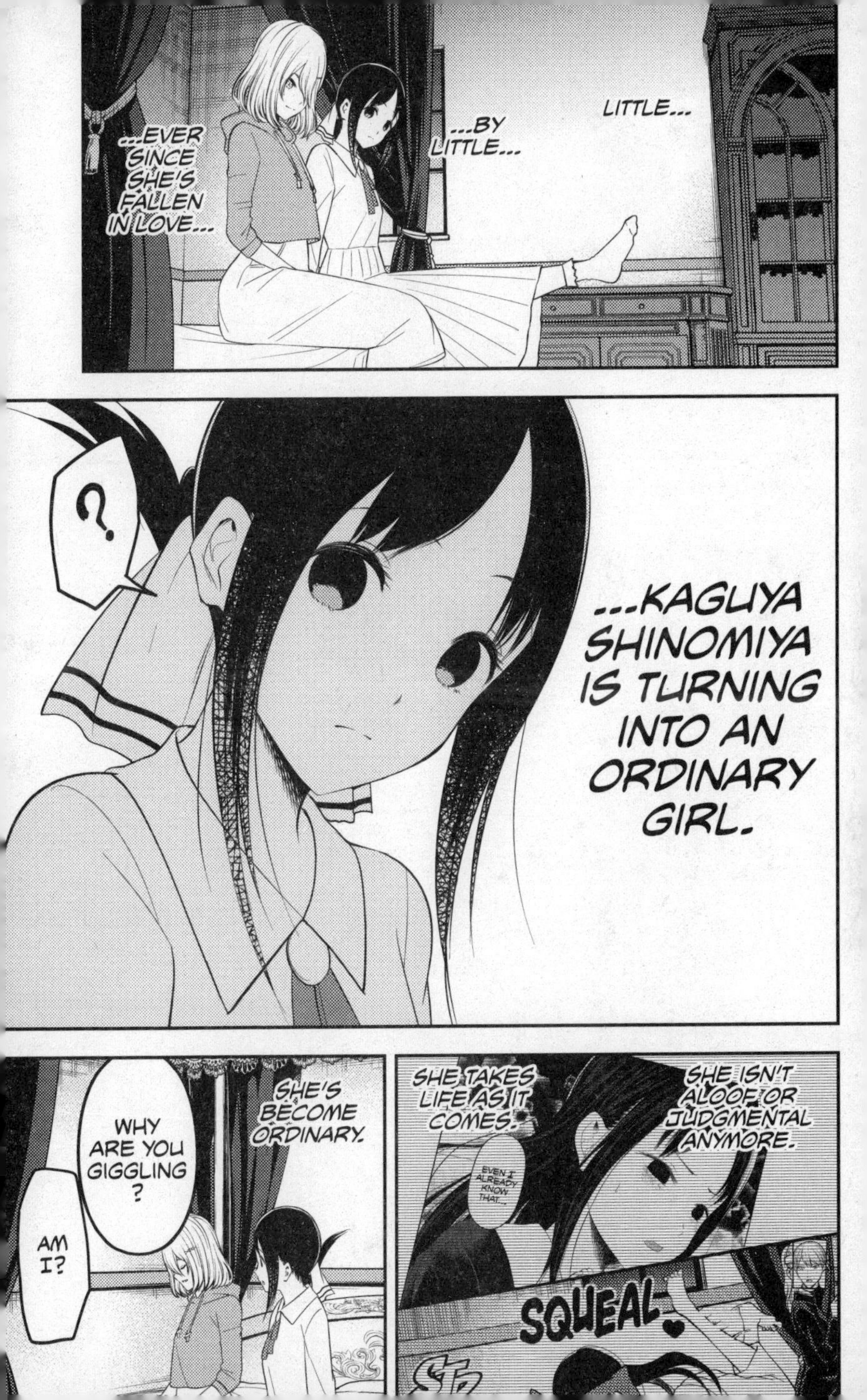
LITTLE...
...BY LITTLE...
...EVER SINCE SHE'S FALLEN IN LOVE...
...KAGUYA SHINOMIYA IS TURNING INTO AN ORDINARY GIRL.
?
SHE ISN'T ALOOF OR JUDGMENTAL ANYMORE.
SHE TAKES LIFE AS IT COMES.
EVEN I ALREADY KNOW THAT...
SQUEAL
SHE'S BECOME ORDINARY.
WHY ARE YOU GIGGLING?
AM I?

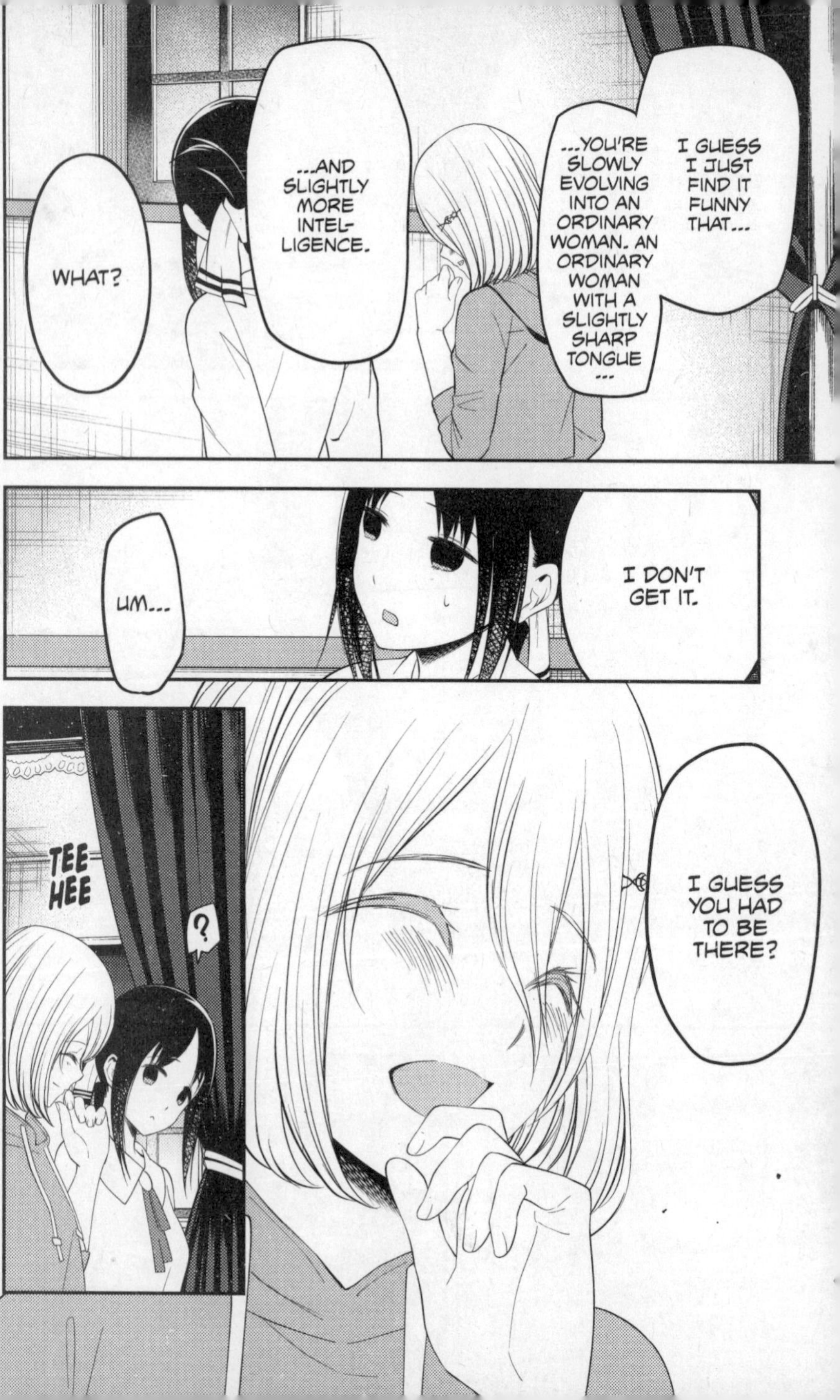
I GUESS I JUST FIND IT FUNNY THAT...
...YOU'RE SLOWLY EVOLVING INTO AN ORDINARY WOMAN. AN ORDINARY WOMAN WITH A SLIGHTLY SHARP TONGUE...
...AND SLIGHTLY MORE INTEL-LIGENCE.
WHAT?
I DON'T GET IT.
UM...
I GUESS YOU HAD TO BE THERE?
TEE-HEE
?

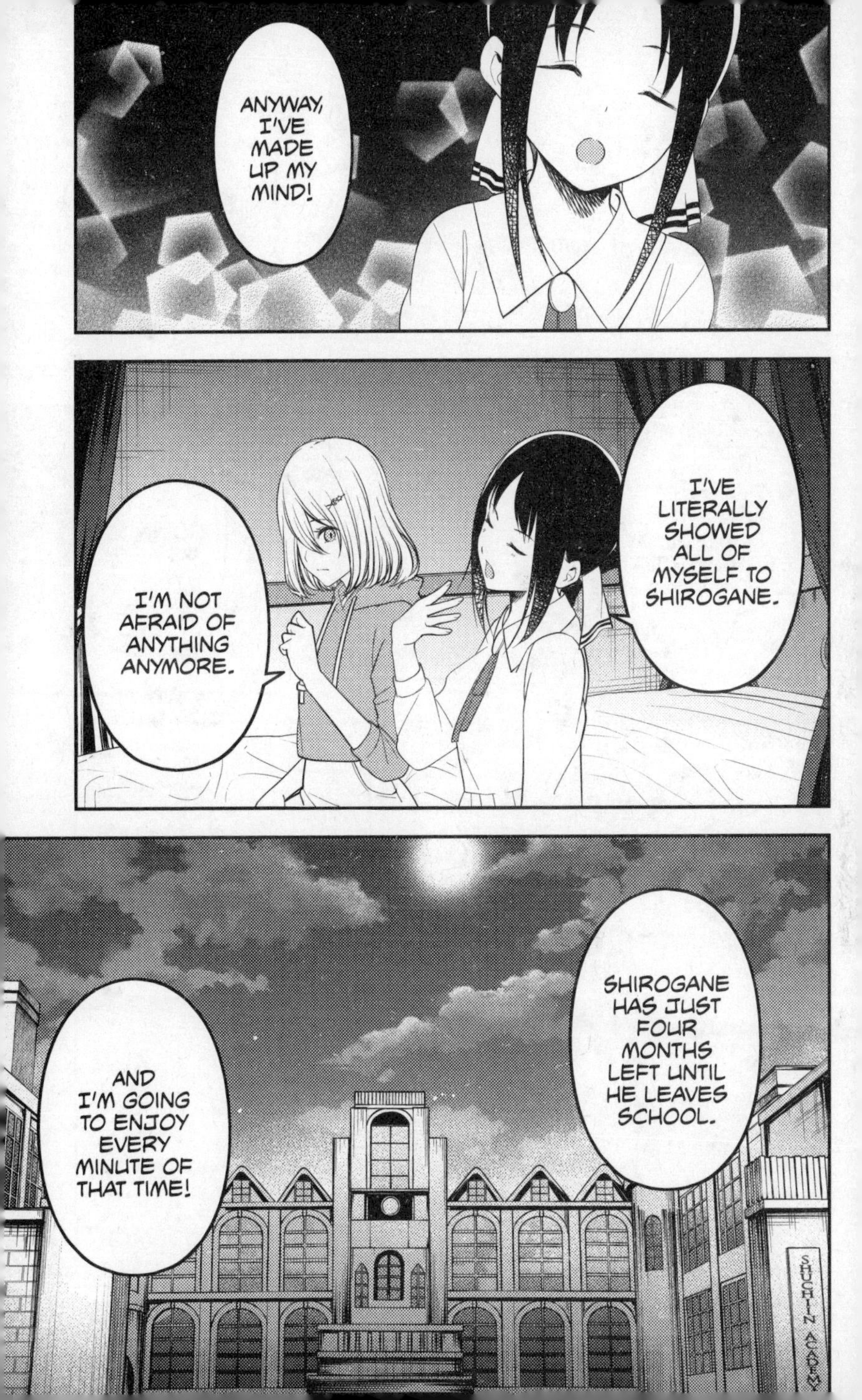
ANYWAY, I'VE MADE UP MY MIND!
I'VE LITERALLY SHOWED ALL OF MYSELF TO SHIROGANE.
I'M NOT AFRAID OF ANYTHING ANYMORE.
SHIROGANE HAS JUST FOUR MONTHS LEFT UNTIL HE LEAVES SCHOOL.
AND I'M GOING TO ENJOY EVERY MINUTE OF THAT TIME!
SHUCHIIN ACADEMY

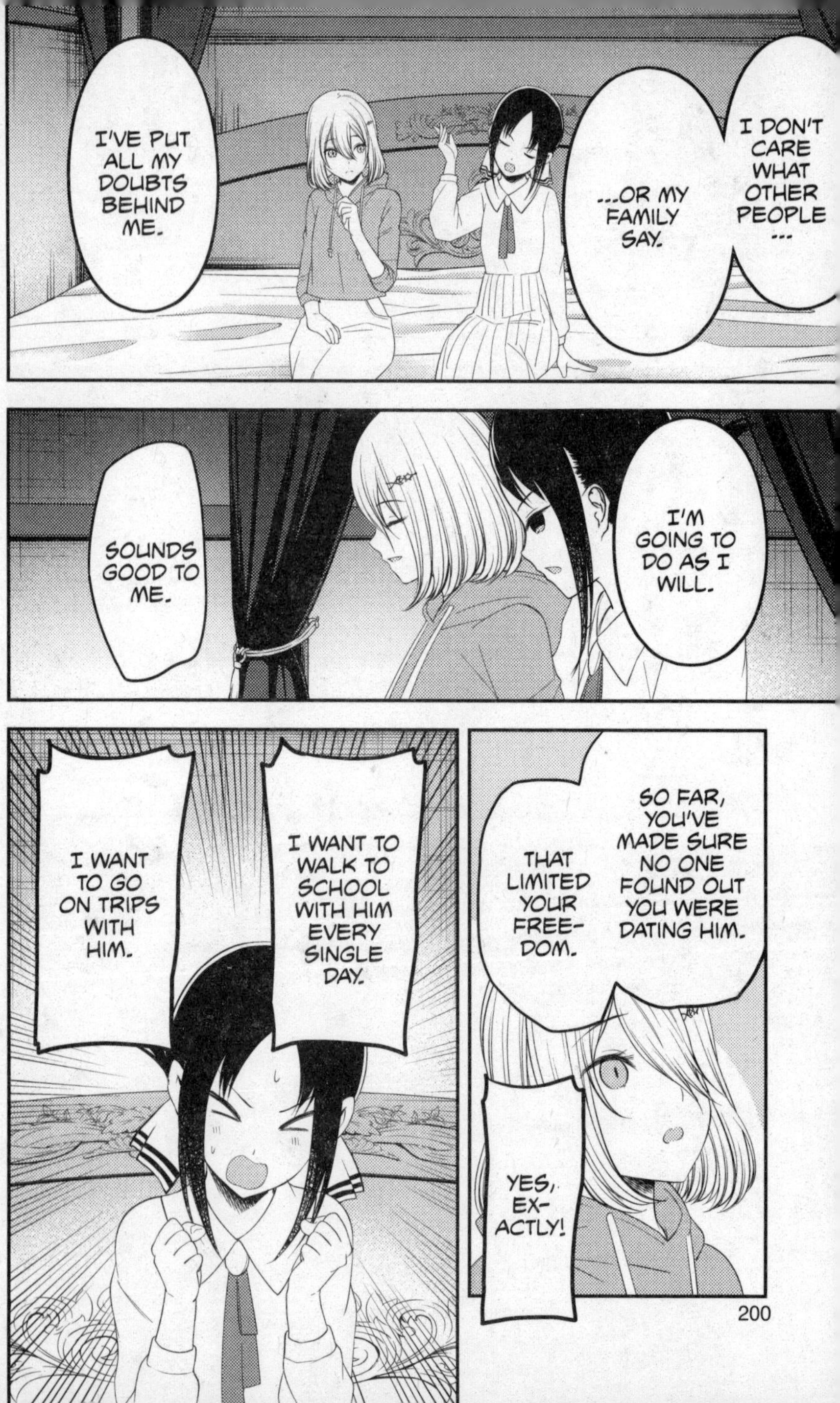
I DON'T CARE WHAT OTHER PEOPLE ...
...OR MY FAMILY SAY.
I'VE PUT ALL MY DOUBTS BEHIND ME.
I'M GOING TO DO AS I WILL.
SOUNDS GOOD TO ME.
SO FAR, YOU'VE MADE SURE NO ONE FOUND OUT YOU WERE DATING HIM.
THAT LIMITED YOUR FREE-DOM.
YES, EX-ACTLY!
I WANT TO WALK TO SCHOOL WITH HIM EVERY SINGLE DAY.
I WANT TO GO ON TRIPS WITH HIM.

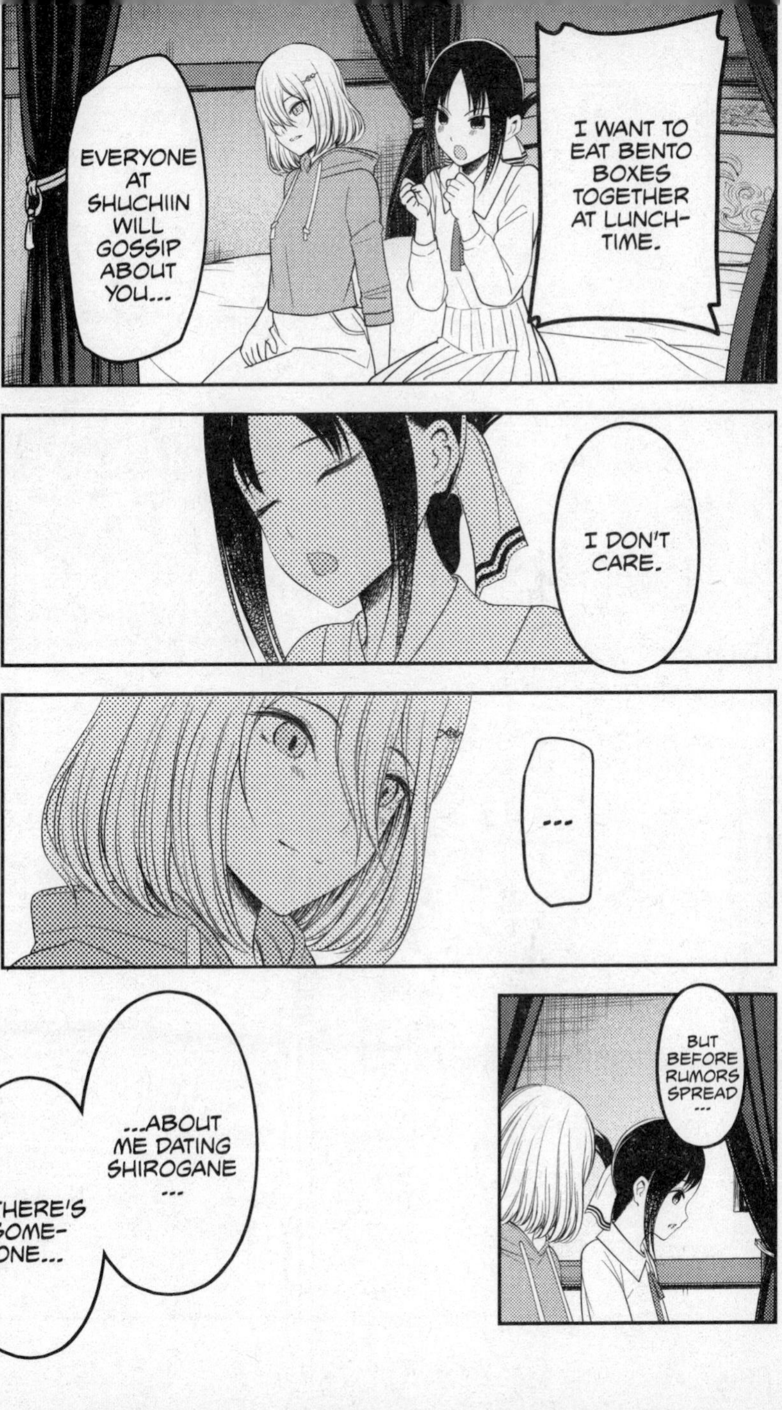
I WANT TO EAT BENTO BOXES TOGETHER AT LUNCH-TIME.
EVERYONE AT SHUCHIIN WILL GOSSIP ABOUT YOU...
I DON'T CARE.
...
BUT BEFORE RUMORS SPREAD...
...ABOUT ME DATING SHIROGANE...
...THERE'S SOME-ONE...

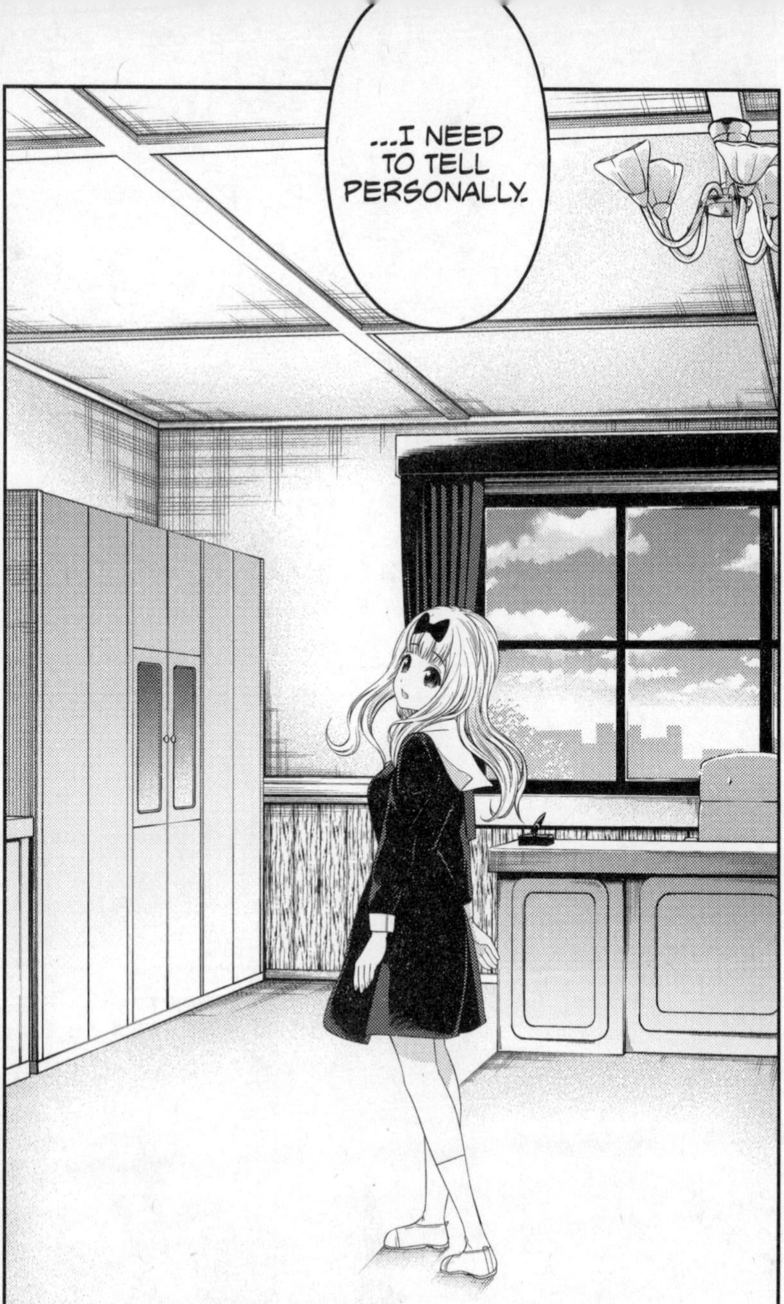
...I NEED TO TELL PERSONALLY.

To be
continued...

AN INTELLIGENT DECISION DOESN'T ALWAYS TURN OUT TO BE RIGHT. CONVERSELY, A FOOLISH DECISION DOESN'T ALWAYS TURN OUT TO BE WRONG.

Aka Akasaka

Aka Akasaka got his start as an assistant to Jinsei Kataoka and Kazuma Kondou, the creators of *Deadman Wonderland*. His first serialized manga was an adaptation of the light novel series *Sayonara Piano Sonata*, published by Kadokawa in 2011. *Kaguya-sama: Love Is War* began serialization in *Miracle Jump* in 2015 but was later moved to *Weekly Young Jump* in 2016 due to its popularity.

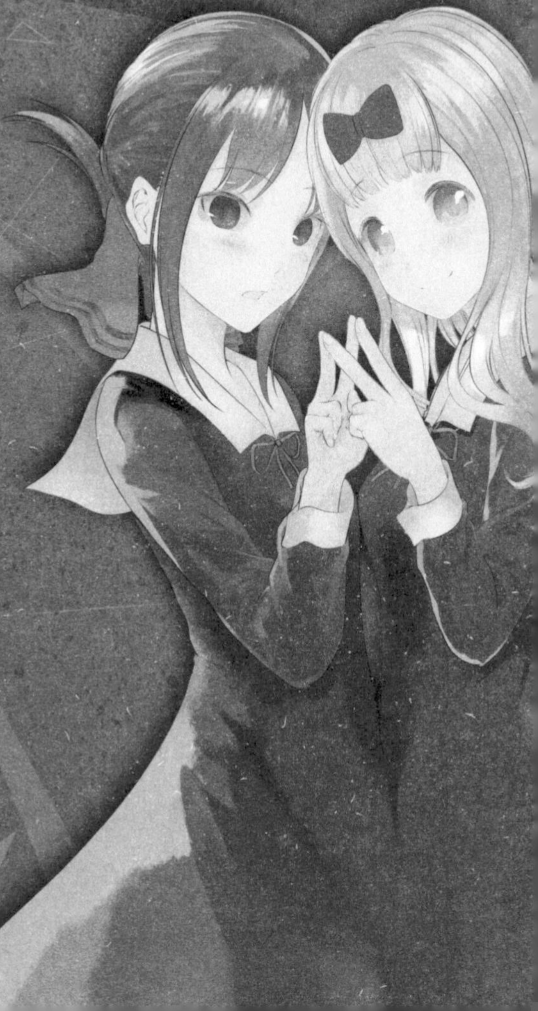

About the Final Story Arc

Kaguya-sama: Love Is War is entering its last stage. I'm not sure how long the final arc will be, but I already see the path before me. I'll check in on how each character is doing, and the story will take detours every now and then while moving toward the finish line.

This is my afterword as the creator of *Kaguya-sama*. The reason I'm writing it now is because I believe the star of a manga is the manga itself. It doesn't seem right for me to have the last word in the final volume. That's why I'd like to take this opportunity to express my gratitude to all the parties involved, even though my timing might seem premature.

In *Kaguya-sama*, each character has their own principles, personality, and background. Some of the characters behave in ways that go against my principles. To put that in a positive light, the characters do as they like. My role is to be their pain-in-the-neck friend—the one who meddles with people in love and stirs things up.

Kaguya-sama has a spin-off manga and has been adapted into anime and live-action films. A lot of merchandise has been created. This series involved a lot of people and has had a good run.

So many others worked hard on this. I'm grateful they've been so considerate to my characters.

I think all good reviews should be proffered to the characters, not the creator.

I'm an ordinary person, not a millionaire, so for the past six years, I've worried that my weaknesses would reflect badly on my characters.

I celebrated my tenth anniversary as a manga artist the other day.

Over the past decade, I've drawn a weekly series that got adapted into both anime and film, started another series, got married, then divorced, had some mental health issues, then recovered. I've gone through a lot.

Drawing a weekly series is grueling. I pretend it isn't, but the work is hard. I often feel like quitting, retiring, and moving somewhere overseas where the cost of living is low.

But I do love manga, so I guess I'll still be drawing it ten years from now.

Kaguya-sama is entering its final stage.

The story reached a climax of sorts at the end of volume 14. What follows is the story of two people in a romantic relationship after confessing their feelings for each other.

Until volume 14, I was drawing a story about the miscommunication between people who are attracted to each other. I'm continuing beyond that point because I believe you can't explore the complexities of a romantic relationship without telling what happens after its inception.

The focus has shifted to how all the characters (each of them with their own personal history) find answers to their questions and solve their problems.

This means the manga is less of a lighthearted rom-com than before. But it's my way of taking responsibility for the fates of the whole cast of characters. I hope you'll keep reading.

From now on, this will be Kaguya and Shirogane's story, not a rom-com about a couple in love.

I have no idea if this is the direction it should go. But the characters made this choice for themselves, so I'm going to watch over them as if I'm a reader of the story myself. I hope they keep their momentum in pursuit of their goals, let the consequences be damned! And I hope all their stories have a happy ending.

Aka Akasaka

KAGUYA-SAMA
LOVE IS WAR

SHONEN JUMP EDITION

22

STORY AND ART BY
AKA AKASAKA

Translation/Tomo Kimura
English Adaptation/Annette Roman
Touch-Up Art & Lettering/Steve Dutro
Cover & Interior Design/Alice Lewis
Editor/Annette Roman

KAGUYA-SAMA WA KOKURASETAI~TENSAITACHI NO REN'AI ZUNO SEN~
© 2015 by Aka Akasaka
All rights reserved.
First published in Japan in 2015 by SHUEISHA Inc., Tokyo.
English translation rights arranged by SHUEISHA Inc.

Printed in the U.S.A.

Published by VIZ Media, LLC
P.O. Box 77010
San Francisco, CA 94107

10 9 8 7 6 5 4 3 2 1
First printing, April 2022

COMING NEXT VOLUME

23

KAGUYA-SAMA
LOVE IS WAR

23

STORY & ART BY
AKA AKASAKA

Will Miyuki replace Chika in Kaguya's heart? When dense Chika belatedly finds out they're dating, she certainly thinks so. Then, Kaguya learns of an unexpected source of support in her battle against her family, Miko tries various approaches to get Yu to fall in love with her, and Kobachi turns out to be more complicated than she appears.

Sometimes, it's good to play games with people.